Itsuwaribito・空・

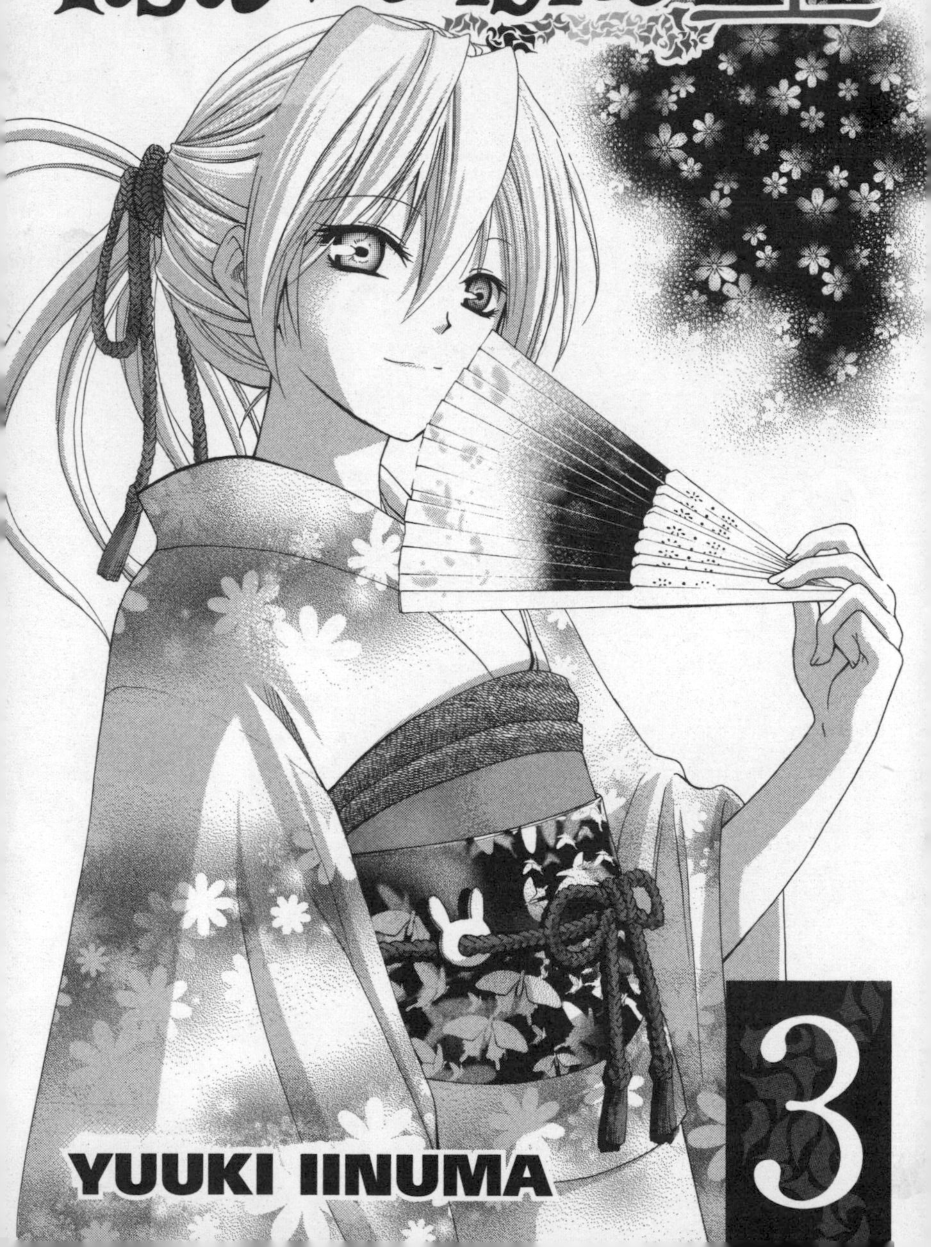

3

YUUKI IINUMA

Contents

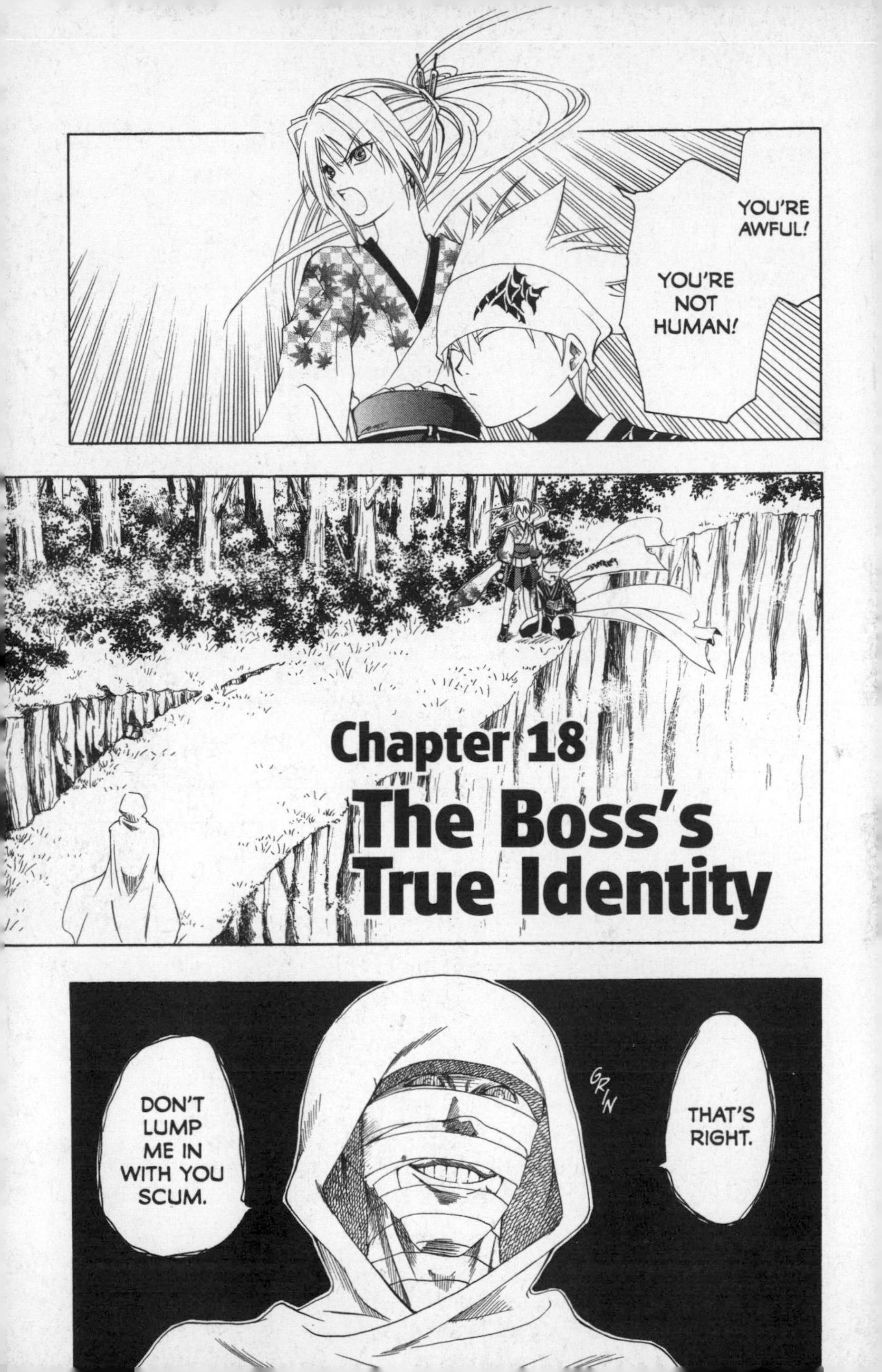
YOU'RE AWFUL!
YOU'RE NOT HUMAN!
Chapter 18
The Boss's True Identity
THAT'S RIGHT.
GRIN
DON'T LUMP ME IN WITH YOU SCUM.

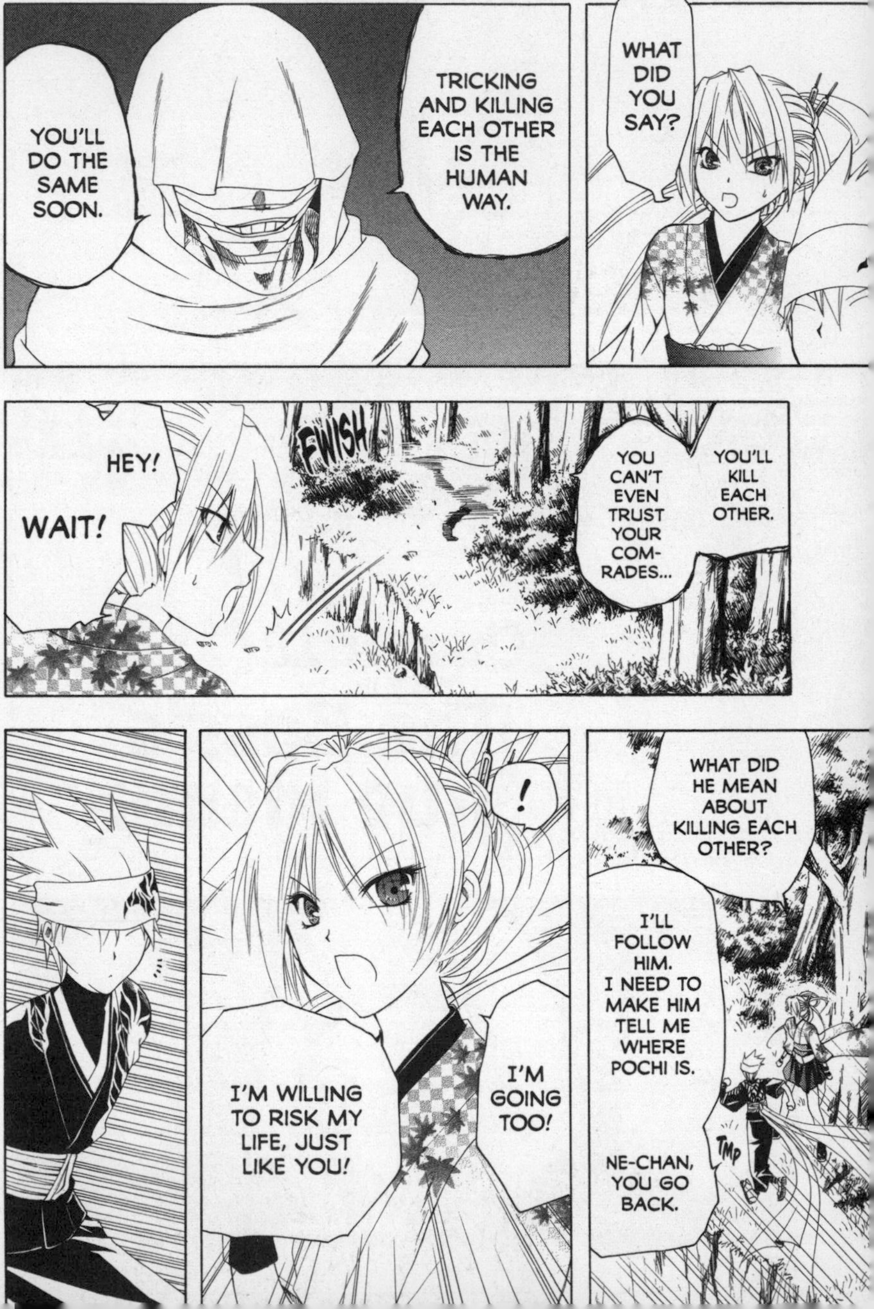
WHAT DID YOU SAY?
TRICKING AND KILLING EACH OTHER IS THE HUMAN WAY.
YOU'LL DO THE SAME SOON.
YOU'LL KILL EACH OTHER.
YOU CAN'T EVEN TRUST YOUR COM-RADES...
FWISH
HEY!
WAIT!
WHAT DID HE MEAN ABOUT KILLING EACH OTHER?
I'LL FOLLOW HIM. I NEED TO MAKE HIM TELL ME WHERE POCHI IS.
TMP
NE-CHAN, YOU GO BACK.
!
I'M GOING TOO!
I'M WILLING TO RISK MY LIFE, JUST LIKE YOU!

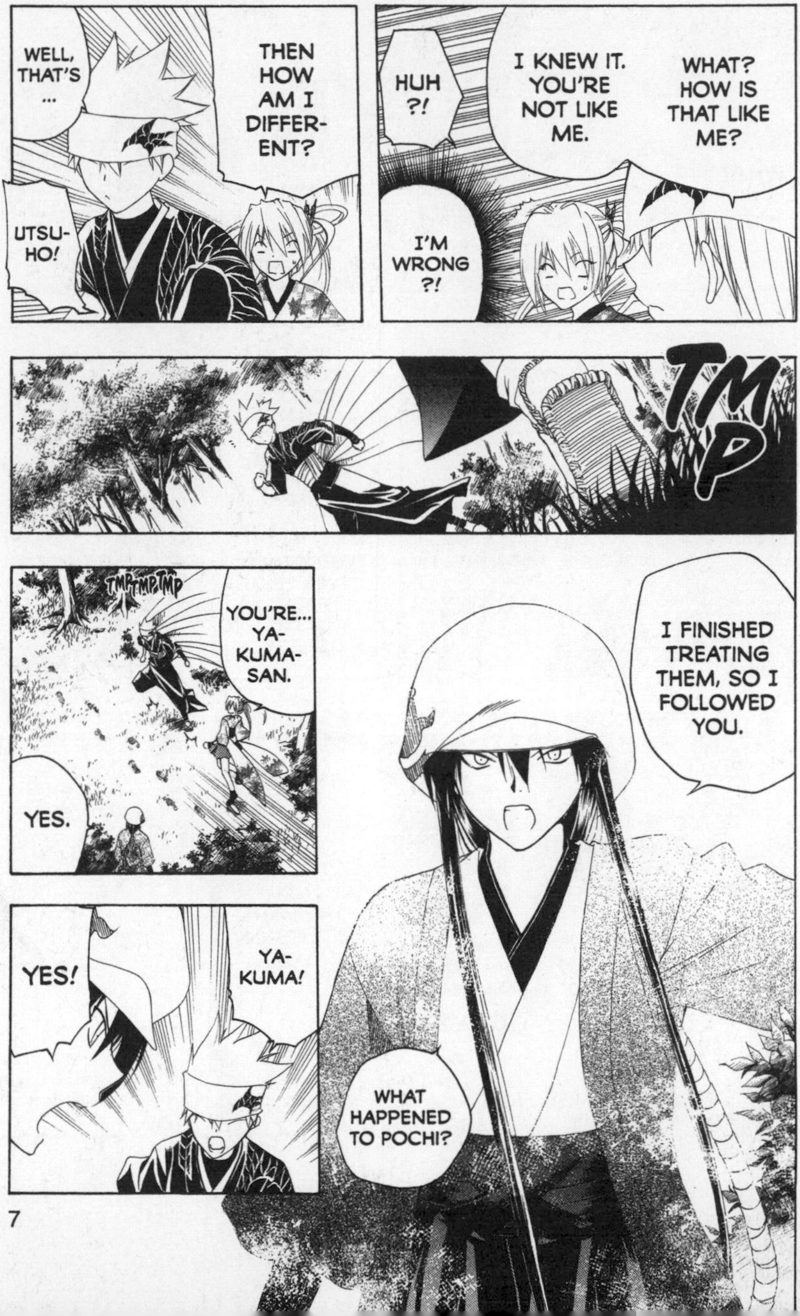
WHAT? HOW IS THAT LIKE ME?
I KNEW IT. YOU'RE NOT LIKE ME.
HUH ?!
I'M WRONG ?!
THEN HOW AM I DIFFER-ENT?
WELL, THAT'S ...
UTSU-HO!
TMP
I FINISHED TREATING THEM, SO I FOLLOWED YOU.
WHAT HAPPENED TO POCHI?
TMP TMP TMP
YOU'RE... YA-KUMA-SAN.
YES.
YA-KUMA!
YES!

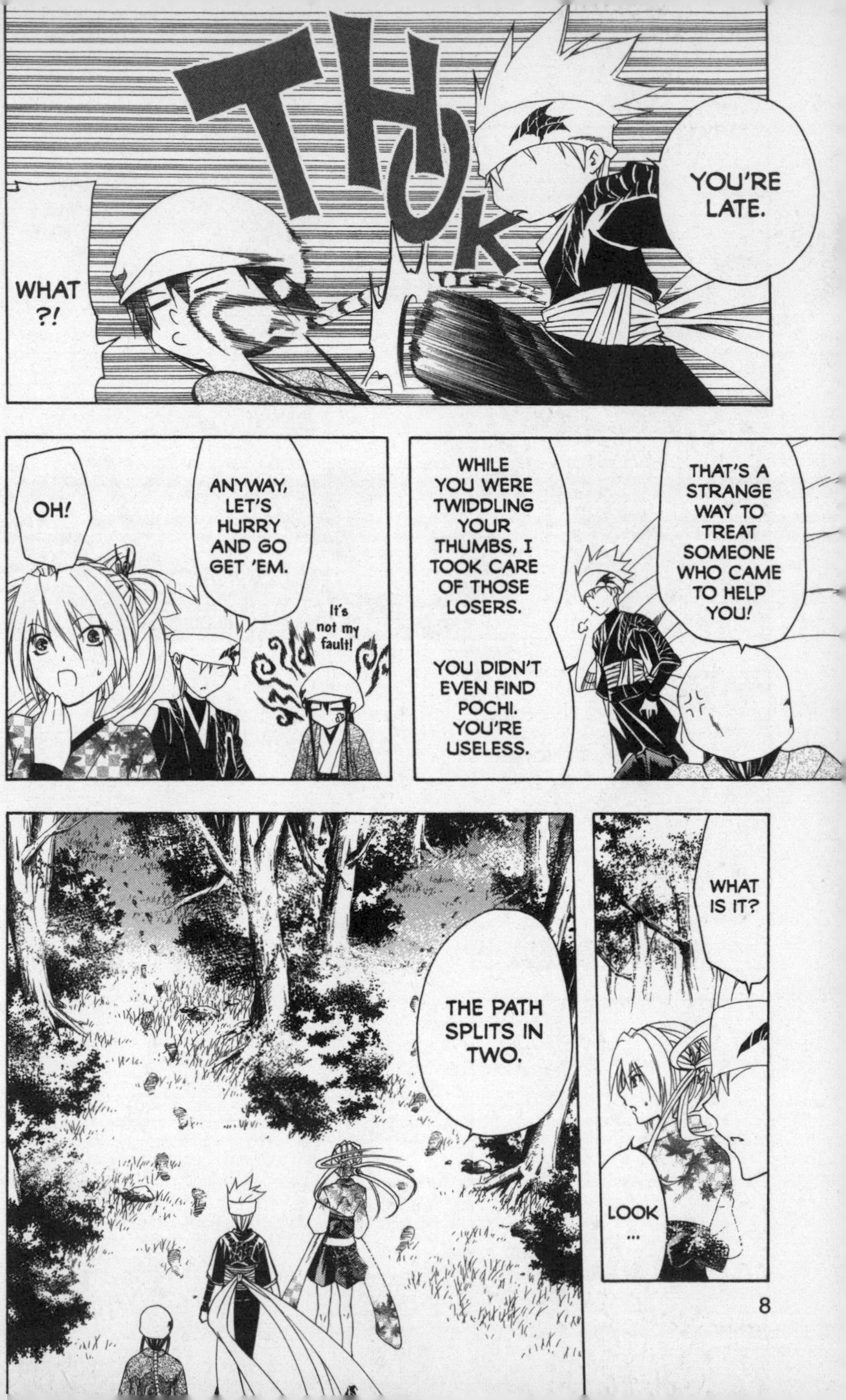
YOU'RE LATE.
THUK
WHAT ?!
THAT'S A STRANGE WAY TO TREAT SOMEONE WHO CAME TO HELP YOU!
WHILE YOU WERE TWIDDLING YOUR THUMBS, I TOOK CARE OF THOSE LOSERS.
YOU DIDN'T EVEN FIND POCHI. YOU'RE USELESS.
ANYWAY, LET'S HURRY AND GO GET 'EM.
OH!
It's not my fault!
WHAT IS IT?
LOOK ...
THE PATH SPLITS IN TWO.

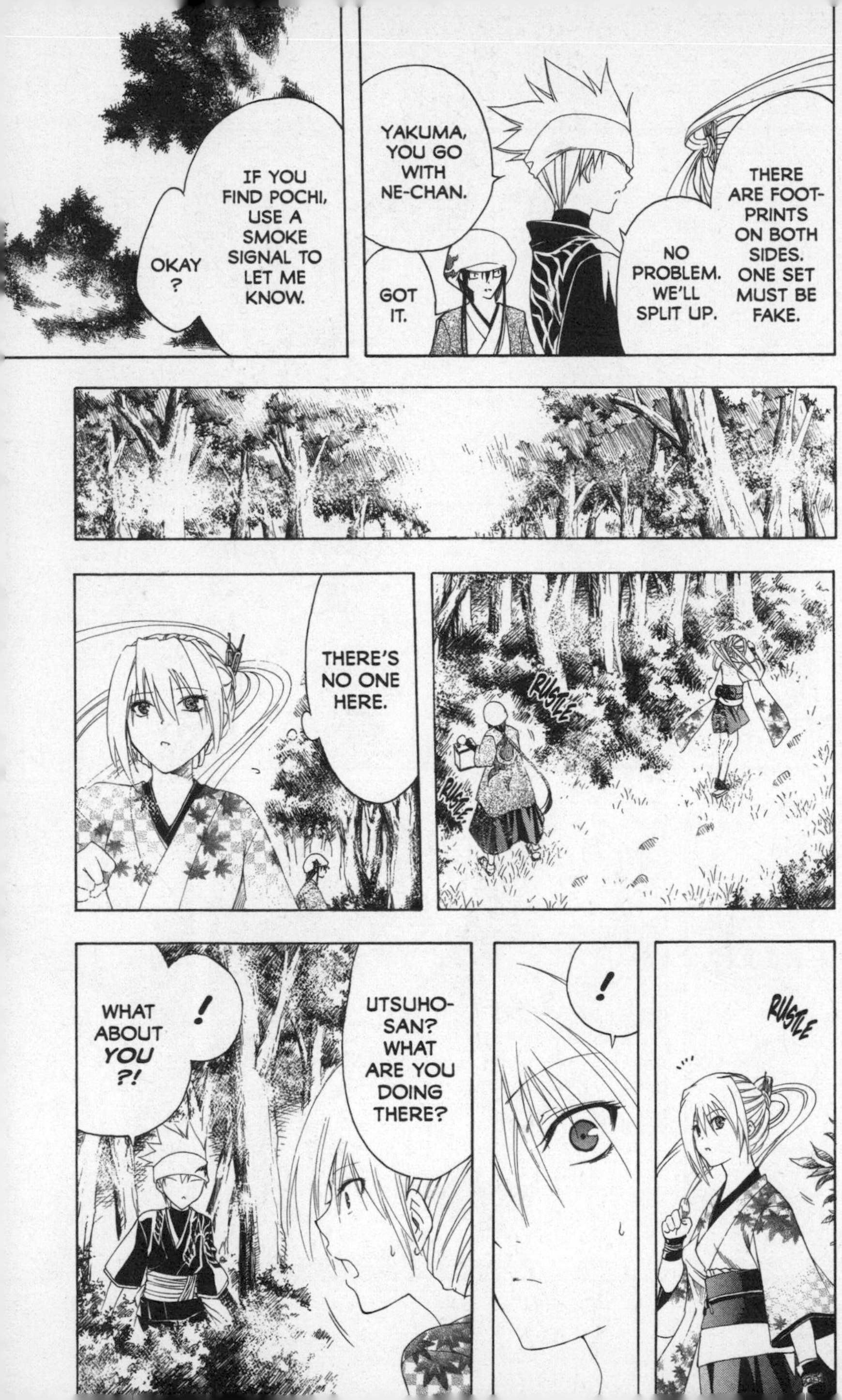
THERE ARE FOOT-PRINTS ON BOTH SIDES. ONE SET MUST BE FAKE.
NO PROBLEM. WE'LL SPLIT UP.
YAKUMA, YOU GO WITH NE-CHAN.
GOT IT.
IF YOU FIND POCHI, USE A SMOKE SIGNAL TO LET ME KNOW.
OKAY?
RUSTLE
RUSTLE
THERE'S NO ONE HERE.
RUSTLE
!
UTSUHO-SAN? WHAT ARE YOU DOING THERE?
!
WHAT ABOUT *YOU*?!

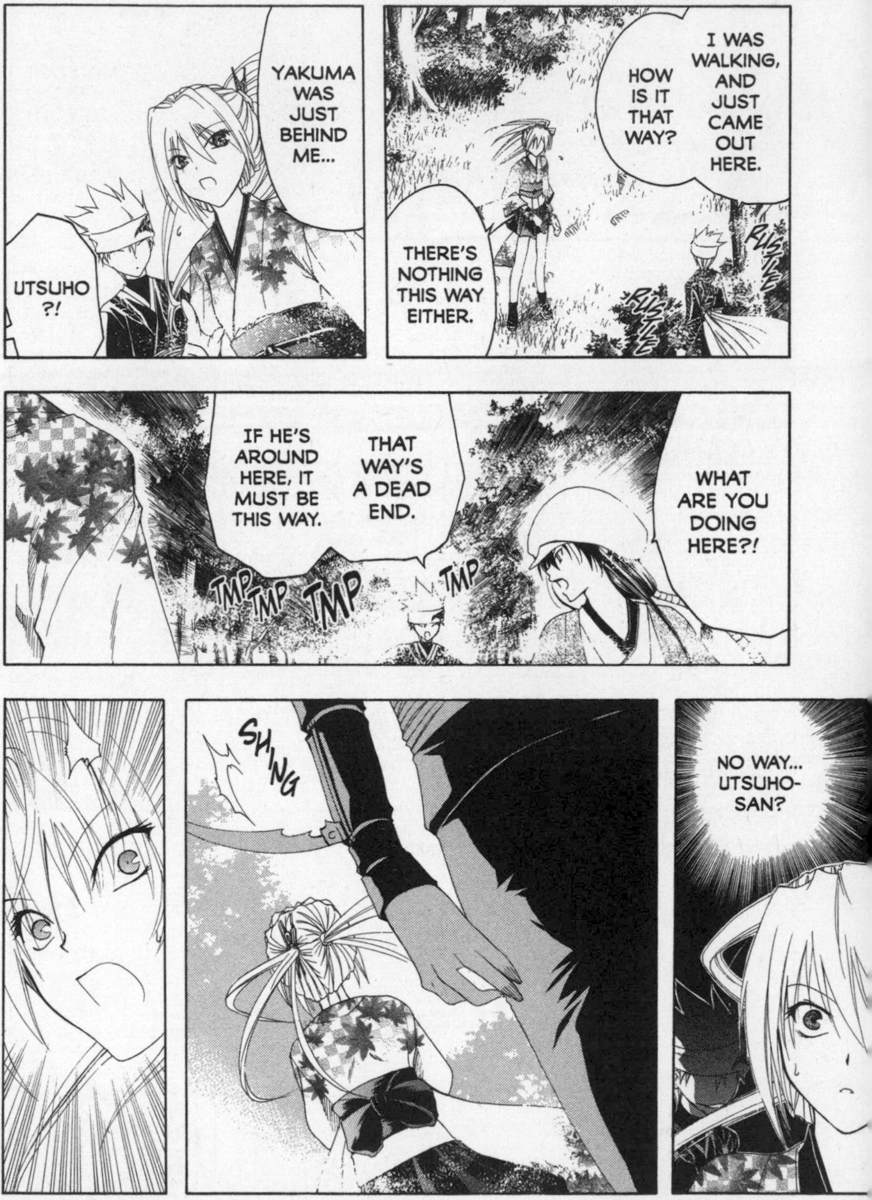
I WAS WALKING, AND JUST CAME OUT HERE.
HOW IS IT THAT WAY?
RUSTLE
RUSTLE
THERE'S NOTHING THIS WAY EITHER.
YAKUMA WAS JUST BEHIND ME...
UTSUHO ?!
WHAT ARE YOU DOING HERE?!
THAT WAY'S A DEAD END.
IF HE'S AROUND HERE, IT MUST BE THIS WAY.
TMP TMP TMP TMP
NO WAY... UTSUHO-SAN?
SHING

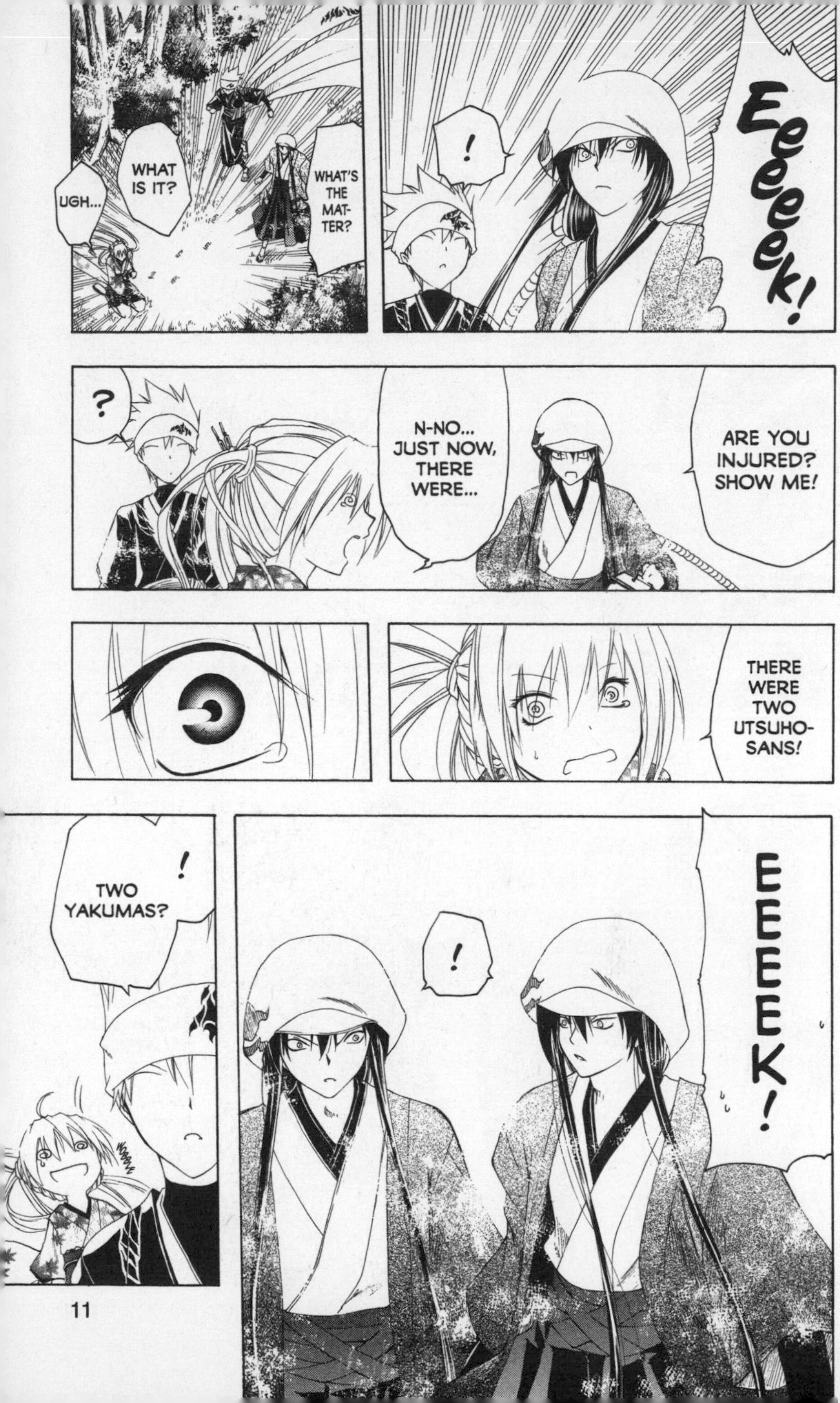
Eeeeek!
!
WHAT'S THE MATTER?
WHAT IS IT?
UGH...
ARE YOU INJURED? SHOW ME!
N-NO... JUST NOW, THERE WERE...
?
THERE WERE TWO UTSUHO-SANS!
EEEEK!
!
TWO YAKUMAS?
!

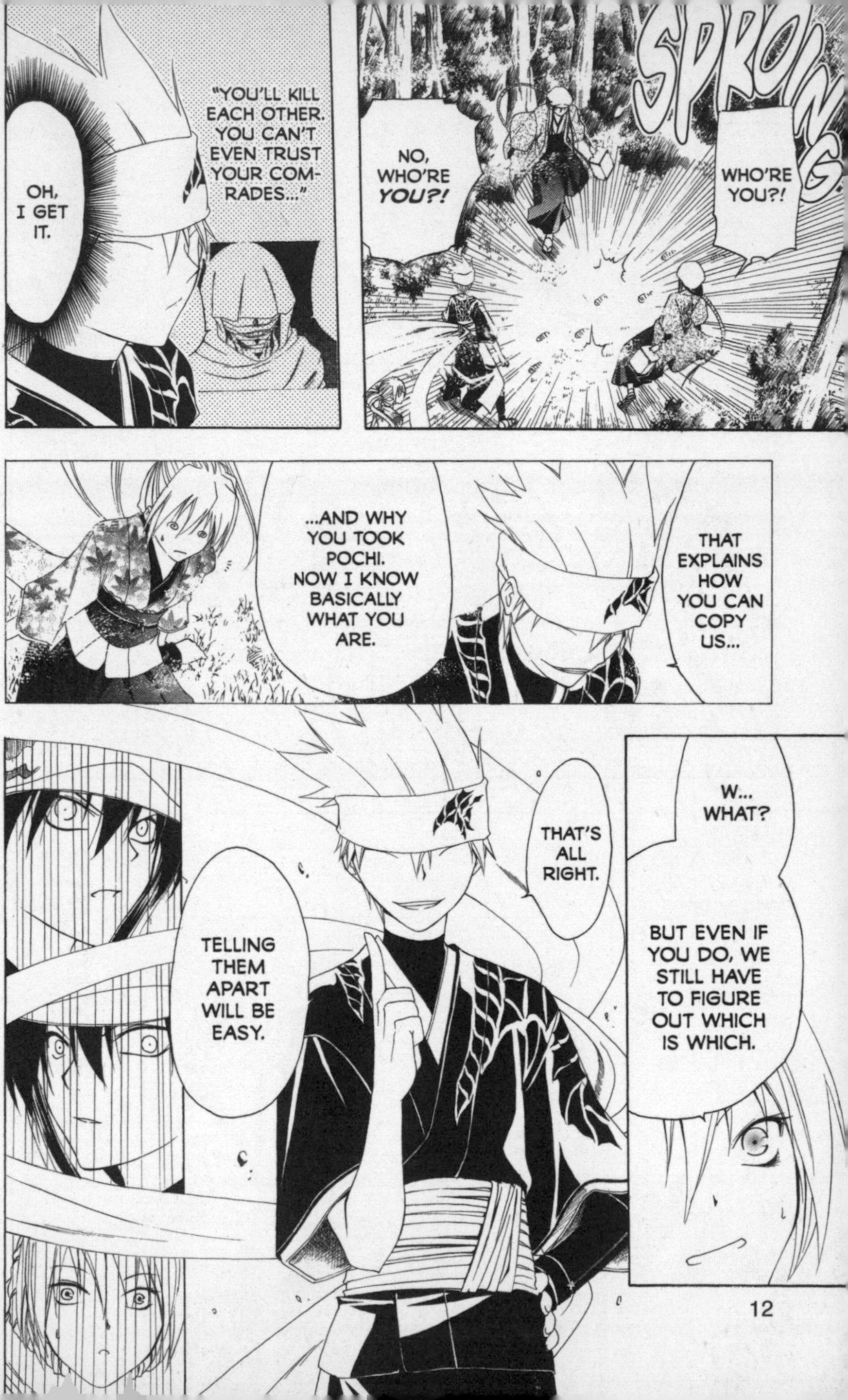
SPRONG
WHO'RE YOU?!
NO, WHO'RE *YOU?!*
"YOU'LL KILL EACH OTHER. YOU CAN'T EVEN TRUST YOUR COM-RADES..."
OH, I GET IT.
THAT EXPLAINS HOW YOU CAN COPY US...
...AND WHY YOU TOOK POCHI. NOW I KNOW BASICALLY WHAT YOU ARE.
W... WHAT?
BUT EVEN IF YOU DO, WE STILL HAVE TO FIGURE OUT WHICH IS WHICH.
THAT'S ALL RIGHT.
TELLING THEM APART WILL BE EASY.

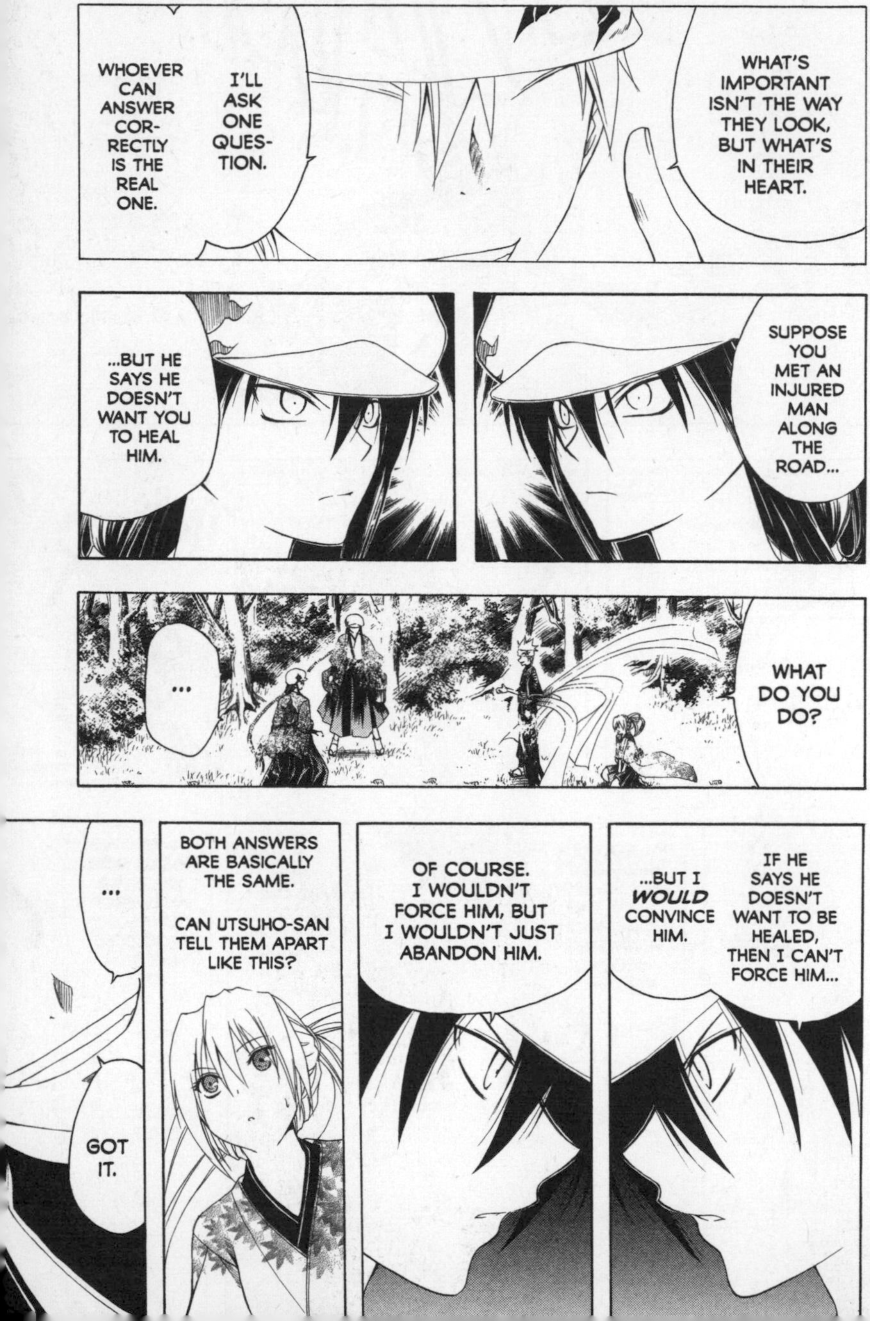
WHAT'S IMPORTANT ISN'T THE WAY THEY LOOK, BUT WHAT'S IN THEIR HEART.
I'LL ASK ONE QUES-TION.
WHOEVER CAN ANSWER COR-RECTLY IS THE REAL ONE.
SUPPOSE YOU MET AN INJURED MAN ALONG THE ROAD...
...BUT HE SAYS HE DOESN'T WANT YOU TO HEAL HIM.
WHAT DO YOU DO?
...
IF HE SAYS HE DOESN'T WANT TO BE HEALED, THEN I CAN'T FORCE HIM...
...BUT I *WOULD* CONVINCE HIM.
OF COURSE. I WOULDN'T FORCE HIM, BUT I WOULDN'T JUST ABANDON HIM.
BOTH ANSWERS ARE BASICALLY THE SAME.
CAN UTSUHO-SAN TELL THEM APART LIKE THIS?
...
GOT IT.

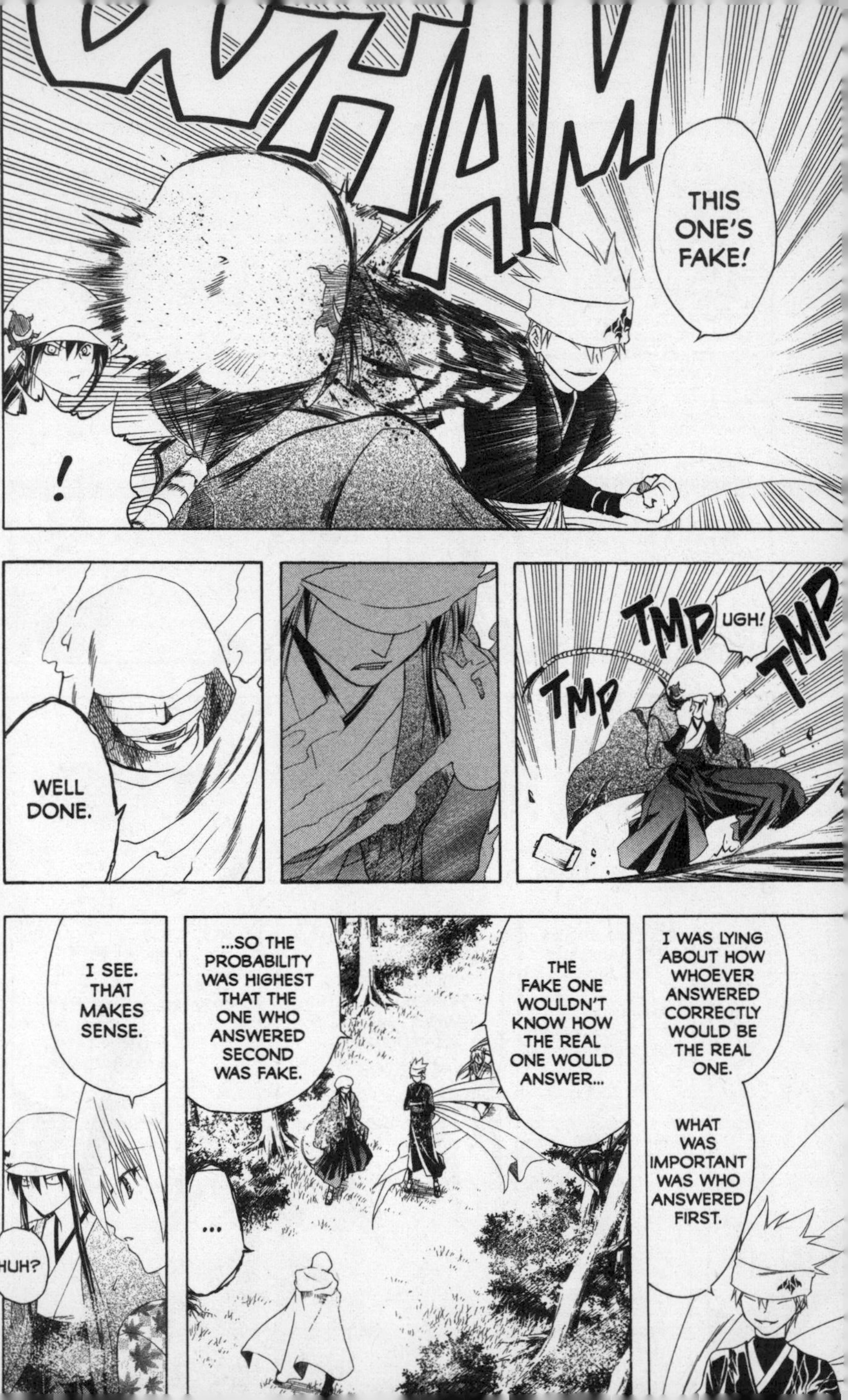
WHAM
THIS ONE'S FAKE!
!
TMP
TMP
UGH!
TMP
WELL DONE.
I WAS LYING ABOUT HOW WHOEVER ANSWERED CORRECTLY WOULD BE THE REAL ONE.
WHAT WAS IMPORTANT WAS WHO ANSWERED FIRST.
THE FAKE ONE WOULDN'T KNOW HOW THE REAL ONE WOULD ANSWER...
...SO THE PROBABILITY WAS HIGHEST THAT THE ONE WHO ANSWERED SECOND WAS FAKE.
...
I SEE. THAT MAKES SENSE.
HUH?

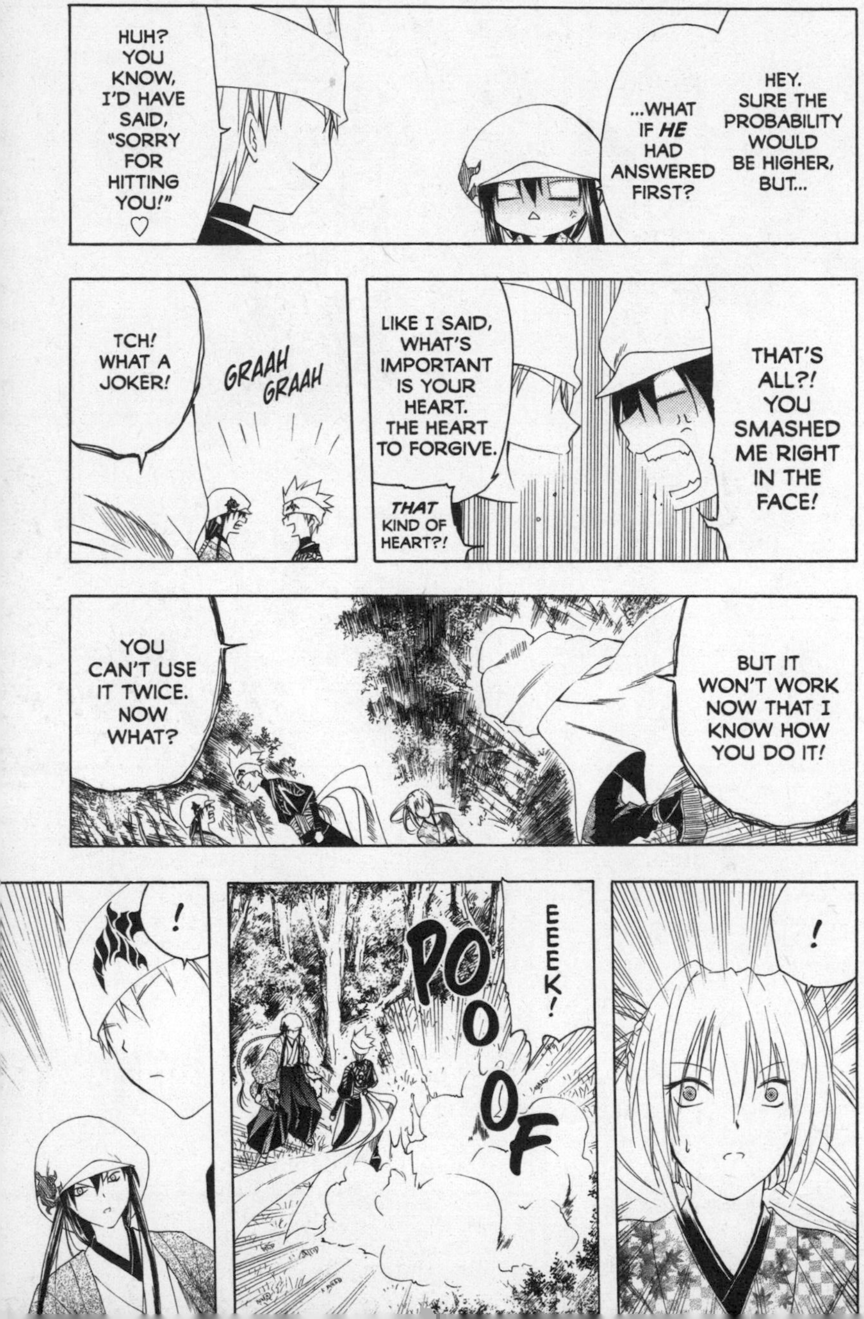
HEY. SURE THE PROBABILITY WOULD BE HIGHER, BUT...
...WHAT IF *HE* HAD ANSWERED FIRST?
HUH? YOU KNOW, I'D HAVE SAID, "SORRY FOR HITTING YOU!" ♡
THAT'S ALL?! YOU SMASHED ME RIGHT IN THE FACE!
LIKE I SAID, WHAT'S IMPORTANT IS YOUR HEART. THE HEART TO FORGIVE.
THAT KIND OF HEART?!
TCH! WHAT A JOKER!
GRAAH GRAAH
BUT IT WON'T WORK NOW THAT I KNOW HOW YOU DO IT!
YOU CAN'T USE IT TWICE. NOW WHAT?
!
EEEK!
POOOF
!

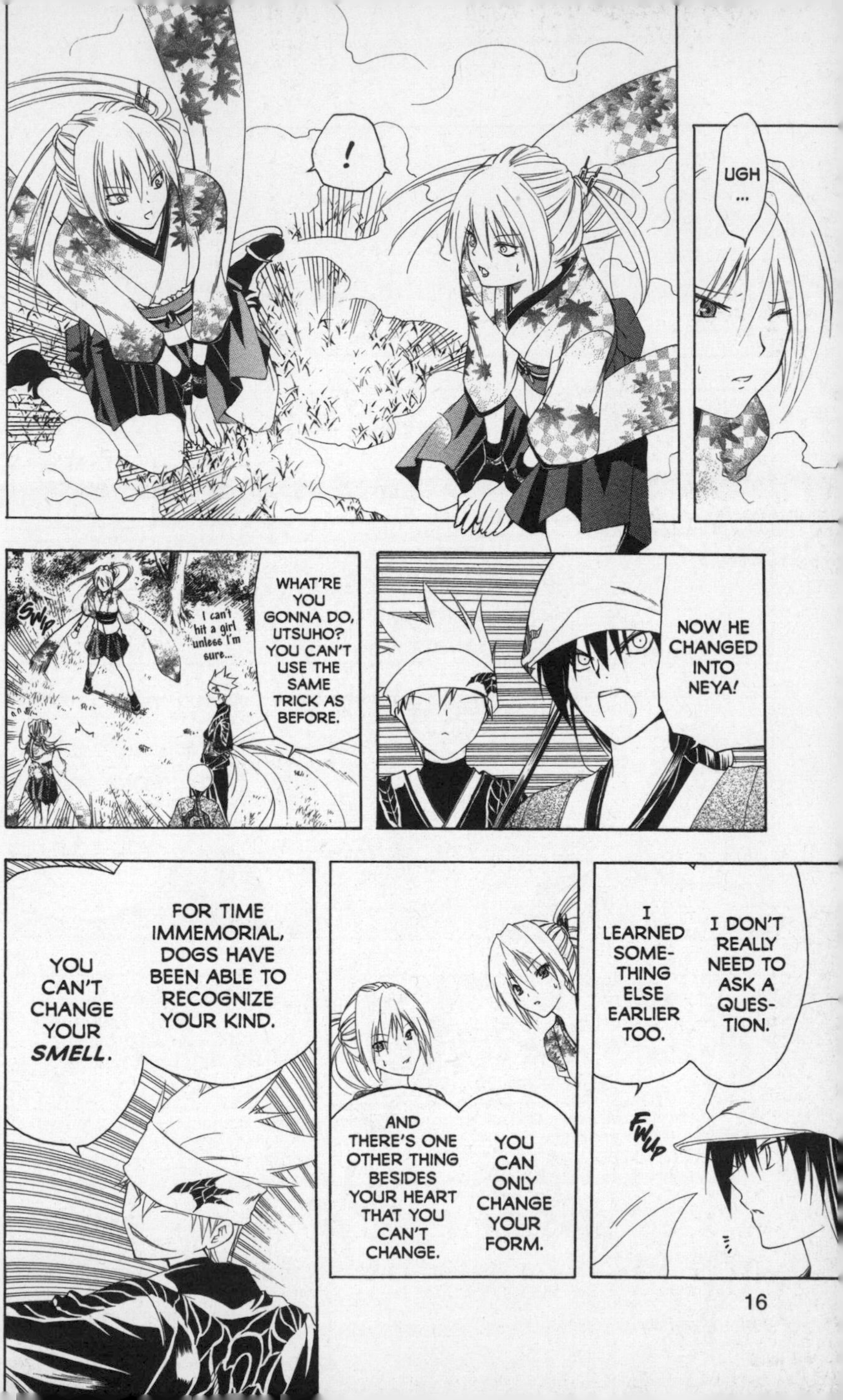
UGH ...
!
NOW HE CHANGED INTO NEYA!
WHAT'RE YOU GONNA DO, UTSUHO? YOU CAN'T USE THE SAME TRICK AS BEFORE.
I can't hit a girl unless I'm sure...
SWIP
I DON'T REALLY NEED TO ASK A QUES-TION.
I LEARNED SOME-THING ELSE EARLIER TOO.
FWUP
YOU CAN ONLY CHANGE YOUR FORM.
AND THERE'S ONE OTHER THING BESIDES YOUR HEART THAT YOU CAN'T CHANGE.
FOR TIME IMMEMORIAL, DOGS HAVE BEEN ABLE TO RECOGNIZE YOUR KIND.
YOU CAN'T CHANGE YOUR SMELL.

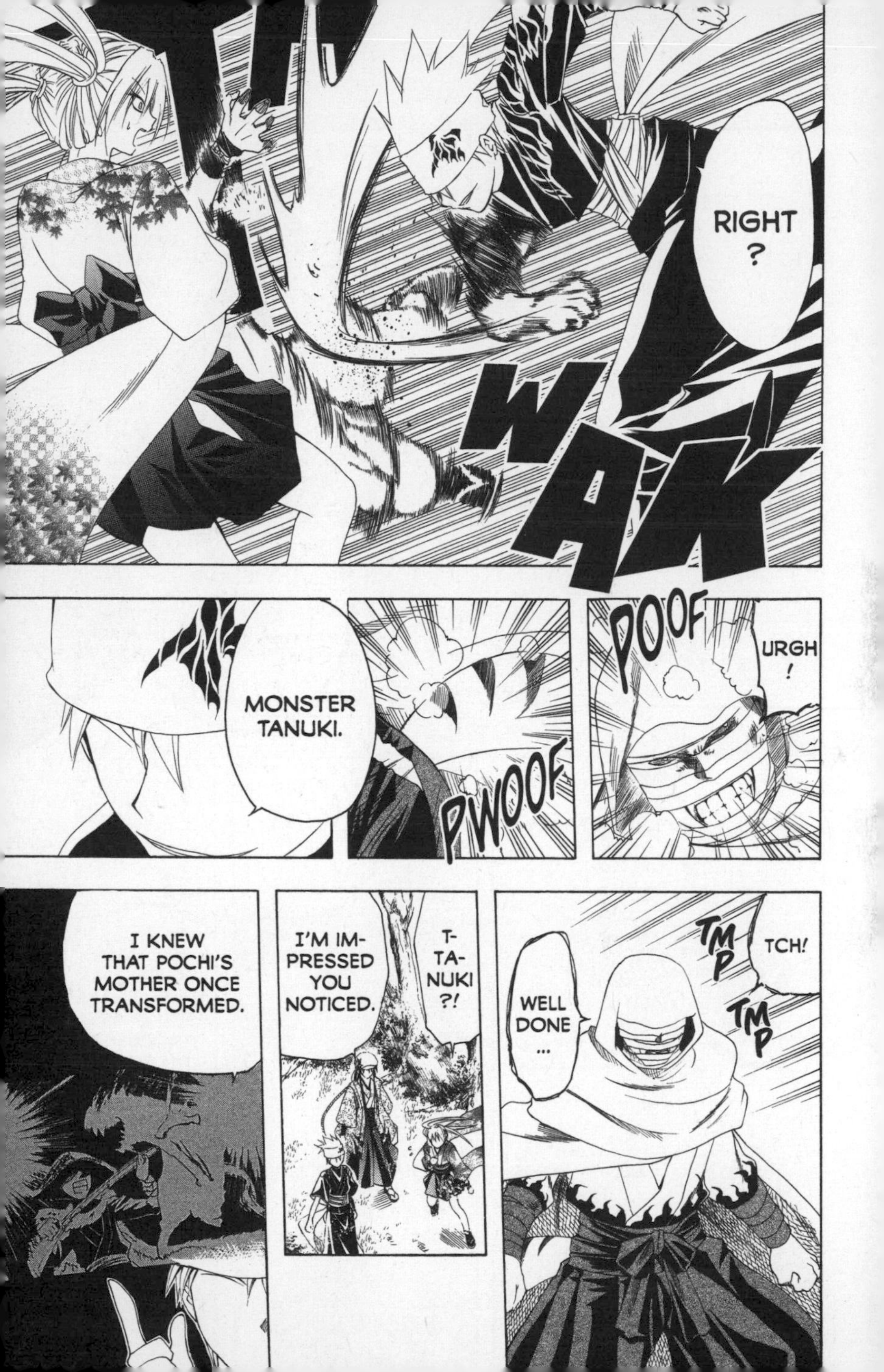
RIGHT?
WAK
POOF
URGH!
PWOOF
MONSTER TANUKI.
TMP
TCH!
TMP
WELL DONE...
T-TANUKI?!
I'M IMPRESSED YOU NOTICED.
I KNEW THAT POCHI'S MOTHER ONCE TRANSFORMED.

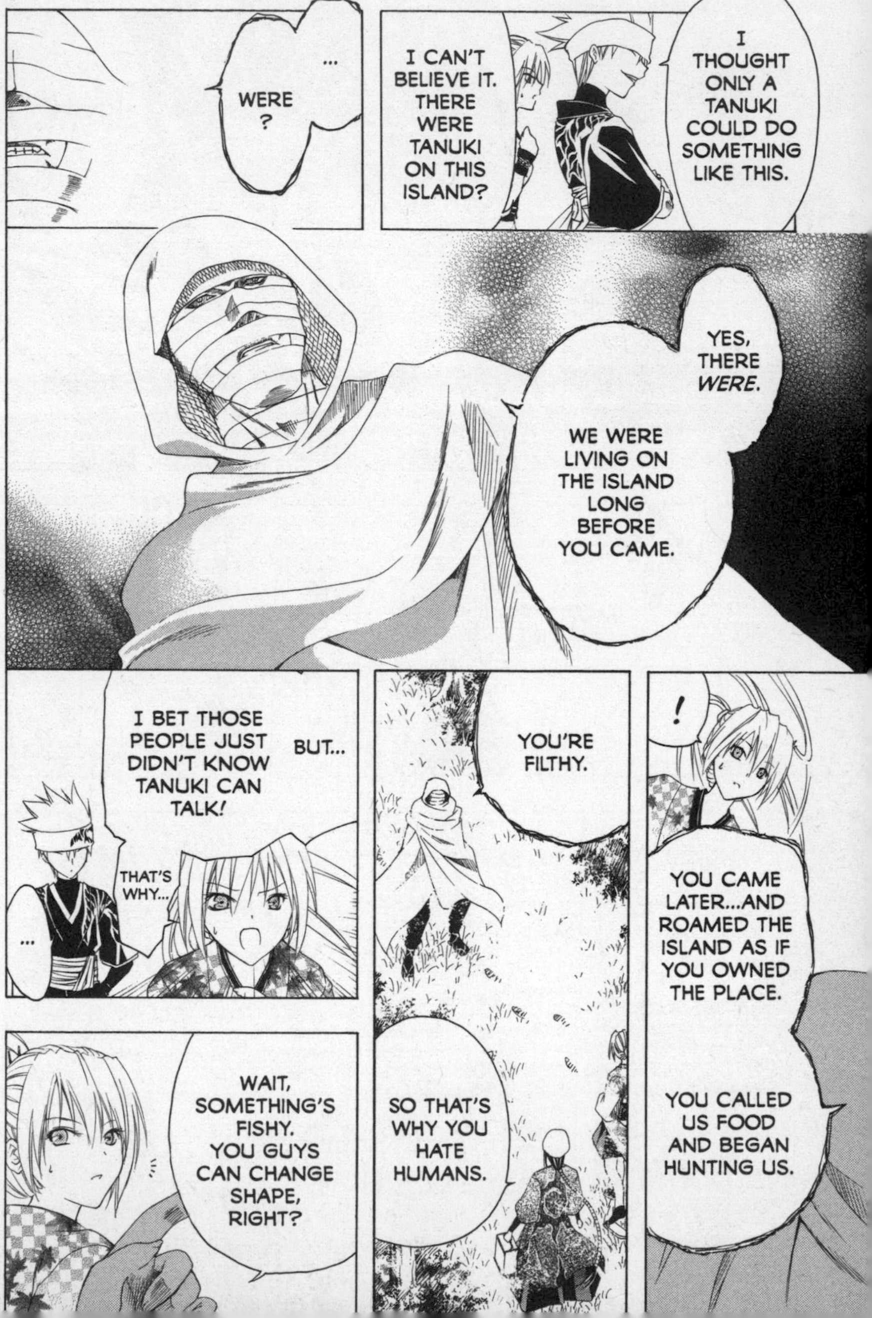
I THOUGHT ONLY A TANUKI COULD DO SOMETHING LIKE THIS.
I CAN'T BELIEVE IT. THERE WERE TANUKI ON THIS ISLAND?
... WERE ?
YES, THERE *WERE*.
WE WERE LIVING ON THE ISLAND LONG BEFORE YOU CAME.
!
YOU CAME LATER...AND ROAMED THE ISLAND AS IF YOU OWNED THE PLACE.
YOU CALLED US FOOD AND BEGAN HUNTING US.
YOU'RE FILTHY.
SO THAT'S WHY YOU HATE HUMANS.
BUT...
I BET THOSE PEOPLE JUST DIDN'T KNOW TANUKI CAN TALK!
THAT'S WHY...
...
WAIT, SOMETHING'S FISHY. YOU GUYS CAN CHANGE SHAPE, RIGHT?

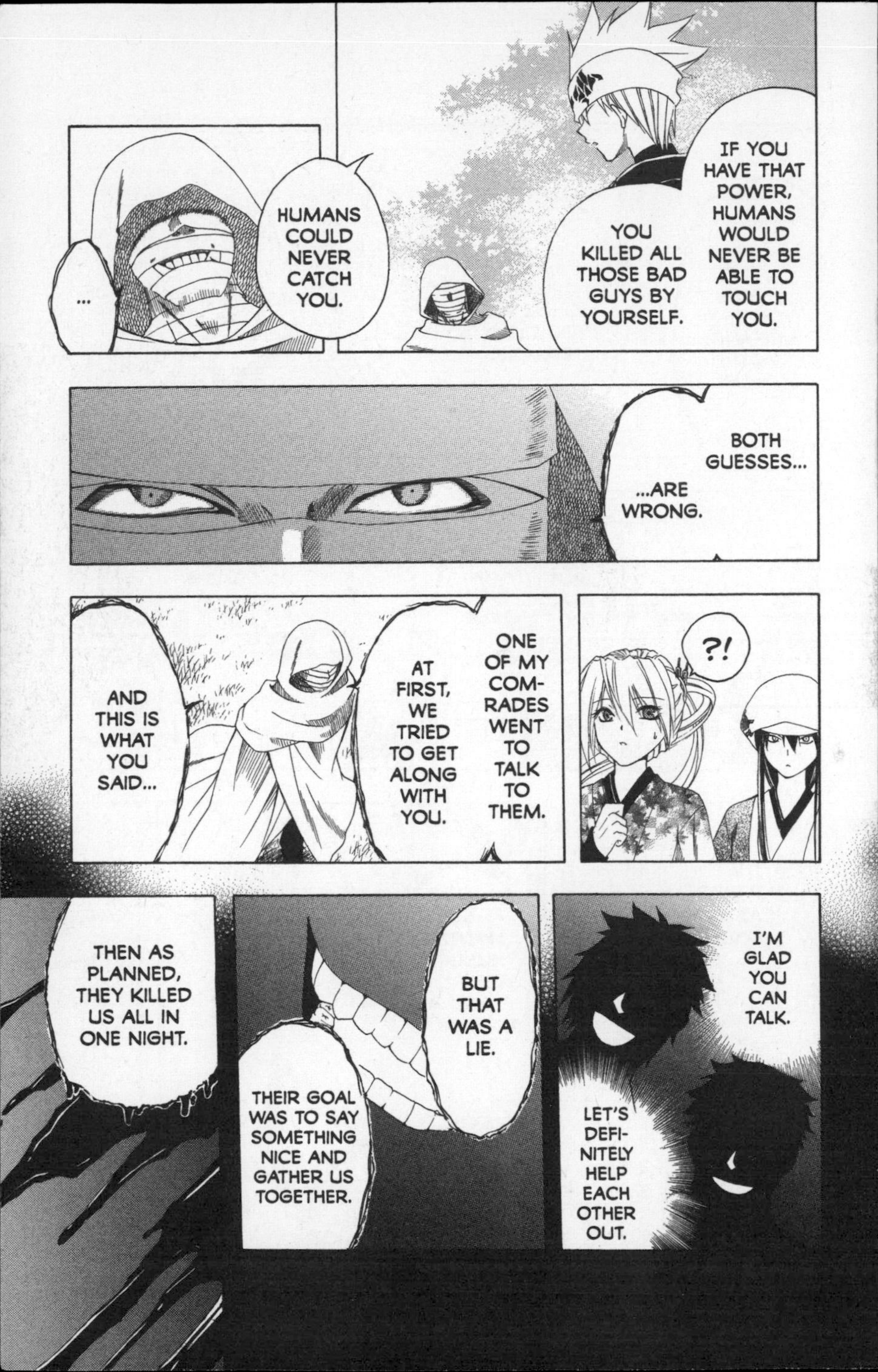
IF YOU HAVE THAT POWER, HUMANS WOULD NEVER BE ABLE TO TOUCH YOU.
YOU KILLED ALL THOSE BAD GUYS BY YOURSELF.
HUMANS COULD NEVER CATCH YOU.
...
BOTH GUESSES...
...ARE WRONG.
?!
ONE OF MY COM-RADES WENT TO TALK TO THEM.
AT FIRST, WE TRIED TO GET ALONG WITH YOU.
AND THIS IS WHAT YOU SAID...
I'M GLAD YOU CAN TALK.
LET'S DEFI-NITELY HELP EACH OTHER OUT.
BUT THAT WAS A LIE.
THEIR GOAL WAS TO SAY SOMETHING NICE AND GATHER US TOGETHER.
THEN AS PLANNED, THEY KILLED US ALL IN ONE NIGHT.

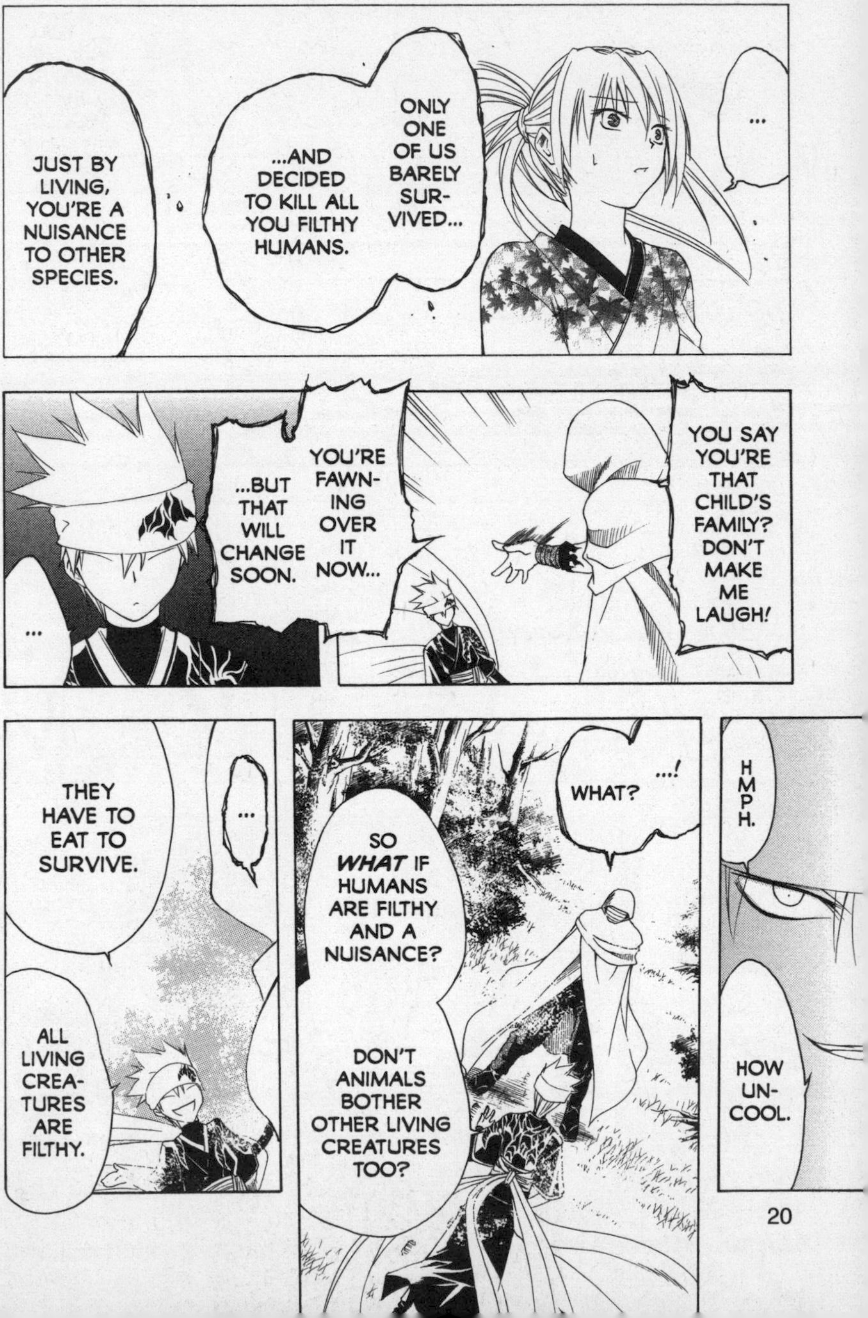
...
ONLY ONE OF US BARELY SURVIVED...
...AND DECIDED TO KILL ALL YOU FILTHY HUMANS.
JUST BY LIVING, YOU'RE A NUISANCE TO OTHER SPECIES.
YOU SAY YOU'RE THAT CHILD'S FAMILY? DON'T MAKE ME LAUGH!
YOU'RE FAWNING OVER IT NOW...
...BUT THAT WILL CHANGE SOON.
...
HMPH.
HOW UN-COOL.
...!
WHAT?
SO *WHAT* IF HUMANS ARE FILTHY AND A NUISANCE?
DON'T ANIMALS BOTHER OTHER LIVING CREATURES TOO?
...
THEY HAVE TO EAT TO SURVIVE.
ALL LIVING CREATURES ARE FILTHY.

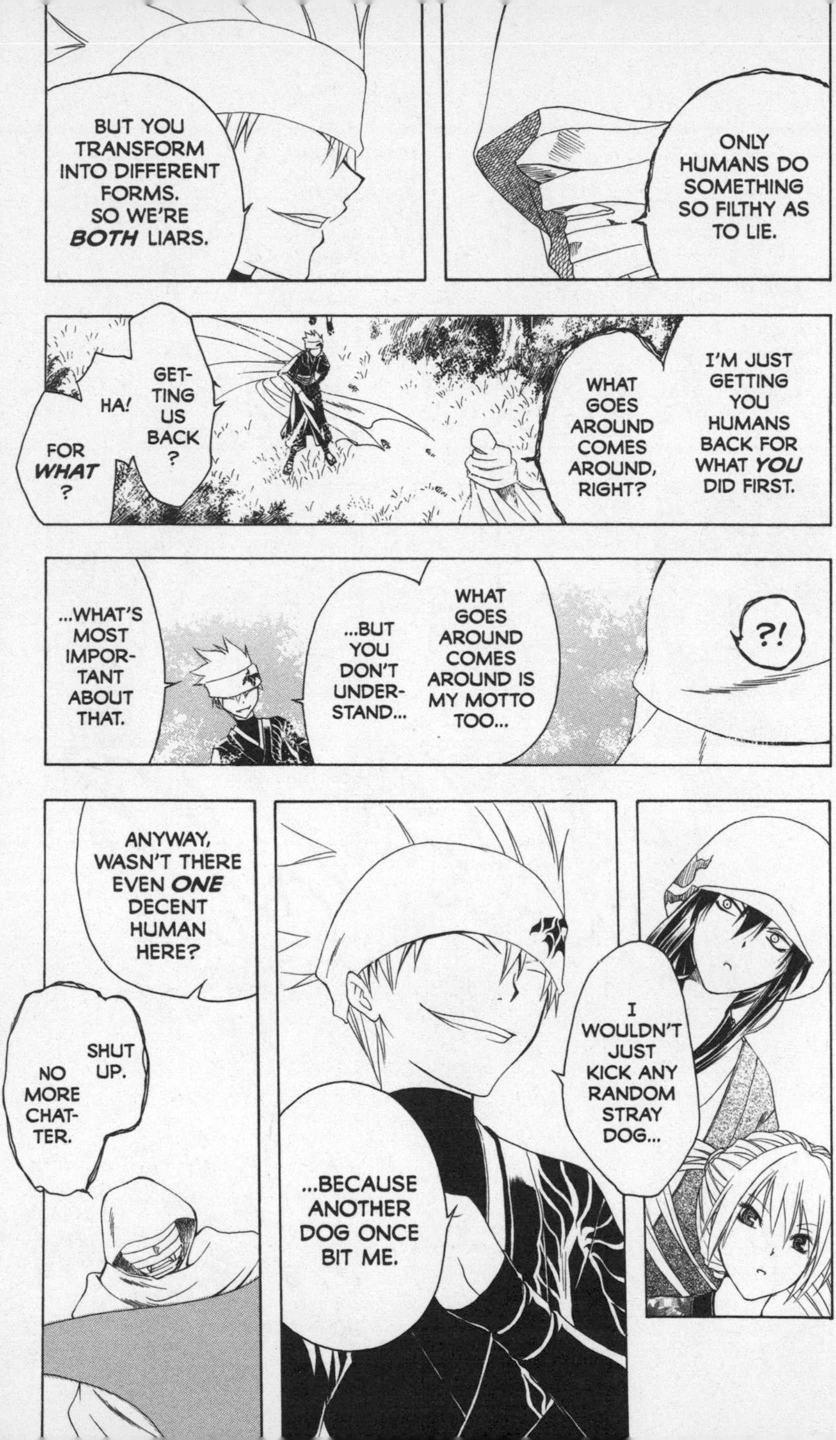
ONLY HUMANS DO SOMETHING SO FILTHY AS TO LIE.
BUT YOU TRANSFORM INTO DIFFERENT FORMS. SO WE'RE *BOTH* LIARS.
I'M JUST GETTING YOU HUMANS BACK FOR WHAT *YOU* DID FIRST.
WHAT GOES AROUND COMES AROUND, RIGHT?
GETTING US BACK?
HA! FOR *WHAT*?
?!
WHAT GOES AROUND COMES AROUND IS MY MOTTO TOO...
...BUT YOU DON'T UNDERSTAND...
...WHAT'S MOST IMPORTANT ABOUT THAT.
I WOULDN'T JUST KICK ANY RANDOM STRAY DOG...
...BECAUSE ANOTHER DOG ONCE BIT ME.
ANYWAY, WASN'T THERE EVEN *ONE* DECENT HUMAN HERE?
SHUT UP. NO MORE CHATTER.

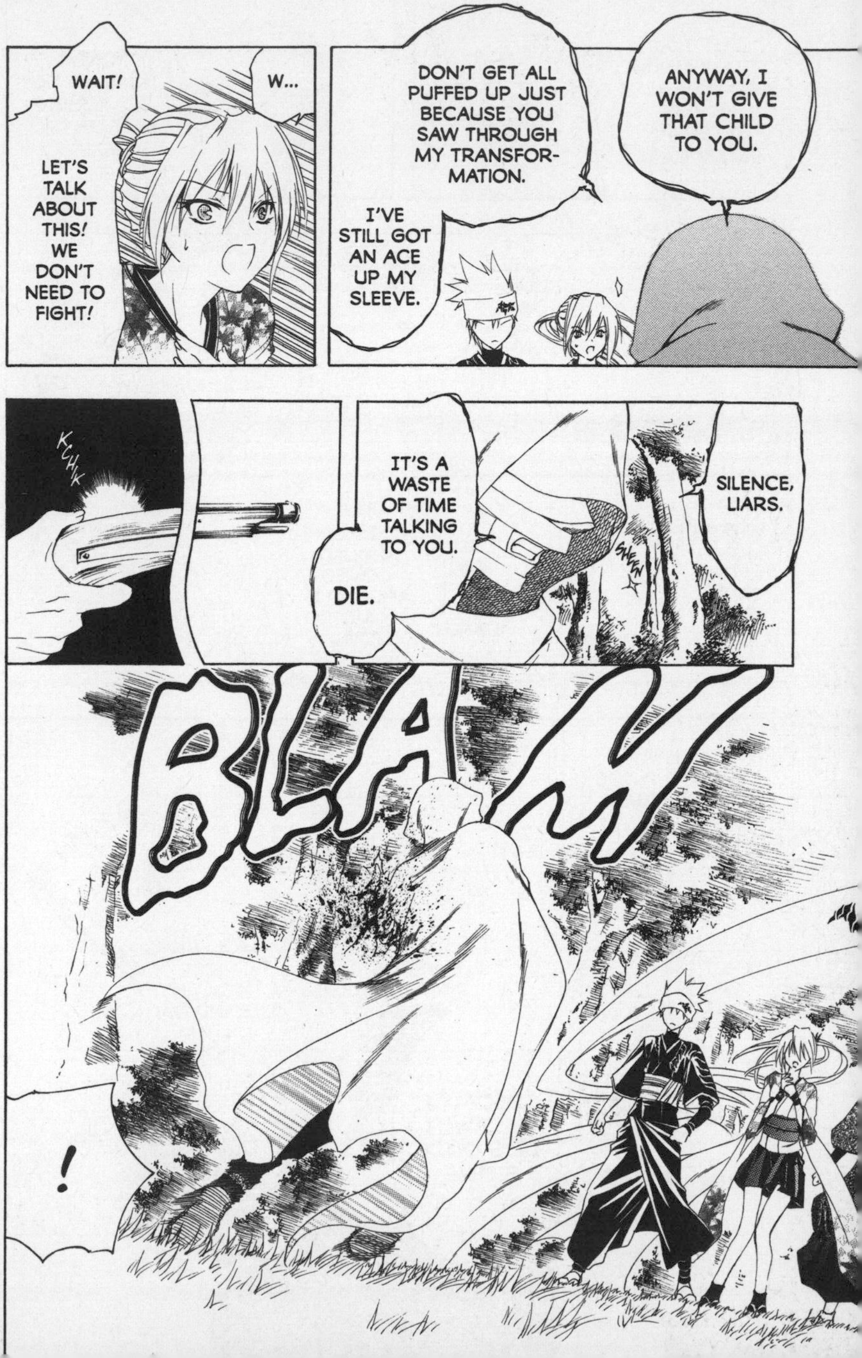
ANYWAY, I WON'T GIVE THAT CHILD TO YOU.
DON'T GET ALL PUFFED UP JUST BECAUSE YOU SAW THROUGH MY TRANSFOR-MATION.
I'VE STILL GOT AN ACE UP MY SLEEVE.
W...
WAIT!
LET'S TALK ABOUT THIS! WE DON'T NEED TO FIGHT!
SILENCE, LIARS.
SHEEN
IT'S A WASTE OF TIME TALKING TO YOU.
DIE.
KCHIK
BLAM
!

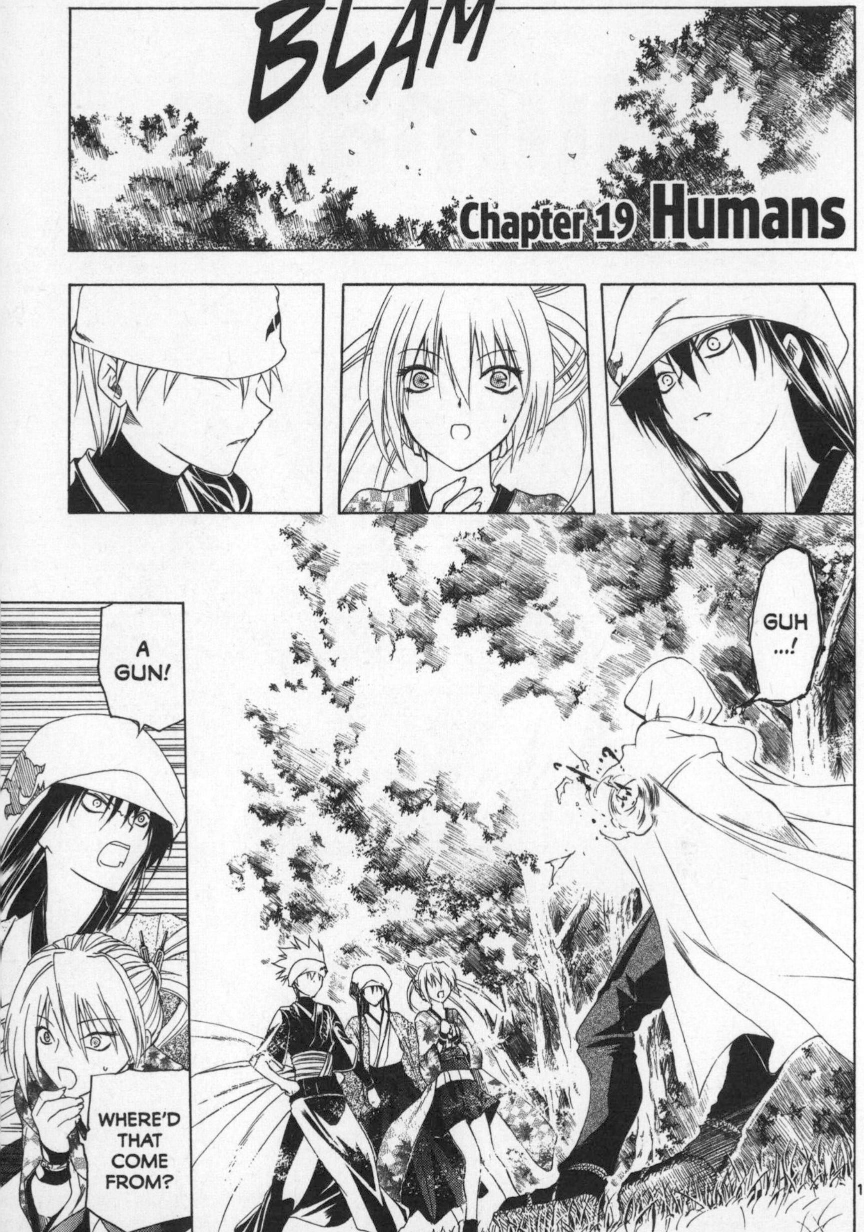
BLAM
Chapter 19 Humans
GUH ...!
A GUN!
WHERE'D THAT COME FROM?

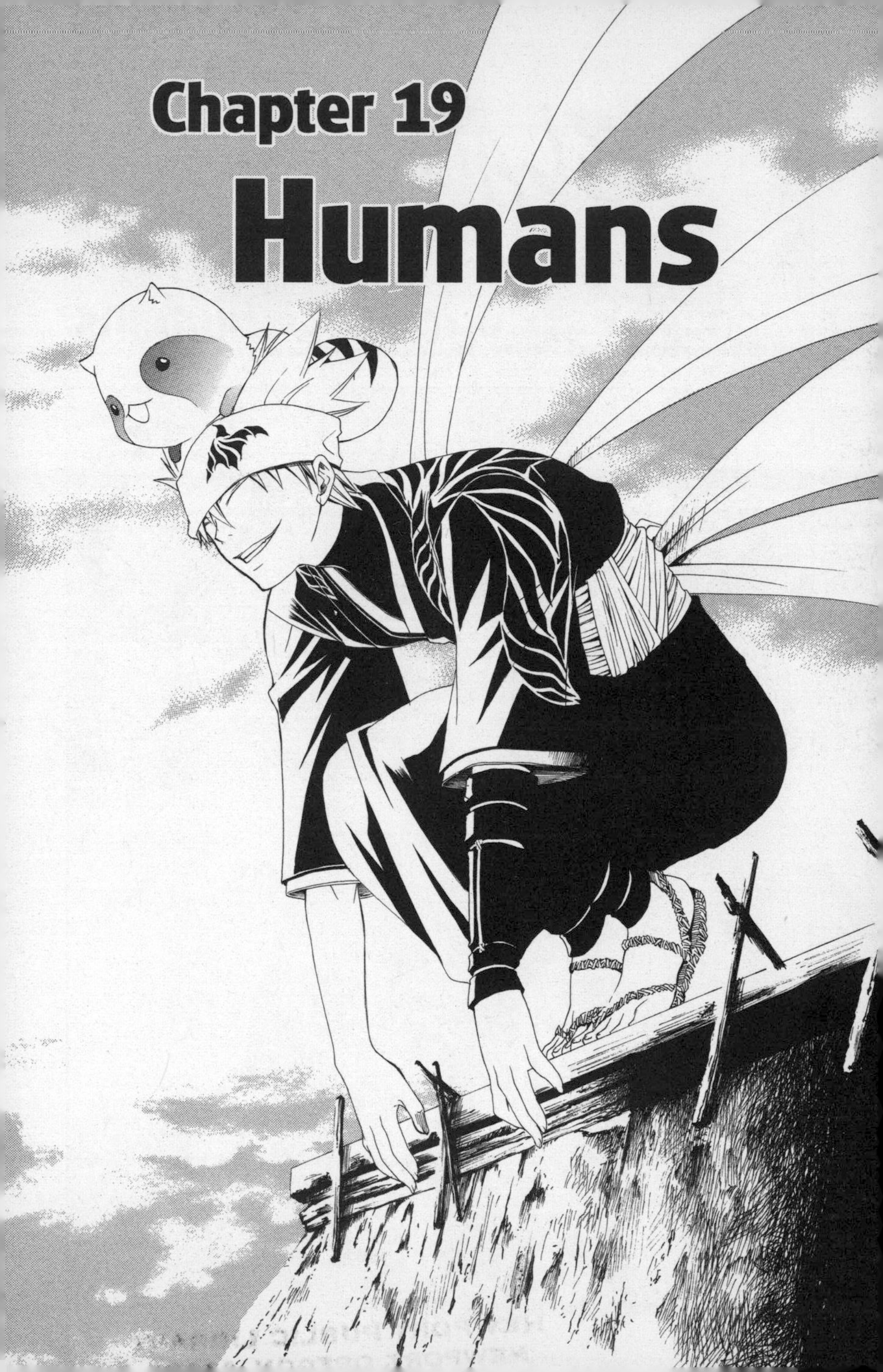

Chapter 19
Humans

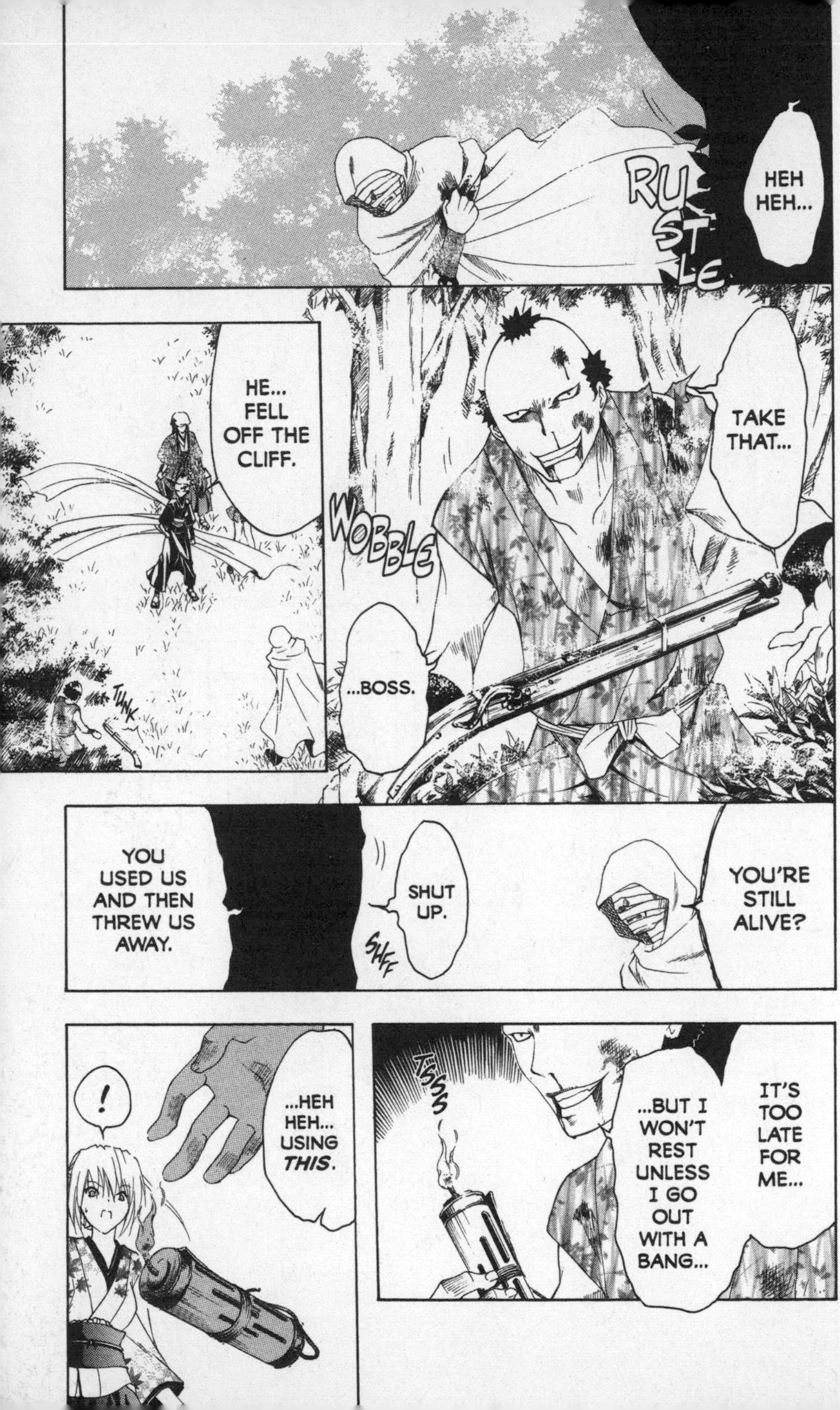
HEH HEH...
RUSTLE
TAKE THAT...
WOBBLE
...BOSS.
HE... FELL OFF THE CLIFF.
TUNK
YOU'RE STILL ALIVE?
SHUT UP.
SHFF
YOU USED US AND THEN THREW US AWAY.
IT'S TOO LATE FOR ME...
...BUT I WON'T REST UNLESS I GO OUT WITH A BANG...
TSSS
...HEH HEH... USING *THIS*.
!

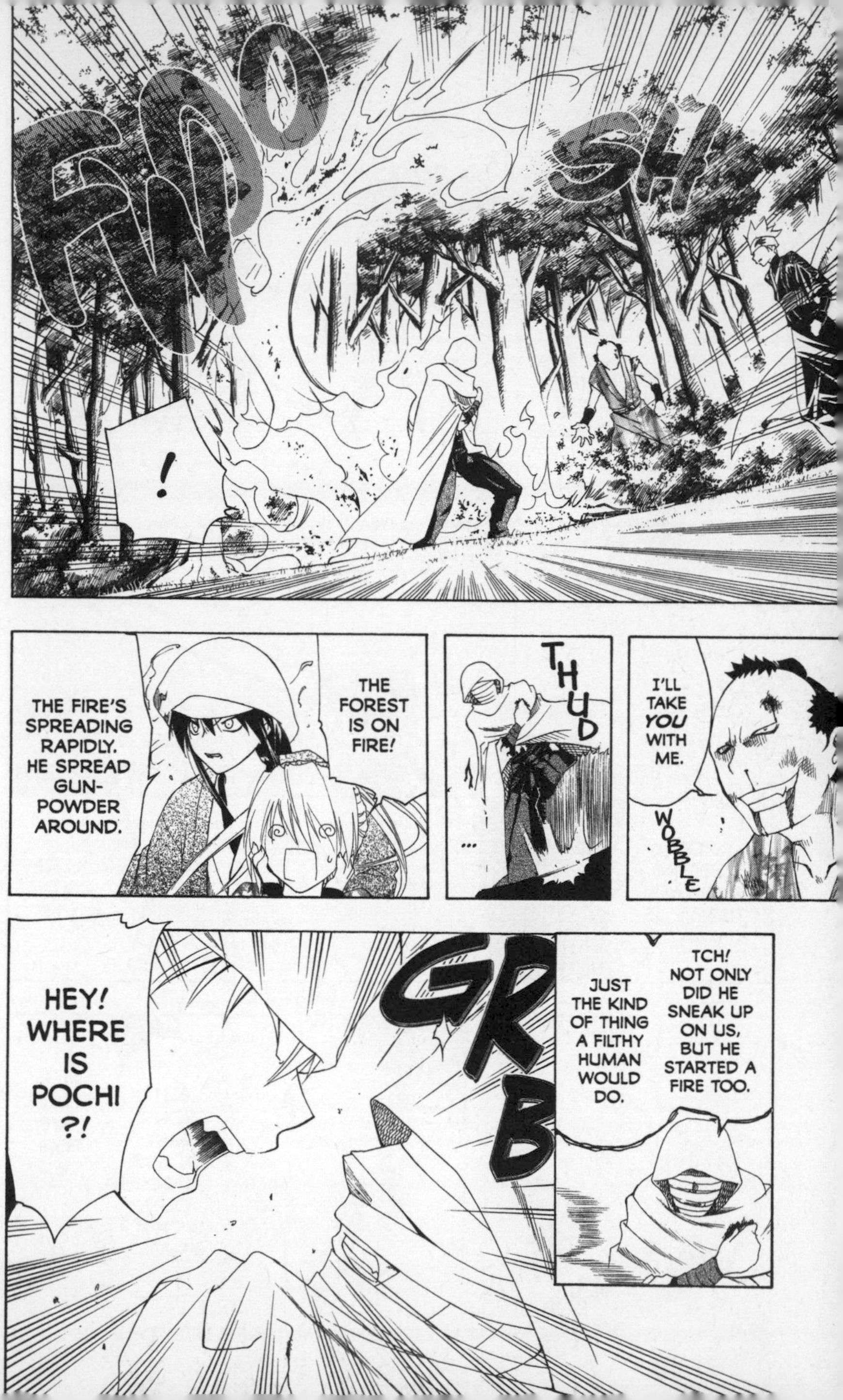
FWOOSH!
!
I'LL TAKE *YOU* WITH ME.
WOBBLE
THUD
...
THE FOREST IS ON FIRE!
THE FIRE'S SPREADING RAPIDLY. HE SPREAD GUN-POWDER AROUND.
TCH! NOT ONLY DID HE SNEAK UP ON US, BUT HE STARTED A FIRE TOO.
JUST THE KIND OF THING A FILTHY HUMAN WOULD DO.
GRB
HEY! WHERE IS POCHI?!

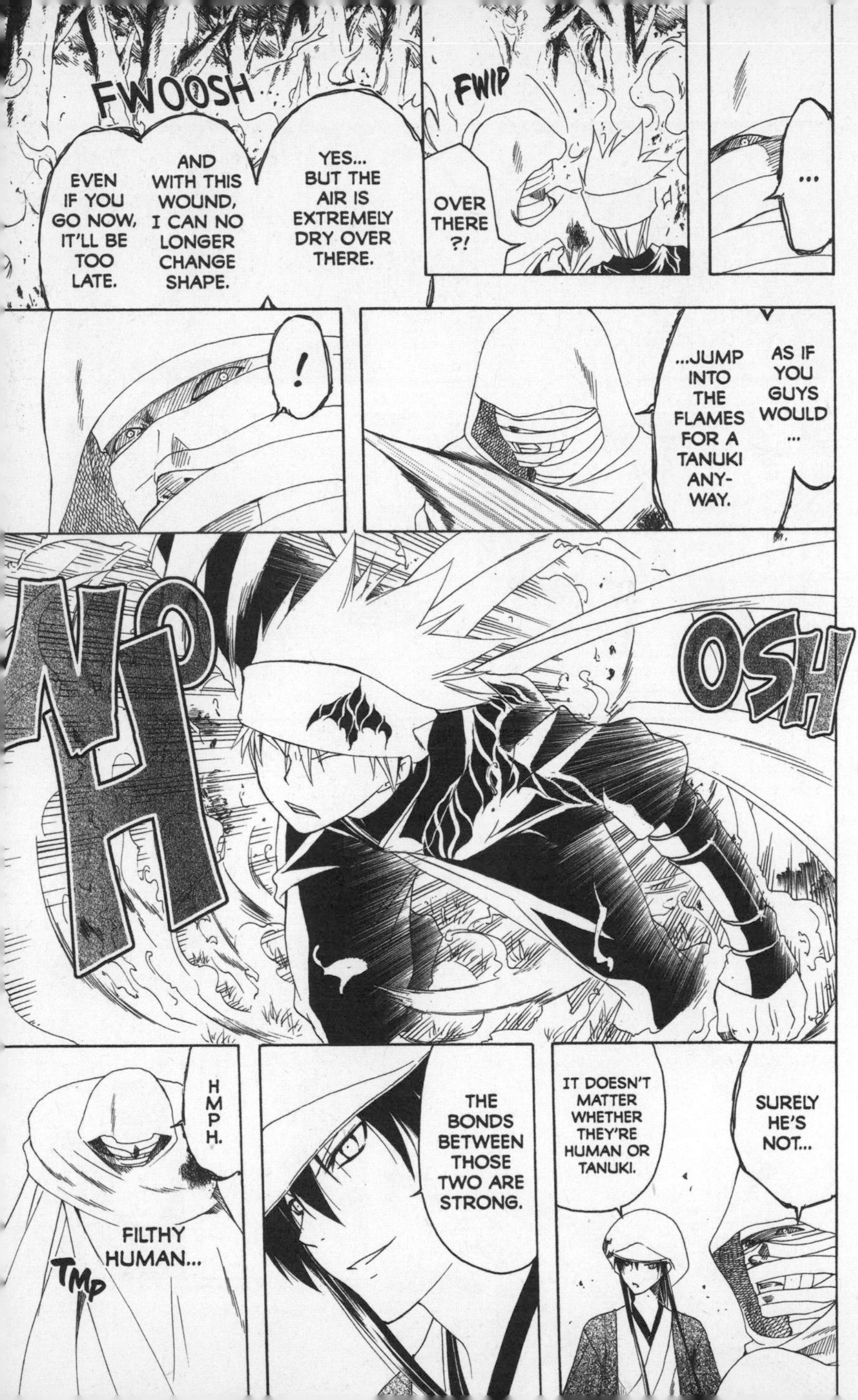
...
FWIP
OVER THERE?!
YES... BUT THE AIR IS EXTREMELY DRY OVER THERE.
AND WITH THIS WOUND, I CAN NO LONGER CHANGE SHAPE.
EVEN IF YOU GO NOW, IT'LL BE TOO LATE.
FWOOSH
AS IF YOU GUYS WOULD...
...JUMP INTO THE FLAMES FOR A TANUKI ANY-WAY.
!
WHOOSH
SURELY HE'S NOT...
IT DOESN'T MATTER WHETHER THEY'RE HUMAN OR TANUKI.
THE BONDS BETWEEN THOSE TWO ARE STRONG.
HMPH.
FILTHY HUMAN...
TMP

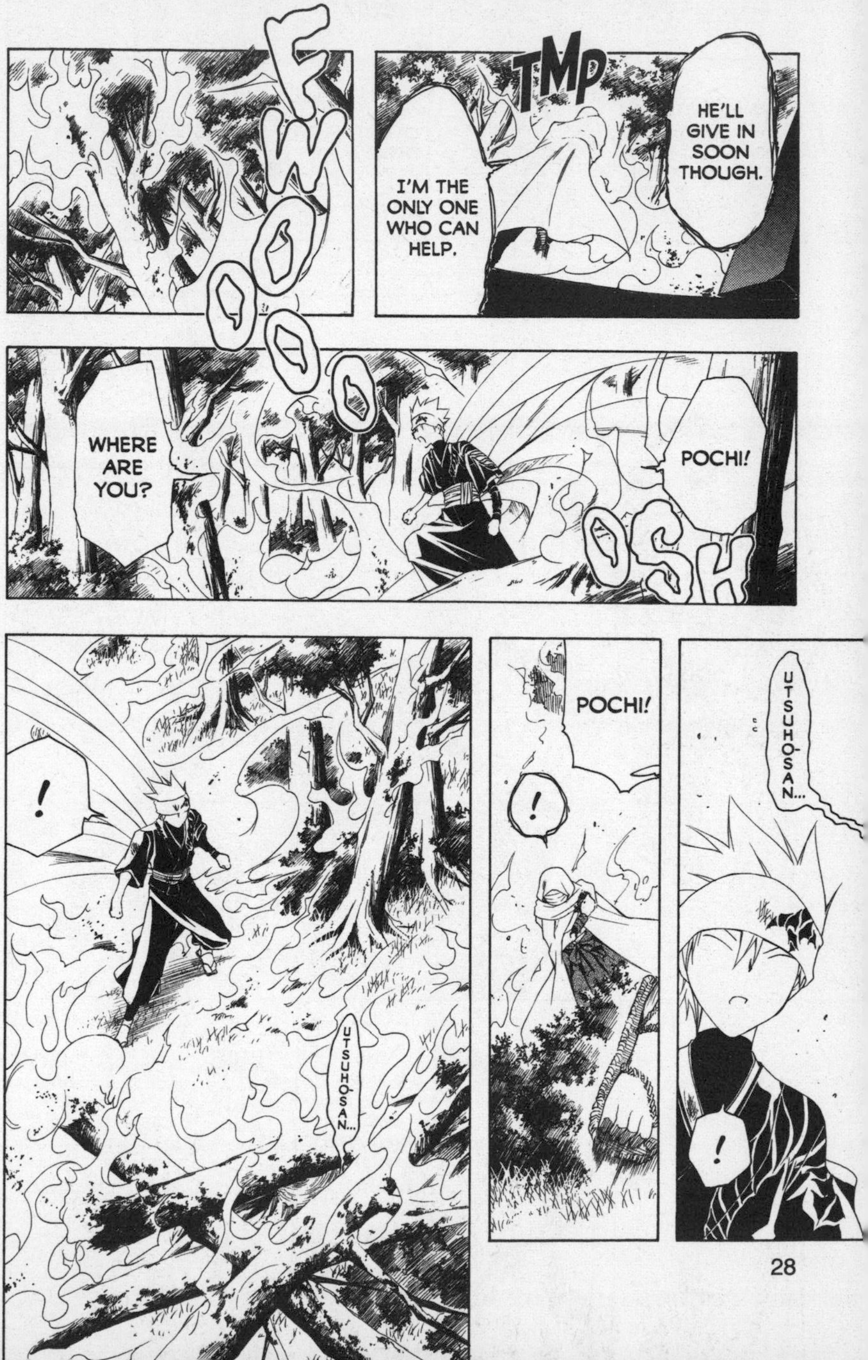
TMP
HE'LL GIVE IN SOON THOUGH.
I'M THE ONLY ONE WHO CAN HELP.
FWOOOO
POCHI!
OSH
WHERE ARE YOU?
UTSUHO-SAN...
!
POCHI!
!
!
UTSUHO-SAN...

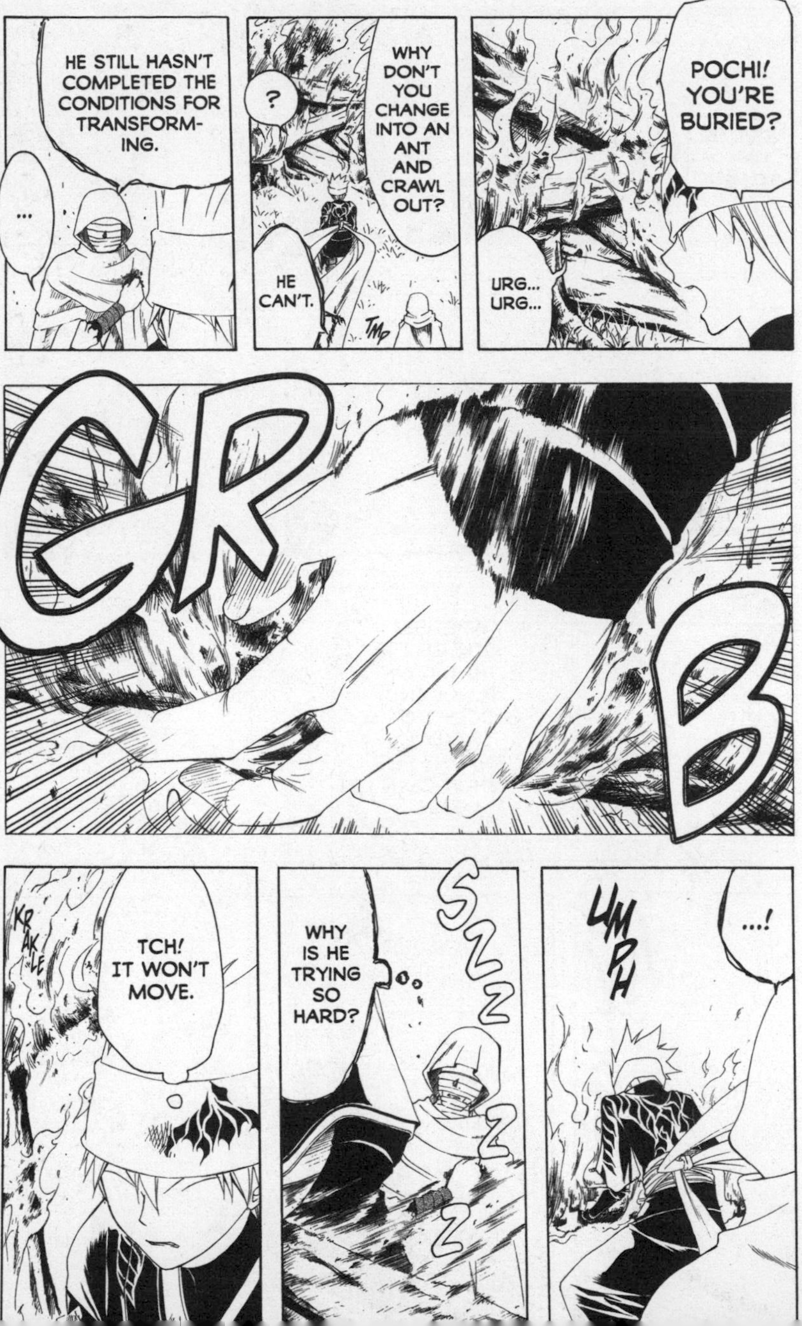
POCHI! YOU'RE BURIED?
URG... URG...
WHY DON'T YOU CHANGE INTO AN ANT AND CRAWL OUT?
?
HE CAN'T.
TMP
HE STILL HASN'T COMPLETED THE CONDITIONS FOR TRANSFORMING.
...
CR
B
UMPH
...!
SZZZZZ
WHY IS HE TRYING SO HARD?
TCH! IT WON'T MOVE.
KRAKLE

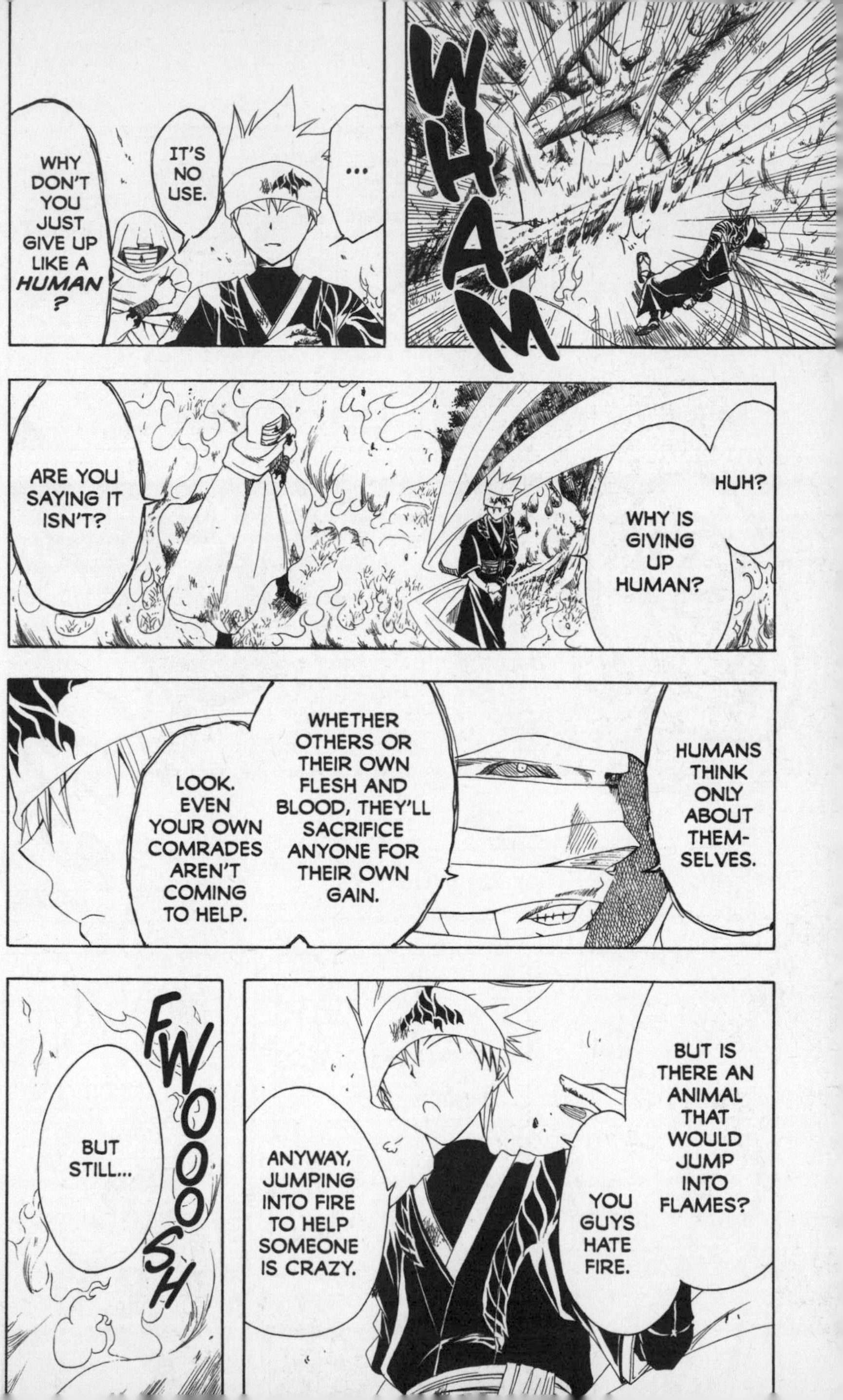
WHAM
...
IT'S NO USE.
WHY DON'T YOU JUST GIVE UP LIKE A *HUMAN*?
HUH?
WHY IS GIVING UP HUMAN?
ARE YOU SAYING IT ISN'T?
HUMANS THINK ONLY ABOUT THEMSELVES.
WHETHER OTHERS OR THEIR OWN FLESH AND BLOOD, THEY'LL SACRIFICE ANYONE FOR THEIR OWN GAIN.
LOOK. EVEN YOUR OWN COMRADES AREN'T COMING TO HELP.
BUT IS THERE AN ANIMAL THAT WOULD JUMP INTO FLAMES?
YOU GUYS HATE FIRE.
ANYWAY, JUMPING INTO FIRE TO HELP SOMEONE IS CRAZY.
FWOOOSH
BUT STILL...

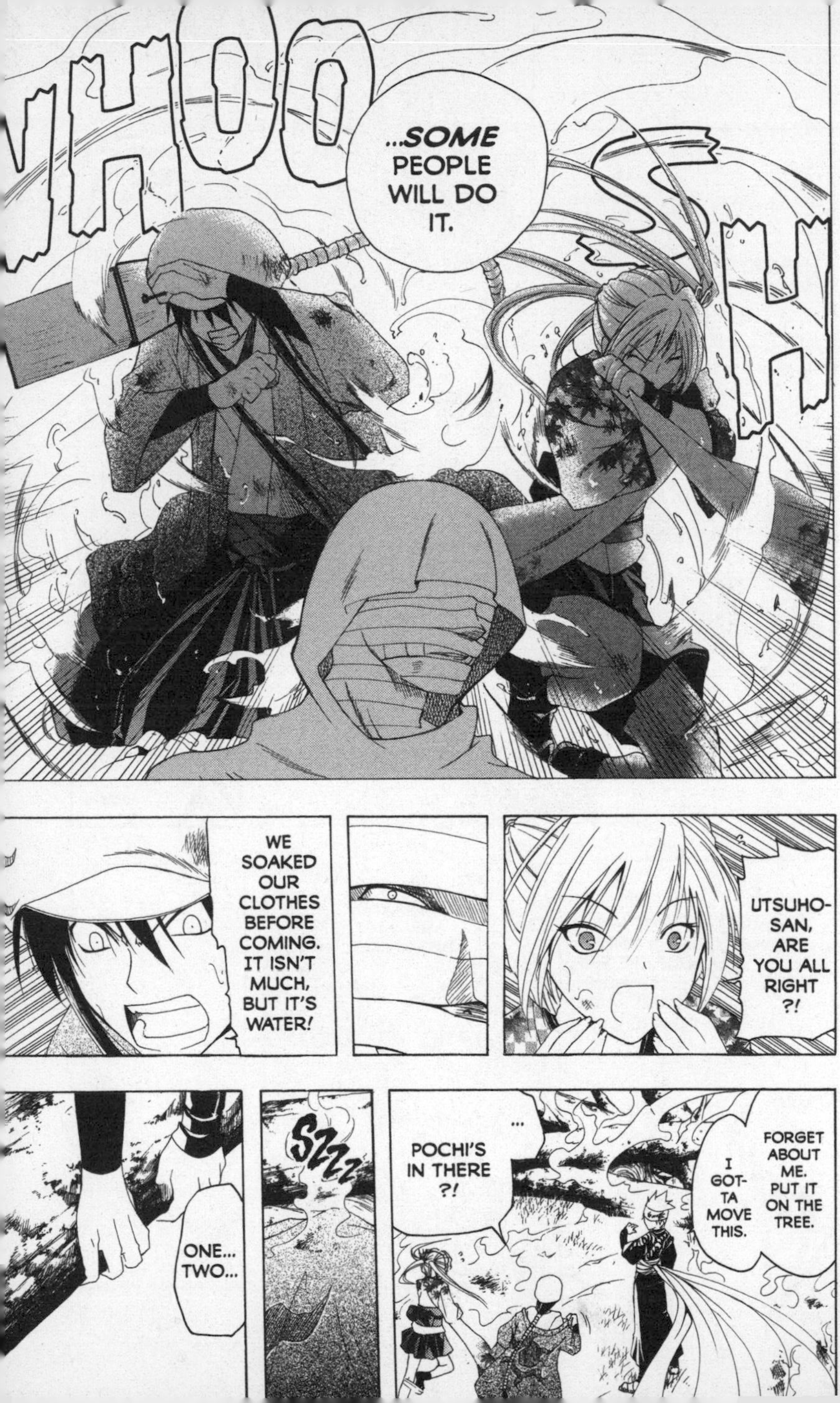
WHOOSH
...*SOME* PEOPLE WILL DO IT.
UTSUHO-SAN, ARE YOU ALL RIGHT ?!
WE SOAKED OUR CLOTHES BEFORE COMING. IT ISN'T MUCH, BUT IT'S WATER!
FORGET ABOUT ME. PUT IT ON THE TREE.
I GOT-TA MOVE THIS.
...
POCHI'S IN THERE ?!
SZZZ
ONE... TWO...

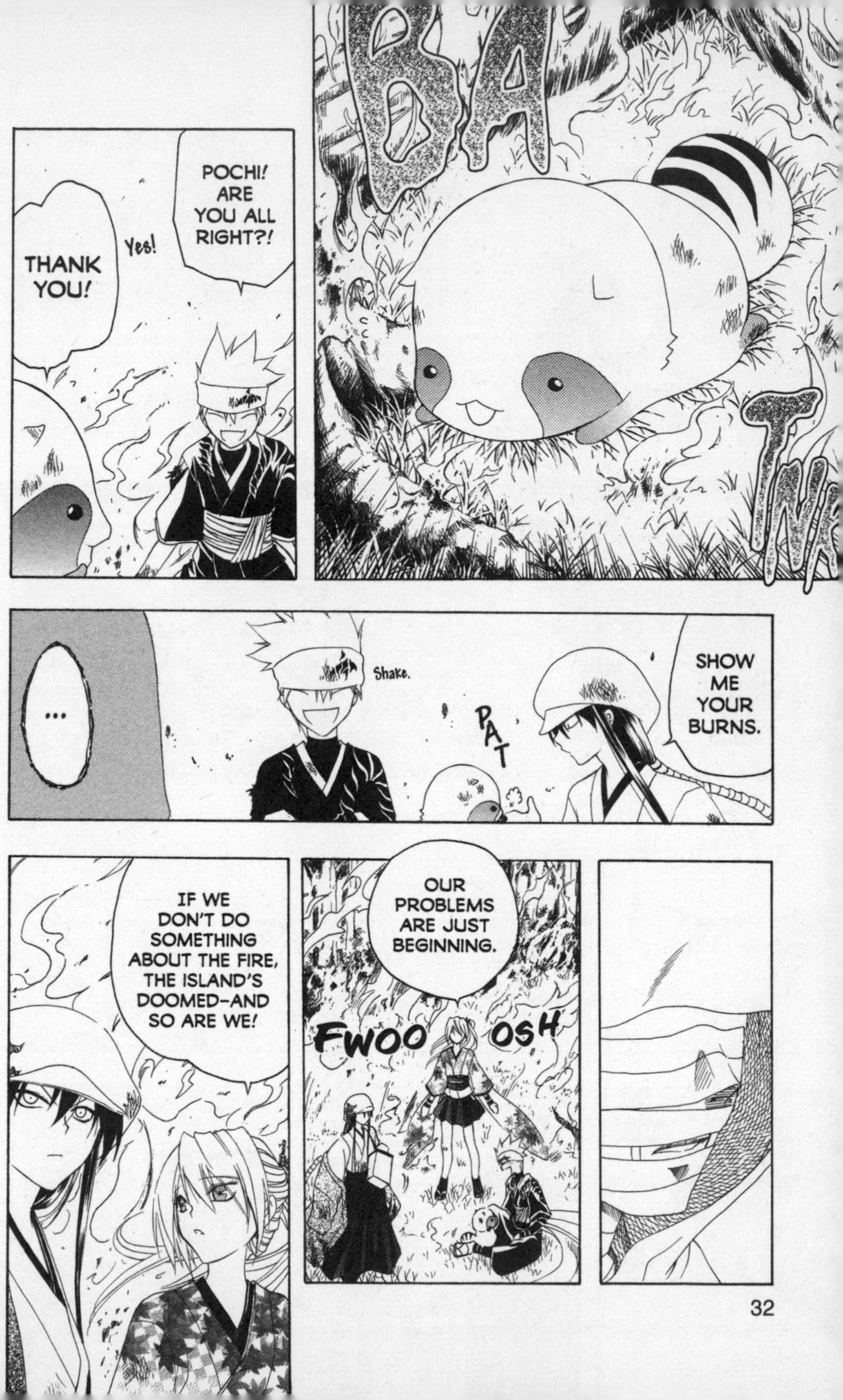
BA
POCHI! ARE YOU ALL RIGHT?!
Yes!
THANK YOU!
SHOW ME YOUR BURNS.
PAT
Shake.
...
OUR PROBLEMS ARE JUST BEGINNING.
FWOOOSH
IF WE DON'T DO SOMETHING ABOUT THE FIRE, THE ISLAND'S DOOMED–AND SO ARE WE!

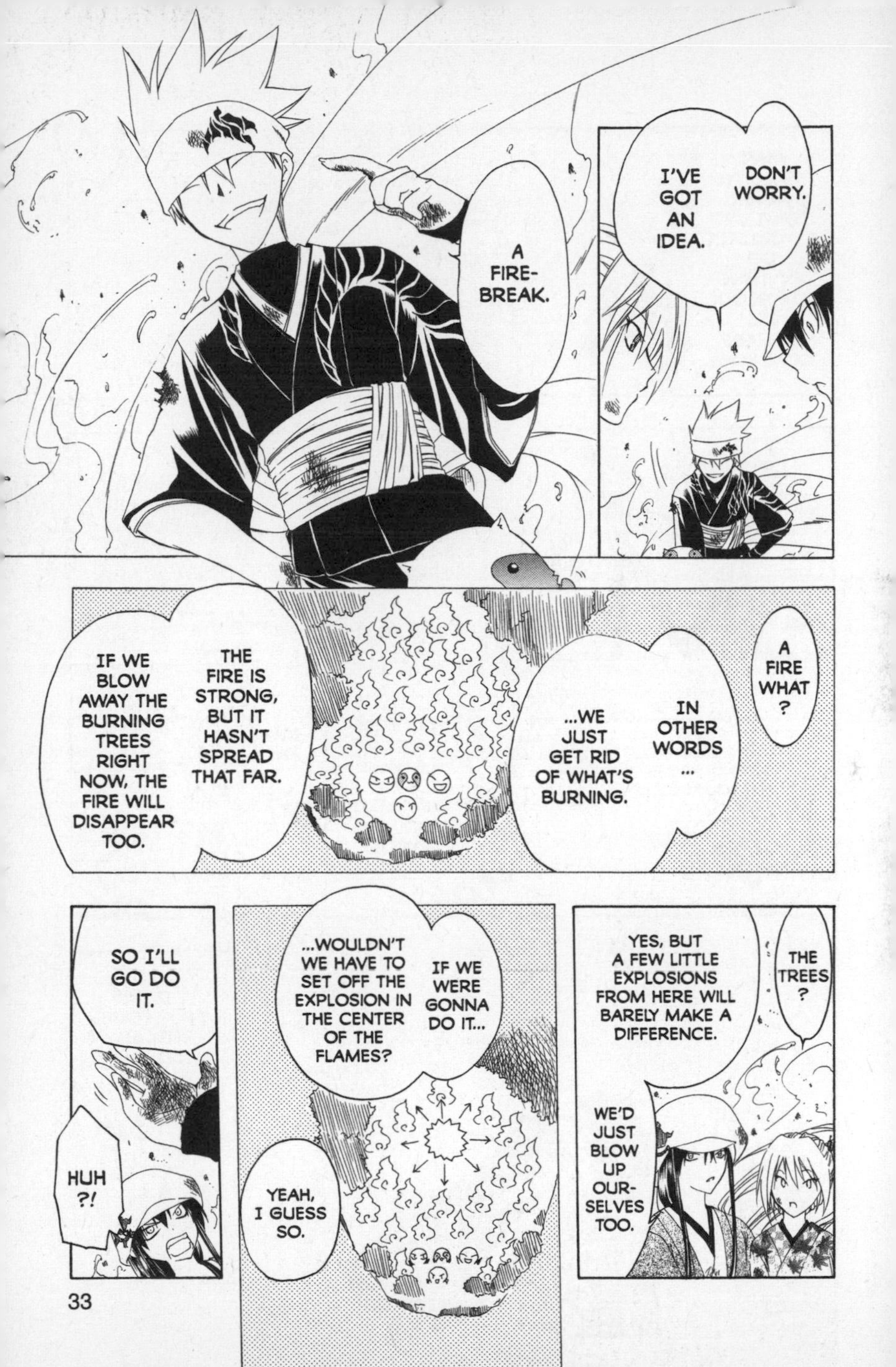
DON'T WORRY.
I'VE GOT AN IDEA.
A FIRE-BREAK.
A FIRE WHAT?
IN OTHER WORDS...
...WE JUST GET RID OF WHAT'S BURNING.
THE FIRE IS STRONG, BUT IT HASN'T SPREAD THAT FAR.
IF WE BLOW AWAY THE BURNING TREES RIGHT NOW, THE FIRE WILL DISAPPEAR TOO.
THE TREES?
YES, BUT A FEW LITTLE EXPLOSIONS FROM HERE WILL BARELY MAKE A DIFFERENCE.
WE'D JUST BLOW UP OUR-SELVES TOO.
IF WE WERE GONNA DO IT...
...WOULDN'T WE HAVE TO SET OFF THE EXPLOSION IN THE CENTER OF THE FLAMES?
YEAH, I GUESS SO.
SO I'LL GO DO IT.
HUH?!

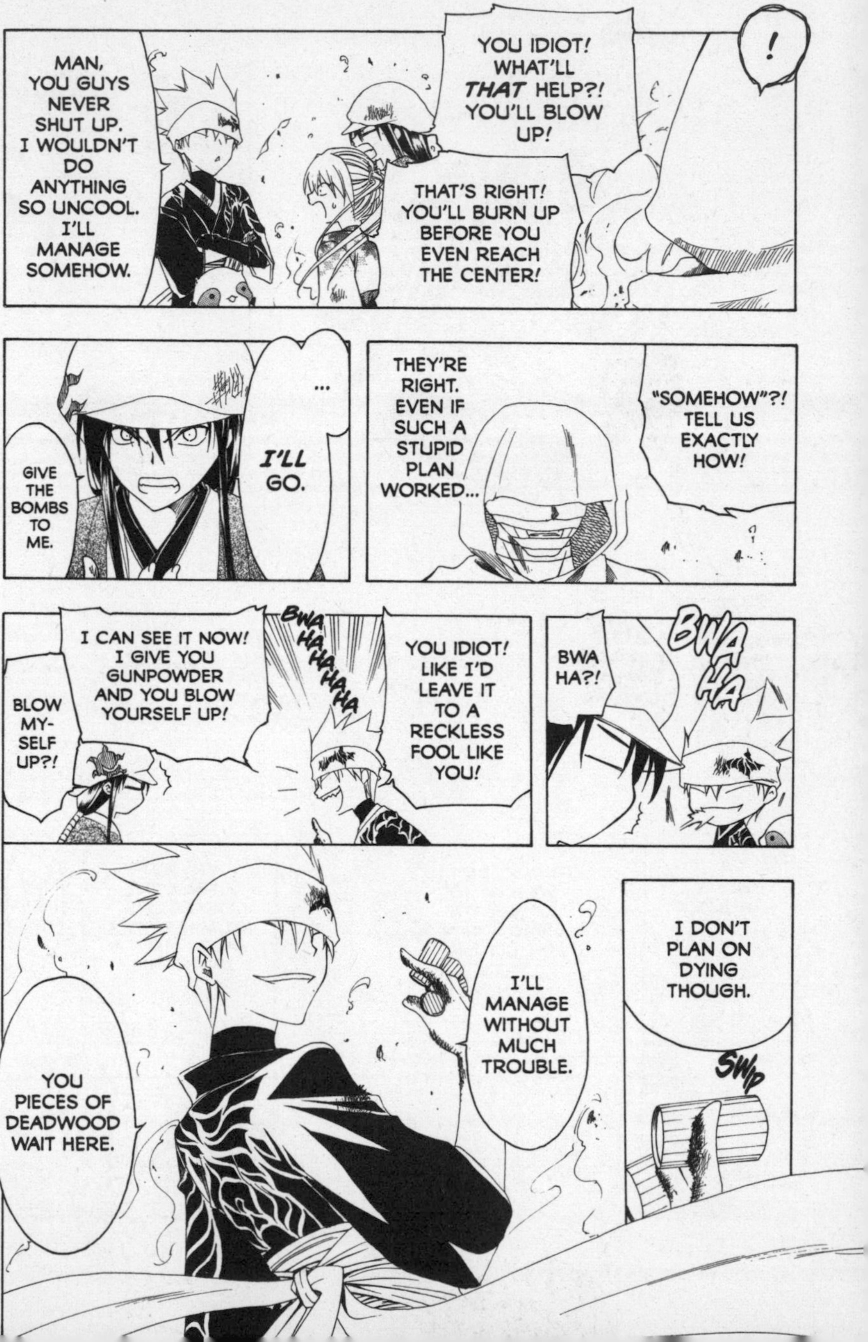
!
YOU IDIOT! WHAT'LL *THAT* HELP?! YOU'LL BLOW UP!
THAT'S RIGHT! YOU'LL BURN UP BEFORE YOU EVEN REACH THE CENTER!
MAN, YOU GUYS NEVER SHUT UP. I WOULDN'T DO ANYTHING SO UNCOOL. I'LL MANAGE SOMEHOW.
"SOMEHOW"?! TELL US EXACTLY HOW!
THEY'RE RIGHT. EVEN IF SUCH A STUPID PLAN WORKED...
...
I'LL GO.
GIVE THE BOMBS TO ME.
BWA HA
BWA HA?!
YOU IDIOT! LIKE I'D LEAVE IT TO A RECKLESS FOOL LIKE YOU!
BWA HA HA HA HA HA
I CAN SEE IT NOW! I GIVE YOU GUNPOWDER AND YOU BLOW YOURSELF UP!
BLOW MY-SELF UP?!
I DON'T PLAN ON DYING THOUGH.
SWIP
I'LL MANAGE WITHOUT MUCH TROUBLE.
YOU PIECES OF DEADWOOD WAIT HERE.

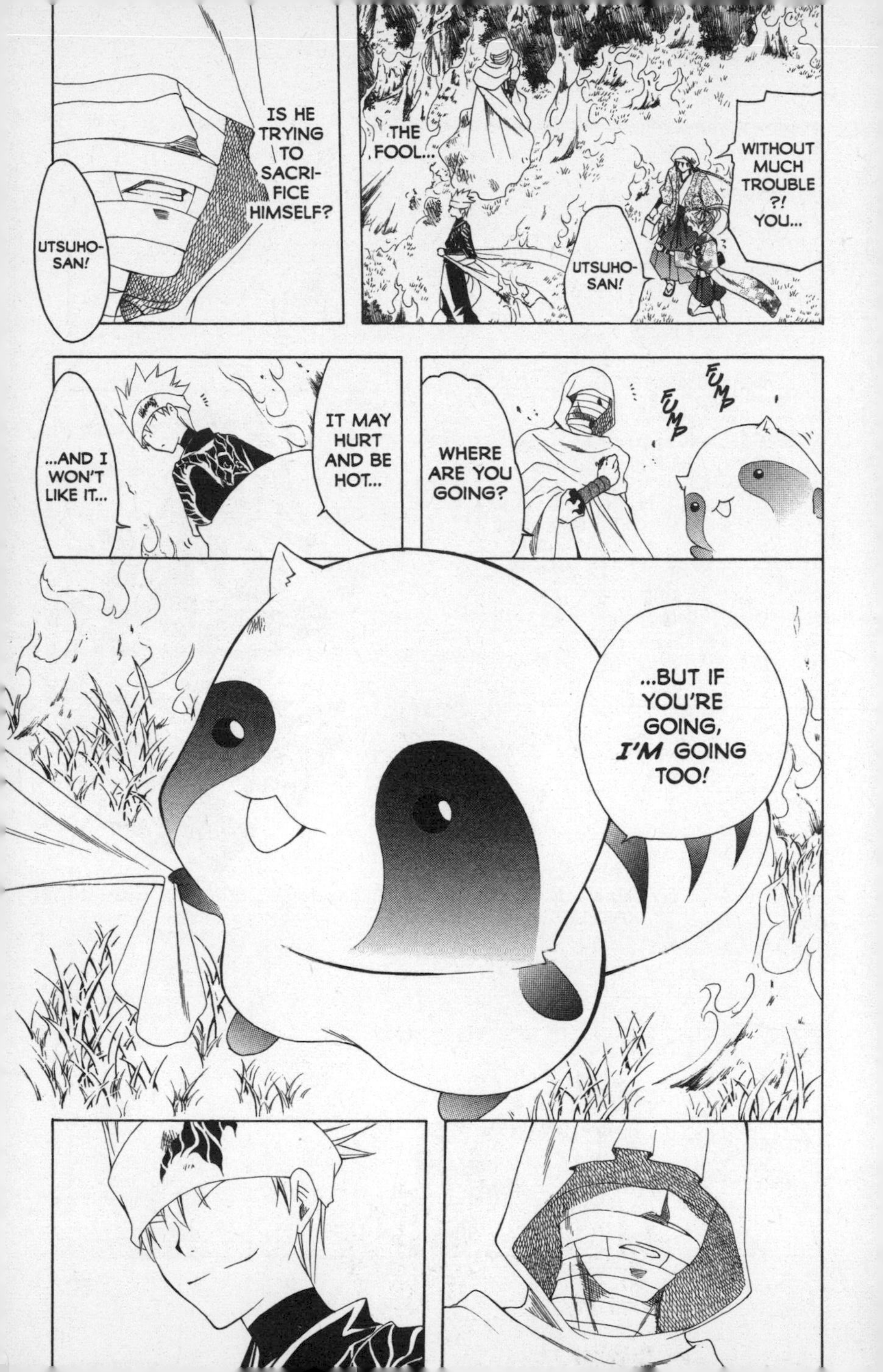
WITHOUT MUCH TROUBLE?! YOU...
UTSUHO-SAN!
THE FOOL...
IS HE TRYING TO SACRIFICE HIMSELF?
UTSUHO-SAN!
FUMP
FUMP
WHERE ARE YOU GOING?
IT MAY HURT AND BE HOT...
...AND I WON'T LIKE IT...
...BUT IF YOU'RE GOING, *I'M* GOING TOO!

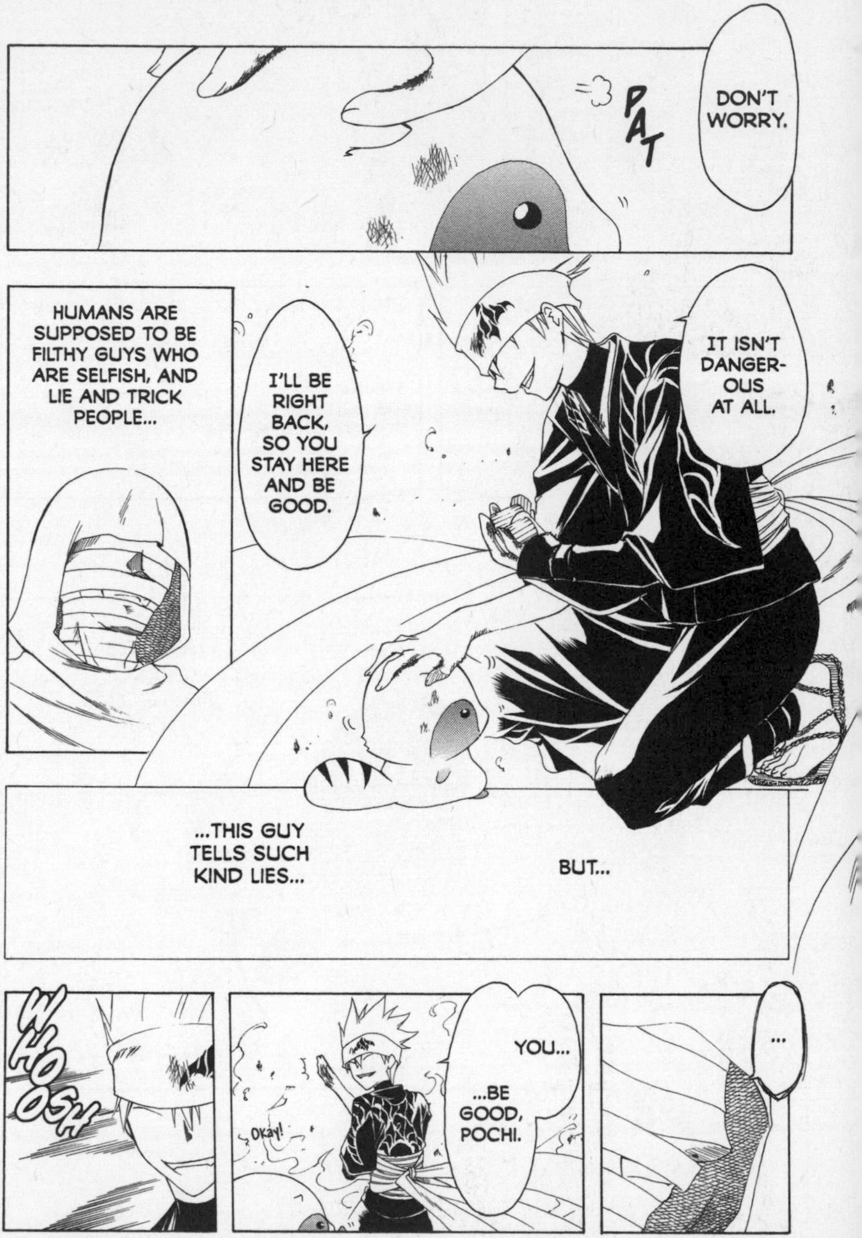
DON'T WORRY.
PAT
IT ISN'T DANGER-OUS AT ALL.
I'LL BE RIGHT BACK, SO YOU STAY HERE AND BE GOOD.
HUMANS ARE SUPPOSED TO BE FILTHY GUYS WHO ARE SELFISH, AND LIE AND TRICK PEOPLE...
BUT...
...THIS GUY TELLS SUCH KIND LIES...
...
YOU...
...BE GOOD, POCHI.
Okay!
WHOSH

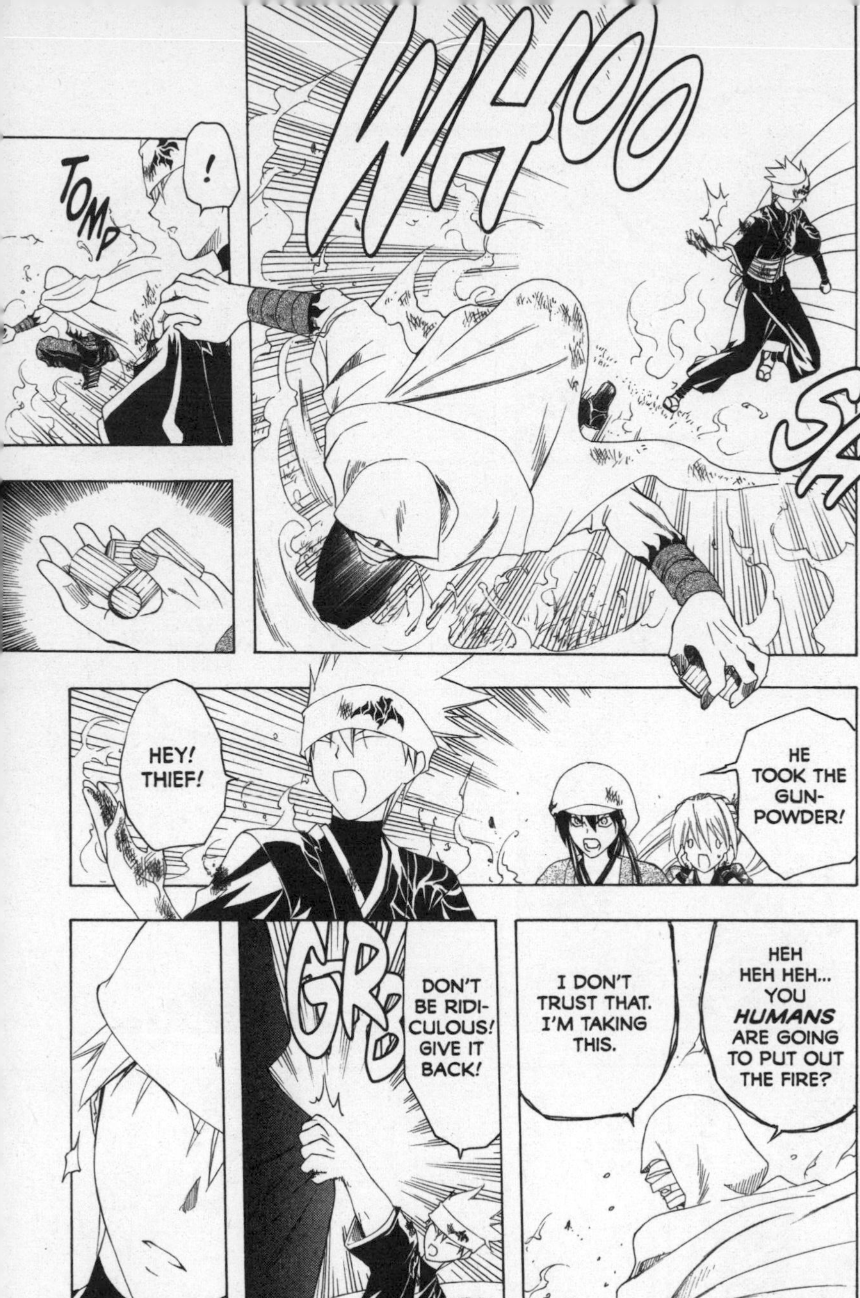
WHOOO
SH
TOMP
!
HE TOOK THE GUN-POWDER!
HEY! THIEF!
HEH HEH HEH... YOU **HUMANS** ARE GOING TO PUT OUT THE FIRE?
I DON'T TRUST THAT. I'M TAKING THIS.
DON'T BE RIDI-CULOUS! GIVE IT BACK!
GR

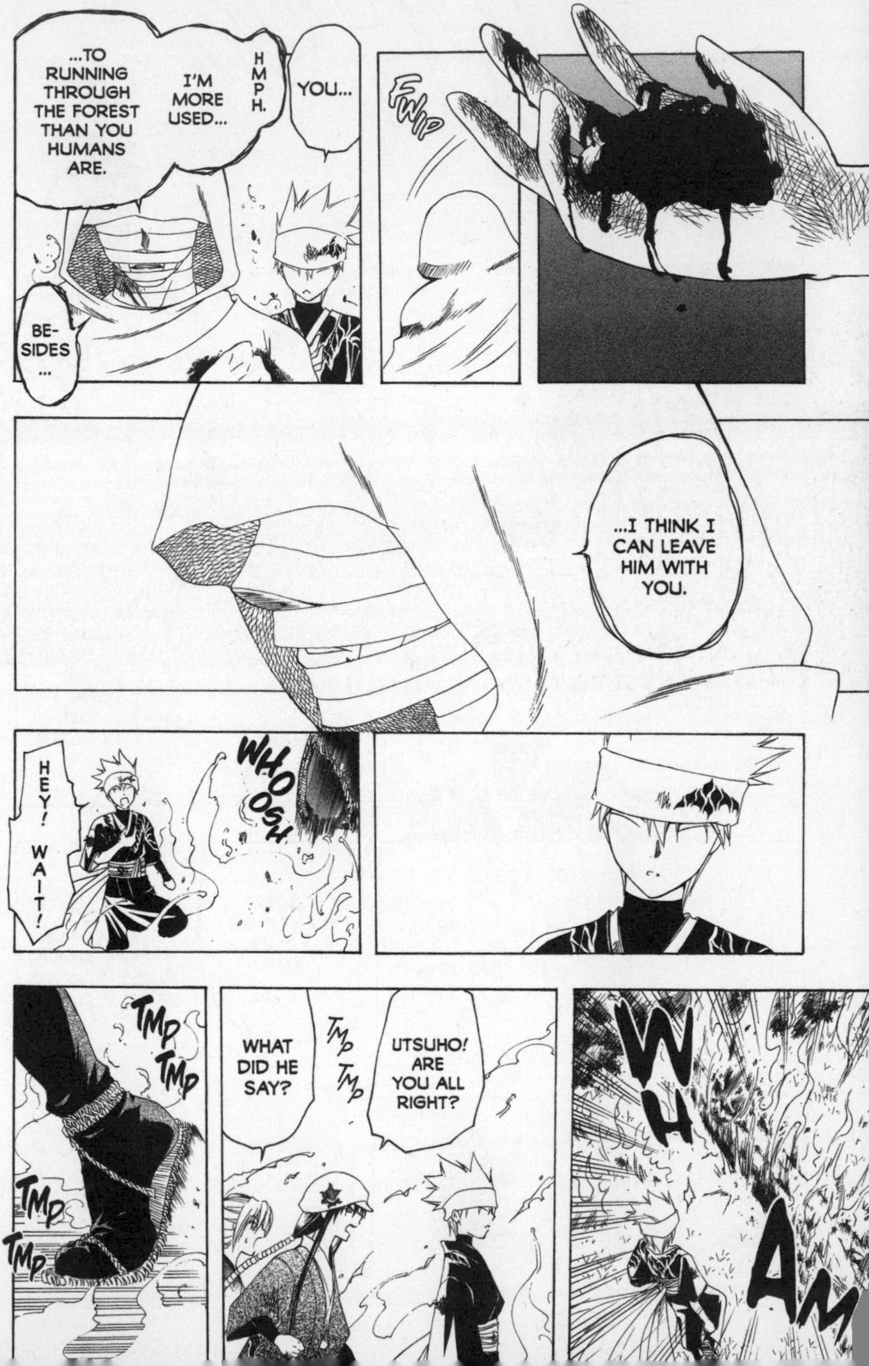
FWIP
YOU...
HMPH.
I'M MORE USED...
...TO RUNNING THROUGH THE FOREST THAN YOU HUMANS ARE.
BE-SIDES...
...I THINK I CAN LEAVE HIM WITH YOU.
WHOOSH
HEY! WAIT!
WHAM
UTSUHO! ARE YOU ALL RIGHT?
TMP TMP
WHAT DID HE SAY?
TMP TMP
TMP TMP

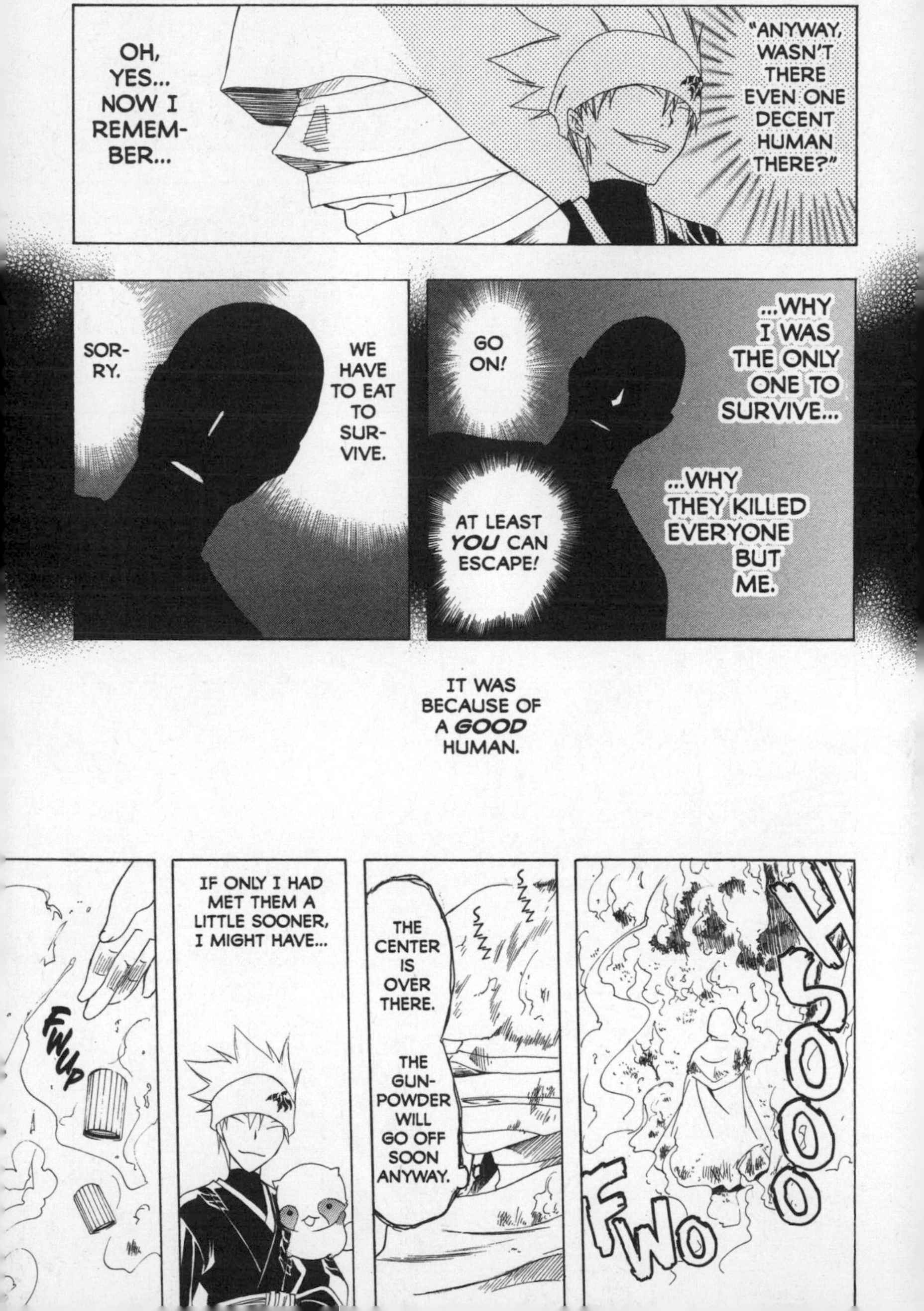
"ANYWAY, WASN'T THERE EVEN ONE DECENT HUMAN THERE?"
OH, YES... NOW I REMEMBER...
...WHY I WAS THE ONLY ONE TO SURVIVE...
GO ON!
...WHY THEY KILLED EVERYONE BUT ME.
AT LEAST *YOU* CAN ESCAPE!
WE HAVE TO EAT TO SURVIVE.
SORRY.
IT WAS BECAUSE OF A *GOOD* HUMAN.
FWOOOOSH
ZZZ
ZZZ
THE CENTER IS OVER THERE.
THE GUNPOWDER WILL GO OFF SOON ANYWAY.
IF ONLY I HAD MET THEM A LITTLE SOONER, I MIGHT HAVE...
FWUP

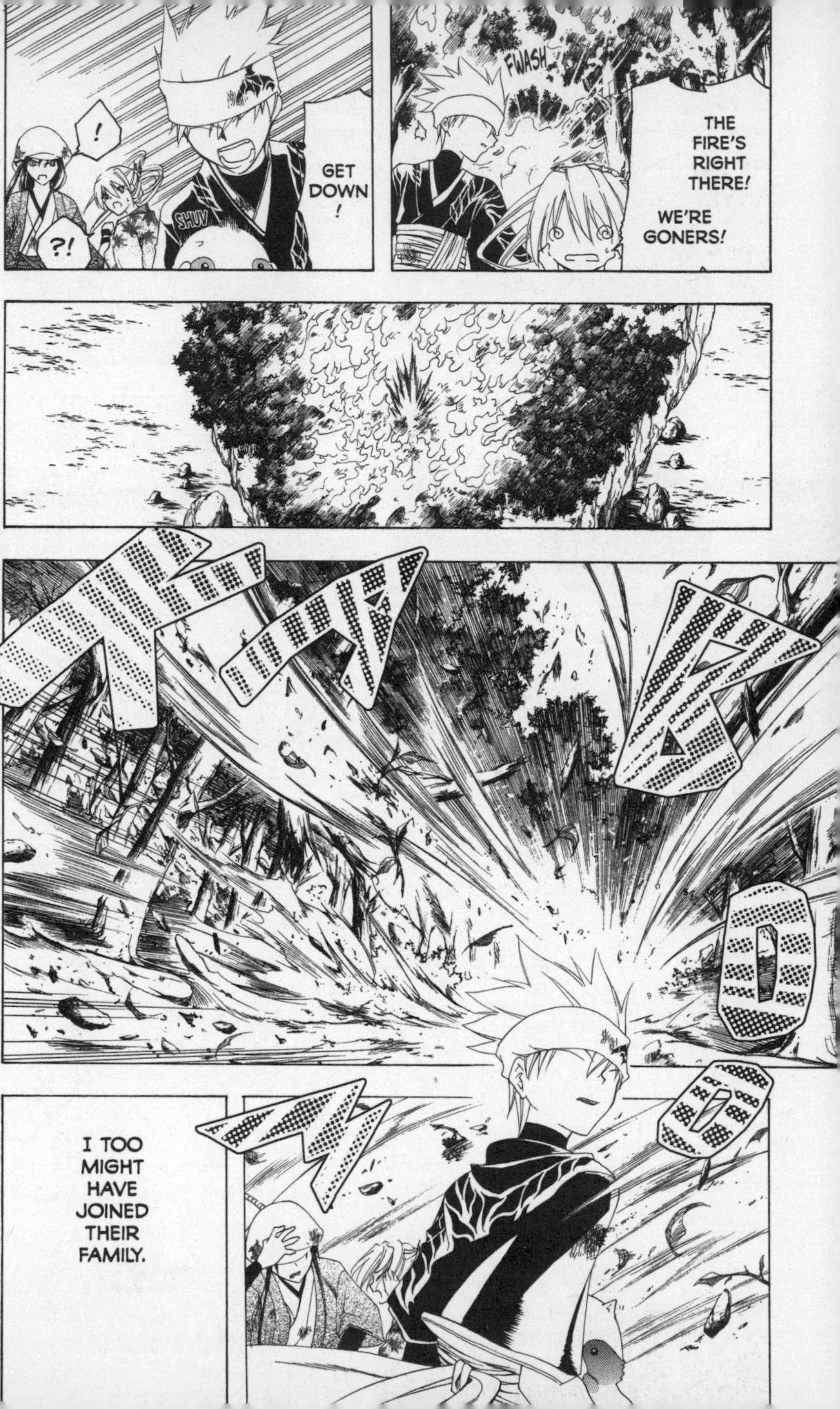
FWASH
THE FIRE'S RIGHT THERE!
WE'RE GONERS!
GET DOWN!
!
?!
SHUV
I TOO MIGHT HAVE JOINED THEIR FAMILY.

Chapter 20 Neya's Agony

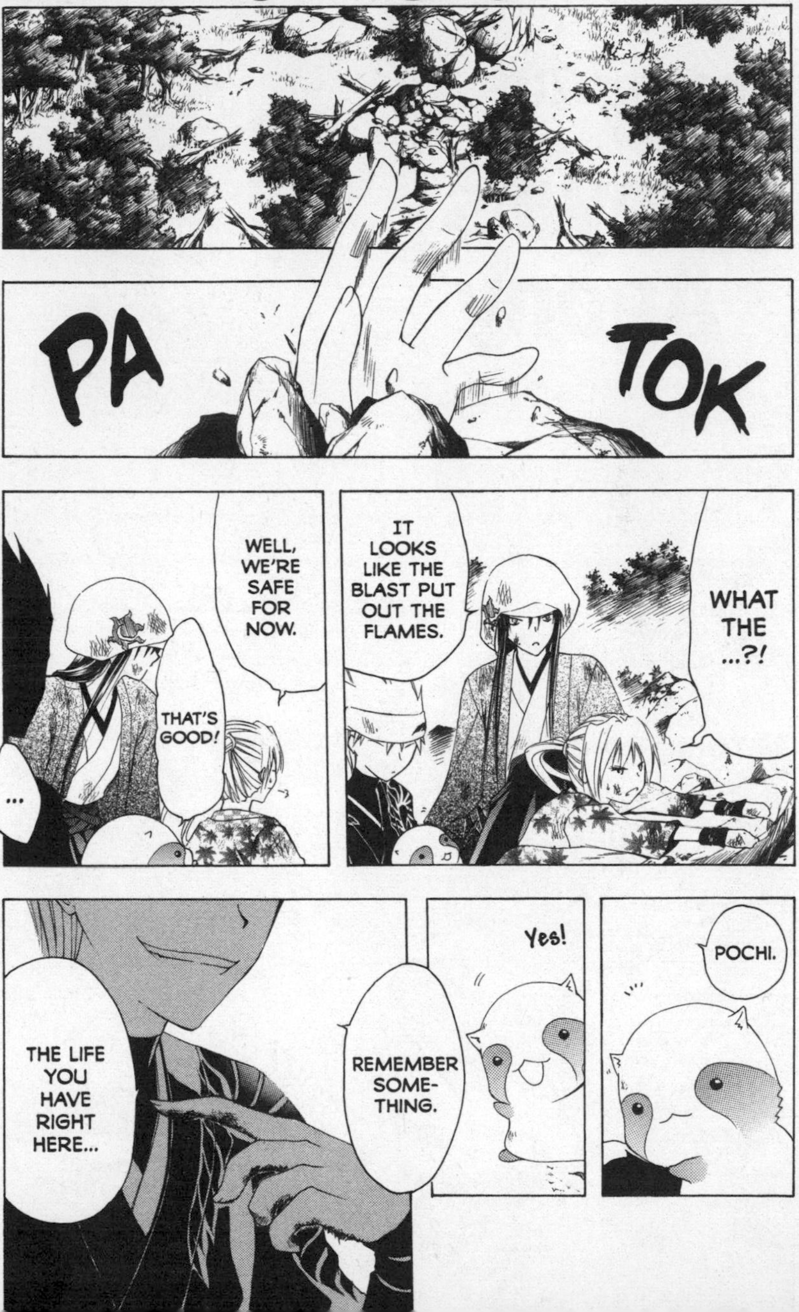
PA TOK
WHAT THE ...?!
IT LOOKS LIKE THE BLAST PUT OUT THE FLAMES.
WELL, WE'RE SAFE FOR NOW.
THAT'S GOOD!
...
POCHI.
Yes!
REMEMBER SOMETHING.
THE LIFE YOU HAVE RIGHT HERE...

Chapter 20

Neya's Agony

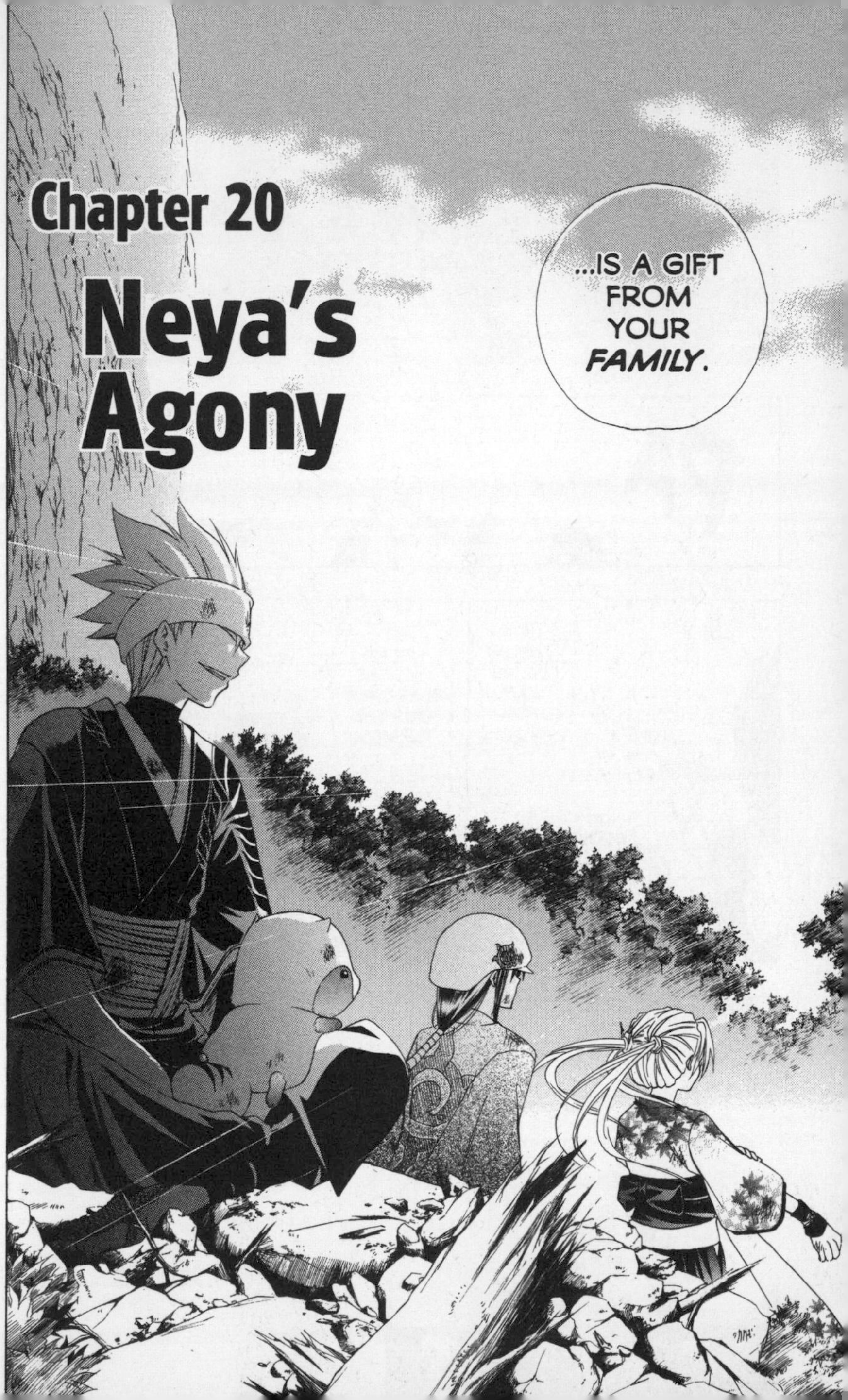
...IS A GIFT FROM YOUR *FAMILY*.

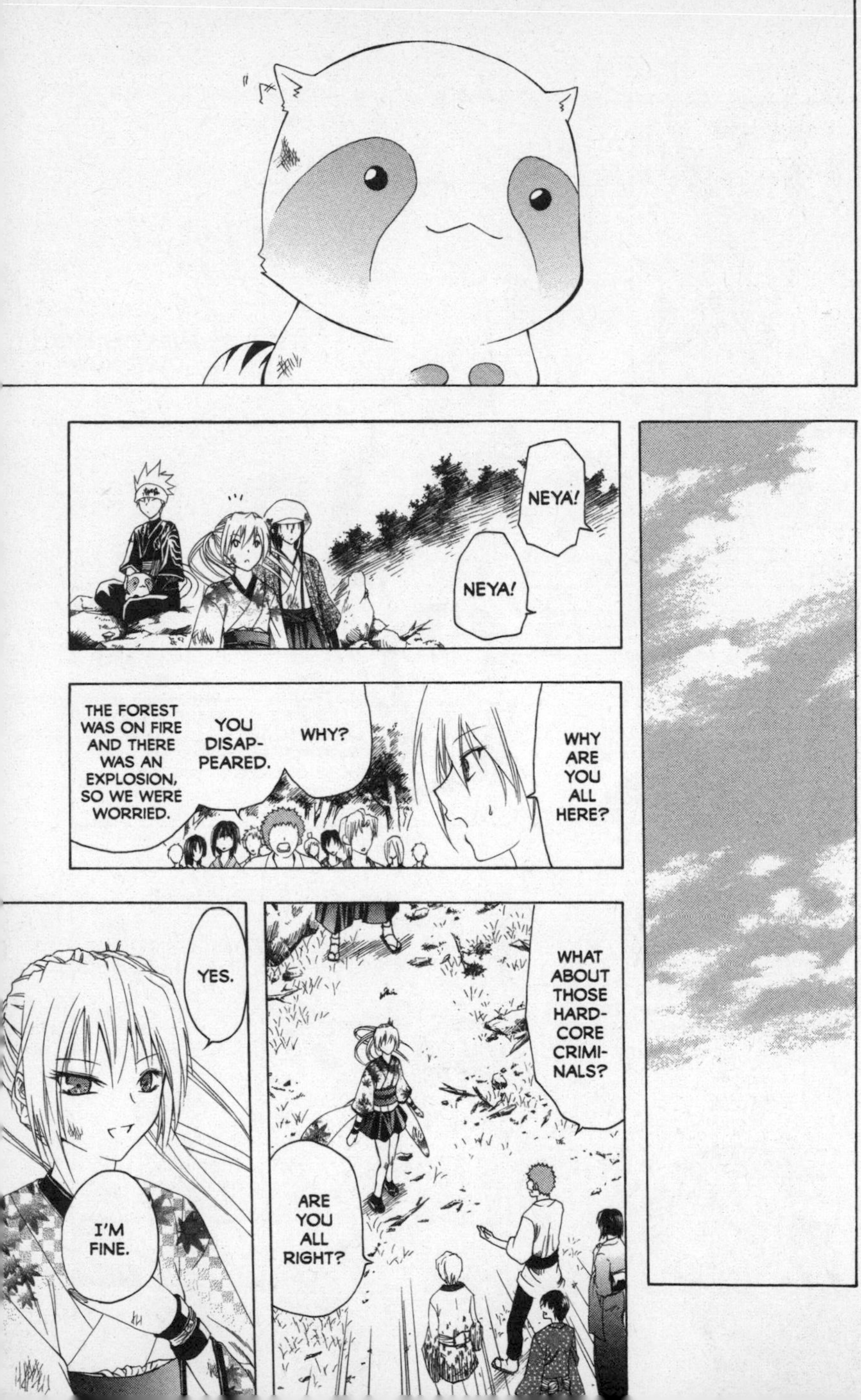
NEYA!
NEYA!
WHY ARE YOU ALL HERE?
WHY?
YOU DISAPPEARED.
THE FOREST WAS ON FIRE AND THERE WAS AN EXPLOSION, SO WE WERE WORRIED.
WHAT ABOUT THOSE HARDCORE CRIMINALS?
ARE YOU ALL RIGHT?
YES.
I'M FINE.

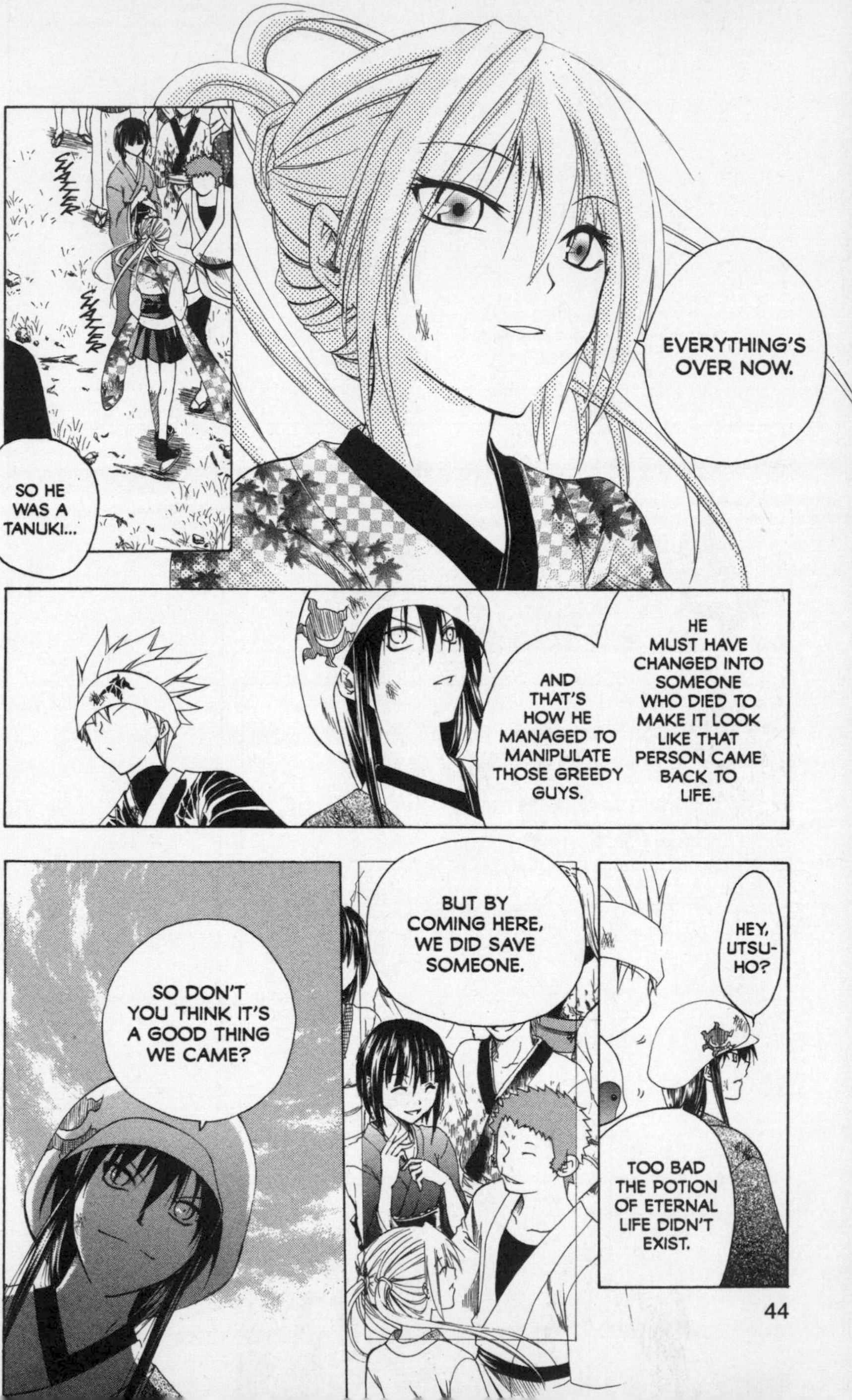
EVERYTHING'S OVER NOW.
SO HE WAS A TANUKI...
HE MUST HAVE CHANGED INTO SOMEONE WHO DIED TO MAKE IT LOOK LIKE THAT PERSON CAME BACK TO LIFE.
AND THAT'S HOW HE MANAGED TO MANIPULATE THOSE GREEDY GUYS.
HEY, UTSU-HO?
TOO BAD THE POTION OF ETERNAL LIFE DIDN'T EXIST.
BUT BY COMING HERE, WE DID SAVE SOMEONE.
SO DON'T YOU THINK IT'S A GOOD THING WE CAME?

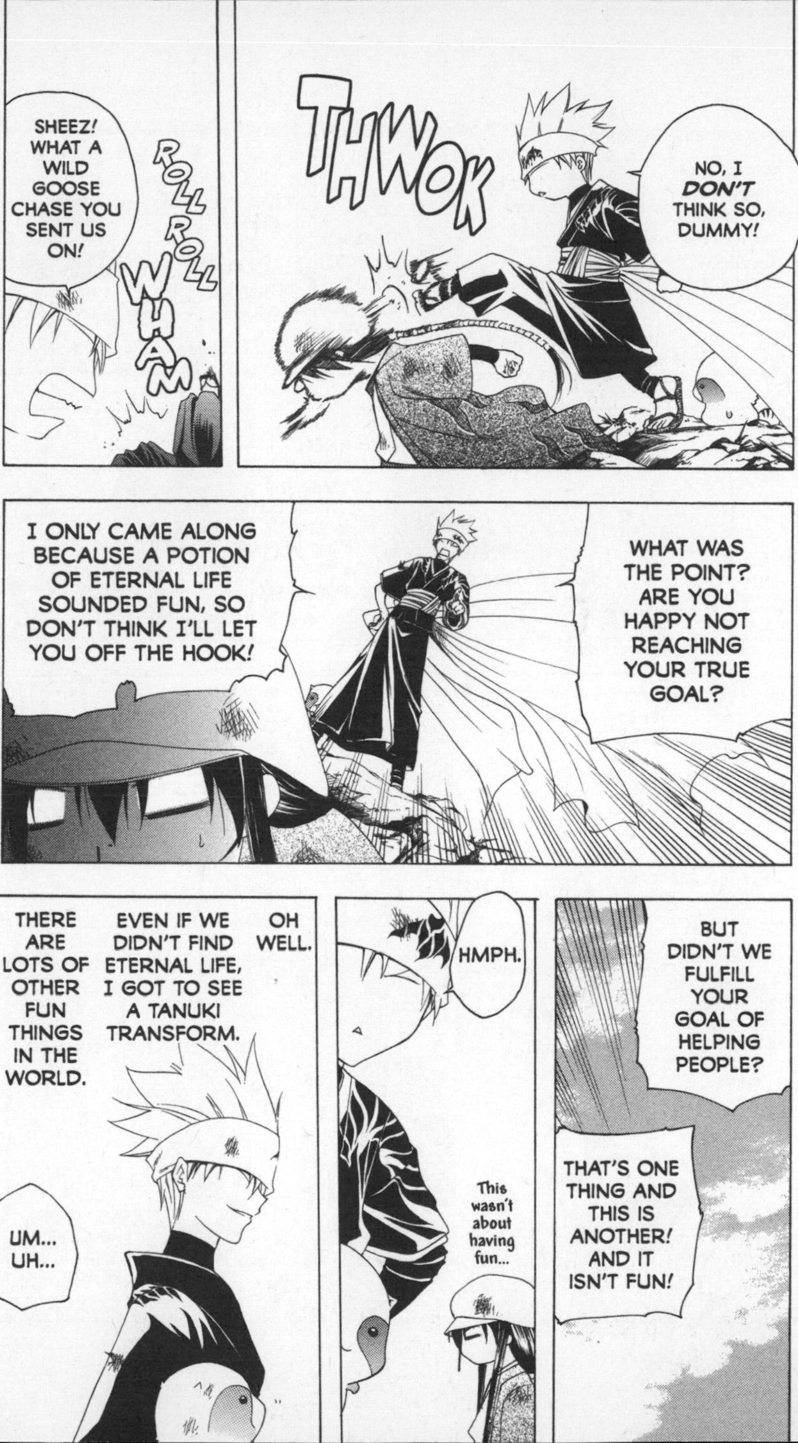
THWOK
NO, I *DON'T* THINK SO, DUMMY!
SHEEZ! WHAT A WILD GOOSE CHASE YOU SENT US ON!
ROLL ROLL
WHAM
WHAT WAS THE POINT? ARE YOU HAPPY NOT REACHING YOUR TRUE GOAL?
I ONLY CAME ALONG BECAUSE A POTION OF ETERNAL LIFE SOUNDED FUN, SO DON'T THINK I'LL LET YOU OFF THE HOOK!
BUT DIDN'T WE FULFILL YOUR GOAL OF HELPING PEOPLE?
THAT'S ONE THING AND THIS IS ANOTHER! AND IT ISN'T FUN!
HMPH.
This wasn't about having fun...
OH WELL.
EVEN IF WE DIDN'T FIND ETERNAL LIFE, I GOT TO SEE A TANUKI TRANSFORM.
THERE ARE LOTS OF OTHER FUN THINGS IN THE WORLD.
UM... UH...

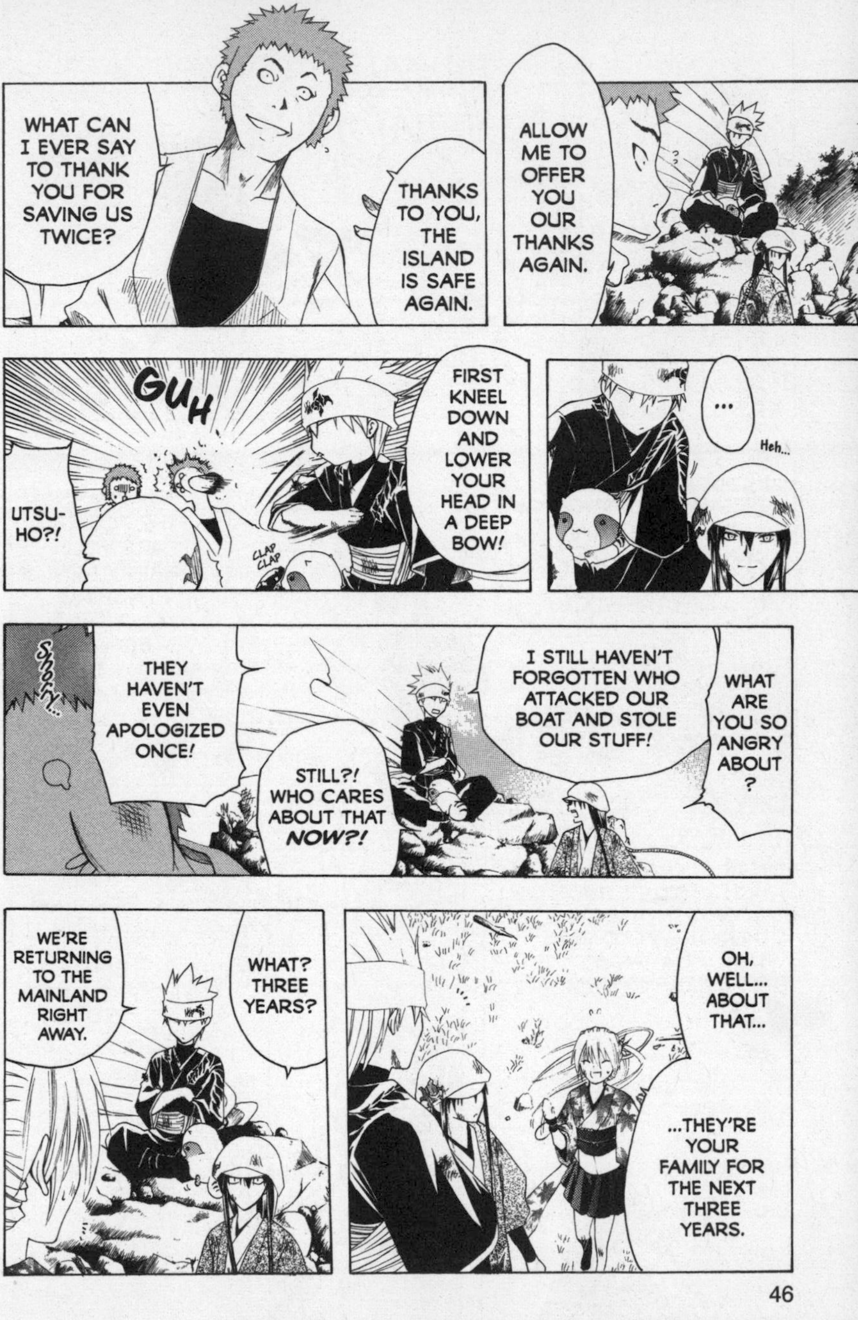
ALLOW ME TO OFFER YOU OUR THANKS AGAIN.
THANKS TO YOU, THE ISLAND IS SAFE AGAIN.
WHAT CAN I EVER SAY TO THANK YOU FOR SAVING US TWICE?
...
Heh...
FIRST KNEEL DOWN AND LOWER YOUR HEAD IN A DEEP BOW!
GUH
UTSU-HO?!
CLAP CLAP
WHAT ARE YOU SO ANGRY ABOUT?
I STILL HAVEN'T FORGOTTEN WHO ATTACKED OUR BOAT AND STOLE OUR STUFF!
THEY HAVEN'T EVEN APOLOGIZED ONCE!
Snort...
STILL?! WHO CARES ABOUT THAT *NOW?!*
OH, WELL... ABOUT THAT...
...THEY'RE YOUR FAMILY FOR THE NEXT THREE YEARS.
WHAT? THREE YEARS?
WE'RE RETURNING TO THE MAINLAND RIGHT AWAY.

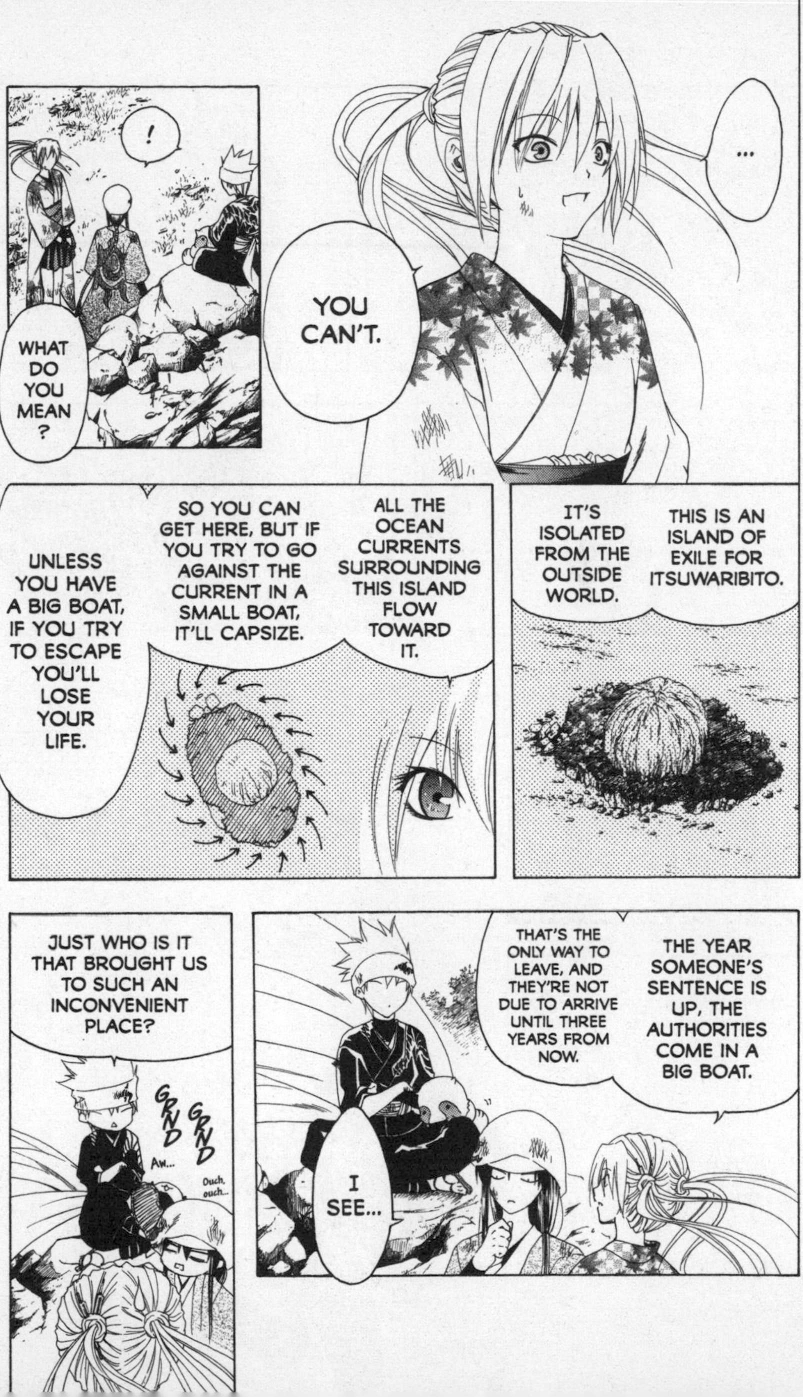
...
YOU CAN'T.
!
WHAT DO YOU MEAN?
THIS IS AN ISLAND OF EXILE FOR ITSUWARIBITO.
IT'S ISOLATED FROM THE OUTSIDE WORLD.
ALL THE OCEAN CURRENTS SURROUNDING THIS ISLAND FLOW TOWARD IT.
SO YOU CAN GET HERE, BUT IF YOU TRY TO GO AGAINST THE CURRENT IN A SMALL BOAT, IT'LL CAPSIZE.
UNLESS YOU HAVE A BIG BOAT, IF YOU TRY TO ESCAPE YOU'LL LOSE YOUR LIFE.
THE YEAR SOMEONE'S SENTENCE IS UP, THE AUTHORITIES COME IN A BIG BOAT.
THAT'S THE ONLY WAY TO LEAVE, AND THEY'RE NOT DUE TO ARRIVE UNTIL THREE YEARS FROM NOW.
I SEE...
JUST WHO IS IT THAT BROUGHT US TO SUCH AN INCONVENIENT PLACE?
GRND GRND
Aw...
Ouch, ouch...

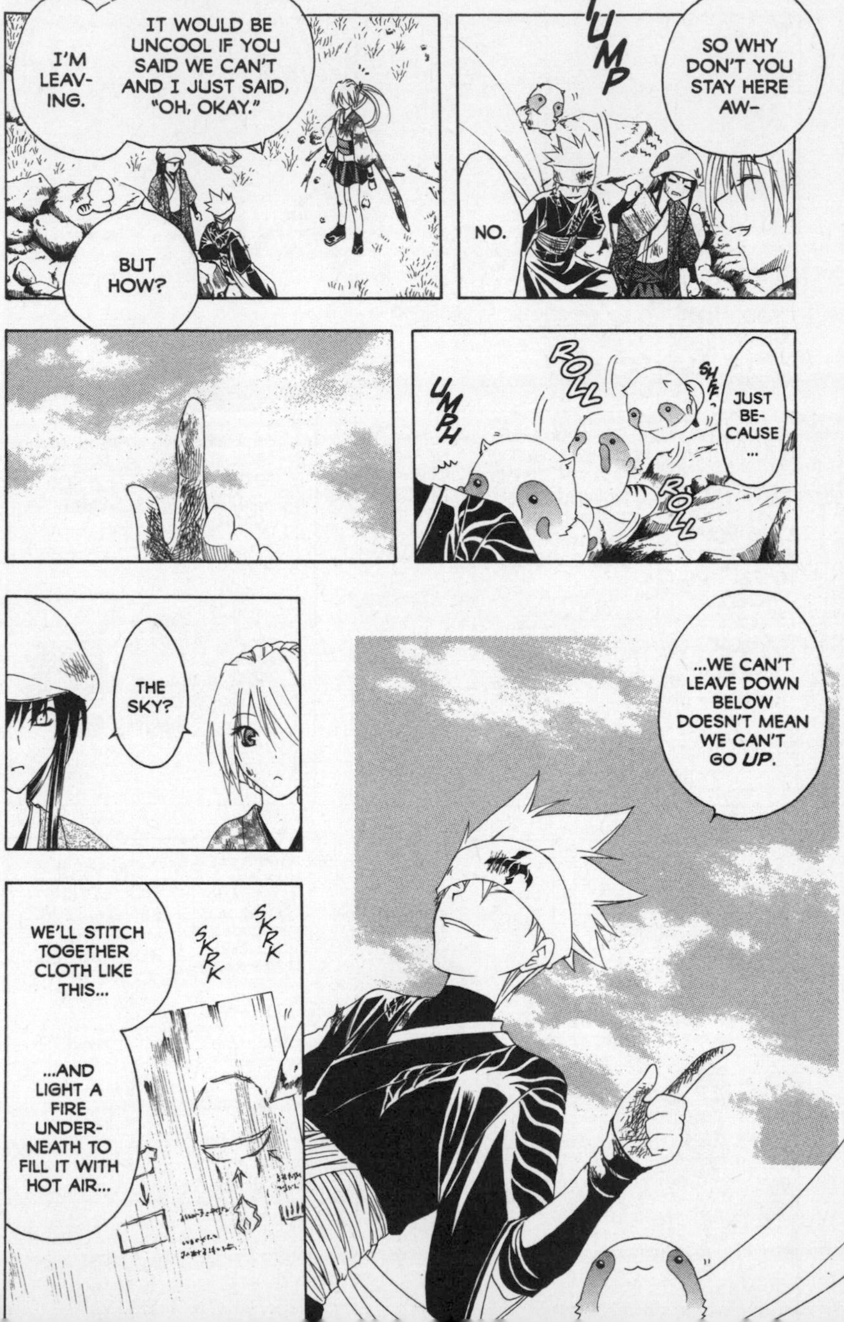
TUMP
SO WHY DON'T YOU STAY HERE AW-
NO.
IT WOULD BE UNCOOL IF YOU SAID WE CAN'T AND I JUST SAID, "OH, OKAY."
I'M LEAV-ING.
BUT HOW?
ROLL
SHF
JUST BE-CAUSE ...
UMPH
ROLL
...WE CAN'T LEAVE DOWN BELOW DOESN'T MEAN WE CAN'T GO *UP*.
THE SKY?
SKRK
SKRK
WE'LL STITCH TOGETHER CLOTH LIKE THIS...
...AND LIGHT A FIRE UNDER-NEATH TO FILL IT WITH HOT AIR...

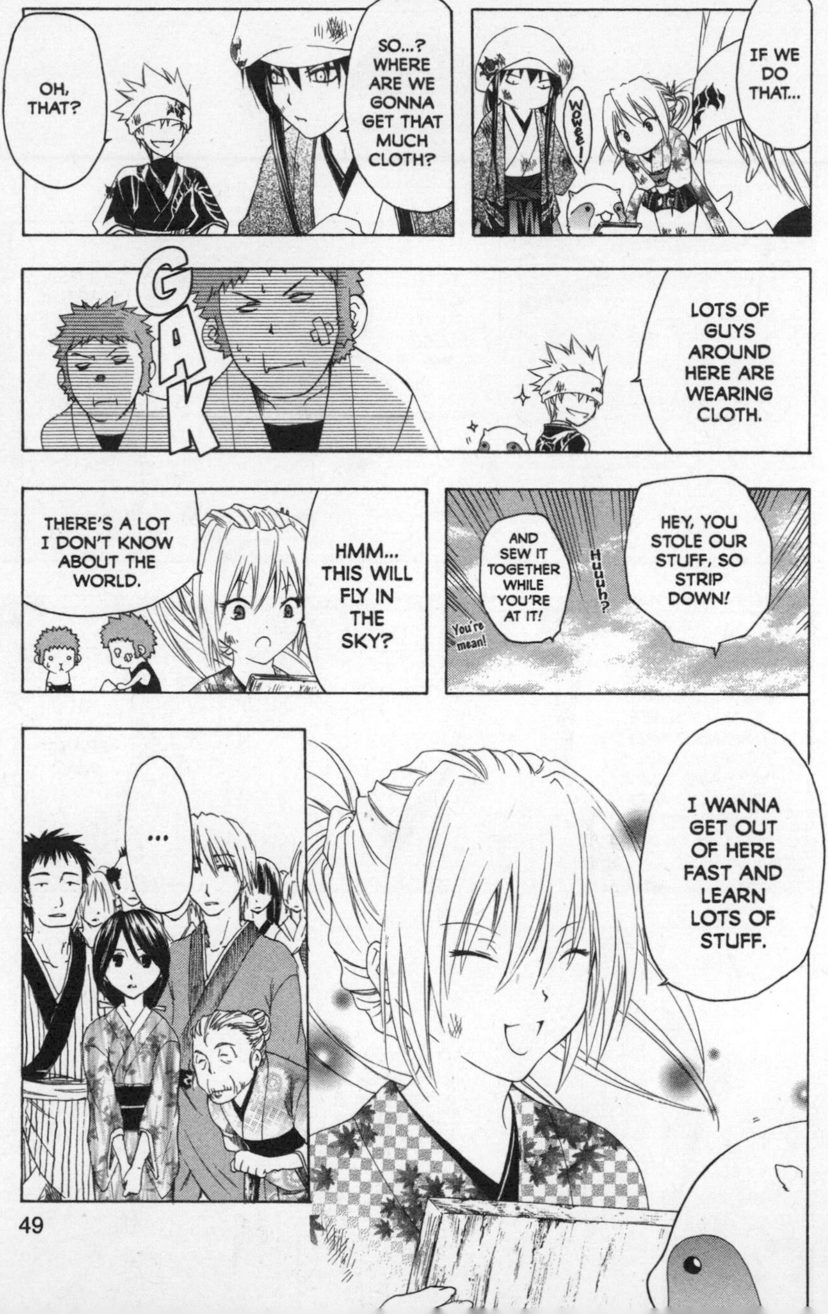
IF WE DO THAT...
Wowee!
SO...? WHERE ARE WE GONNA GET THAT MUCH CLOTH?
OH, THAT?
LOTS OF GUYS AROUND HERE ARE WEARING CLOTH.
GAK
HEY, YOU STOLE OUR STUFF, SO STRIP DOWN!
Huuuh?
AND SEW IT TOGETHER WHILE YOU'RE AT IT!
You're mean!
HMM... THIS WILL FLY IN THE SKY?
THERE'S A LOT I DON'T KNOW ABOUT THE WORLD.
I WANNA GET OUT OF HERE FAST AND LEARN LOTS OF STUFF.
...

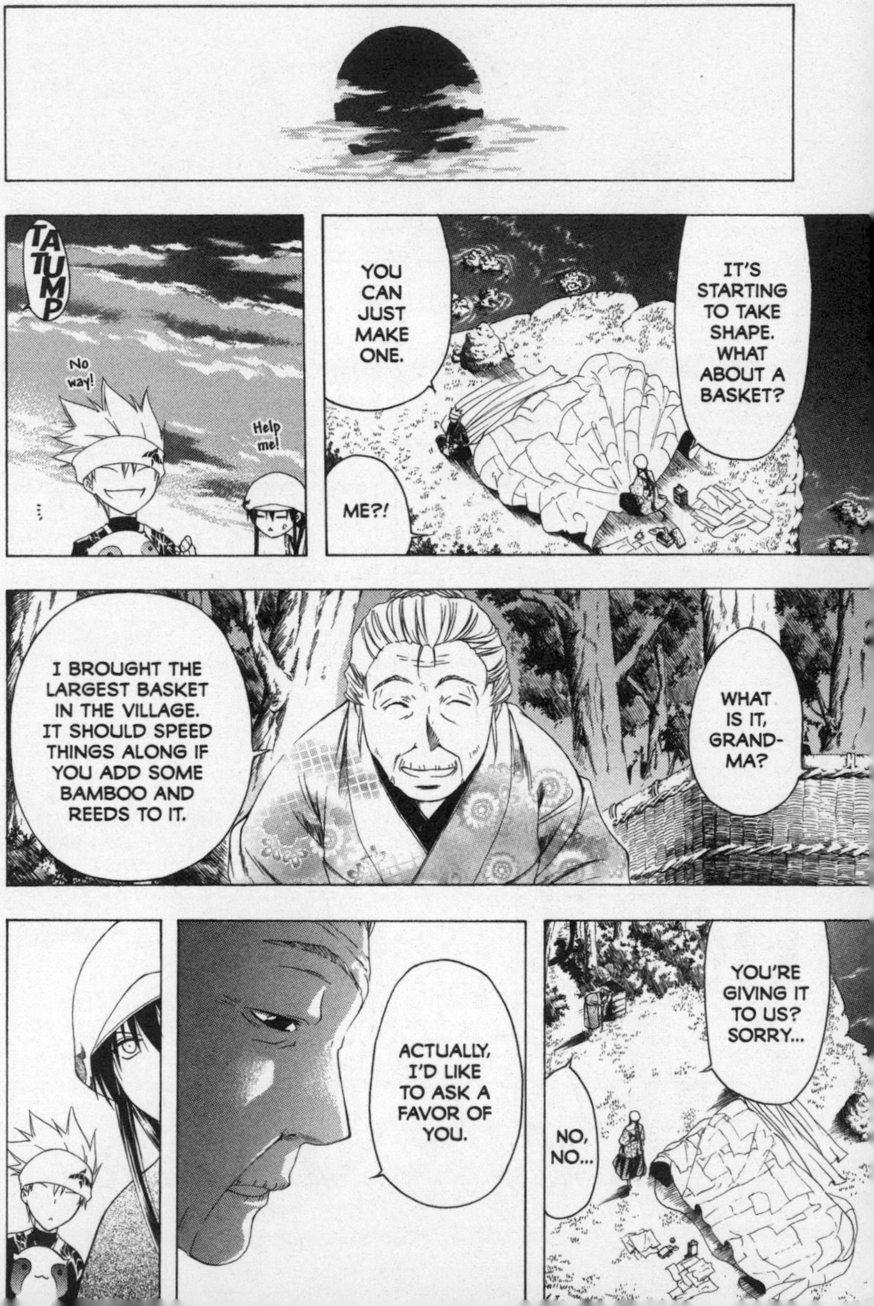
IT'S STARTING TO TAKE SHAPE. WHAT ABOUT A BASKET?
YOU CAN JUST MAKE ONE.
ME?!
TATUMP
No way!
Help me!
WHAT IS IT, GRAND-MA?
I BROUGHT THE LARGEST BASKET IN THE VILLAGE. IT SHOULD SPEED THINGS ALONG IF YOU ADD SOME BAMBOO AND REEDS TO IT.
YOU'RE GIVING IT TO US? SORRY...
NO, NO...
ACTUALLY, I'D LIKE TO ASK A FAVOR OF YOU.

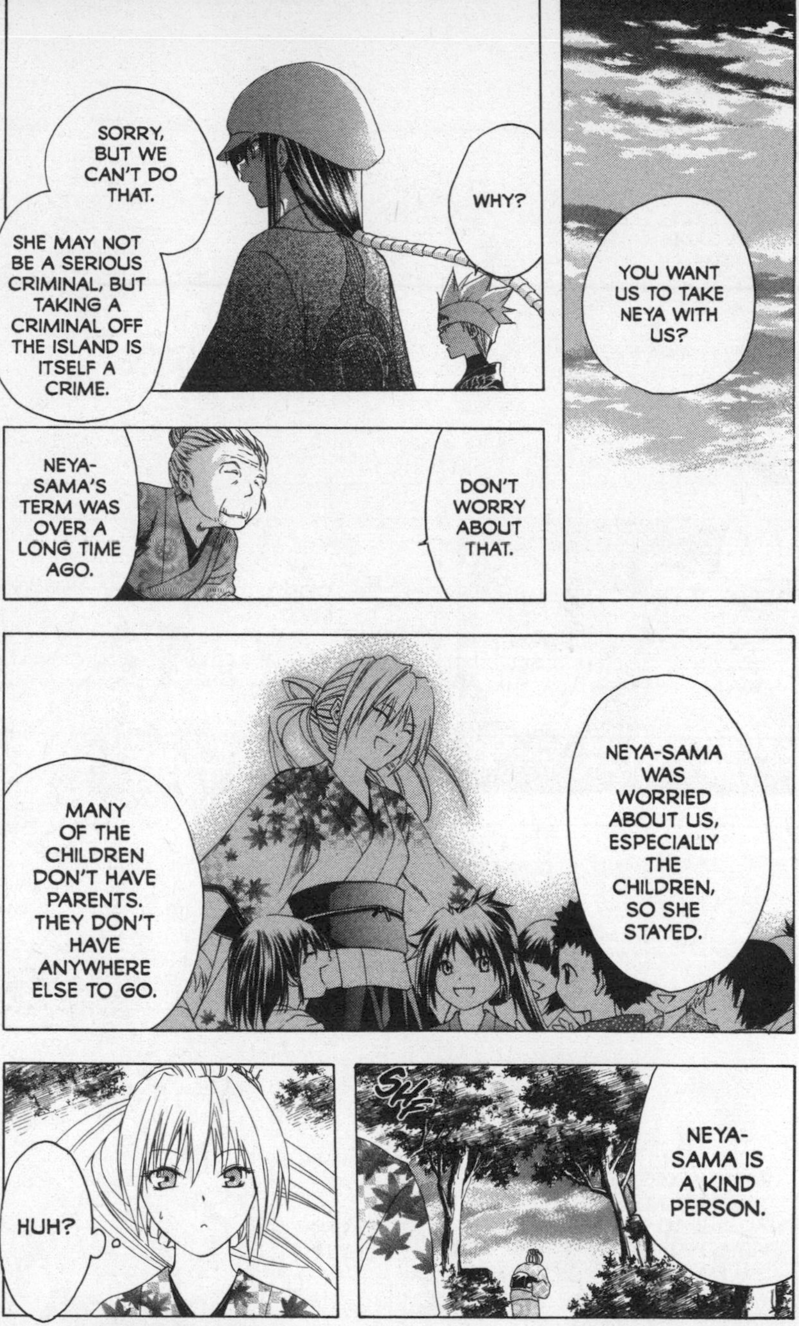
YOU WANT US TO TAKE NEYA WITH US?
WHY?
SORRY, BUT WE CAN'T DO THAT.
SHE MAY NOT BE A SERIOUS CRIMINAL, BUT TAKING A CRIMINAL OFF THE ISLAND IS ITSELF A CRIME.
DON'T WORRY ABOUT THAT.
NEYA-SAMA'S TERM WAS OVER A LONG TIME AGO.
NEYA-SAMA WAS WORRIED ABOUT US, ESPECIALLY THE CHILDREN, SO SHE STAYED.
MANY OF THE CHILDREN DON'T HAVE PARENTS. THEY DON'T HAVE ANYWHERE ELSE TO GO.
SHF
NEYA-SAMA IS A KIND PERSON.
HUH?

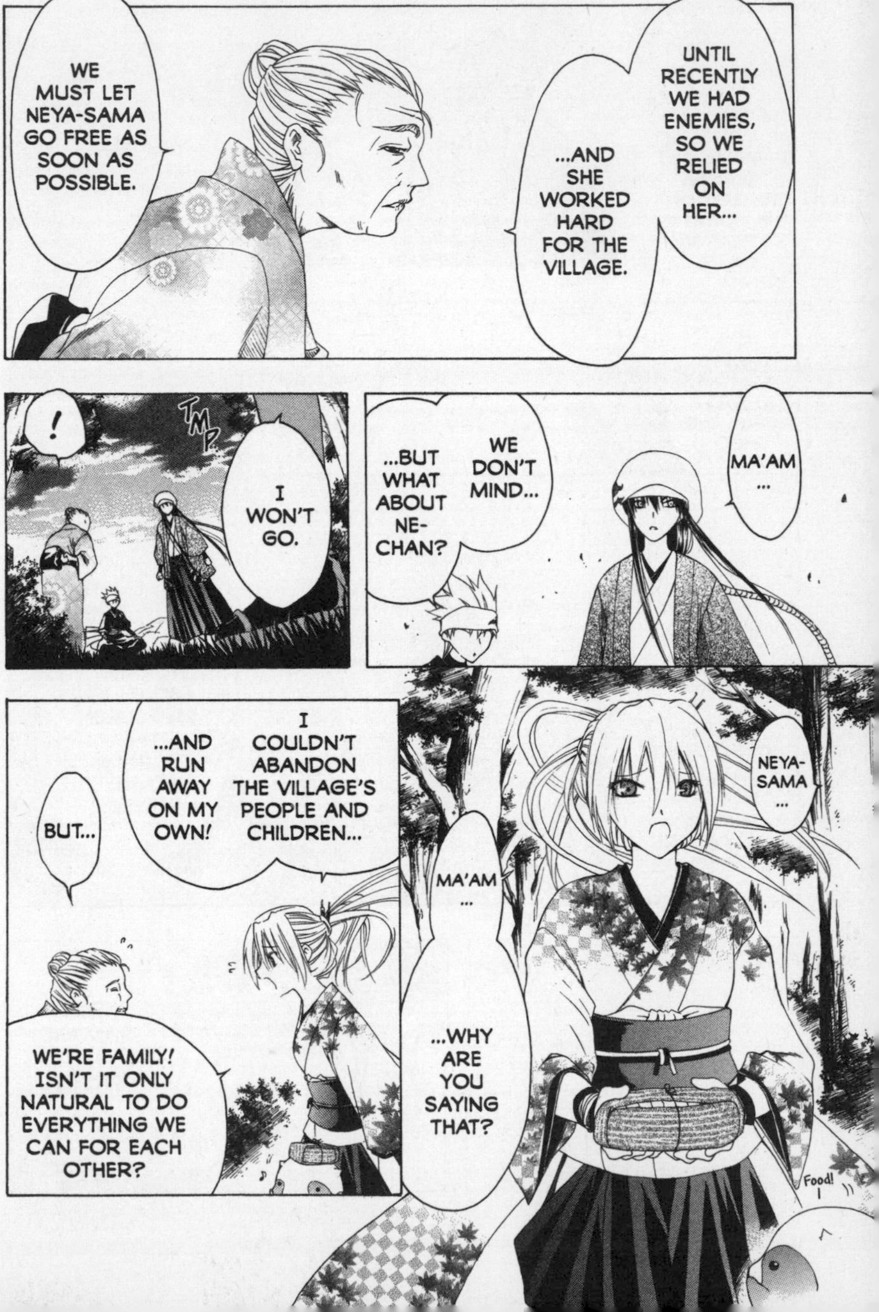
UNTIL RECENTLY WE HAD ENEMIES, SO WE RELIED ON HER...
...AND SHE WORKED HARD FOR THE VILLAGE.
WE MUST LET NEYA-SAMA GO FREE AS SOON AS POSSIBLE.
MA'AM ...
WE DON'T MIND...
...BUT WHAT ABOUT NE-CHAN?
I WON'T GO.
TMP
!
NEYA-SAMA ...
MA'AM ...
...WHY ARE YOU SAYING THAT?
Food!
I COULDN'T ABANDON THE VILLAGE'S PEOPLE AND CHILDREN...
...AND RUN AWAY ON MY OWN!
BUT...
WE'RE FAMILY! ISN'T IT ONLY NATURAL TO DO EVERYTHING WE CAN FOR EACH OTHER?

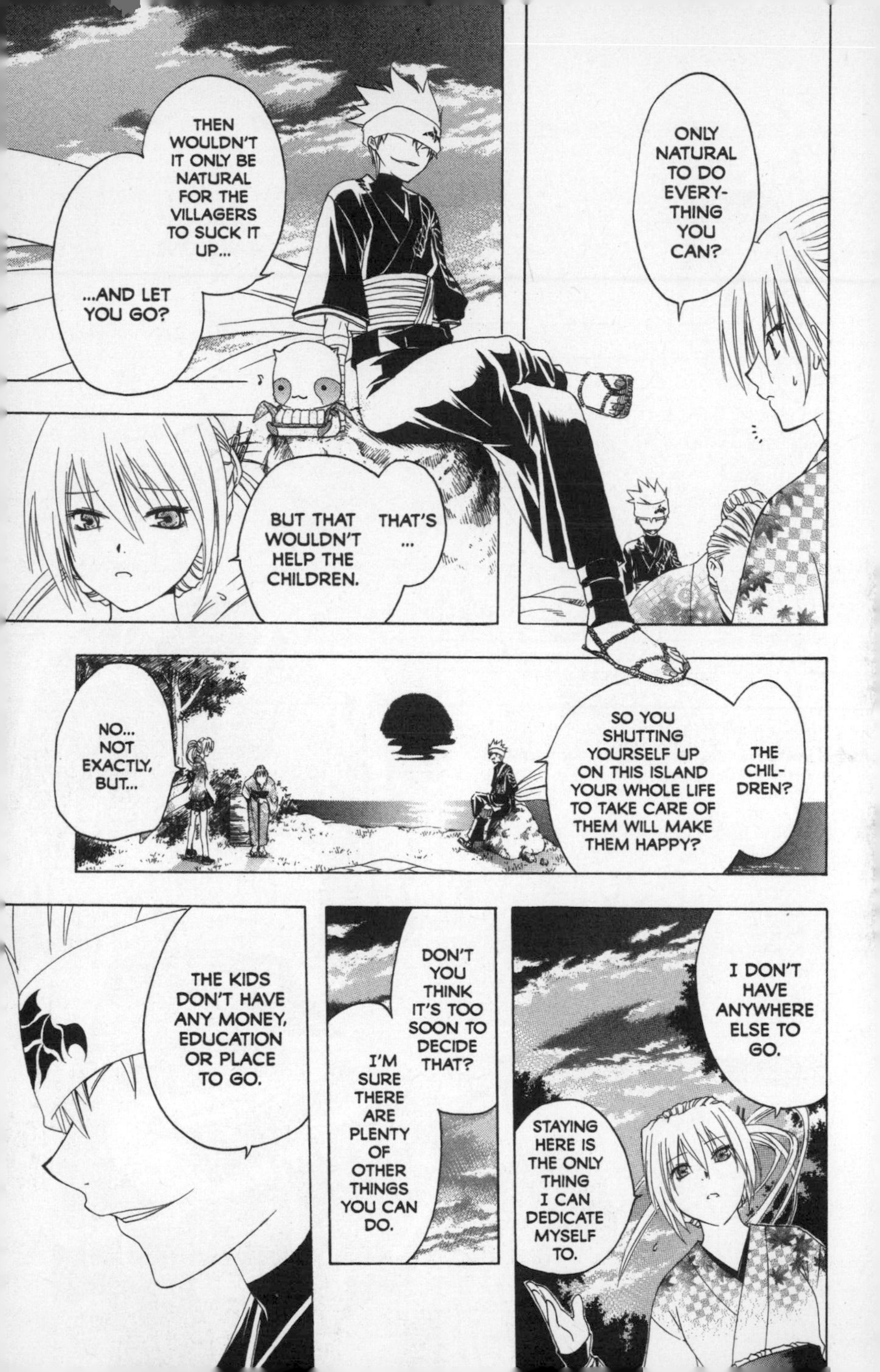
ONLY NATURAL TO DO EVERYTHING YOU CAN?
THEN WOULDN'T IT ONLY BE NATURAL FOR THE VILLAGERS TO SUCK IT UP...
...AND LET YOU GO?
THAT'S...
BUT THAT WOULDN'T HELP THE CHILDREN.
THE CHILDREN?
SO YOU SHUTTING YOURSELF UP ON THIS ISLAND YOUR WHOLE LIFE TO TAKE CARE OF THEM WILL MAKE THEM HAPPY?
NO... NOT EXACTLY, BUT...
I DON'T HAVE ANYWHERE ELSE TO GO.
STAYING HERE IS THE ONLY THING I CAN DEDICATE MYSELF TO.
DON'T YOU THINK IT'S TOO SOON TO DECIDE THAT?
I'M SURE THERE ARE PLENTY OF OTHER THINGS YOU CAN DO.
THE KIDS DON'T HAVE ANY MONEY, EDUCATION OR PLACE TO GO.

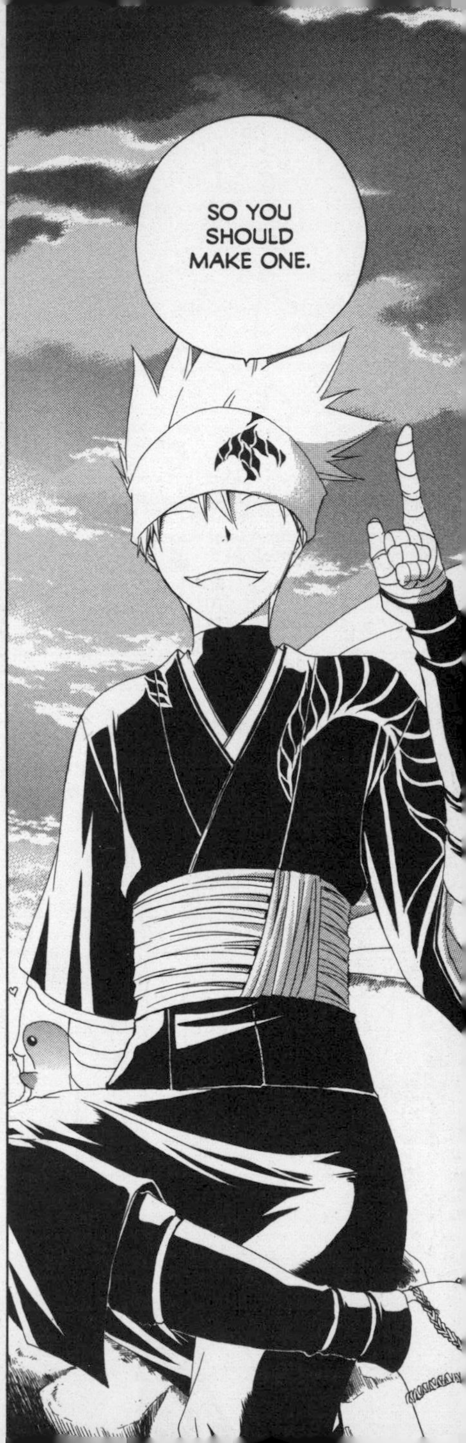
SO YOU SHOULD MAKE ONE.

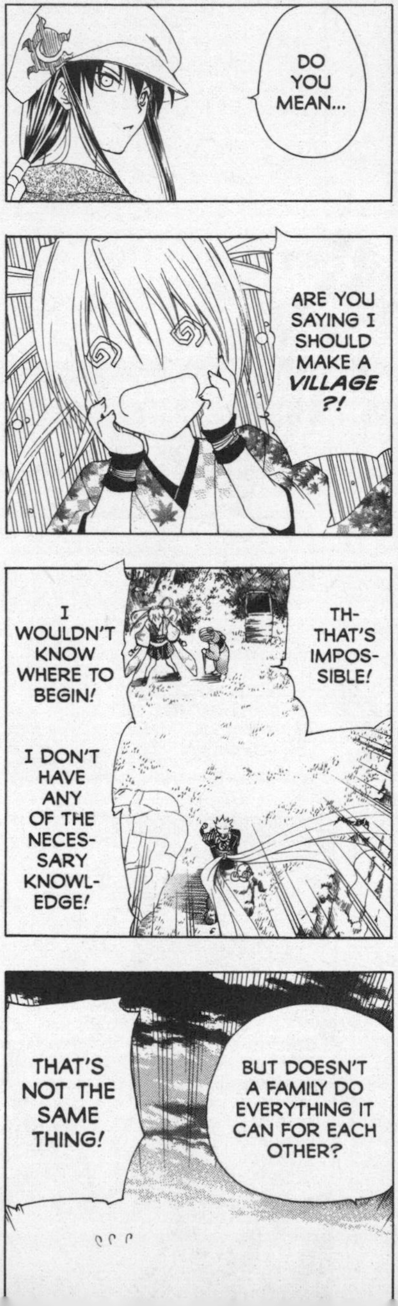
DO YOU MEAN...
ARE YOU SAYING I SHOULD MAKE A *VILLAGE* ?!
TH-THAT'S IMPOSSIBLE!
I WOULDN'T KNOW WHERE TO BEGIN!
I DON'T HAVE ANY OF THE NECES-SARY KNOWL-EDGE!
BUT DOESN'T A FAMILY DO EVERYTHING IT CAN FOR EACH OTHER?
THAT'S NOT THE SAME THING!

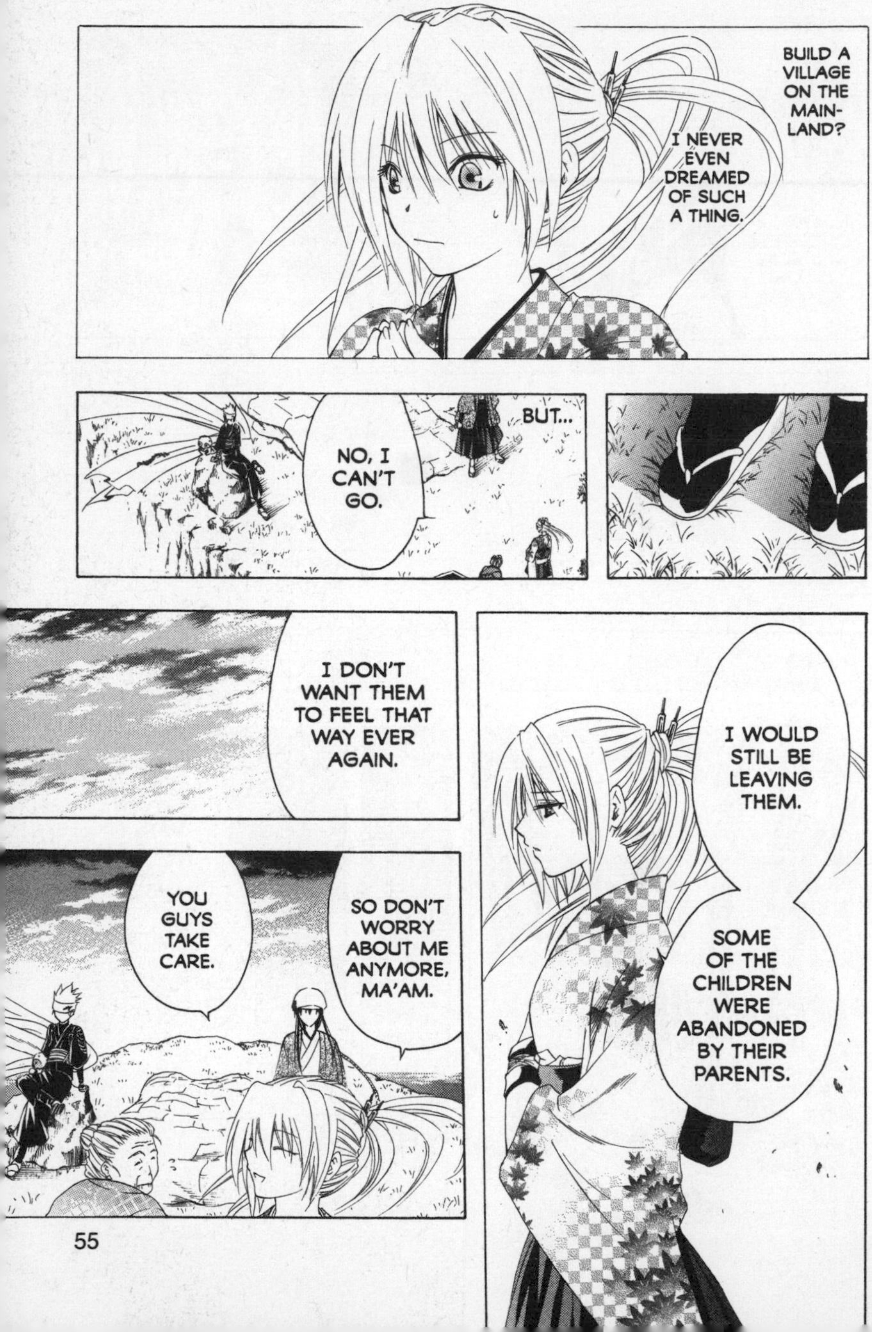
BUILD A VILLAGE ON THE MAIN-LAND?
I NEVER EVEN DREAMED OF SUCH A THING.
BUT...
NO, I CAN'T GO.
I WOULD STILL BE LEAVING THEM.
SOME OF THE CHILDREN WERE ABANDONED BY THEIR PARENTS.
I DON'T WANT THEM TO FEEL THAT WAY EVER AGAIN.
SO DON'T WORRY ABOUT ME ANYMORE, MA'AM.
YOU GUYS TAKE CARE.

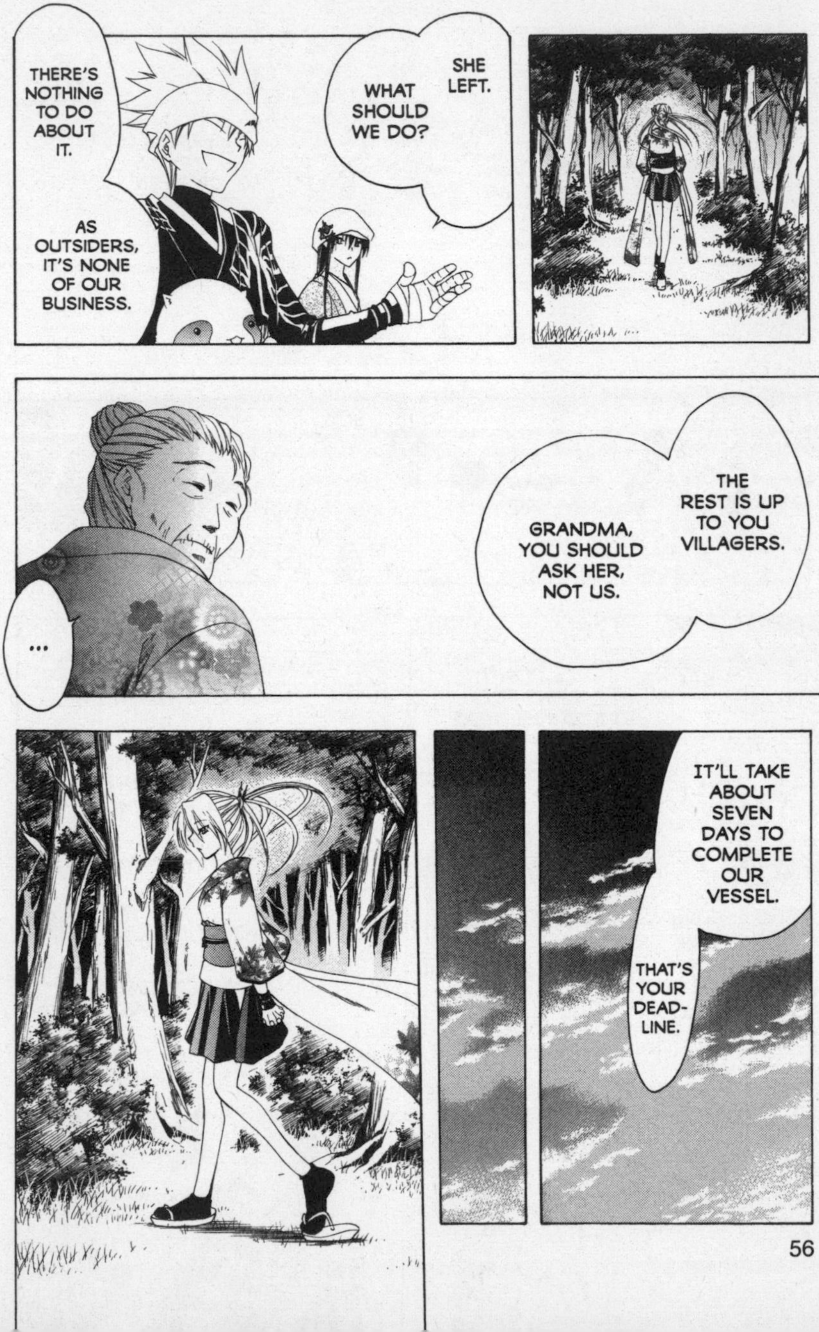
SHE LEFT.
WHAT SHOULD WE DO?
THERE'S NOTHING TO DO ABOUT IT.
AS OUTSIDERS, IT'S NONE OF OUR BUSINESS.
THE REST IS UP TO YOU VILLAGERS.
GRANDMA, YOU SHOULD ASK HER, NOT US.
...
IT'LL TAKE ABOUT SEVEN DAYS TO COMPLETE OUR VESSEL.
THAT'S YOUR DEAD-LINE.

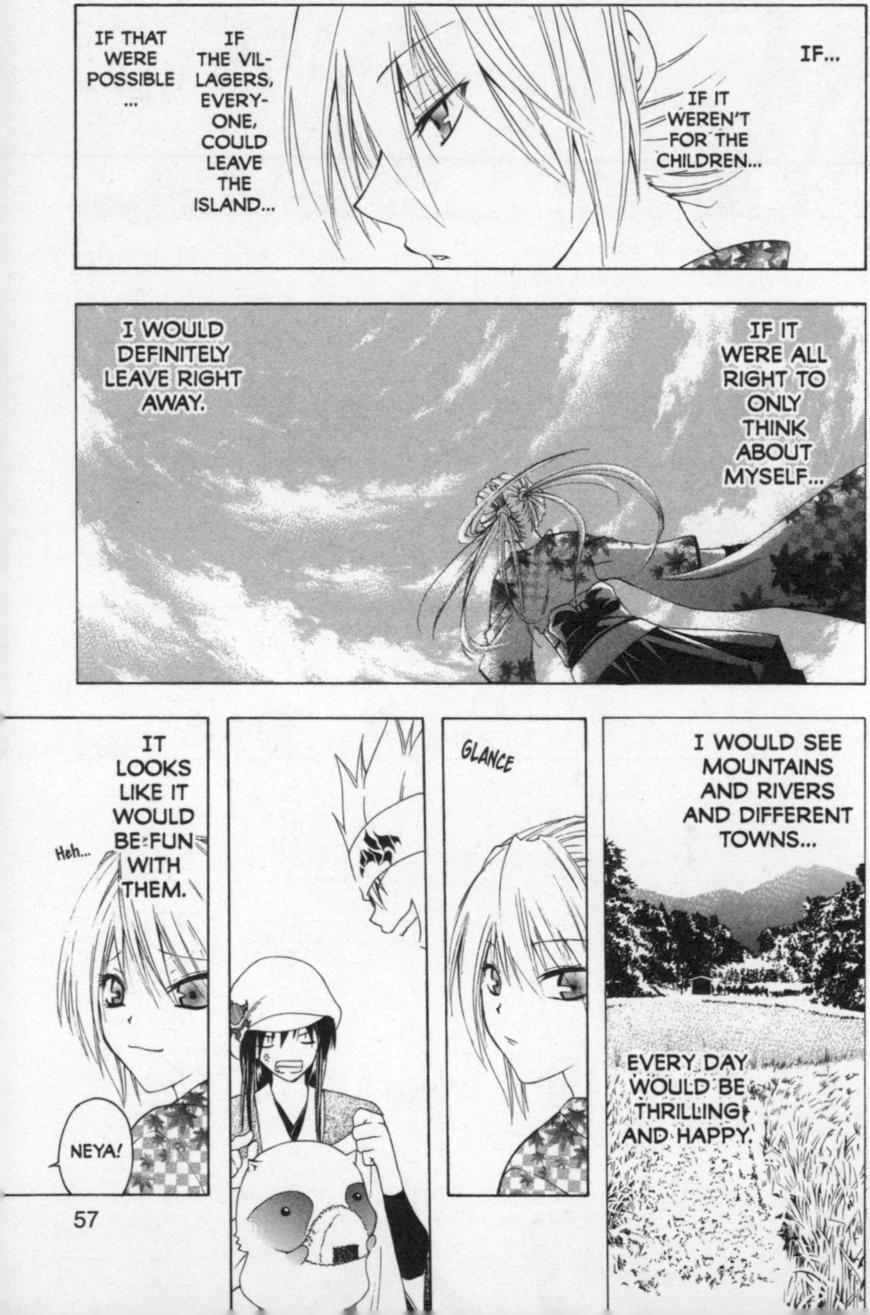
IF...
IF IT WEREN'T FOR THE CHILDREN...
IF THE VIL-LAGERS, EVERY-ONE, COULD LEAVE THE ISLAND...
IF THAT WERE POSSIBLE ...
IF IT WERE ALL RIGHT TO ONLY THINK ABOUT MYSELF...
I WOULD DEFINITELY LEAVE RIGHT AWAY.
I WOULD SEE MOUNTAINS AND RIVERS AND DIFFERENT TOWNS...
EVERY DAY WOULD BE THRILLING AND HAPPY.
GLANCE
IT LOOKS LIKE IT WOULD BE FUN WITH THEM.
Heh...
NEYA!

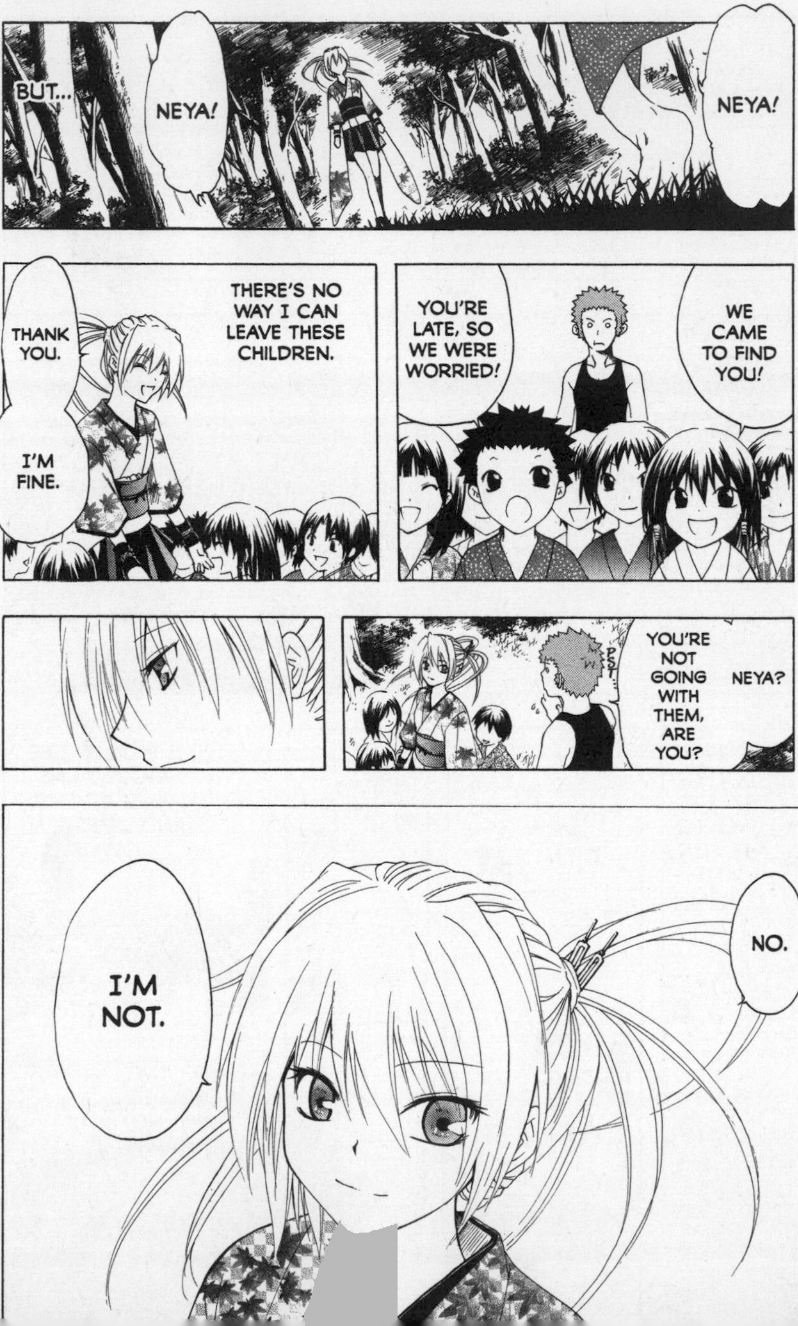
NEYA!
NEYA!
BUT...
WE CAME TO FIND YOU!
YOU'RE LATE, SO WE WERE WORRIED!
THERE'S NO WAY I CAN LEAVE THESE CHILDREN.
THANK YOU.
I'M FINE.
NEYA?
YOU'RE NOT GOING WITH THEM, ARE YOU?
PST...
NO.
I'M NOT.

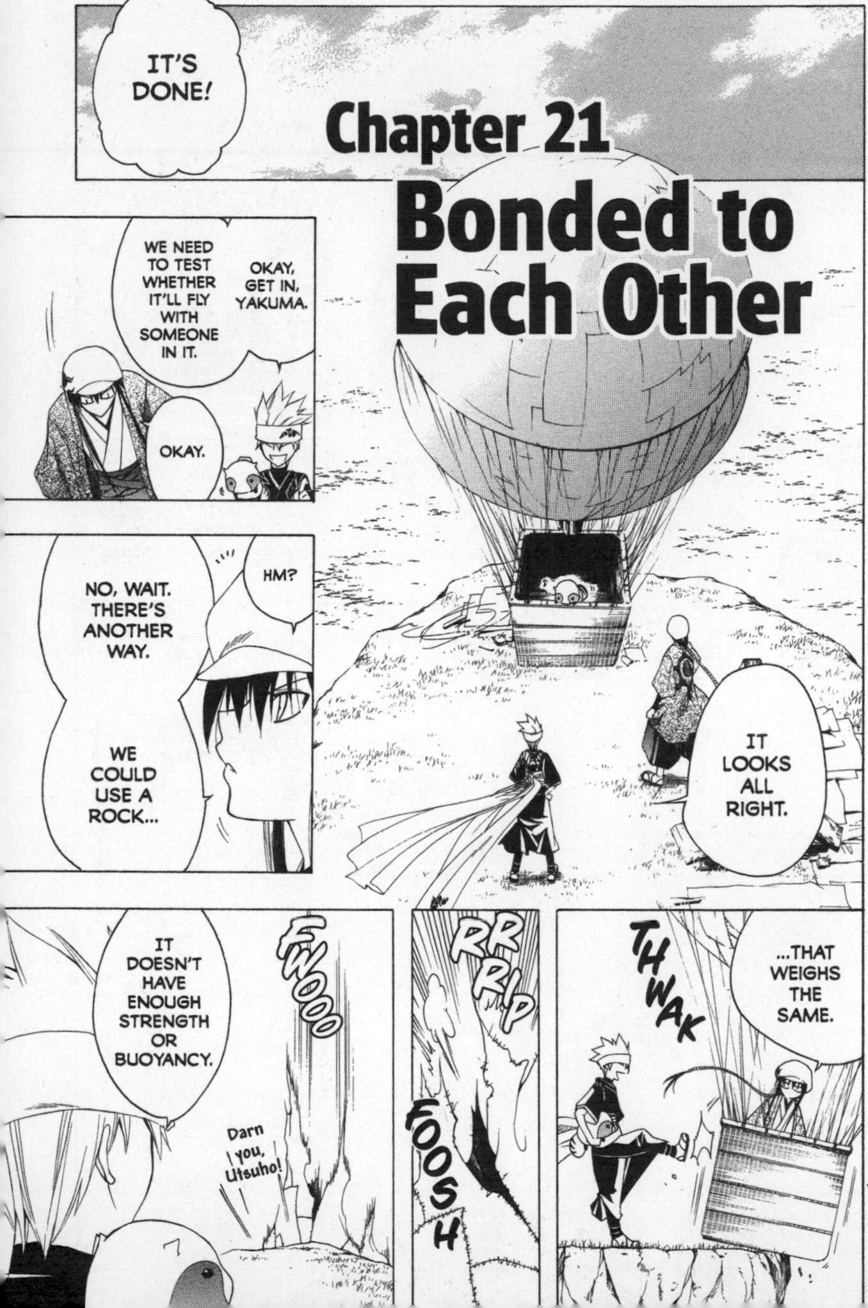
IT'S DONE!
Chapter 21
Bonded to Each Other
IT LOOKS ALL RIGHT.
OKAY, GET IN, YAKUMA.
WE NEED TO TEST WHETHER IT'LL FLY WITH SOMEONE IN IT.
OKAY.
HM?
NO, WAIT. THERE'S ANOTHER WAY.
WE COULD USE A ROCK...
THWAK
...THAT WEIGHS THE SAME.
RRRIP
FOOSH
FWOOO
IT DOESN'T HAVE ENOUGH STRENGTH OR BUOYANCY.
Darn you, Utsuho!

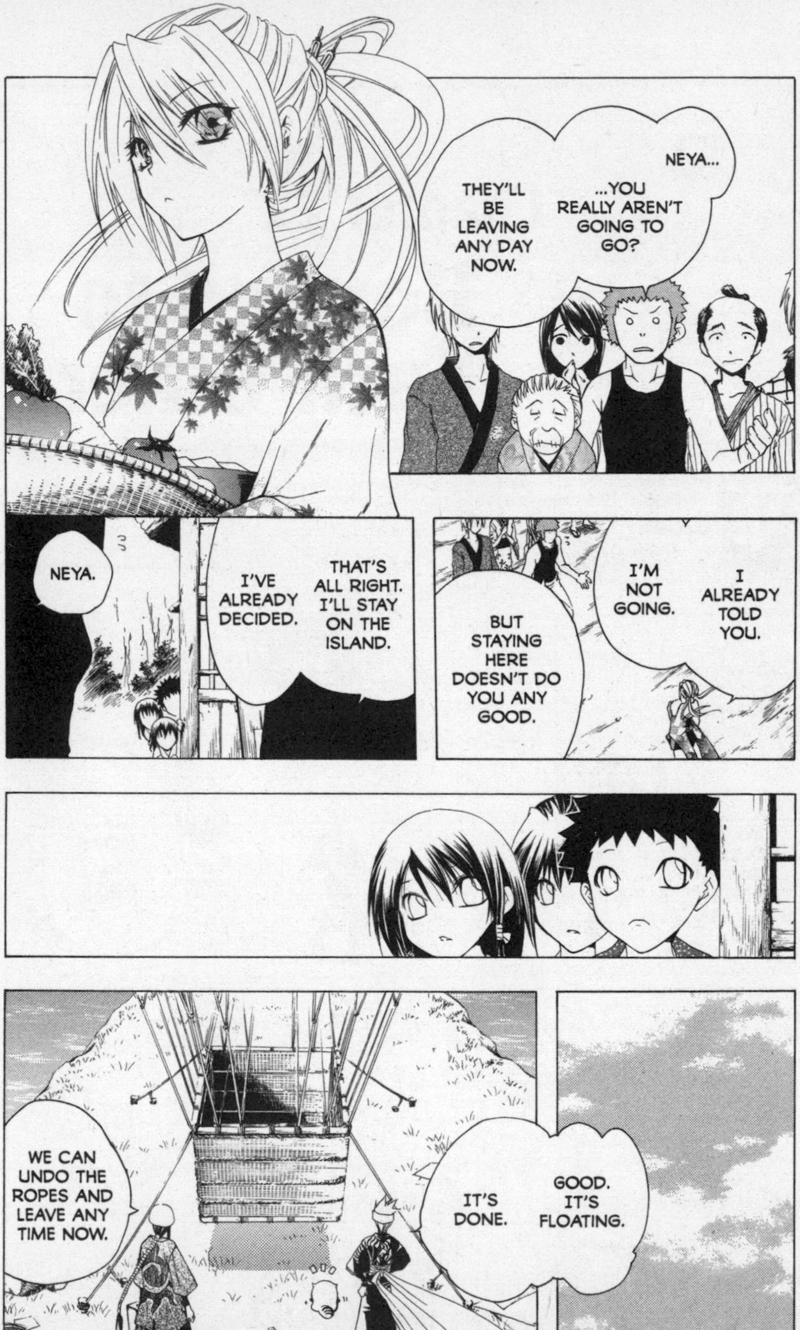
NEYA...
...YOU REALLY AREN'T GOING TO GO?
THEY'LL BE LEAVING ANY DAY NOW.
I ALREADY TOLD YOU.
I'M NOT GOING.
BUT STAYING HERE DOESN'T DO YOU ANY GOOD.
THAT'S ALL RIGHT. I'LL STAY ON THE ISLAND.
I'VE ALREADY DECIDED.
NEYA.
GOOD. IT'S FLOATING.
IT'S DONE.
WE CAN UNDO THE ROPES AND LEAVE ANY TIME NOW.

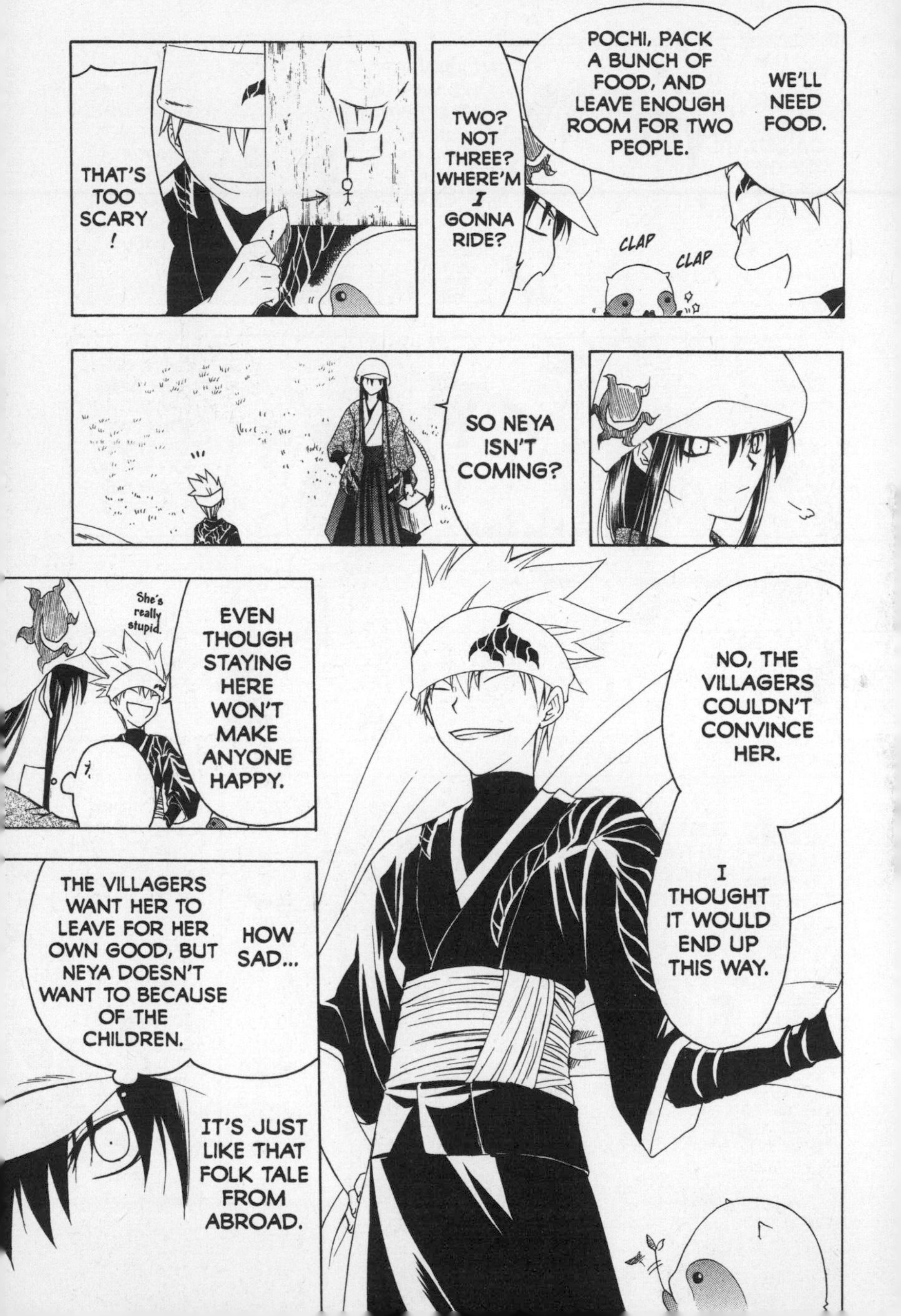
WE'LL NEED FOOD.
POCHI, PACK A BUNCH OF FOOD, AND LEAVE ENOUGH ROOM FOR TWO PEOPLE.
TWO? NOT THREE? WHERE'M I GONNA RIDE?
CLAP
CLAP
THAT'S TOO SCARY!
SO NEYA ISN'T COMING?
NO, THE VILLAGERS COULDN'T CONVINCE HER.
I THOUGHT IT WOULD END UP THIS WAY.
EVEN THOUGH STAYING HERE WON'T MAKE ANYONE HAPPY.
She's really stupid.
HOW SAD...
THE VILLAGERS WANT HER TO LEAVE FOR HER OWN GOOD, BUT NEYA DOESN'T WANT TO BECAUSE OF THE CHILDREN.
IT'S JUST LIKE THAT FOLK TALE FROM ABROAD.

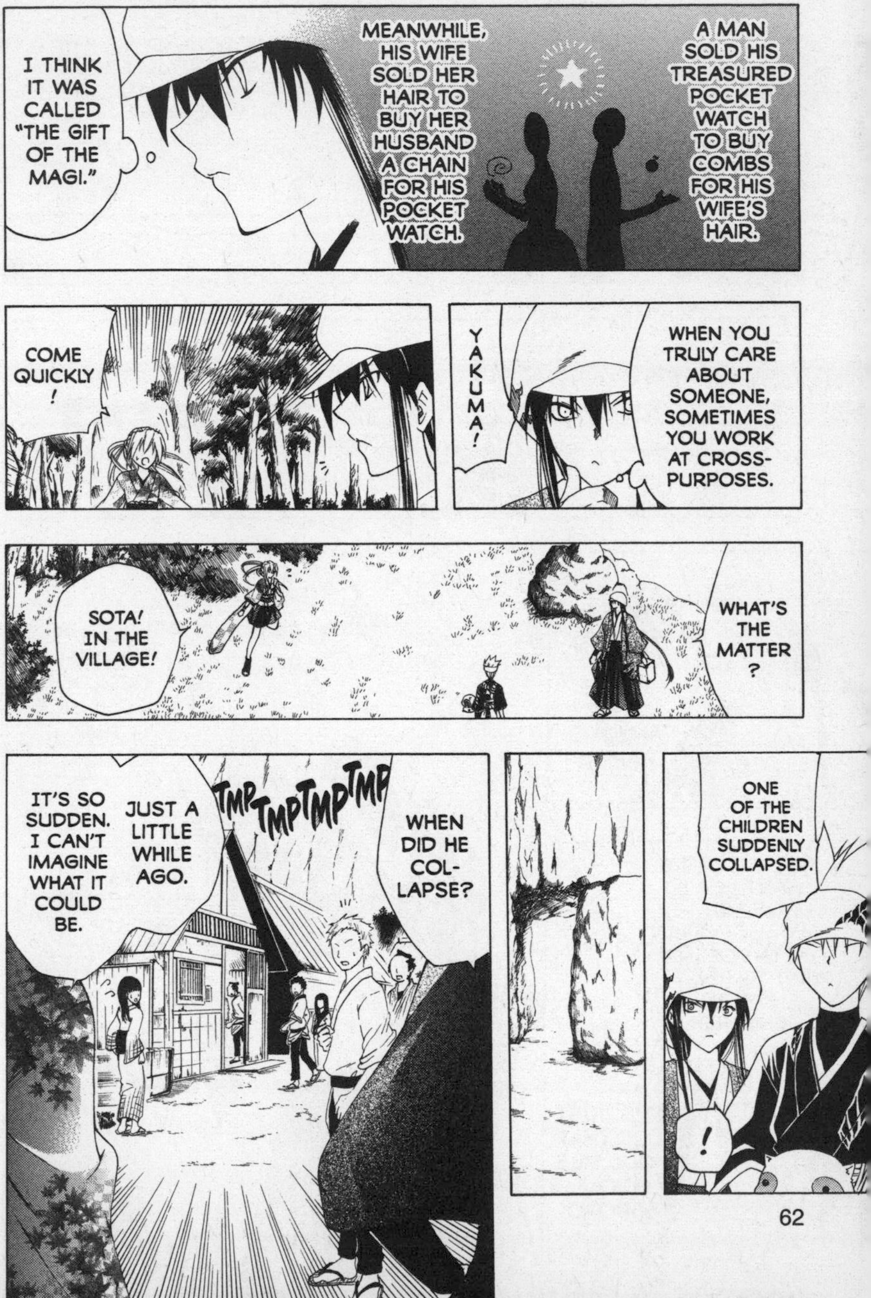
A MAN SOLD HIS TREASURED POCKET WATCH TO BUY COMBS FOR HIS WIFE'S HAIR.
MEANWHILE, HIS WIFE SOLD HER HAIR TO BUY HER HUSBAND A CHAIN FOR HIS POCKET WATCH.
I THINK IT WAS CALLED "THE GIFT OF THE MAGI."
WHEN YOU TRULY CARE ABOUT SOMEONE, SOMETIMES YOU WORK AT CROSS-PURPOSES.
YAKUMA!
COME QUICKLY!
WHAT'S THE MATTER?
SOTA! IN THE VILLAGE!
ONE OF THE CHILDREN SUDDENLY COLLAPSED.
!
WHEN DID HE COLLAPSE?
TMP TMP TMP TMP
JUST A LITTLE WHILE AGO.
IT'S SO SUDDEN. I CAN'T IMAGINE WHAT IT COULD BE.

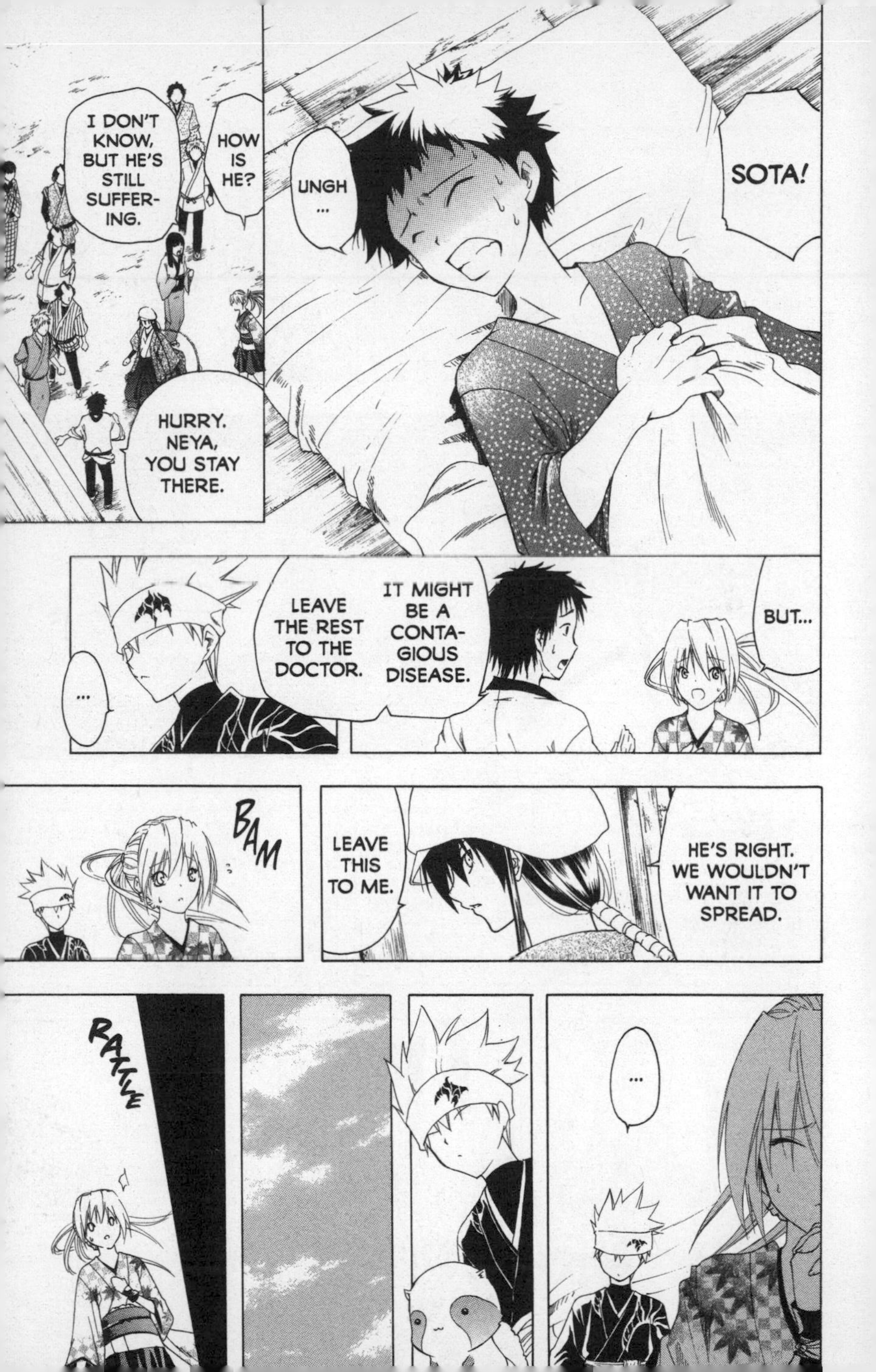
SOTA!
UNGH ...
HOW IS HE?
I DON'T KNOW, BUT HE'S STILL SUFFER-ING.
HURRY. NEYA, YOU STAY THERE.
BUT...
IT MIGHT BE A CONTA-GIOUS DISEASE.
LEAVE THE REST TO THE DOCTOR.
...
HE'S RIGHT. WE WOULDN'T WANT IT TO SPREAD.
LEAVE THIS TO ME.
BAM
...
RATTLE

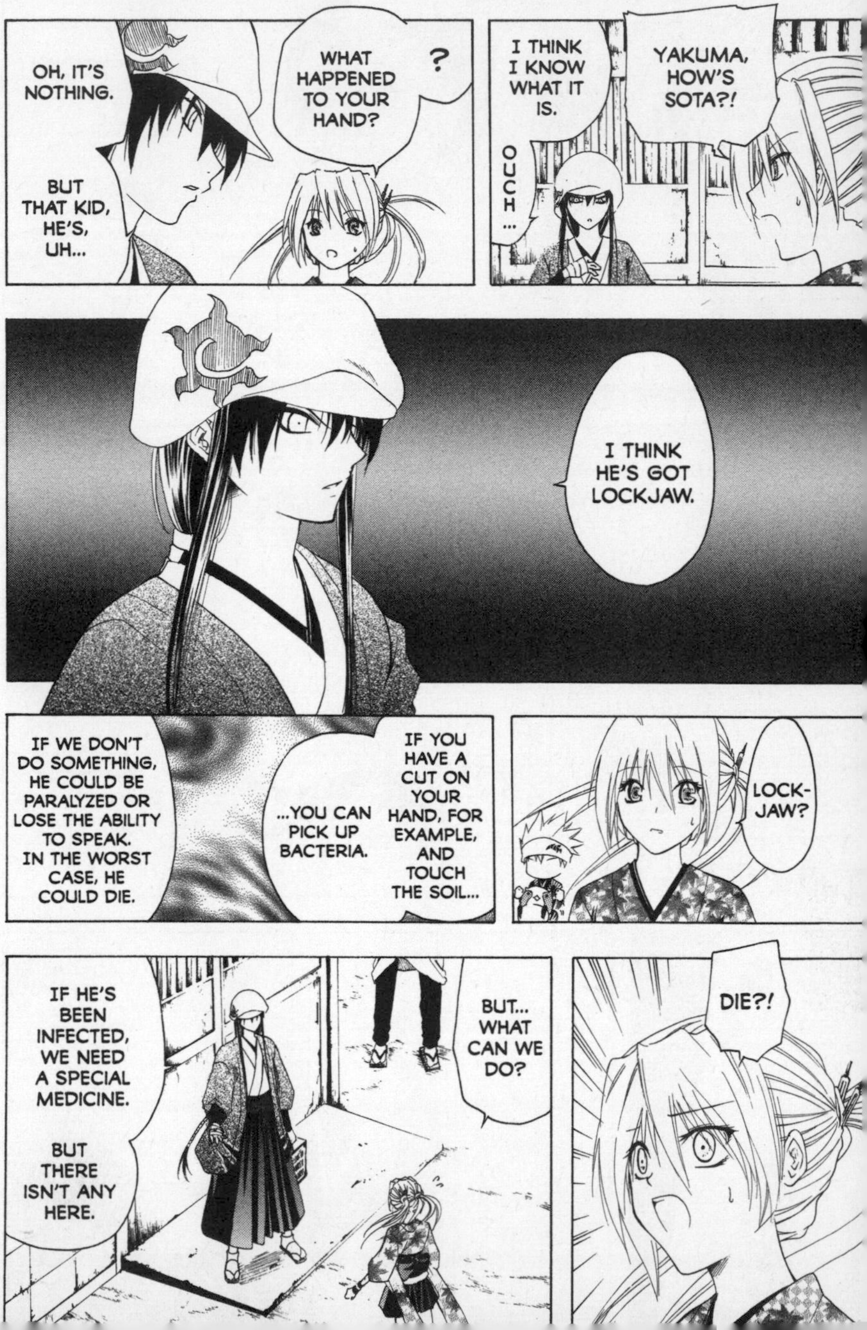
YAKUMA, HOW'S SOTA?!
I THINK I KNOW WHAT IT IS.
OUCH...
WHAT HAPPENED TO YOUR HAND?
?
OH, IT'S NOTHING.
BUT THAT KID, HE'S, UH...
I THINK HE'S GOT LOCKJAW.
LOCK-JAW?
IF YOU HAVE A CUT ON YOUR HAND, FOR EXAMPLE, AND TOUCH THE SOIL...
...YOU CAN PICK UP BACTERIA.
IF WE DON'T DO SOMETHING, HE COULD BE PARALYZED OR LOSE THE ABILITY TO SPEAK. IN THE WORST CASE, HE COULD DIE.
DIE?!
BUT... WHAT CAN WE DO?
IF HE'S BEEN INFECTED, WE NEED A SPECIAL MEDICINE.
BUT THERE ISN'T ANY HERE.

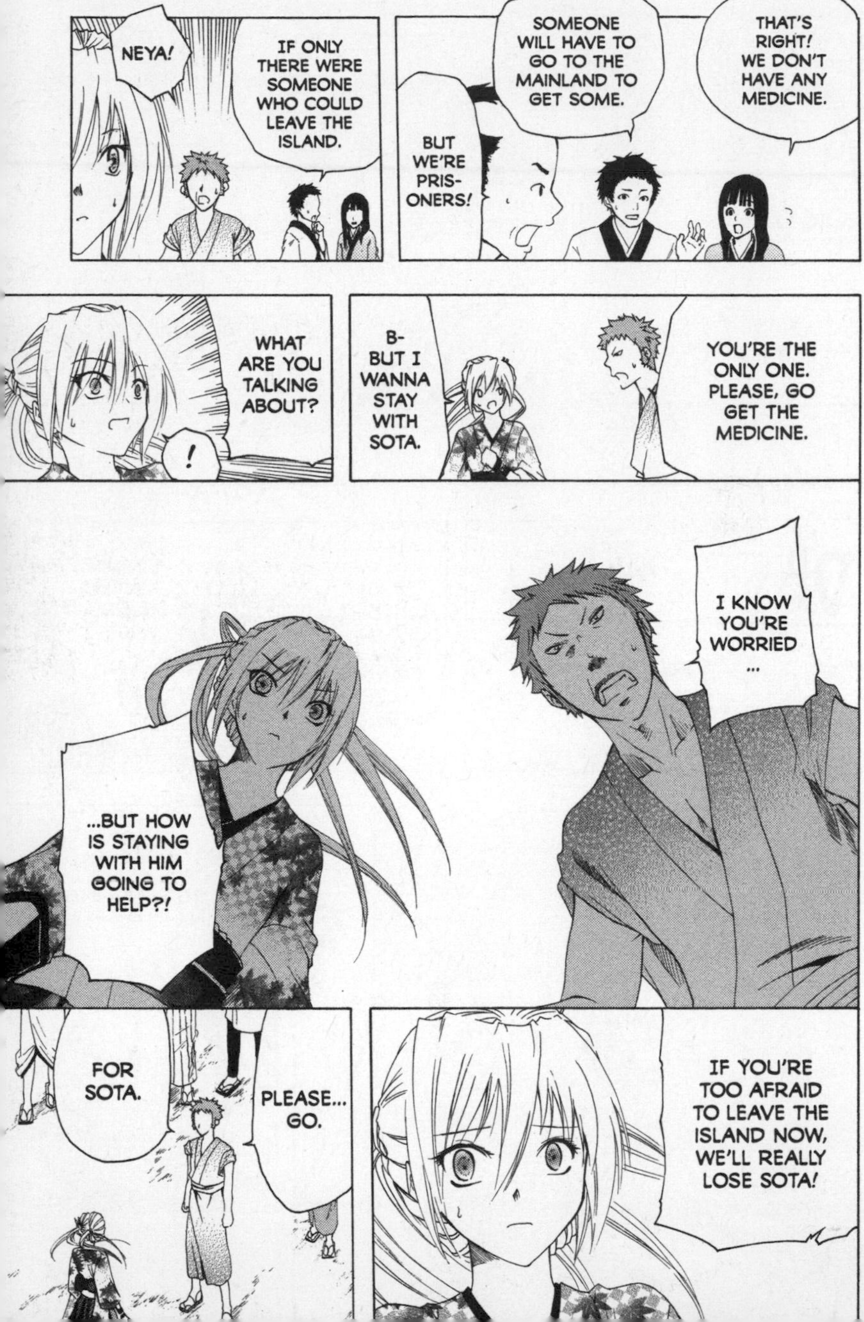
THAT'S RIGHT! WE DON'T HAVE ANY MEDICINE.
SOMEONE WILL HAVE TO GO TO THE MAINLAND TO GET SOME.
BUT WE'RE PRIS-ONERS!
IF ONLY THERE WERE SOMEONE WHO COULD LEAVE THE ISLAND.
NEYA!
YOU'RE THE ONLY ONE. PLEASE, GO GET THE MEDICINE.
B- BUT I WANNA STAY WITH SOTA.
WHAT ARE YOU TALKING ABOUT?
!
I KNOW YOU'RE WORRIED ...
...BUT HOW IS STAYING WITH HIM GOING TO HELP?!
IF YOU'RE TOO AFRAID TO LEAVE THE ISLAND NOW, WE'LL REALLY LOSE SOTA!
PLEASE... GO.
FOR SOTA.

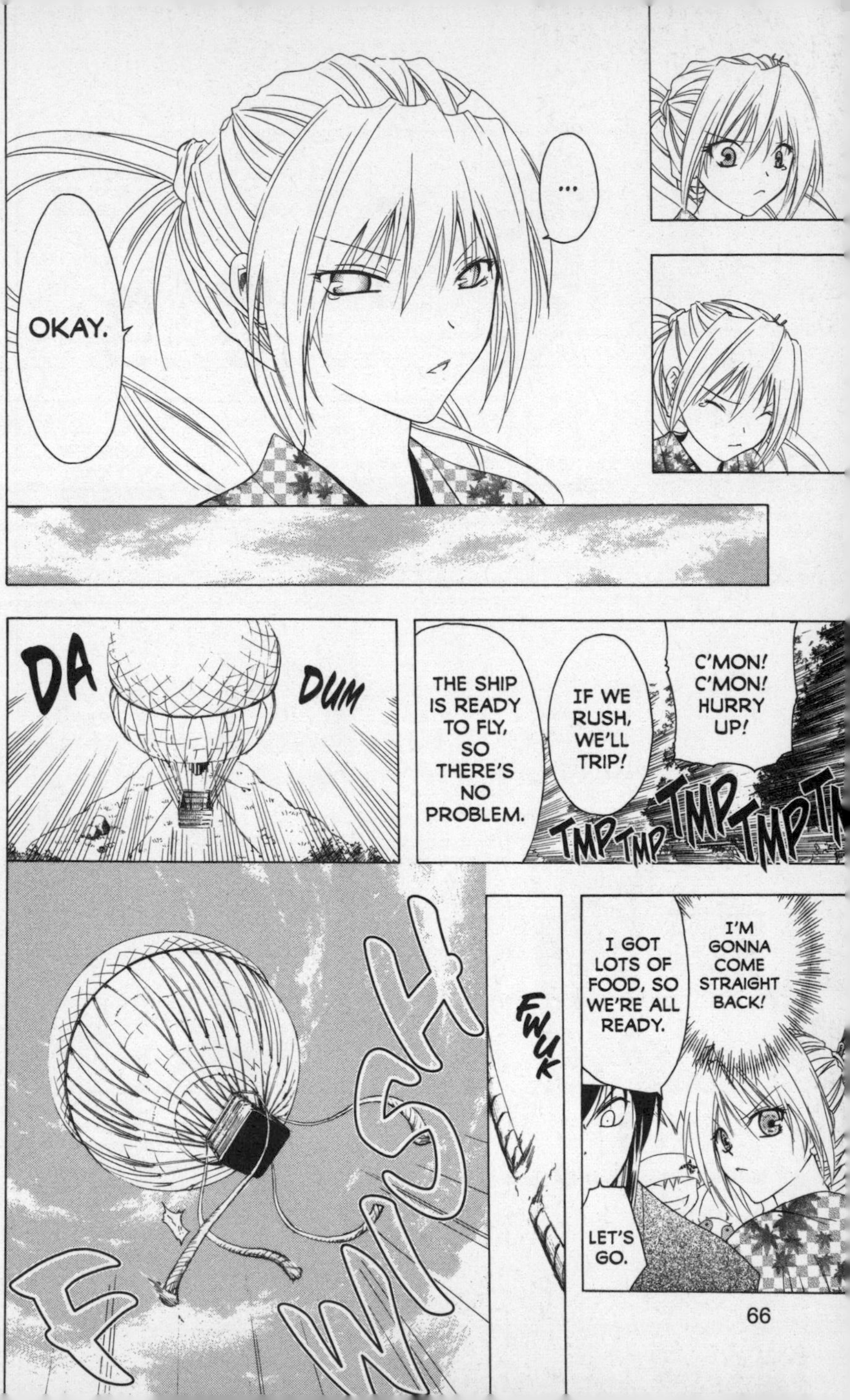
...
OKAY.
C'MON! C'MON! HURRY UP!
IF WE RUSH, WE'LL TRIP!
THE SHIP IS READY TO FLY, SO THERE'S NO PROBLEM.
TMP TMP TMP TMP
DA DUM
I'M GONNA COME STRAIGHT BACK!
I GOT LOTS OF FOOD, SO WE'RE ALL READY.
LET'S GO.
FWUK
FWISH

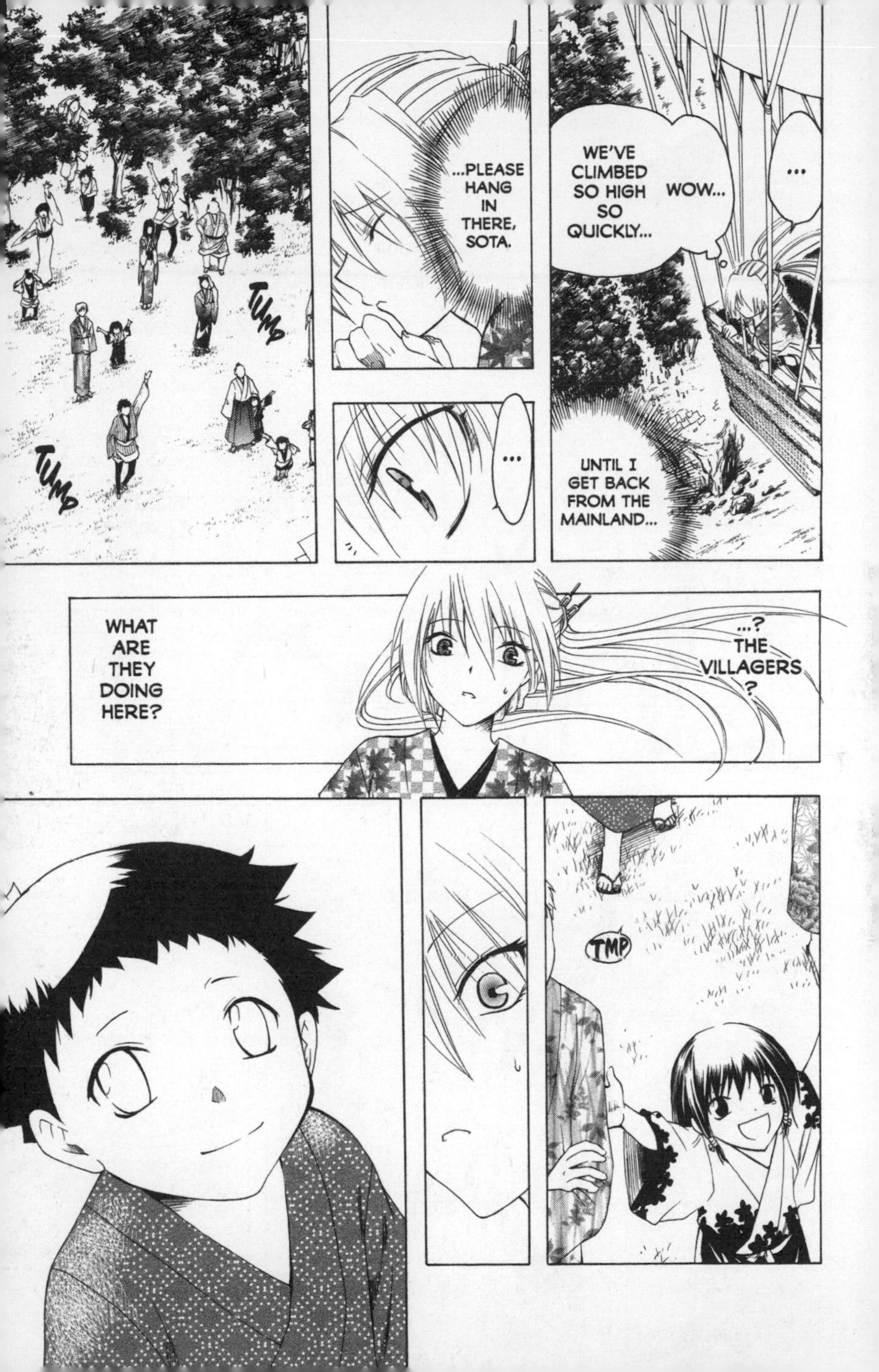
...
WOW...
WE'VE CLIMBED SO HIGH SO QUICKLY...
UNTIL I GET BACK FROM THE MAINLAND...
...PLEASE HANG IN THERE, SOTA.
...
TUMP
TUMP
...? THE VILLAGERS?
WHAT ARE THEY DOING HERE?
TMP

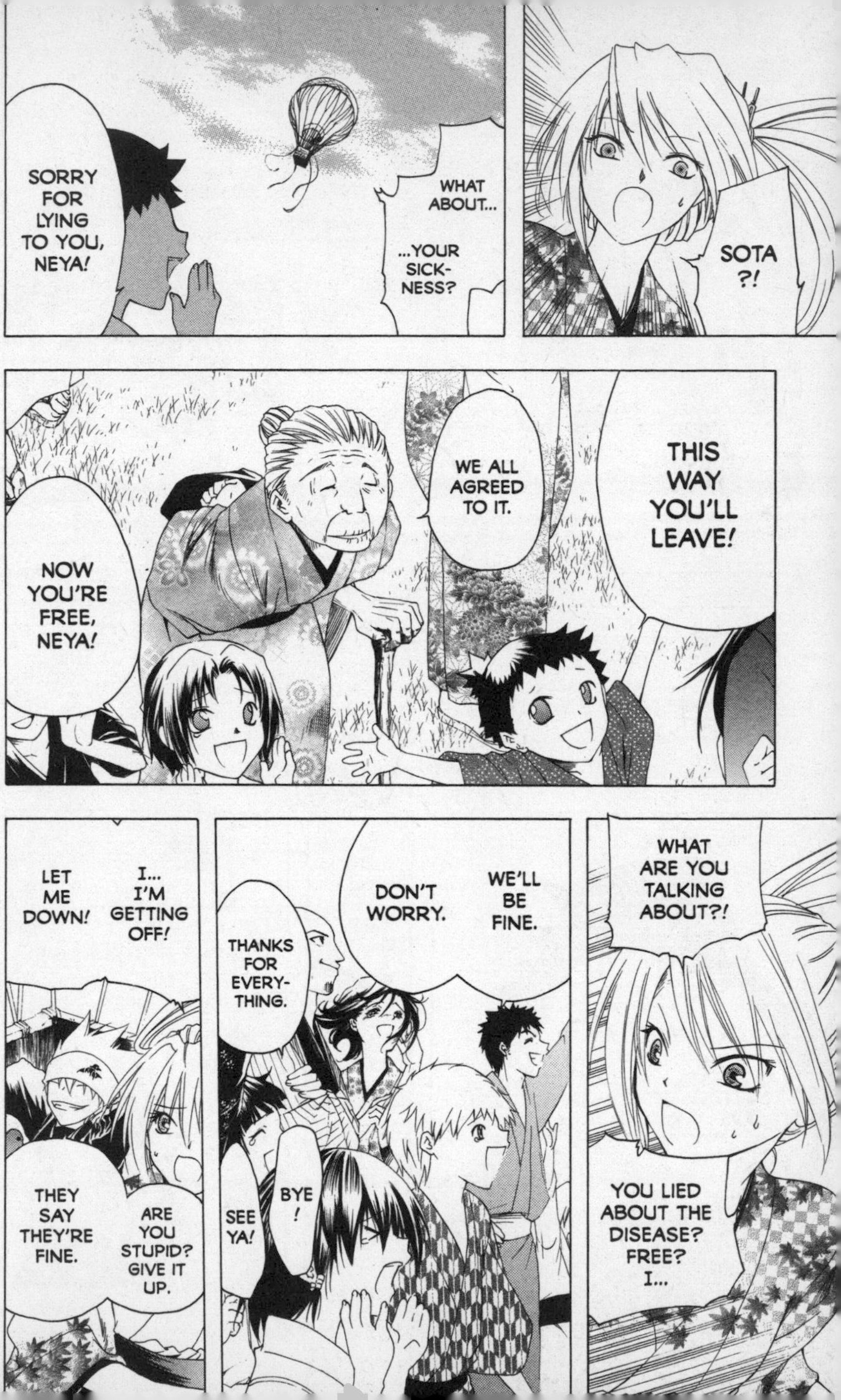
SOTA ?!
WHAT ABOUT...
...YOUR SICK- NESS?
SORRY FOR LYING TO YOU, NEYA!
THIS WAY YOU'LL LEAVE!
WE ALL AGREED TO IT.
NOW YOU'RE FREE, NEYA!
WHAT ARE YOU TALKING ABOUT?!
YOU LIED ABOUT THE DISEASE? FREE? I...
WE'LL BE FINE.
DON'T WORRY.
THANKS FOR EVERY- THING.
BYE!
SEE YA!
I... I'M GETTING OFF!
LET ME DOWN!
ARE YOU STUPID? GIVE IT UP.
THEY SAY THEY'RE FINE.

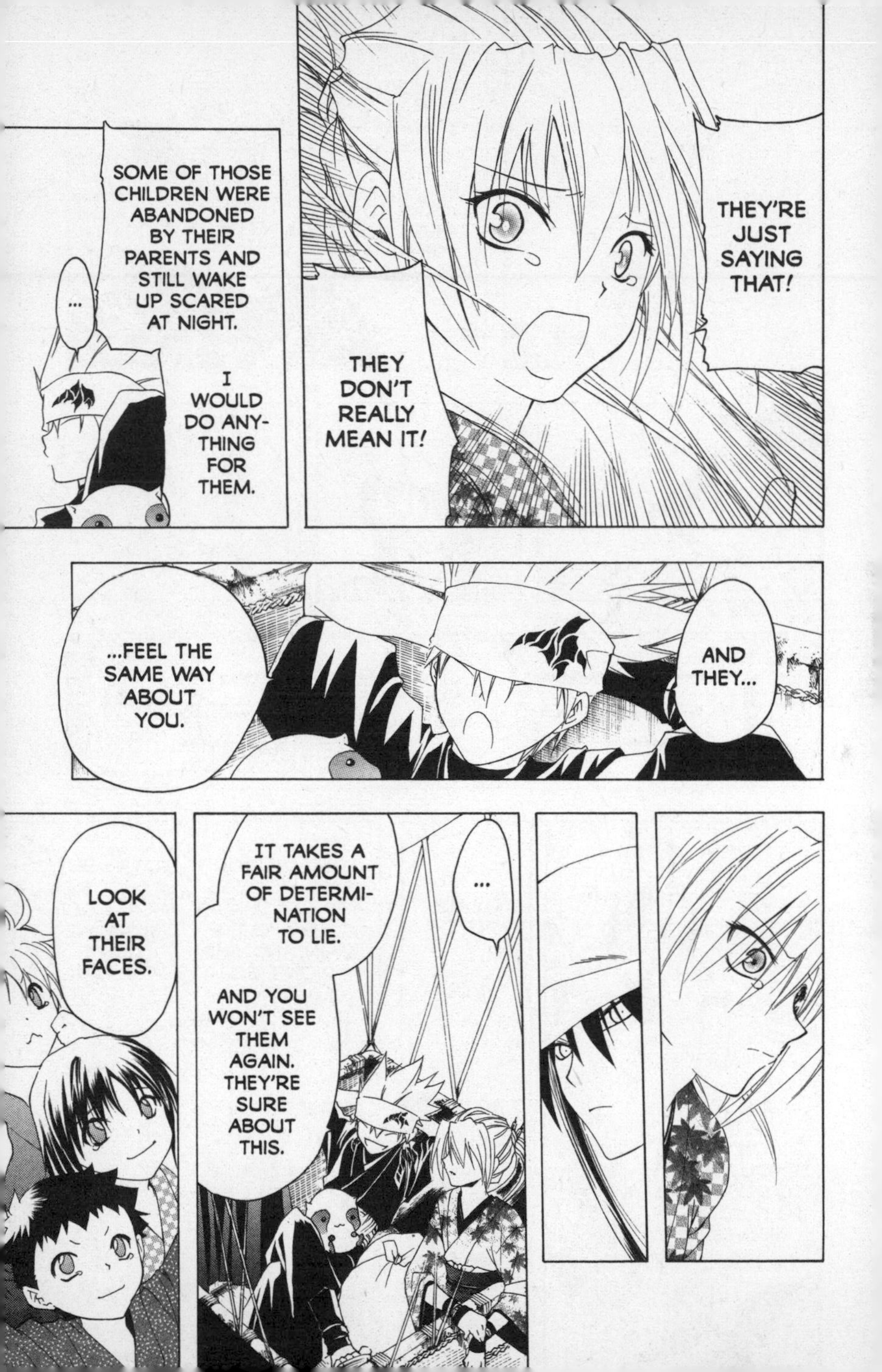
THEY'RE JUST SAYING THAT!
THEY DON'T REALLY MEAN IT!
SOME OF THOSE CHILDREN WERE ABANDONED BY THEIR PARENTS AND STILL WAKE UP SCARED AT NIGHT.
...
I WOULD DO ANYTHING FOR THEM.
AND THEY...
...FEEL THE SAME WAY ABOUT YOU.
...
IT TAKES A FAIR AMOUNT OF DETERMINATION TO LIE.
AND YOU WON'T SEE THEM AGAIN. THEY'RE SURE ABOUT THIS.
LOOK AT THEIR FACES.

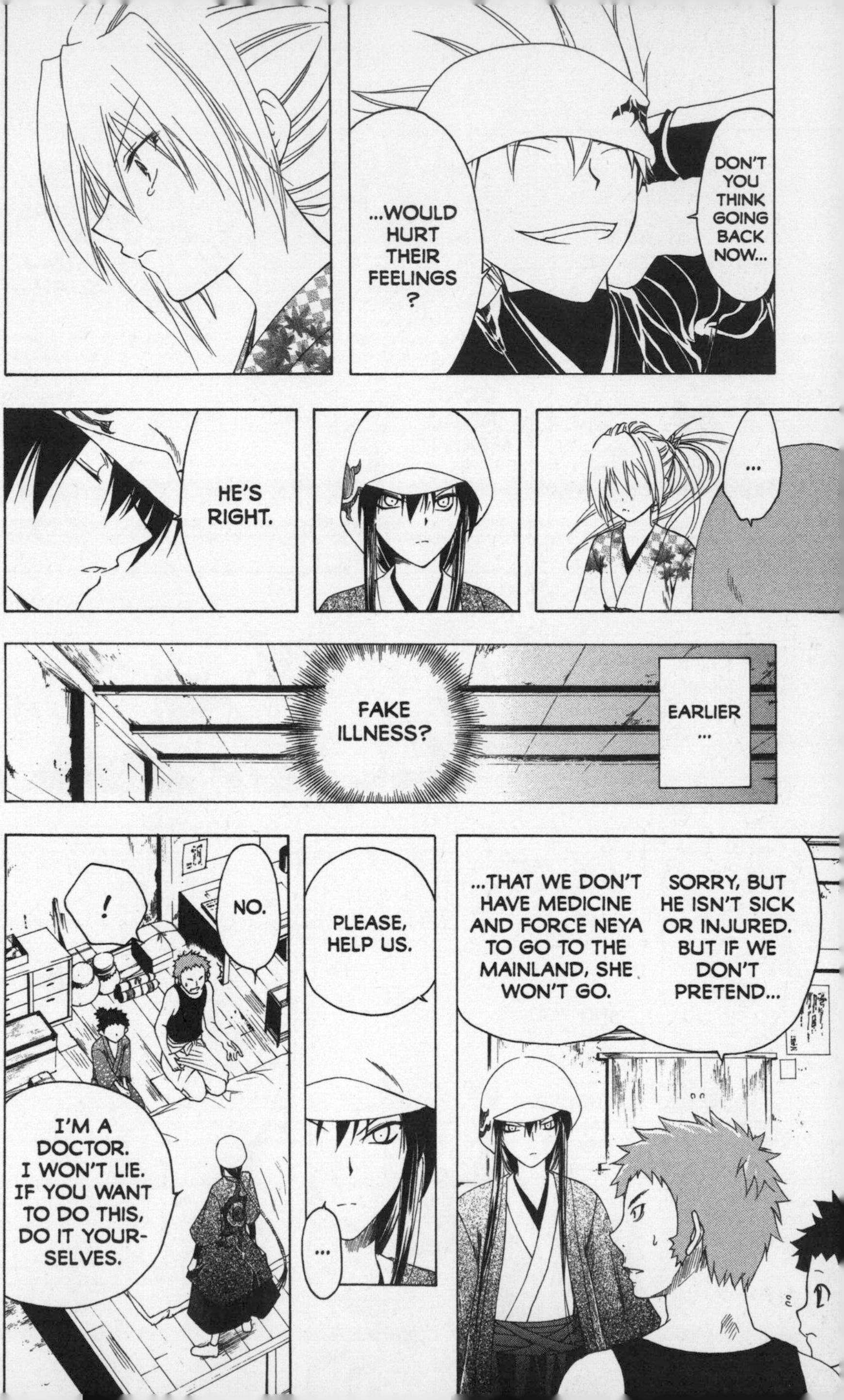
DON'T YOU THINK GOING BACK NOW...
...WOULD HURT THEIR FEELINGS?
...
HE'S RIGHT.
EARLIER ...
FAKE ILLNESS?
SORRY, BUT HE ISN'T SICK OR INJURED. BUT IF WE DON'T PRETEND...
...THAT WE DON'T HAVE MEDICINE AND FORCE NEYA TO GO TO THE MAINLAND, SHE WON'T GO.
PLEASE, HELP US.
...
NO.
!
I'M A DOCTOR. I WON'T LIE. IF YOU WANT TO DO THIS, DO IT YOURSELVES.

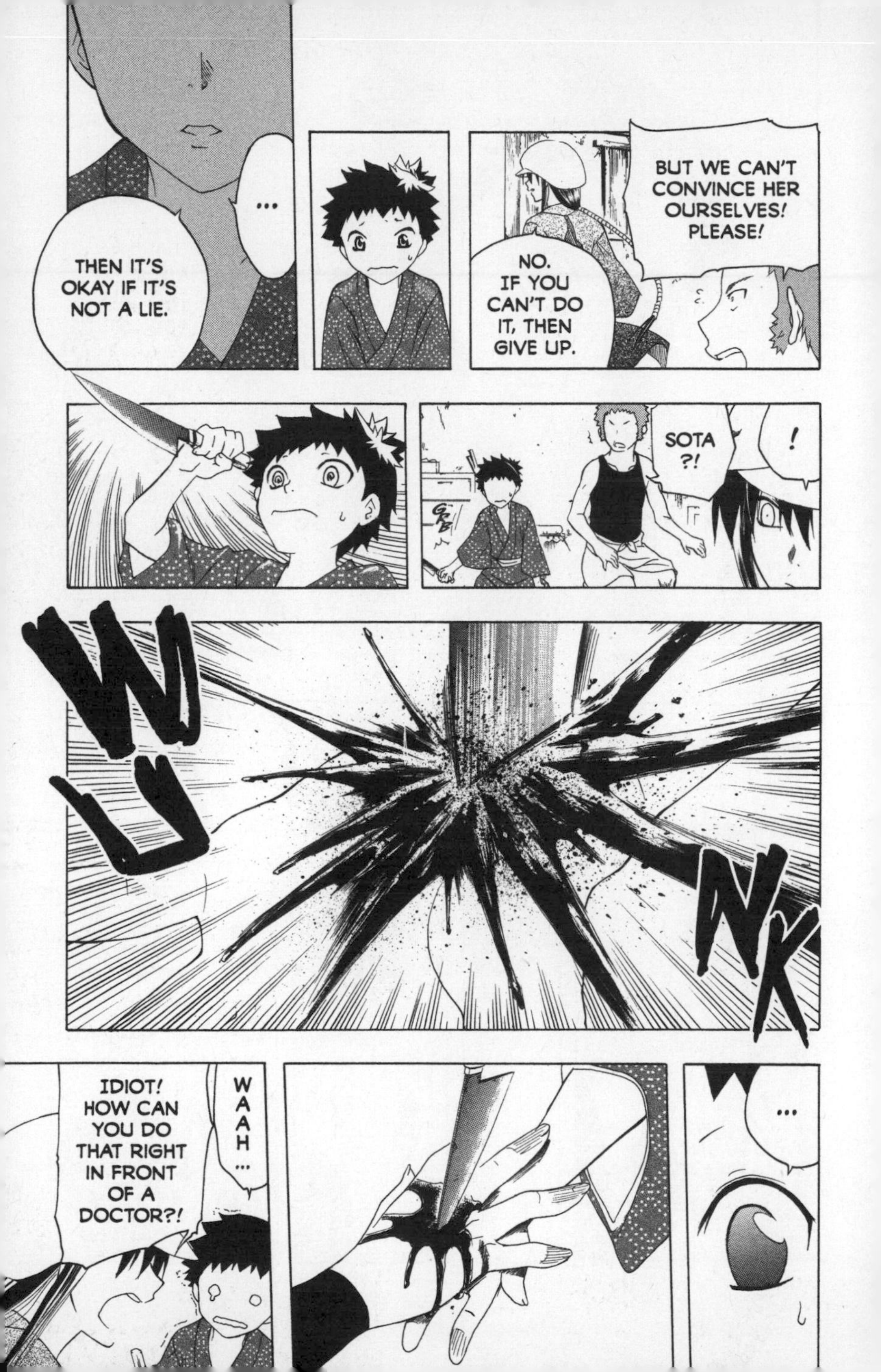
BUT WE CAN'T CONVINCE HER OURSELVES! PLEASE!
NO. IF YOU CAN'T DO IT, THEN GIVE UP.
...
THEN IT'S OKAY IF IT'S NOT A LIE.
!
SOTA ?!
GRB
WUNK
...
WAAH...
IDIOT! HOW CAN YOU DO THAT RIGHT IN FRONT OF A DOCTOR?!

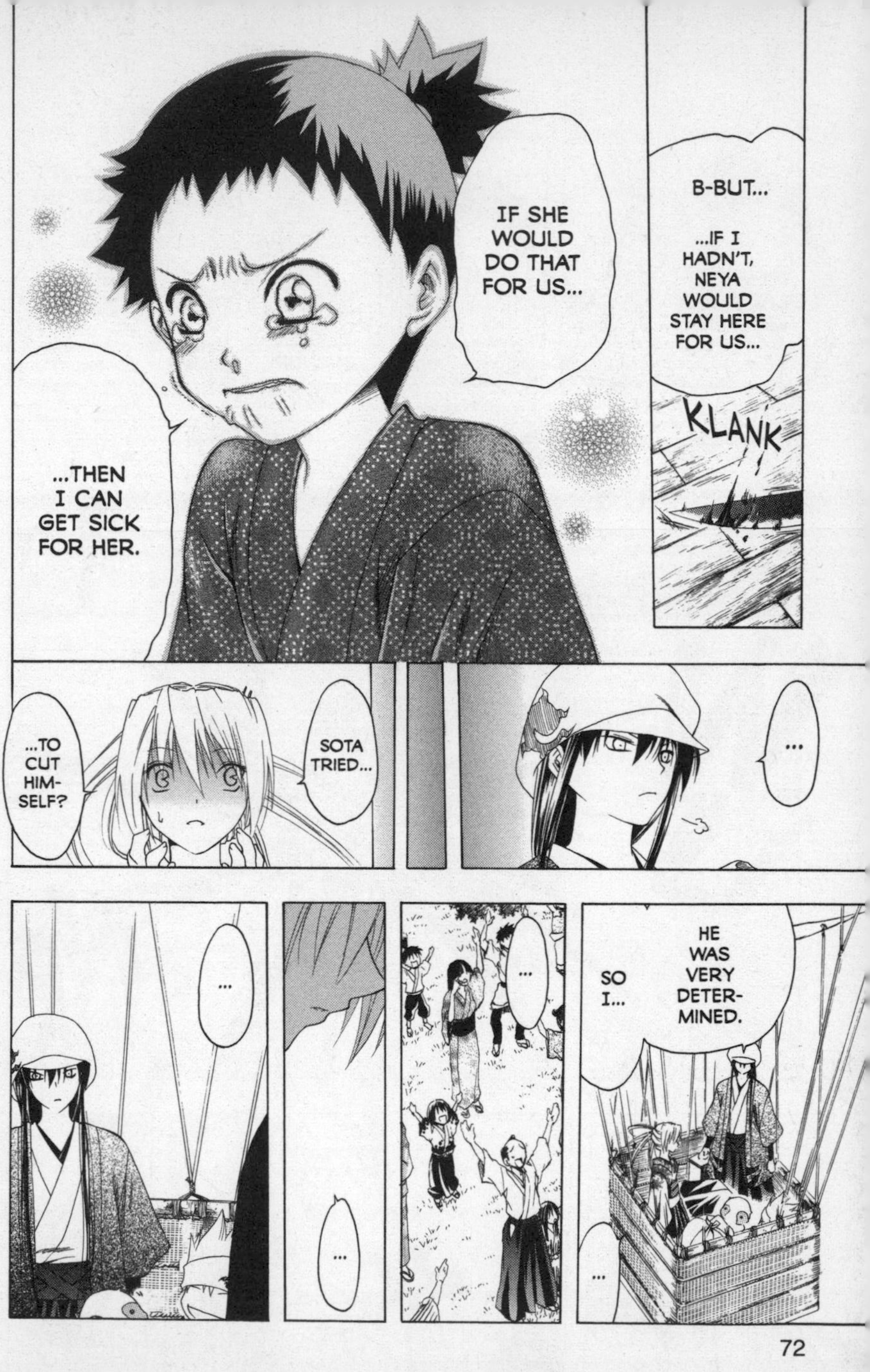
B-BUT...
...IF I HADN'T, NEYA WOULD STAY HERE FOR US...
KLANK
IF SHE WOULD DO THAT FOR US...
...THEN I CAN GET SICK FOR HER.
...
SOTA TRIED...
...TO CUT HIMSELF?
HE WAS VERY DETERMINED.
SO I...
...
...
...
...
...

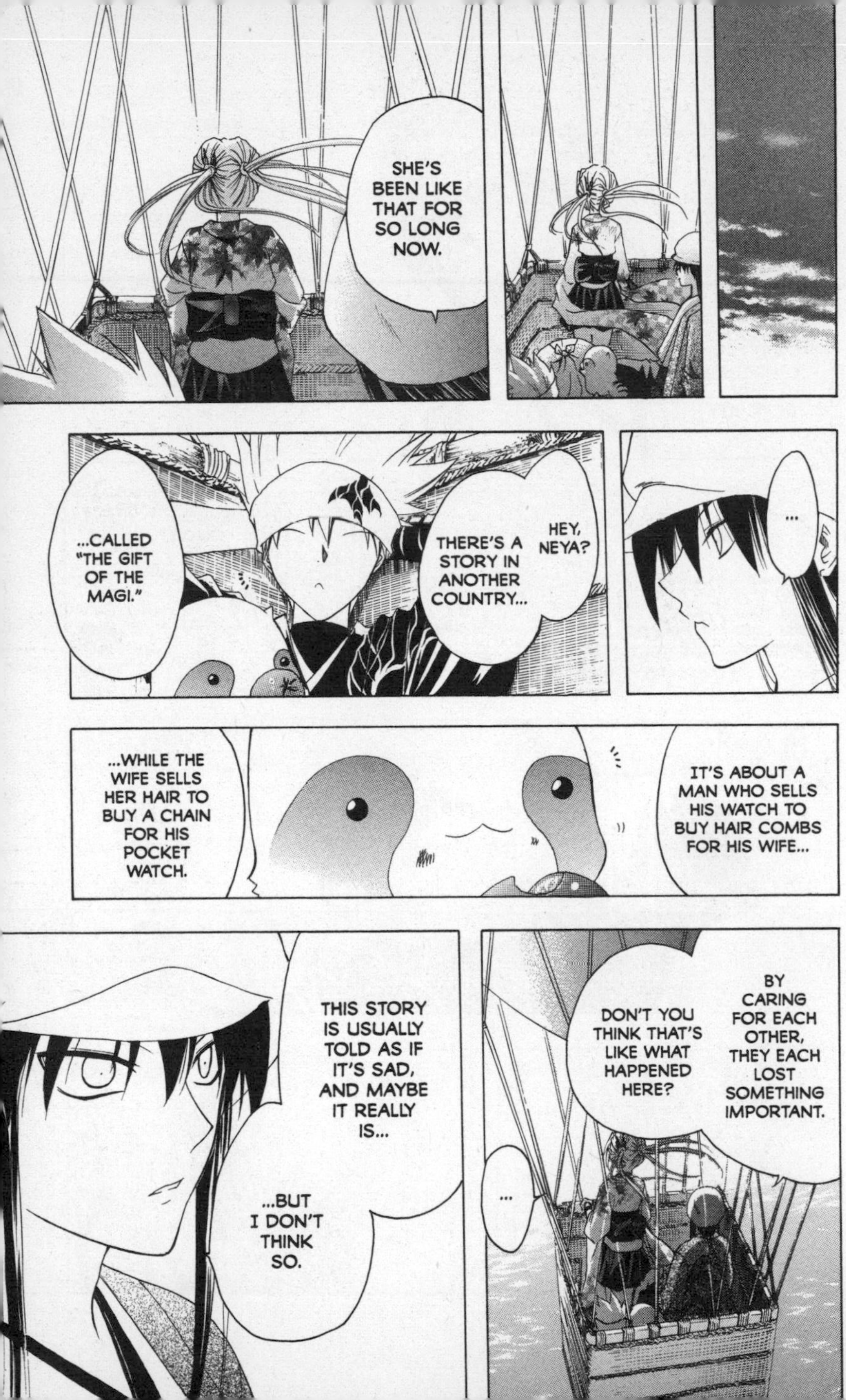
SHE'S BEEN LIKE THAT FOR SO LONG NOW.
...
HEY, NEYA?
THERE'S A STORY IN ANOTHER COUNTRY...
...CALLED "THE GIFT OF THE MAGI."
IT'S ABOUT A MAN WHO SELLS HIS WATCH TO BUY HAIR COMBS FOR HIS WIFE...
...WHILE THE WIFE SELLS HER HAIR TO BUY A CHAIN FOR HIS POCKET WATCH.
BY CARING FOR EACH OTHER, THEY EACH LOST SOMETHING IMPORTANT.
DON'T YOU THINK THAT'S LIKE WHAT HAPPENED HERE?
...
THIS STORY IS USUALLY TOLD AS IF IT'S SAD, AND MAYBE IT REALLY IS...
...BUT I DON'T THINK SO.

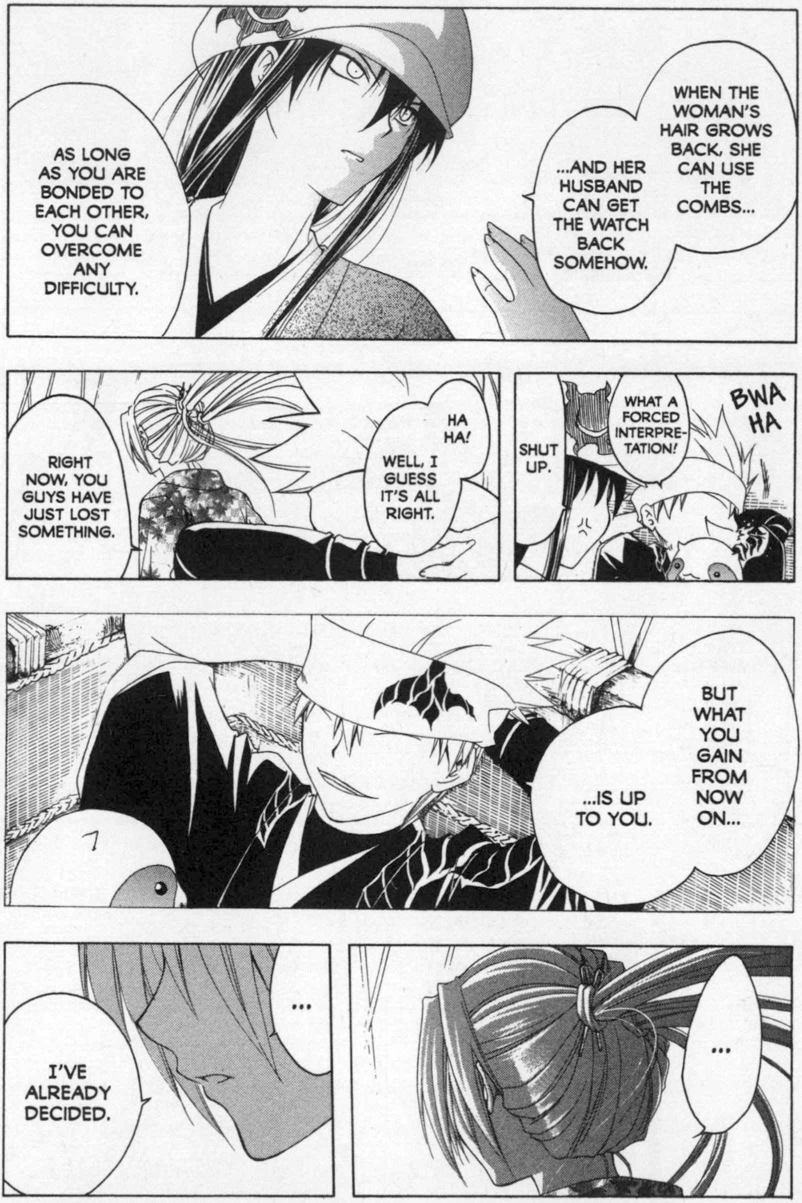

WHEN THE WOMAN'S HAIR GROWS BACK, SHE CAN USE THE COMBS...
...AND HER HUSBAND CAN GET THE WATCH BACK SOMEHOW.
AS LONG AS YOU ARE BONDED TO EACH OTHER, YOU CAN OVERCOME ANY DIFFICULTY.
BWA HA
WHAT A FORCED INTERPRETATION!
SHUT UP.
HA HA!
WELL, I GUESS IT'S ALL RIGHT.
RIGHT NOW, YOU GUYS HAVE JUST LOST SOMETHING.
BUT WHAT YOU GAIN FROM NOW ON...
...IS UP TO YOU.
...
...
I'VE ALREADY DECIDED.

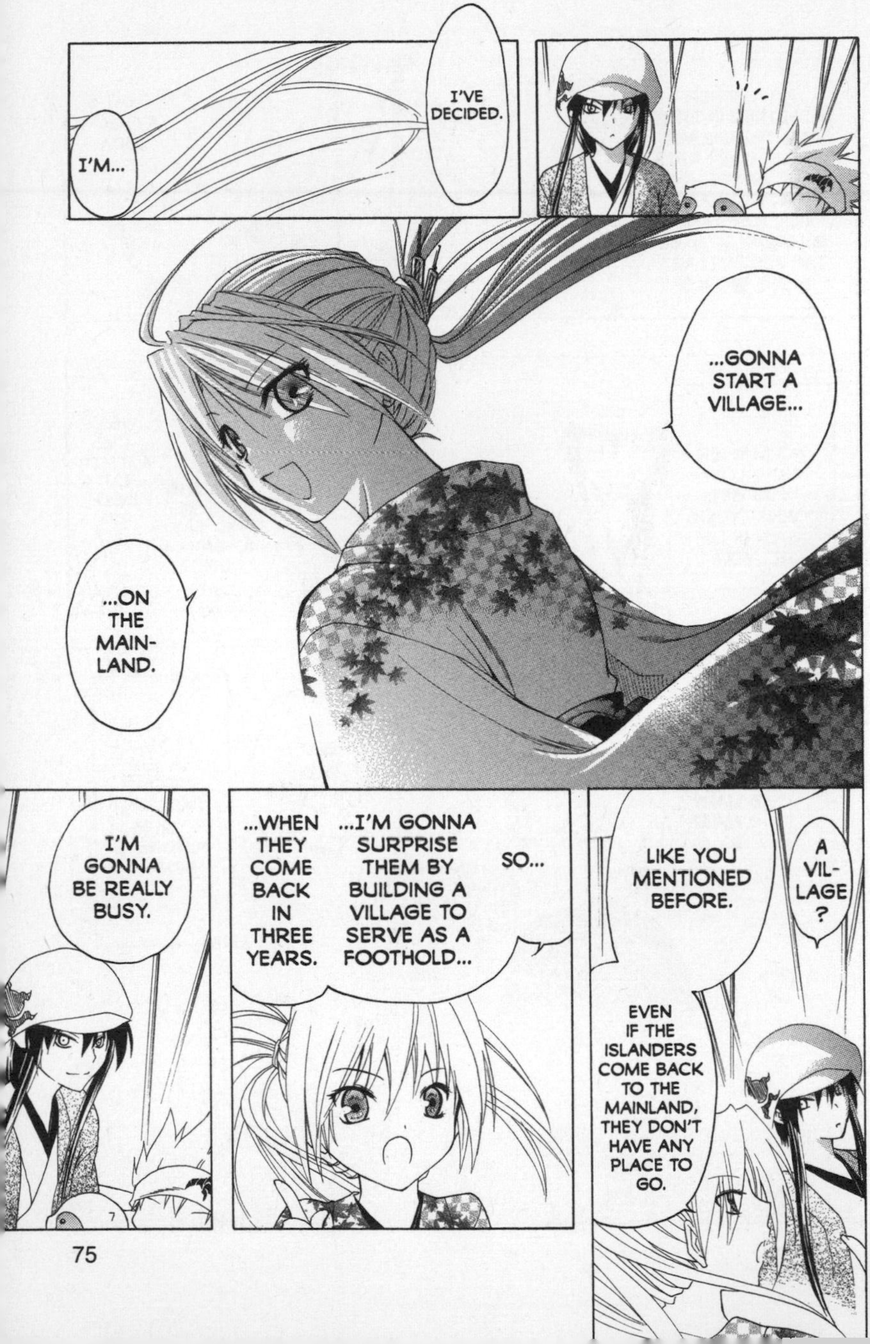
I'VE DECIDED.
I'M...
...GONNA START A VILLAGE...
...ON THE MAINLAND.
A VILLAGE?
LIKE YOU MENTIONED BEFORE.
EVEN IF THE ISLANDERS COME BACK TO THE MAINLAND, THEY DON'T HAVE ANY PLACE TO GO.
SO...
...I'M GONNA SURPRISE THEM BY BUILDING A VILLAGE TO SERVE AS A FOOTHOLD...
...WHEN THEY COME BACK IN THREE YEARS.
I'M GONNA BE REALLY BUSY.

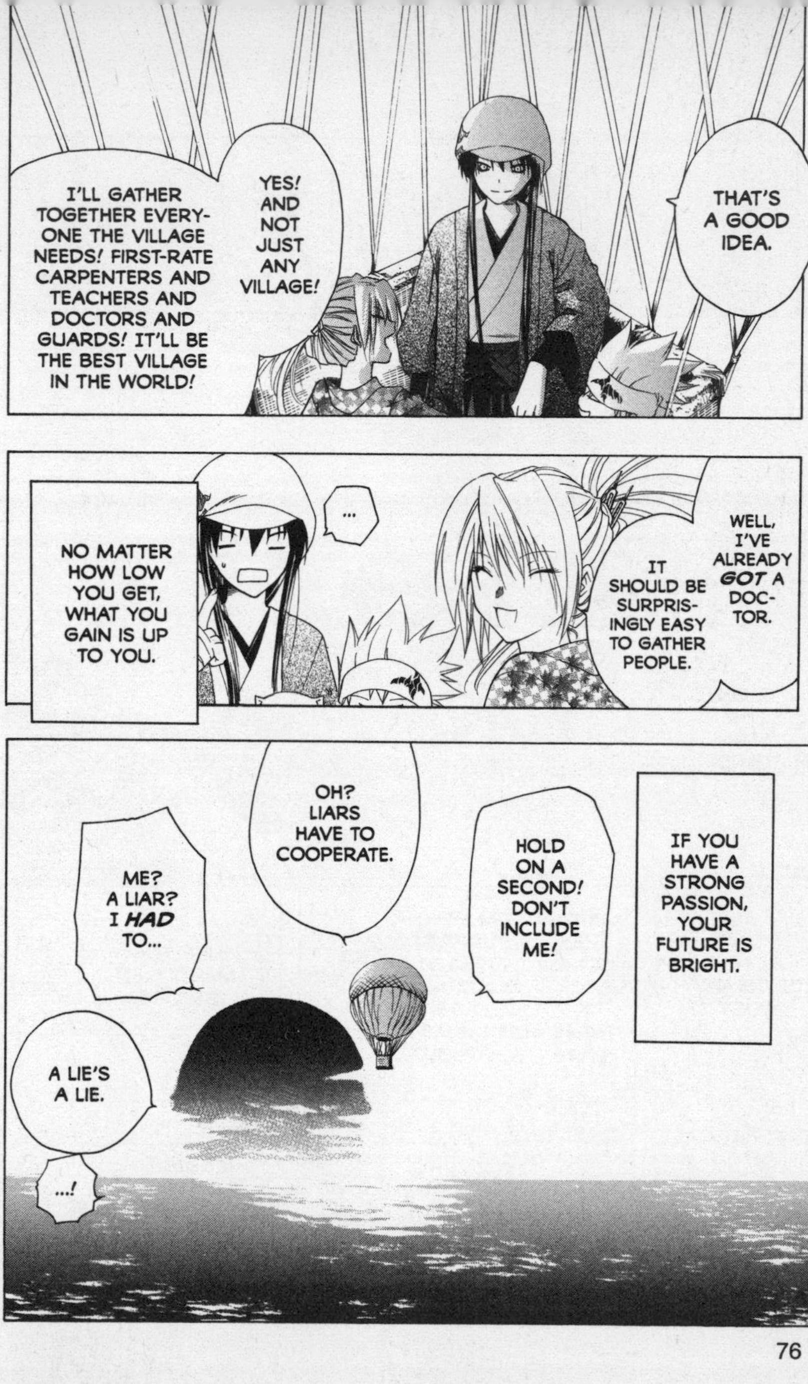
THAT'S A GOOD IDEA.
YES! AND NOT JUST ANY VILLAGE!
I'LL GATHER TOGETHER EVERY-ONE THE VILLAGE NEEDS! FIRST-RATE CARPENTERS AND TEACHERS AND DOCTORS AND GUARDS! IT'LL BE THE BEST VILLAGE IN THE WORLD!
WELL, I'VE ALREADY *GOT* A DOC-TOR.
IT SHOULD BE SURPRIS-INGLY EASY TO GATHER PEOPLE.
...
NO MATTER HOW LOW YOU GET, WHAT YOU GAIN IS UP TO YOU.
IF YOU HAVE A STRONG PASSION, YOUR FUTURE IS BRIGHT.
HOLD ON A SECOND! DON'T INCLUDE ME!
OH? LIARS HAVE TO COOPERATE.
ME? A LIAR? I *HAD* TO...
A LIE'S A LIE.
...!

Chapter 22

The Same as Gramps

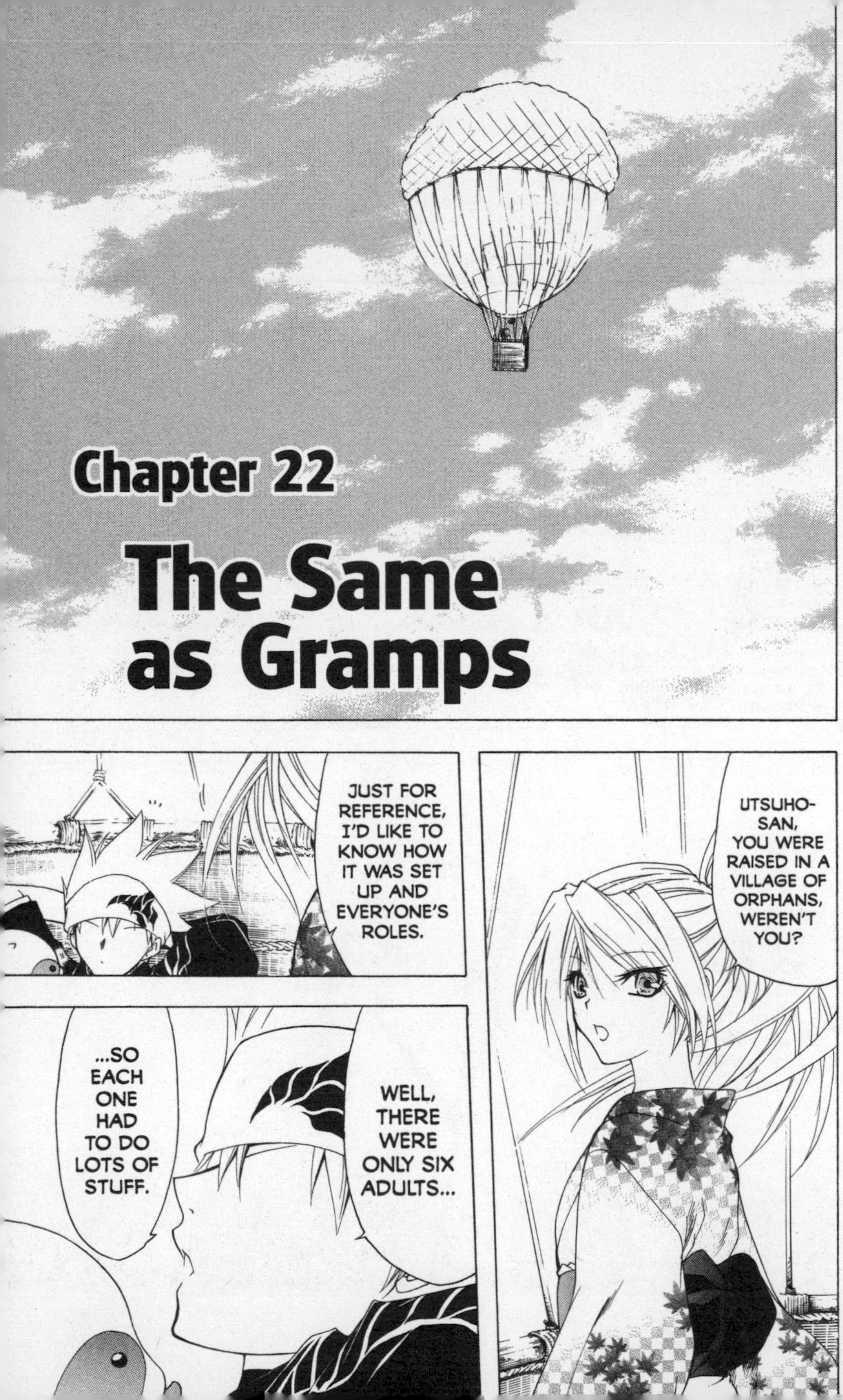
UTSUHO-SAN, YOU WERE RAISED IN A VILLAGE OF ORPHANS, WEREN'T YOU?
JUST FOR REFERENCE, I'D LIKE TO KNOW HOW IT WAS SET UP AND EVERYONE'S ROLES.
WELL, THERE WERE ONLY SIX ADULTS...
...SO EACH ONE HAD TO DO LOTS OF STUFF.

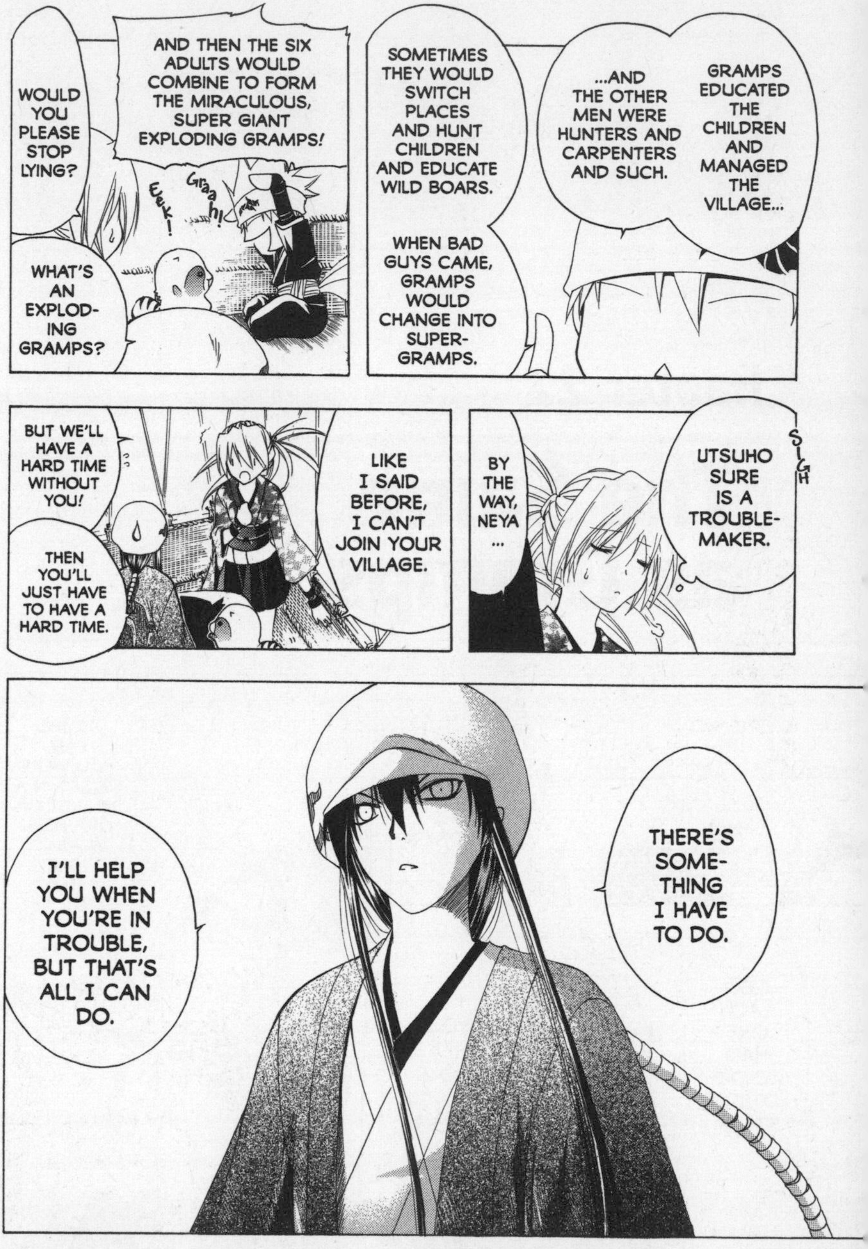
GRAMPS EDUCATED THE CHILDREN AND MANAGED THE VILLAGE...
...AND THE OTHER MEN WERE HUNTERS AND CARPENTERS AND SUCH.
SOMETIMES THEY WOULD SWITCH PLACES AND HUNT CHILDREN AND EDUCATE WILD BOARS.
WHEN BAD GUYS CAME, GRAMPS WOULD CHANGE INTO SUPER-GRAMPS.
AND THEN THE SIX ADULTS WOULD COMBINE TO FORM THE MIRACULOUS, SUPER GIANT EXPLODING GRAMPS!
WOULD YOU PLEASE STOP LYING?
Graah!
Eek!
WHAT'S AN EXPLODING GRAMPS?
SIGH
UTSUHO SURE IS A TROUBLEMAKER.
BY THE WAY, NEYA...
LIKE I SAID BEFORE, I CAN'T JOIN YOUR VILLAGE.
BUT WE'LL HAVE A HARD TIME WITHOUT YOU!
THEN YOU'LL JUST HAVE TO HAVE A HARD TIME.
THERE'S SOMETHING I HAVE TO DO.
I'LL HELP YOU WHEN YOU'RE IN TROUBLE, BUT THAT'S ALL I CAN DO.

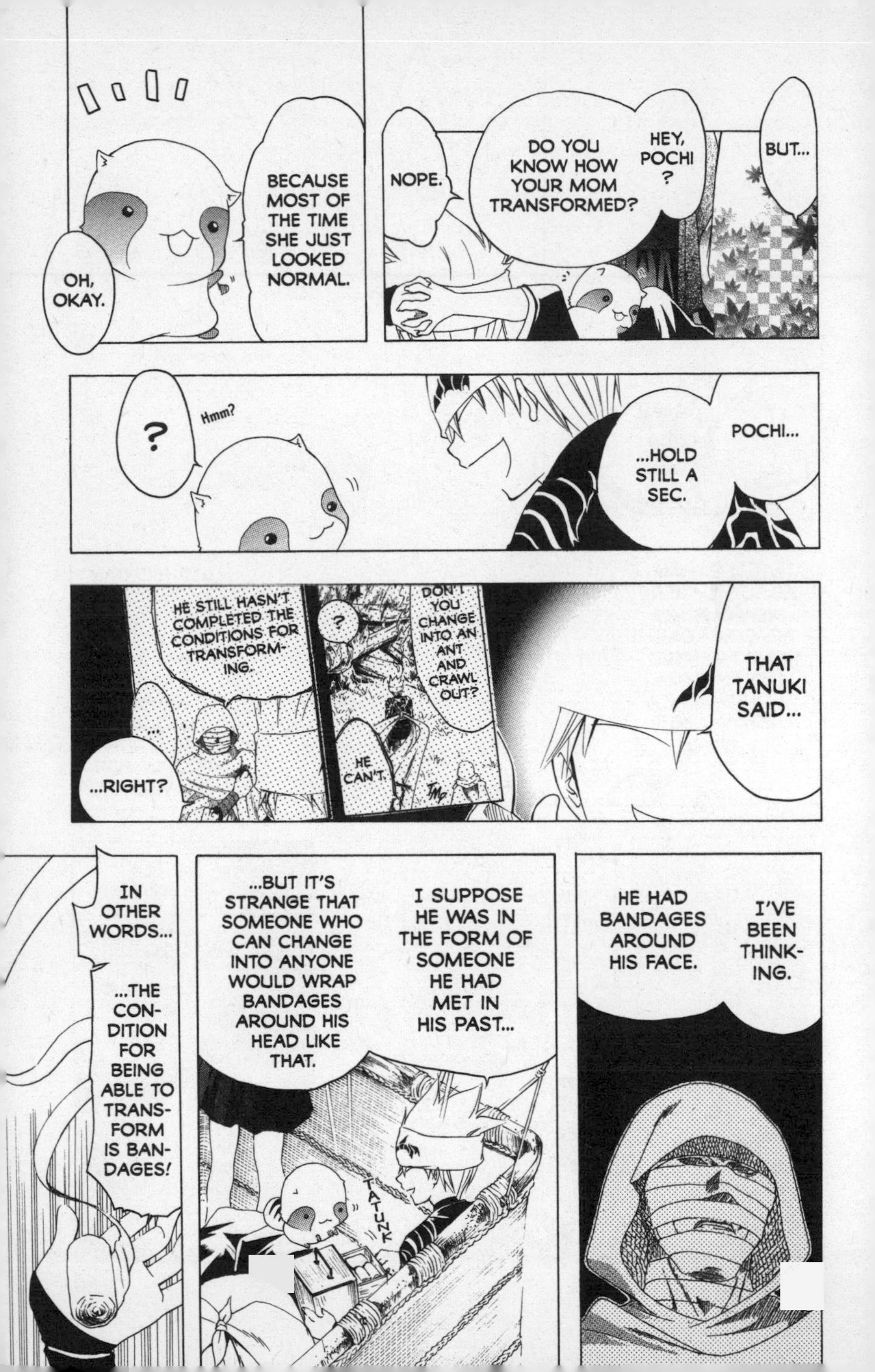
BUT...
HEY, POCHI?
DO YOU KNOW HOW YOUR MOM TRANSFORMED?
NOPE.
BECAUSE MOST OF THE TIME SHE JUST LOOKED NORMAL.
OH, OKAY.
POCHI...
...HOLD STILL A SEC.
Hmm?
?
THAT TANUKI SAID...
DON'T YOU CHANGE INTO AN ANT AND CRAWL OUT?
?
HE CAN'T.
HE STILL HASN'T COMPLETED THE CONDITIONS FOR TRANSFORMING.
...
...RIGHT?
I'VE BEEN THINKING.
HE HAD BANDAGES AROUND HIS FACE.
I SUPPOSE HE WAS IN THE FORM OF SOMEONE HE HAD MET IN HIS PAST...
...BUT IT'S STRANGE THAT SOMEONE WHO CAN CHANGE INTO ANYONE WOULD WRAP BANDAGES AROUND HIS HEAD LIKE THAT.
TATUNK
IN OTHER WORDS...
...THE CONDITION FOR BEING ABLE TO TRANSFORM IS BANDAGES!

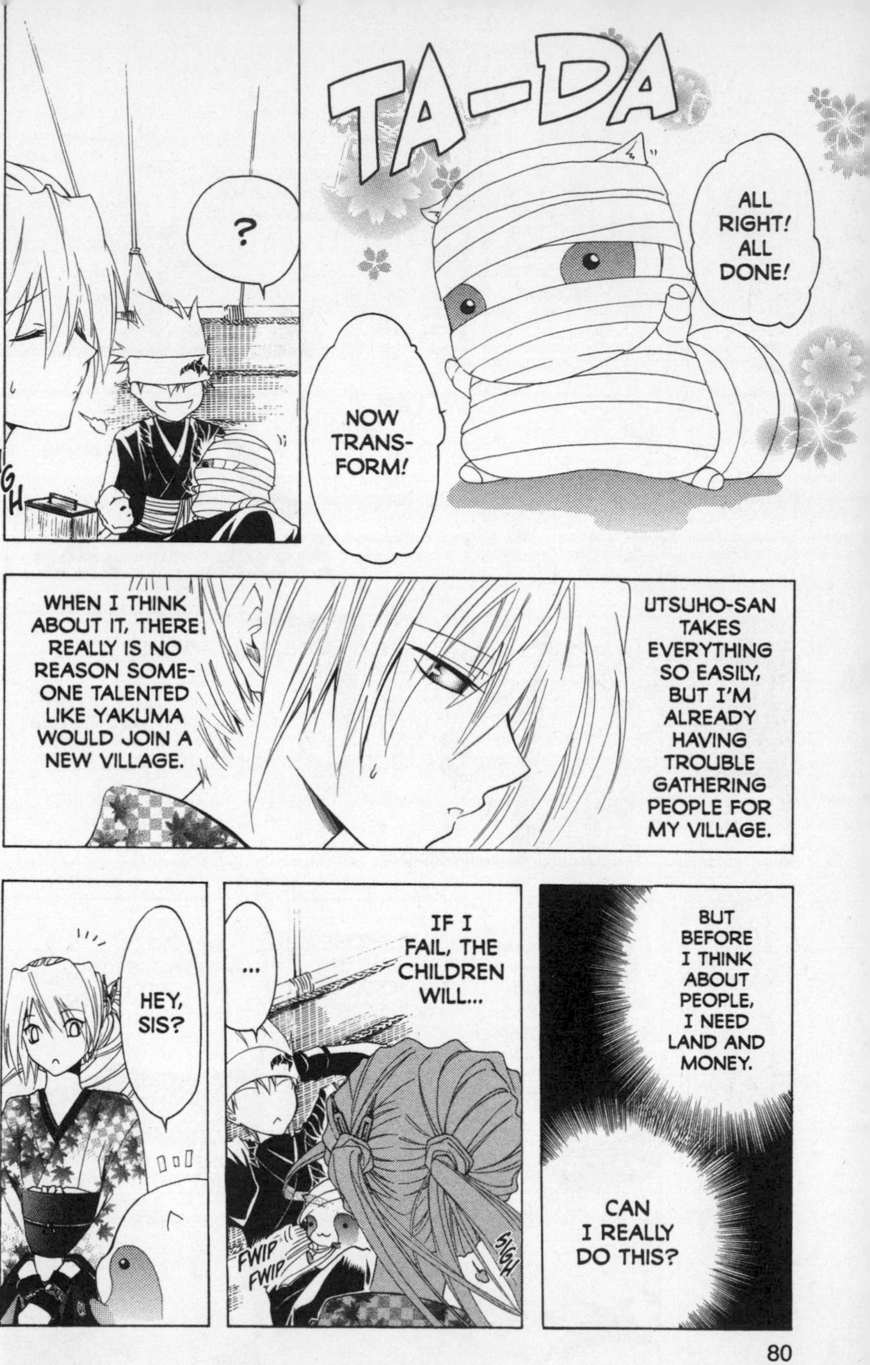
TA-DA
ALL RIGHT! ALL DONE!
NOW TRANS-FORM!
?
SIGH
UTSUHO-SAN TAKES EVERYTHING SO EASILY, BUT I'M ALREADY HAVING TROUBLE GATHERING PEOPLE FOR MY VILLAGE.
WHEN I THINK ABOUT IT, THERE REALLY IS NO REASON SOME-ONE TALENTED LIKE YAKUMA WOULD JOIN A NEW VILLAGE.
BUT BEFORE I THINK ABOUT PEOPLE, I NEED LAND AND MONEY.
CAN I REALLY DO THIS?
IF I FAIL, THE CHILDREN WILL...
...
FWIP FWIP
SIGH
HEY, SIS?

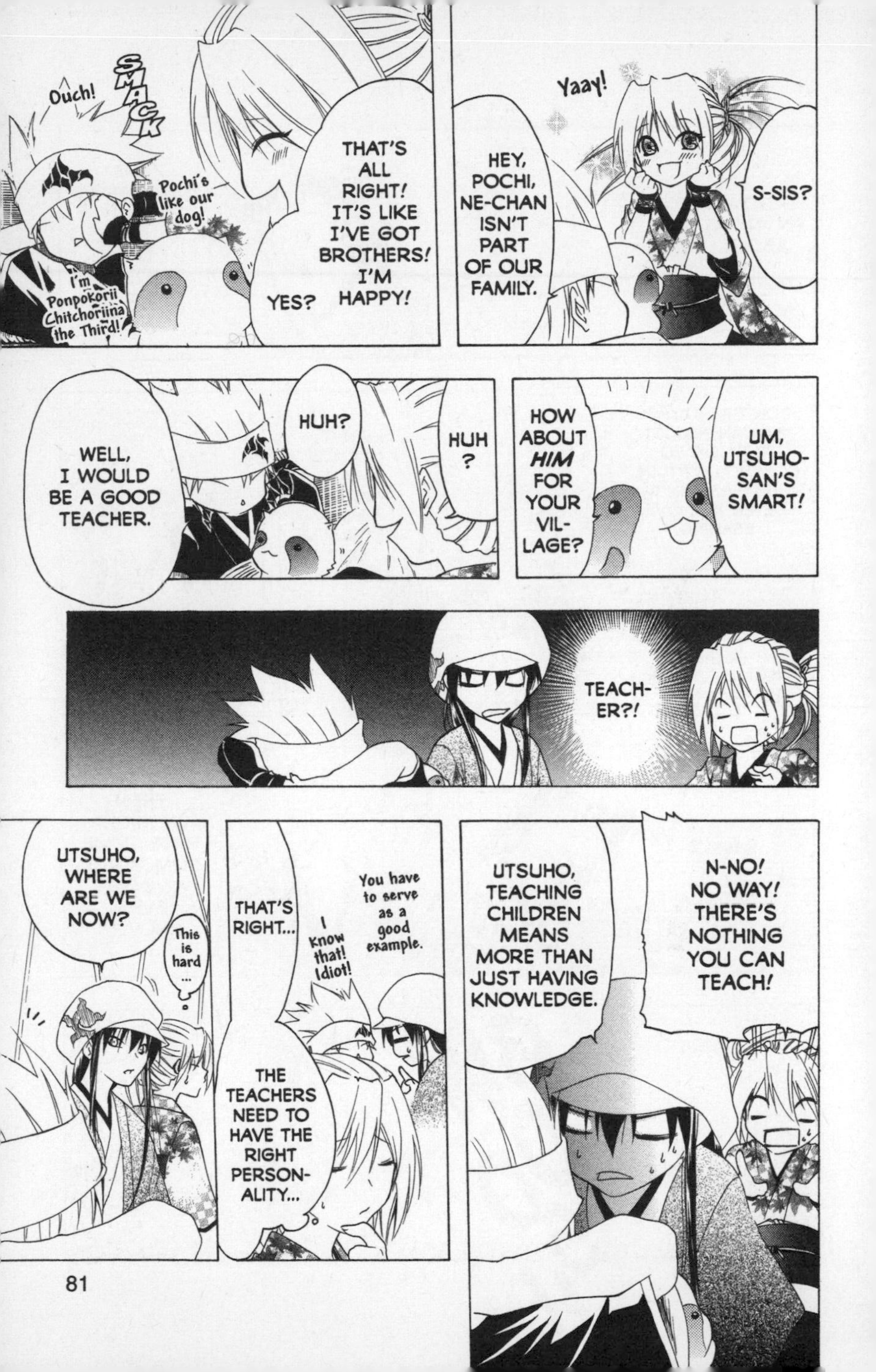
S-SIS?
Yaay!
HEY, POCHI, NE-CHAN ISN'T PART OF OUR FAMILY.
THAT'S ALL RIGHT! IT'S LIKE I'VE GOT BROTHERS! I'M HAPPY!
YES?
SMACK
Ouch!
Pochi's like our dog!
I'm Ponpokorii Chitchoriina the Third!
UM, UTSUHO-SAN'S SMART!
HOW ABOUT *HIM* FOR YOUR VIL-LAGE?
HUH?
HUH?
WELL, I WOULD BE A GOOD TEACHER.
TEACH-ER?!
N-NO! NO WAY! THERE'S NOTHING YOU CAN TEACH!
UTSUHO, TEACHING CHILDREN MEANS MORE THAN JUST HAVING KNOWLEDGE.
You have to serve as a good example.
THAT'S RIGHT...
I know that! Idiot!
THE TEACHERS NEED TO HAVE THE RIGHT PERSON-ALITY...
UTSUHO, WHERE ARE WE NOW?
This is hard...

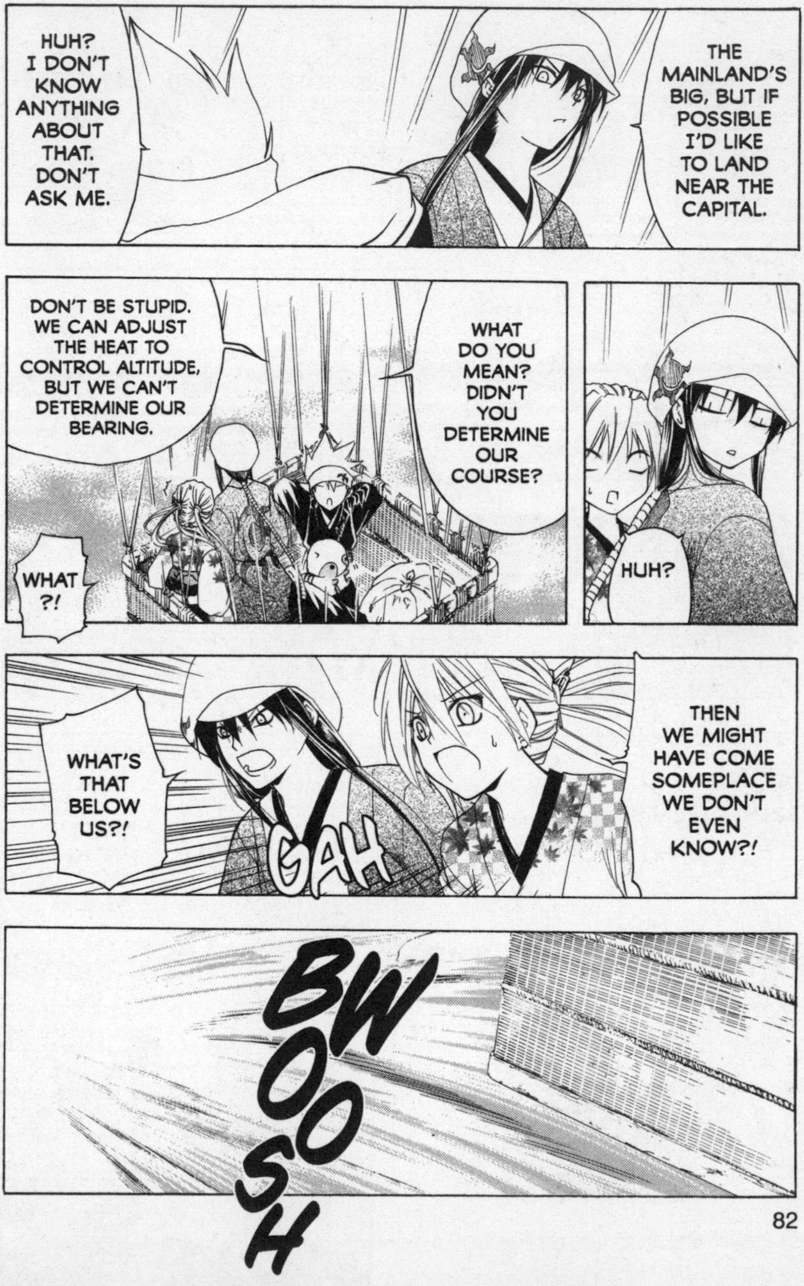
THE MAINLAND'S BIG, BUT IF POSSIBLE I'D LIKE TO LAND NEAR THE CAPITAL.
HUH? I DON'T KNOW ANYTHING ABOUT THAT. DON'T ASK ME.
HUH?
WHAT DO YOU MEAN? DIDN'T YOU DETERMINE OUR COURSE?
DON'T BE STUPID. WE CAN ADJUST THE HEAT TO CONTROL ALTITUDE, BUT WE CAN'T DETERMINE OUR BEARING.
WHAT ?!
THEN WE MIGHT HAVE COME SOMEPLACE WE DON'T EVEN KNOW?!
GAH
WHAT'S THAT BELOW US?!
BWOOSH

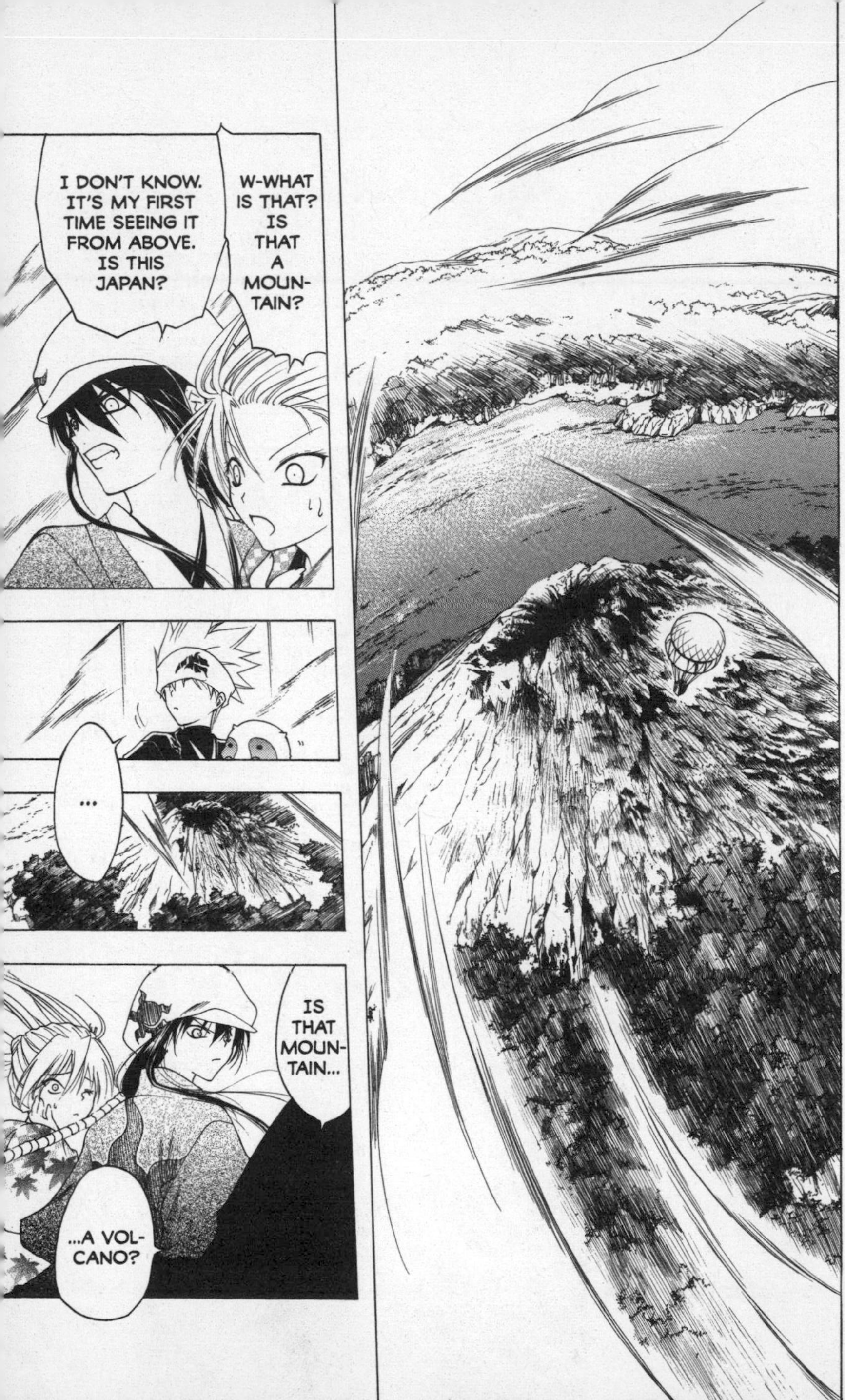
W-WHAT IS THAT? IS THAT A MOUNTAIN?
I DON'T KNOW. IT'S MY FIRST TIME SEEING IT FROM ABOVE. IS THIS JAPAN?
...
IS THAT MOUNTAIN...
...A VOLCANO?

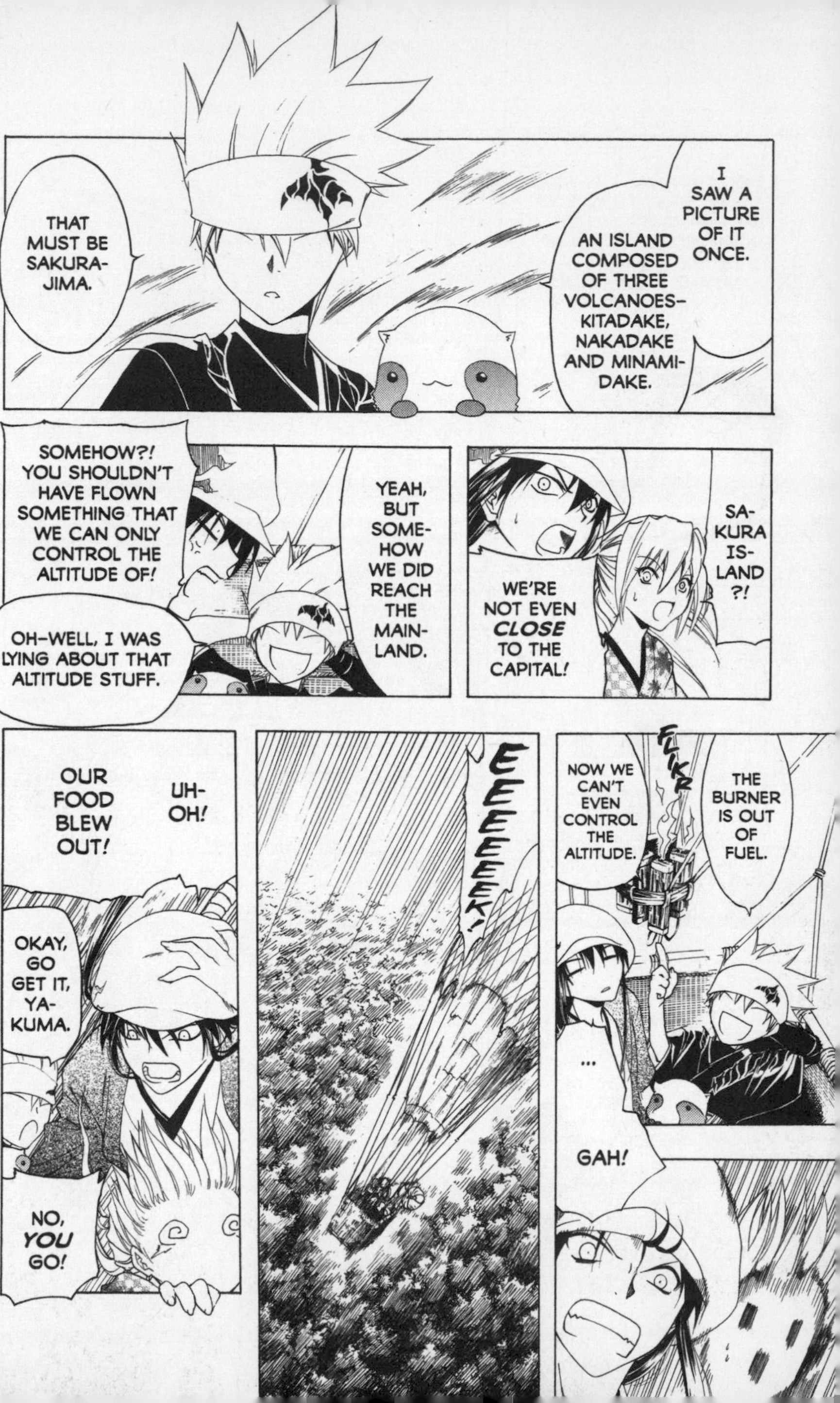
I SAW A PICTURE OF IT ONCE.
AN ISLAND COMPOSED OF THREE VOLCANOES-KITADAKE, NAKADAKE AND MINAMI-DAKE.
THAT MUST BE SAKURA-JIMA.
SA-KURA IS-LAND?!
WE'RE NOT EVEN *CLOSE* TO THE CAPITAL!
YEAH, BUT SOME-HOW WE DID REACH THE MAIN-LAND.
SOMEHOW?! YOU SHOULDN'T HAVE FLOWN SOMETHING THAT WE CAN ONLY CONTROL THE ALTITUDE OF!
OH-WELL, I WAS LYING ABOUT THAT ALTITUDE STUFF.
THE BURNER IS OUT OF FUEL.
FLIKR
NOW WE CAN'T EVEN CONTROL THE ALTITUDE.
...
GAH!
EEEEEEEK!
UH-OH!
OUR FOOD BLEW OUT!
OKAY, GO GET IT, YA-KUMA.
NO, *YOU* GO!

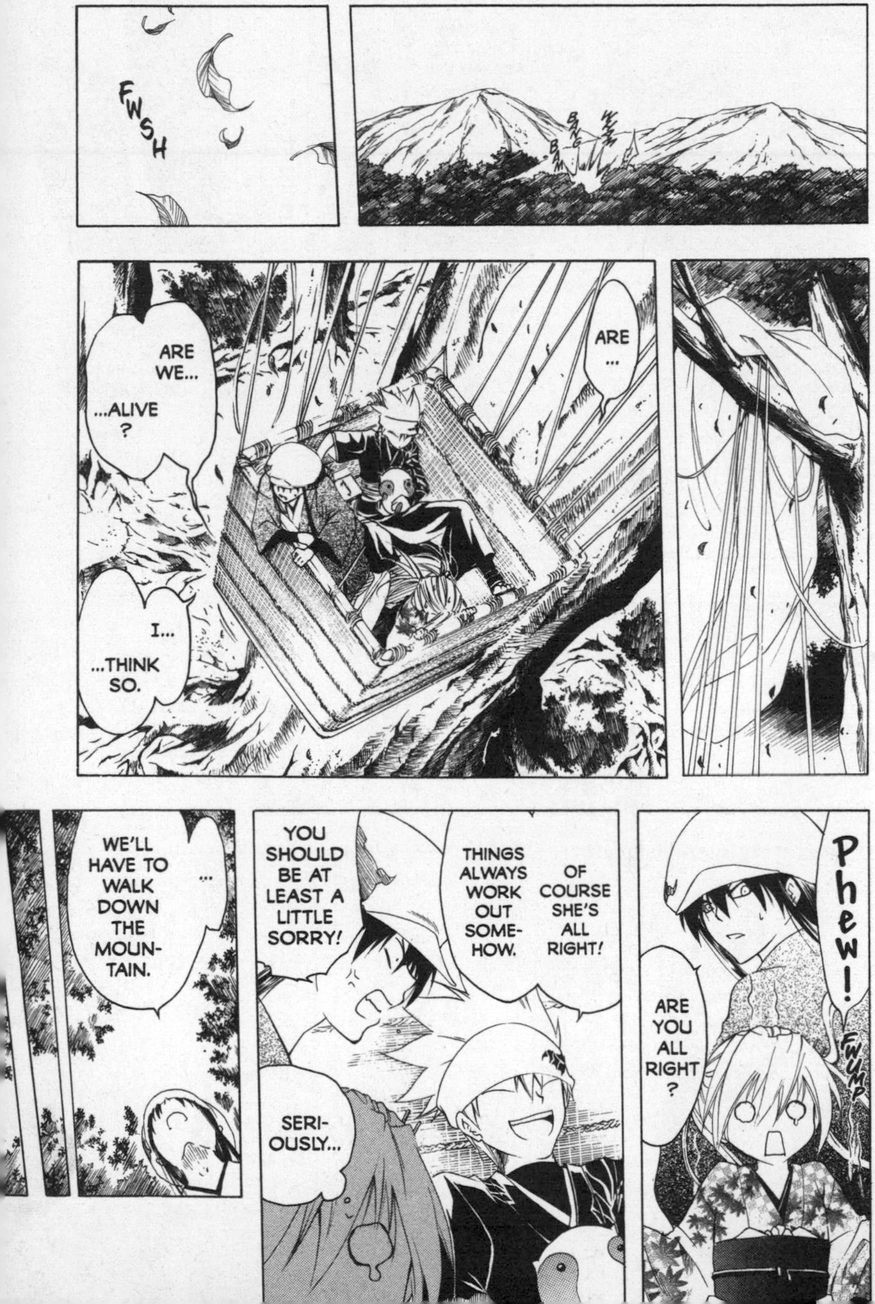
BANG
BAM
FWSH
ARE ...
ARE WE... ...ALIVE ?
I... ...THINK SO.
Phew!
FWUMP
ARE YOU ALL RIGHT ?
OF COURSE SHE'S ALL RIGHT!
THINGS ALWAYS WORK OUT SOME-HOW.
YOU SHOULD BE AT LEAST A LITTLE SORRY!
SERI-OUSLY...
...
WE'LL HAVE TO WALK DOWN THE MOUN-TAIN.

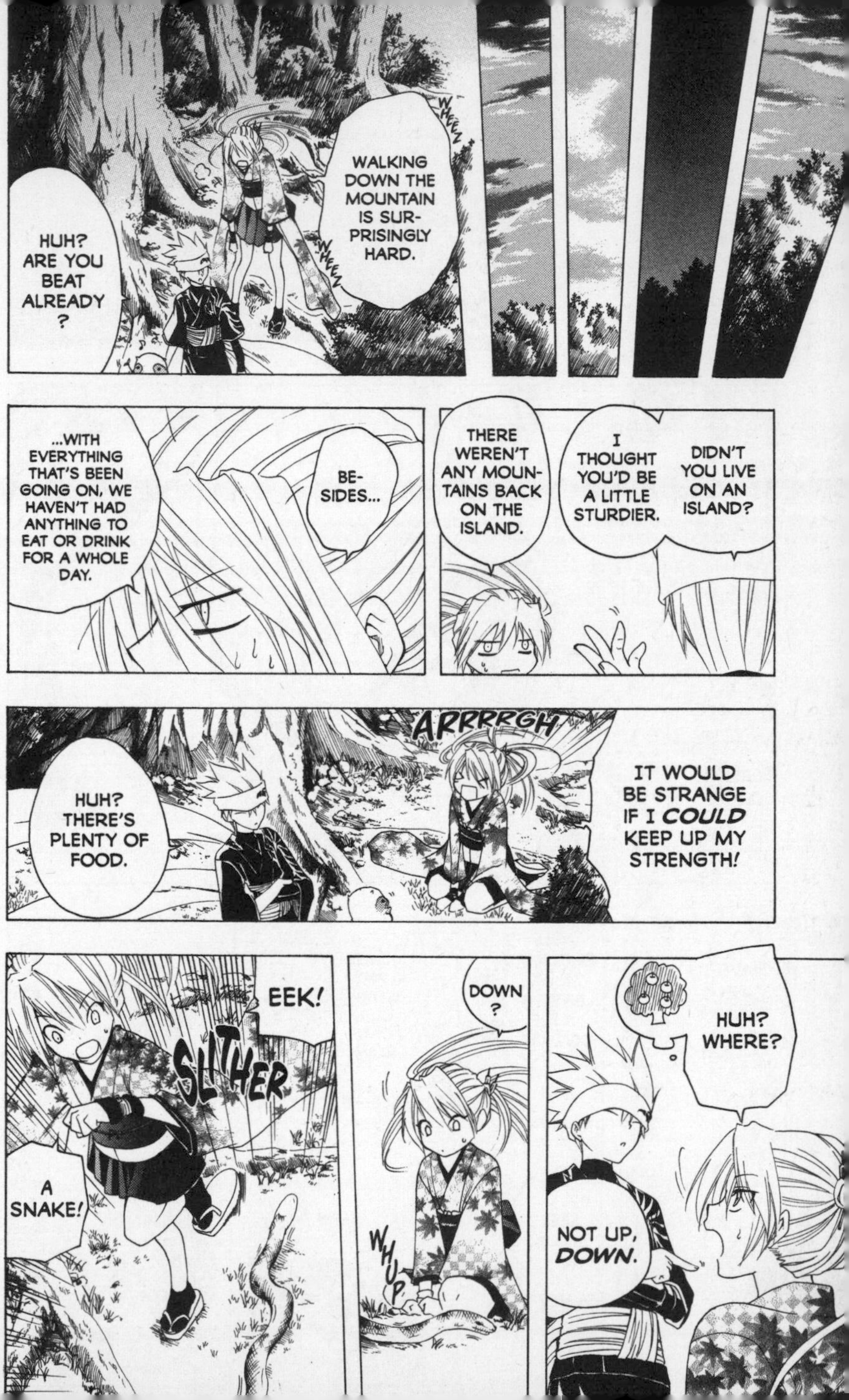
WHEEZ
WALKING DOWN THE MOUNTAIN IS SUR-PRISINGLY HARD.
WHEEZ
HUH? ARE YOU BEAT ALREADY?
DIDN'T YOU LIVE ON AN ISLAND?
I THOUGHT YOU'D BE A LITTLE STURDIER.
THERE WEREN'T ANY MOUN-TAINS BACK ON THE ISLAND.
BE-SIDES...
...WITH EVERYTHING THAT'S BEEN GOING ON, WE HAVEN'T HAD ANYTHING TO EAT OR DRINK FOR A WHOLE DAY.
IT WOULD BE STRANGE IF I *COULD* KEEP UP MY STRENGTH!
ARRRRGH
HUH? THERE'S PLENTY OF FOOD.
HUH? WHERE?
NOT UP, *DOWN*.
DOWN?
WHUP
EEK!
SLITHER
A SNAKE!

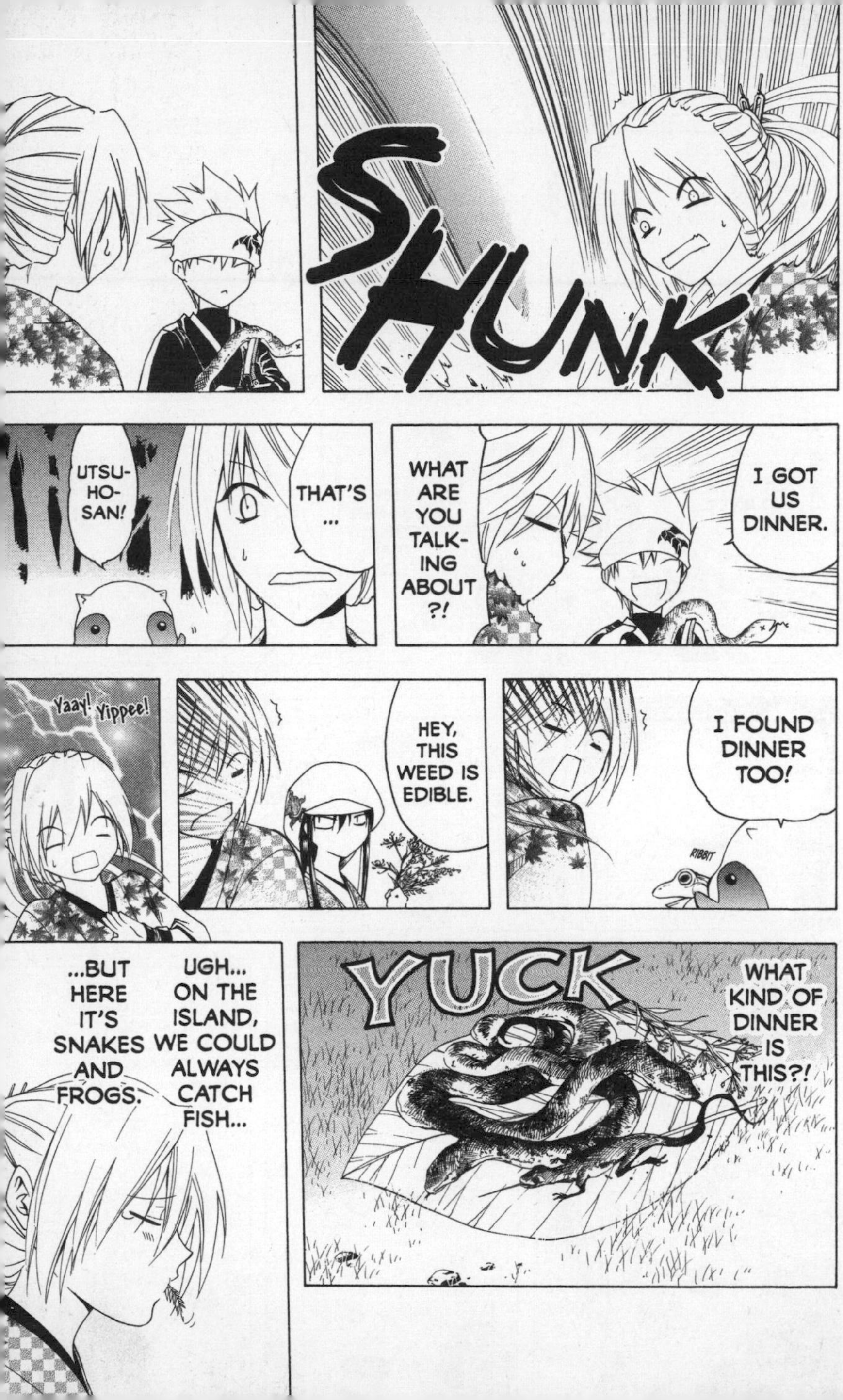
SHUNK
I GOT US DINNER.
WHAT ARE YOU TALKING ABOUT?!
THAT'S ...
UTSU-HO-SAN!
I FOUND DINNER TOO!
RIBBIT
HEY, THIS WEED IS EDIBLE.
Yaay! Yippee!
YUCK
WHAT KIND OF DINNER IS THIS?!
UGH... ON THE ISLAND, WE COULD ALWAYS CATCH FISH...
...BUT HERE IT'S SNAKES AND FROGS.

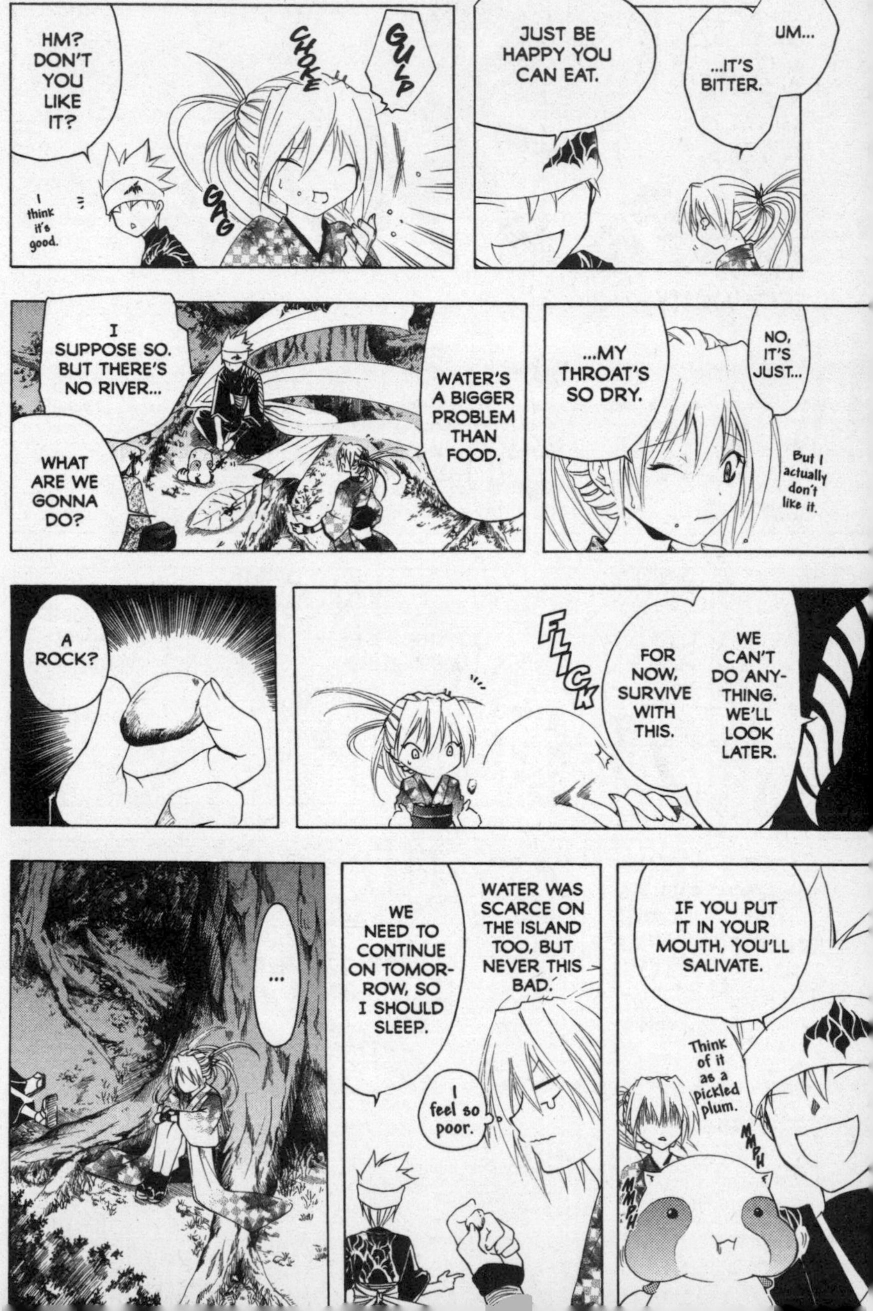
UM...
...IT'S BITTER.
JUST BE HAPPY YOU CAN EAT.
GULP
CHOKE
GAG
HM? DON'T YOU LIKE IT?
I think it's good.
NO, IT'S JUST...
...MY THROAT'S SO DRY.
But I actually don't like it.
WATER'S A BIGGER PROBLEM THAN FOOD.
I SUPPOSE SO. BUT THERE'S NO RIVER...
WHAT ARE WE GONNA DO?
WE CAN'T DO ANY-THING. WE'LL LOOK LATER.
FOR NOW, SURVIVE WITH THIS.
FLICK
A ROCK?
IF YOU PUT IT IN YOUR MOUTH, YOU'LL SALIVATE.
Think of it as a pickled plum.
MMPH
MMPH
WATER WAS SCARCE ON THE ISLAND TOO, BUT NEVER THIS BAD.
WE NEED TO CONTINUE ON TOMOR-ROW, SO I SHOULD SLEEP.
I feel so poor.
...

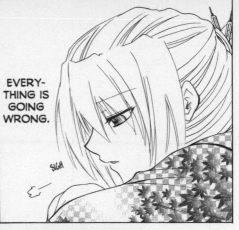

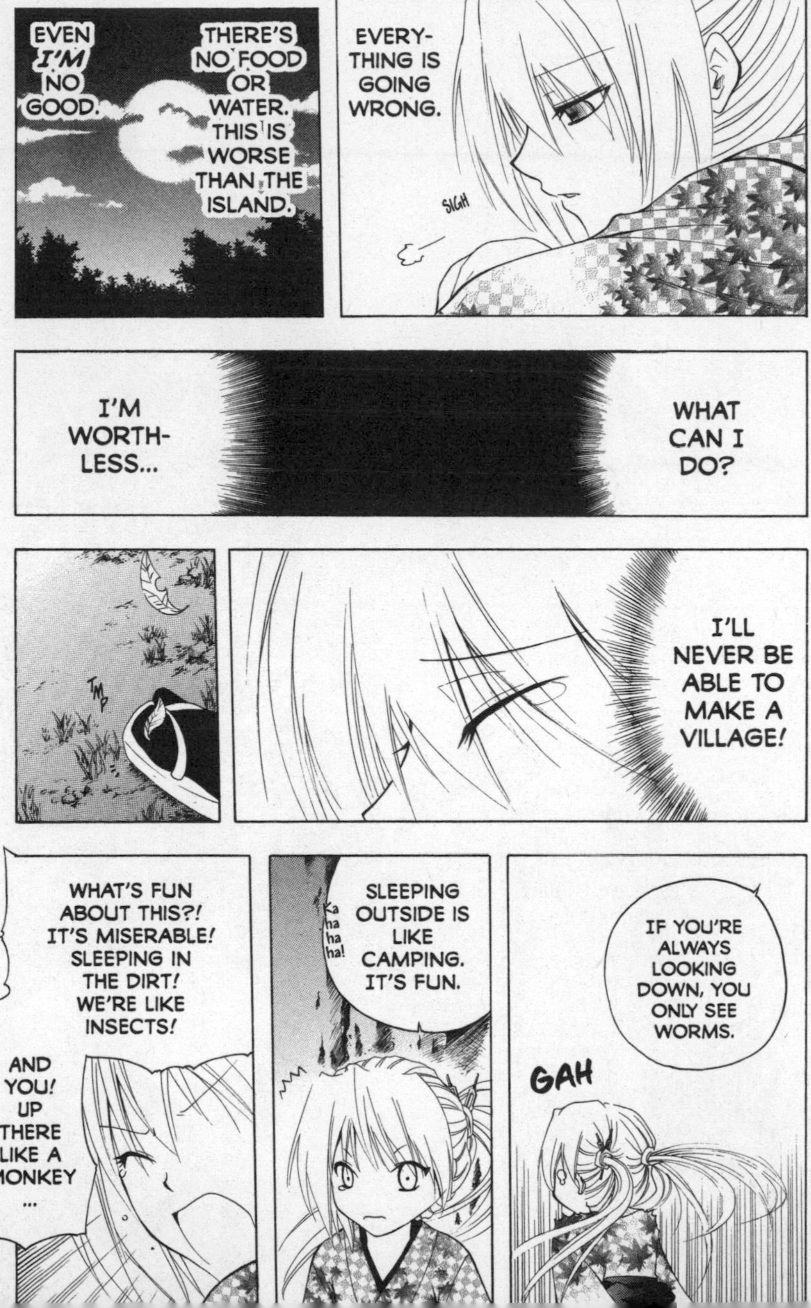
EVERY-THING IS GOING WRONG.
SIGH
THERE'S NO FOOD OR WATER. THIS IS WORSE THAN THE ISLAND.
EVEN I'M NO GOOD.
WHAT CAN I DO?
I'M WORTH-LESS...
I'LL NEVER BE ABLE TO MAKE A VILLAGE!
TMP
IF YOU'RE ALWAYS LOOKING DOWN, YOU ONLY SEE WORMS.
GAH
SLEEPING OUTSIDE IS LIKE CAMPING. IT'S FUN.
Ka ha ha ha!
WHAT'S FUN ABOUT THIS?! IT'S MISERABLE! SLEEPING IN THE DIRT! WE'RE LIKE INSECTS!
AND YOU! UP THERE LIKE A MONKEY ...

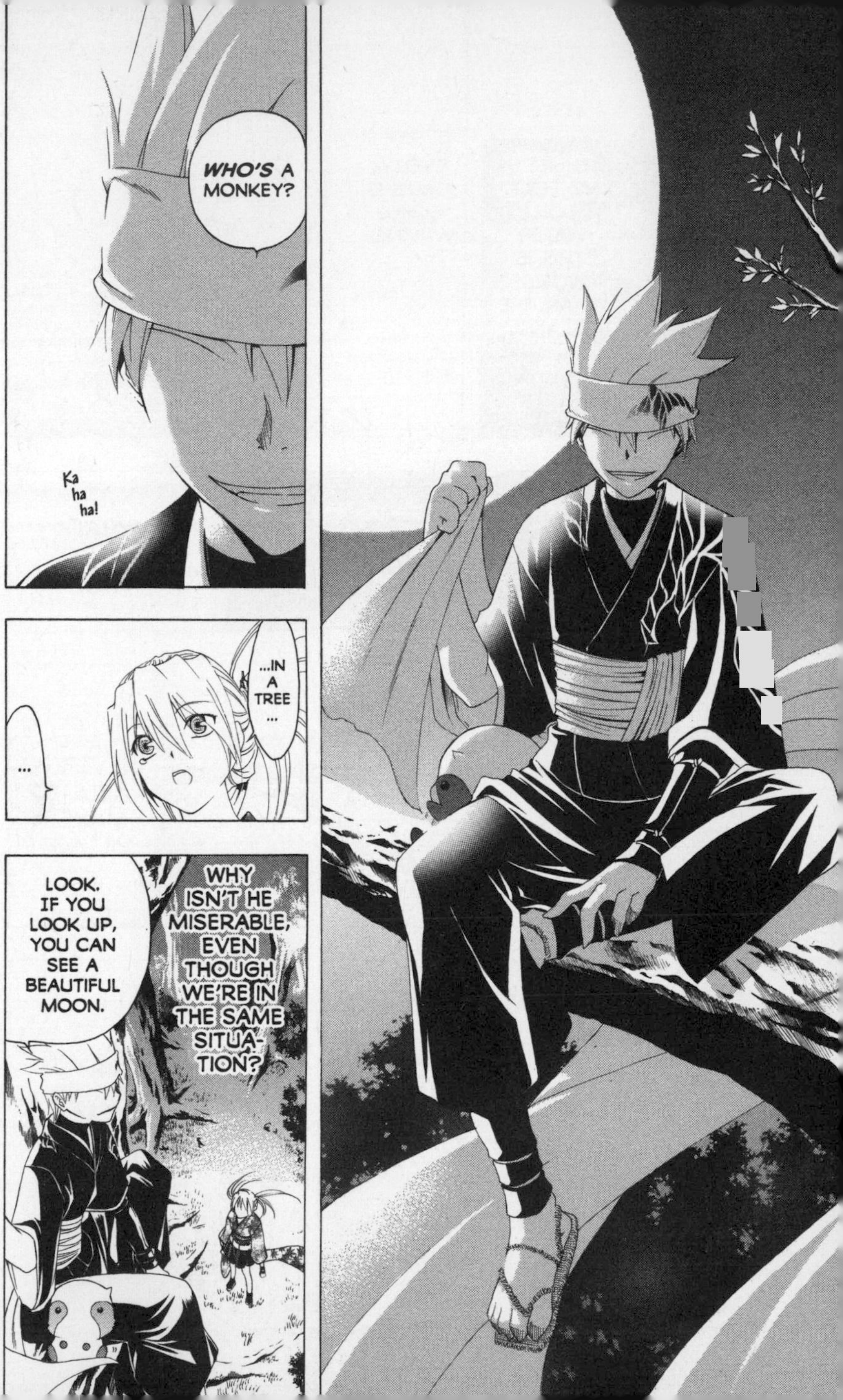

WHO'S A MONKEY?
Ka ha ha!
...IN A TREE ...
...
WHY ISN'T HE MISERABLE, EVEN THOUGH WE'RE IN THE SAME SITUATION?
LOOK. IF YOU LOOK UP, YOU CAN SEE A BEAUTIFUL MOON.

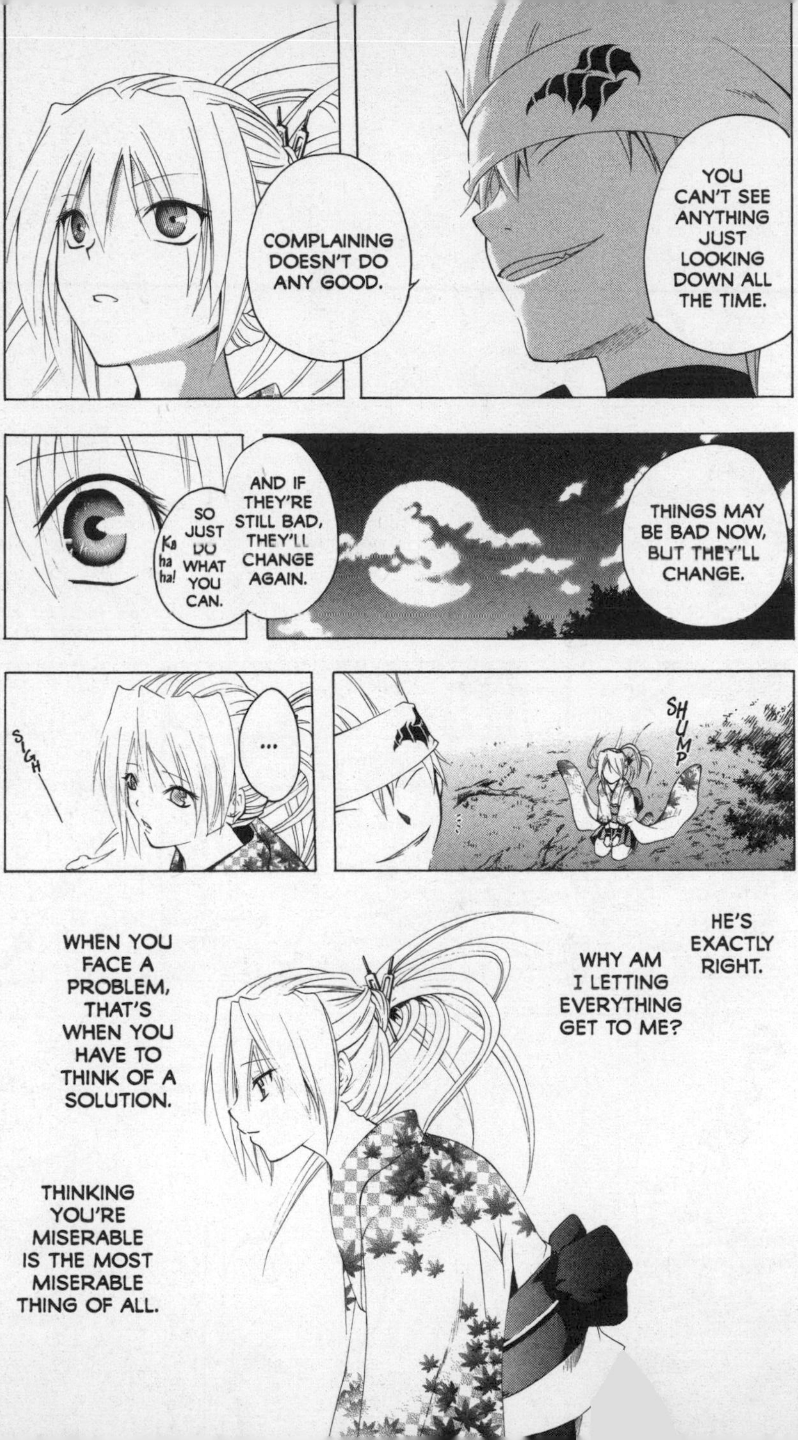
YOU CAN'T SEE ANYTHING JUST LOOKING DOWN ALL THE TIME.
COMPLAINING DOESN'T DO ANY GOOD.
THINGS MAY BE BAD NOW, BUT THEY'LL CHANGE.
AND IF THEY'RE STILL BAD, THEY'LL CHANGE AGAIN.
SO JUST DO WHAT YOU CAN.
Ka ha ha!
SHUMP
...
...
SIGH
HE'S EXACTLY RIGHT.
WHY AM I LETTING EVERYTHING GET TO ME?
WHEN YOU FACE A PROBLEM, THAT'S WHEN YOU HAVE TO THINK OF A SOLUTION.
THINKING YOU'RE MISERABLE IS THE MOST MISERABLE THING OF ALL.

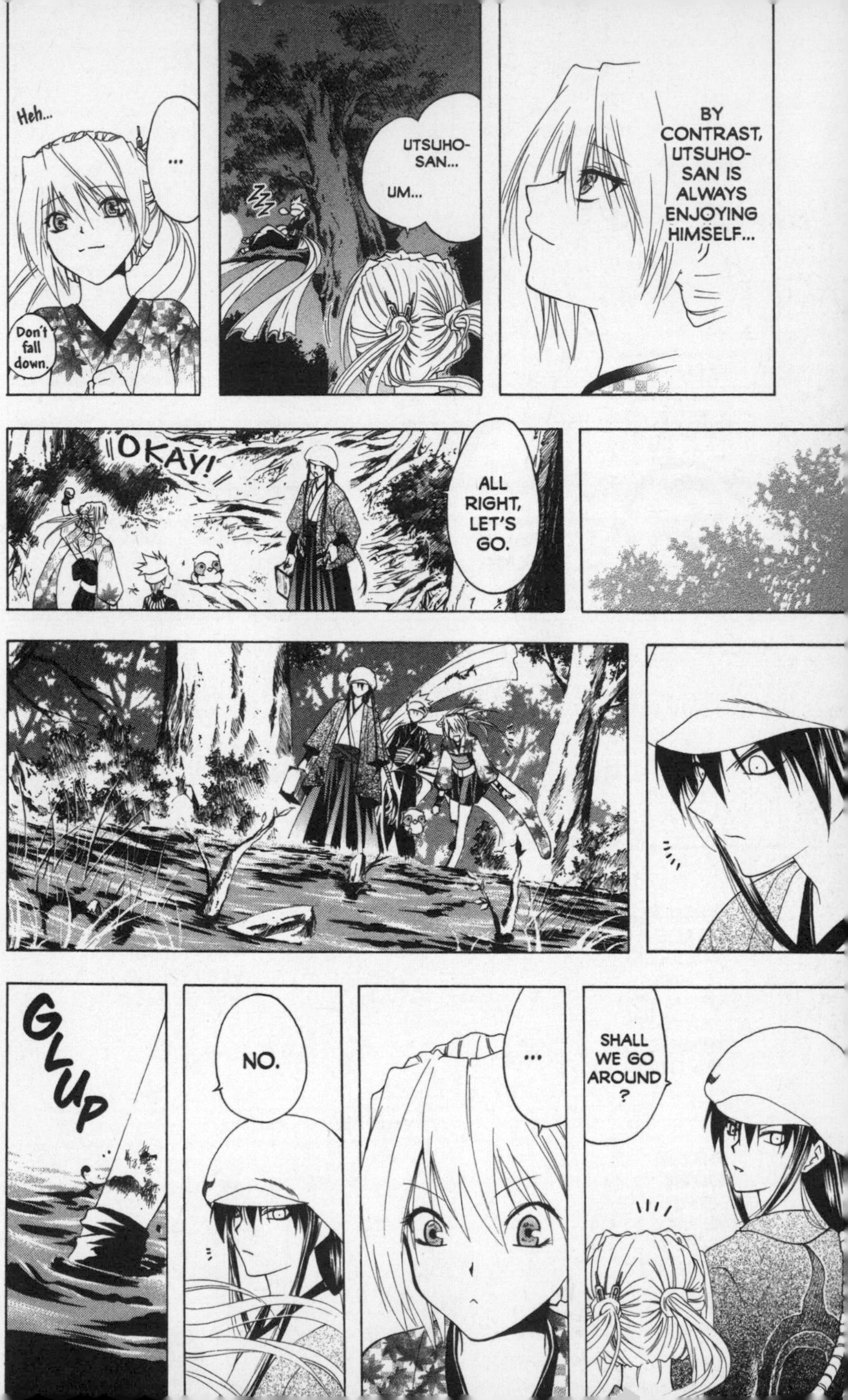
BY CONTRAST, UTSUHO-SAN IS ALWAYS ENJOYING HIMSELF...
UTSUHO-SAN...
UM...
...
Heh...
Don't fall down.
ALL RIGHT, LET'S GO.
OKAY!
SHALL WE GO AROUND?
...
NO.
GLUP

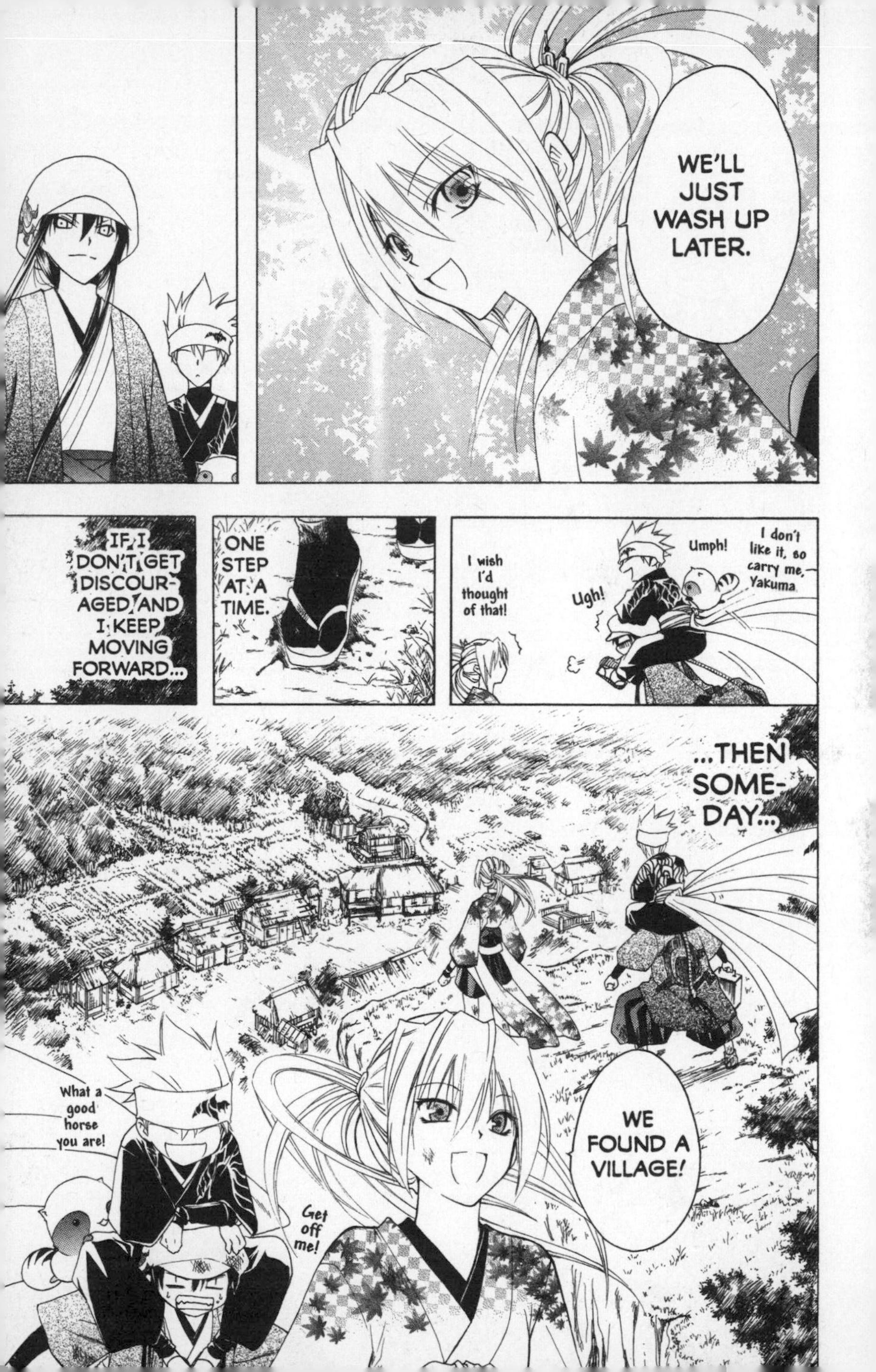
WE'LL JUST WASH UP LATER.
I don't like it, so carry me, Yakuma
Umph!
Ugh!
I wish I'd thought of that!
ONE STEP AT A TIME.
IF I DON'T GET DISCOURAGED AND I KEEP MOVING FORWARD...
...THEN SOME-DAY...
WE FOUND A VILLAGE!
Get off me!
What a good horse you are!

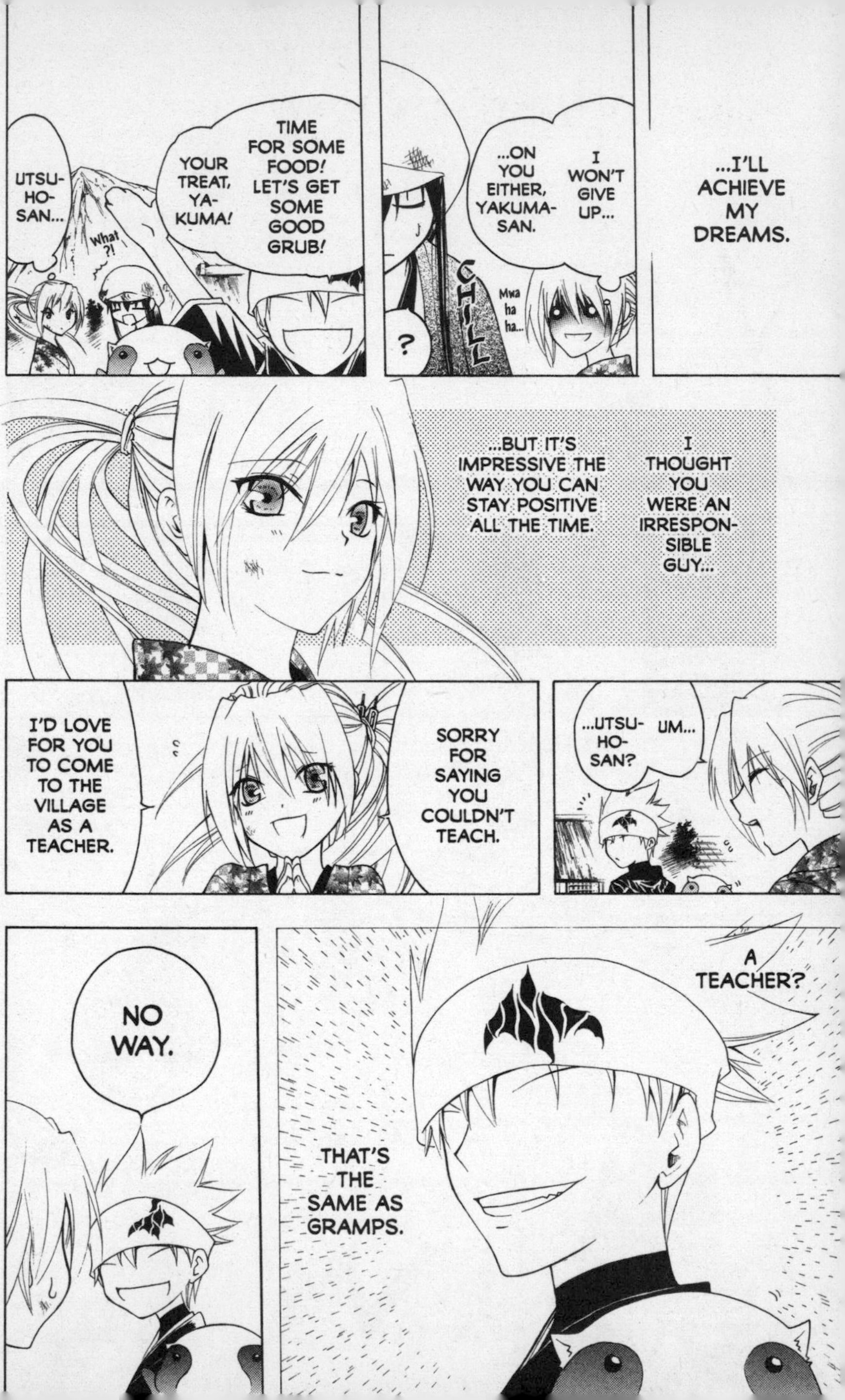
...I'LL ACHIEVE MY DREAMS.
I WON'T GIVE UP...
...ON YOU EITHER, YAKUMA-SAN.
CHILL
Mwa ha ha...
?
TIME FOR SOME FOOD! LET'S GET SOME GOOD GRUB!
YOUR TREAT, YA-KUMA!
What ?!
UTSU-HO-SAN...
I THOUGHT YOU WERE AN IRRESPON-SIBLE GUY...
...BUT IT'S IMPRESSIVE THE WAY YOU CAN STAY POSITIVE ALL THE TIME.
UM...
...UTSU-HO-SAN?
SORRY FOR SAYING YOU COULDN'T TEACH.
I'D LOVE FOR YOU TO COME TO THE VILLAGE AS A TEACHER.
A TEACHER?
THAT'S THE SAME AS GRAMPS.
NO WAY.

Chapter 23 Utsuho's Idea

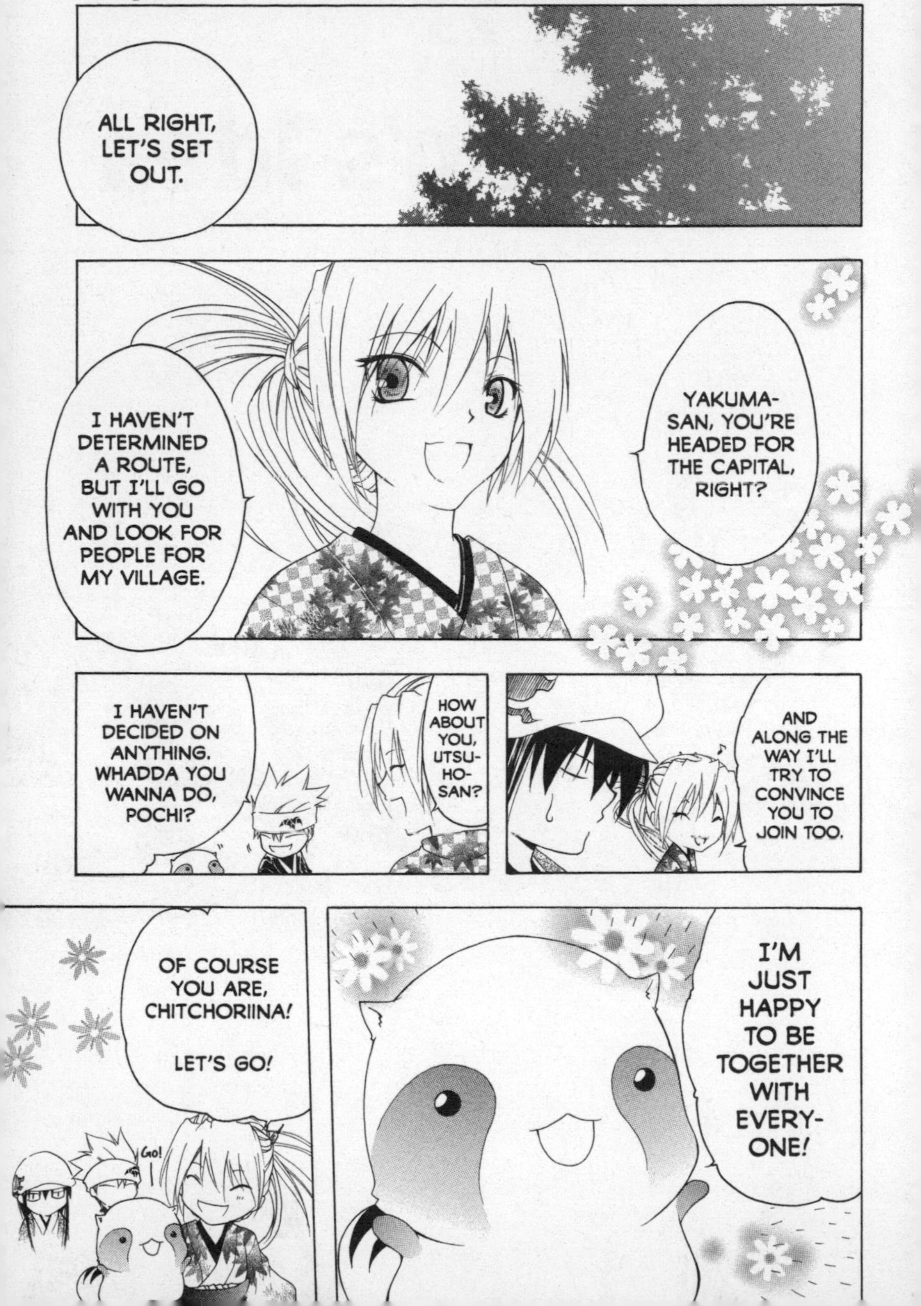
ALL RIGHT, LET'S SET OUT.
YAKUMA-SAN, YOU'RE HEADED FOR THE CAPITAL, RIGHT?
I HAVEN'T DETERMINED A ROUTE, BUT I'LL GO WITH YOU AND LOOK FOR PEOPLE FOR MY VILLAGE.
AND ALONG THE WAY I'LL TRY TO CONVINCE YOU TO JOIN TOO.
HOW ABOUT YOU, UTSUHO-SAN?
I HAVEN'T DECIDED ON ANYTHING. WHADDA YOU WANNA DO, POCHI?
I'M JUST HAPPY TO BE TOGETHER WITH EVERYONE!
OF COURSE YOU ARE, CHITCHORIINA!
LET'S GO!
GO!

Chapter 23
Utsuho's Idea

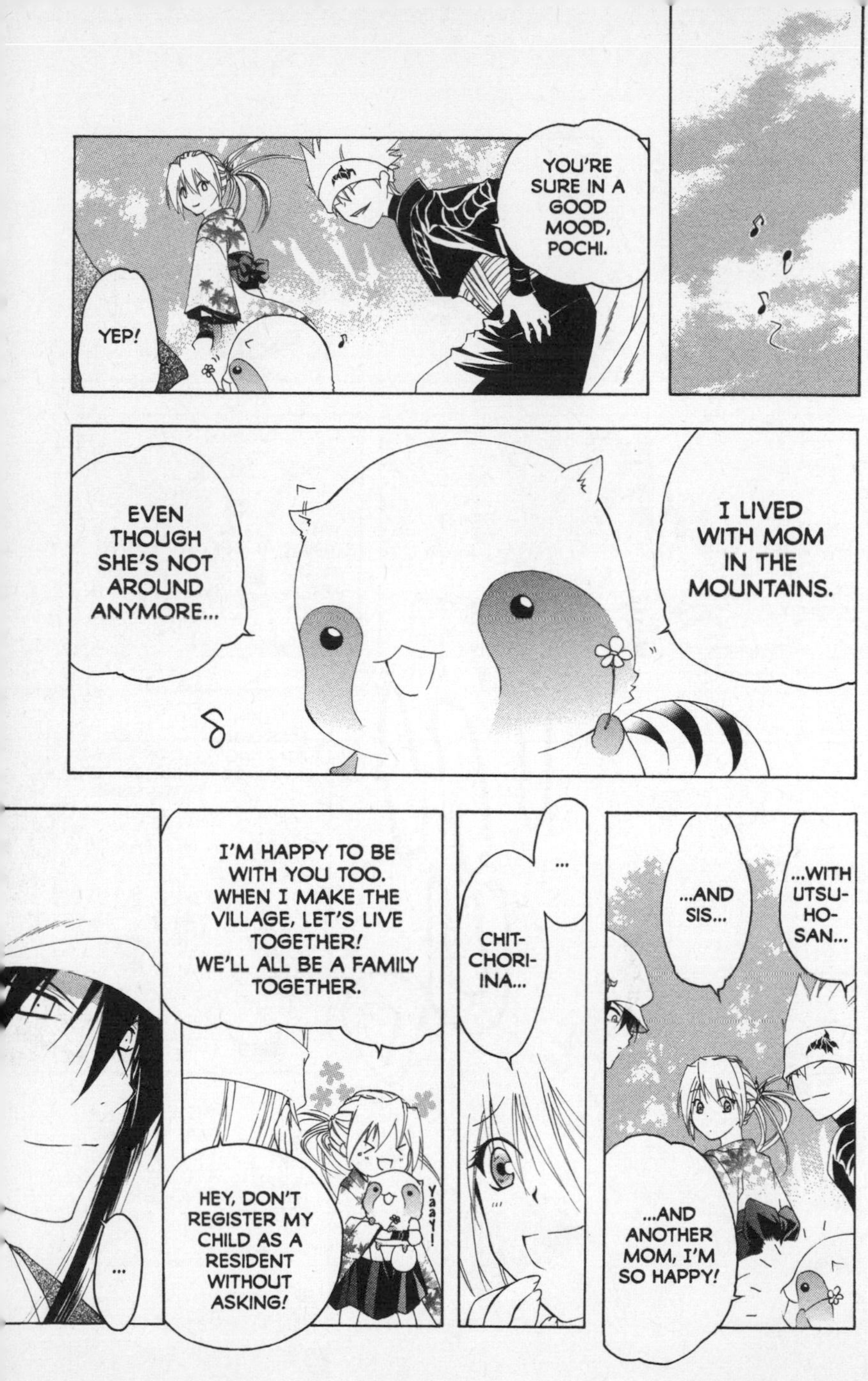
YOU'RE SURE IN A GOOD MOOD, POCHI.
YEP!
I LIVED WITH MOM IN THE MOUNTAINS.
EVEN THOUGH SHE'S NOT AROUND ANYMORE...
...WITH UTSU-HO-SAN...
...AND SIS...
...AND ANOTHER MOM, I'M SO HAPPY!
...
CHIT-CHORI-INA...
I'M HAPPY TO BE WITH YOU TOO. WHEN I MAKE THE VILLAGE, LET'S LIVE TOGETHER! WE'LL ALL BE A FAMILY TOGETHER.
YAAY!
HEY, DON'T REGISTER MY CHILD AS A RESIDENT WITHOUT ASKING!
...

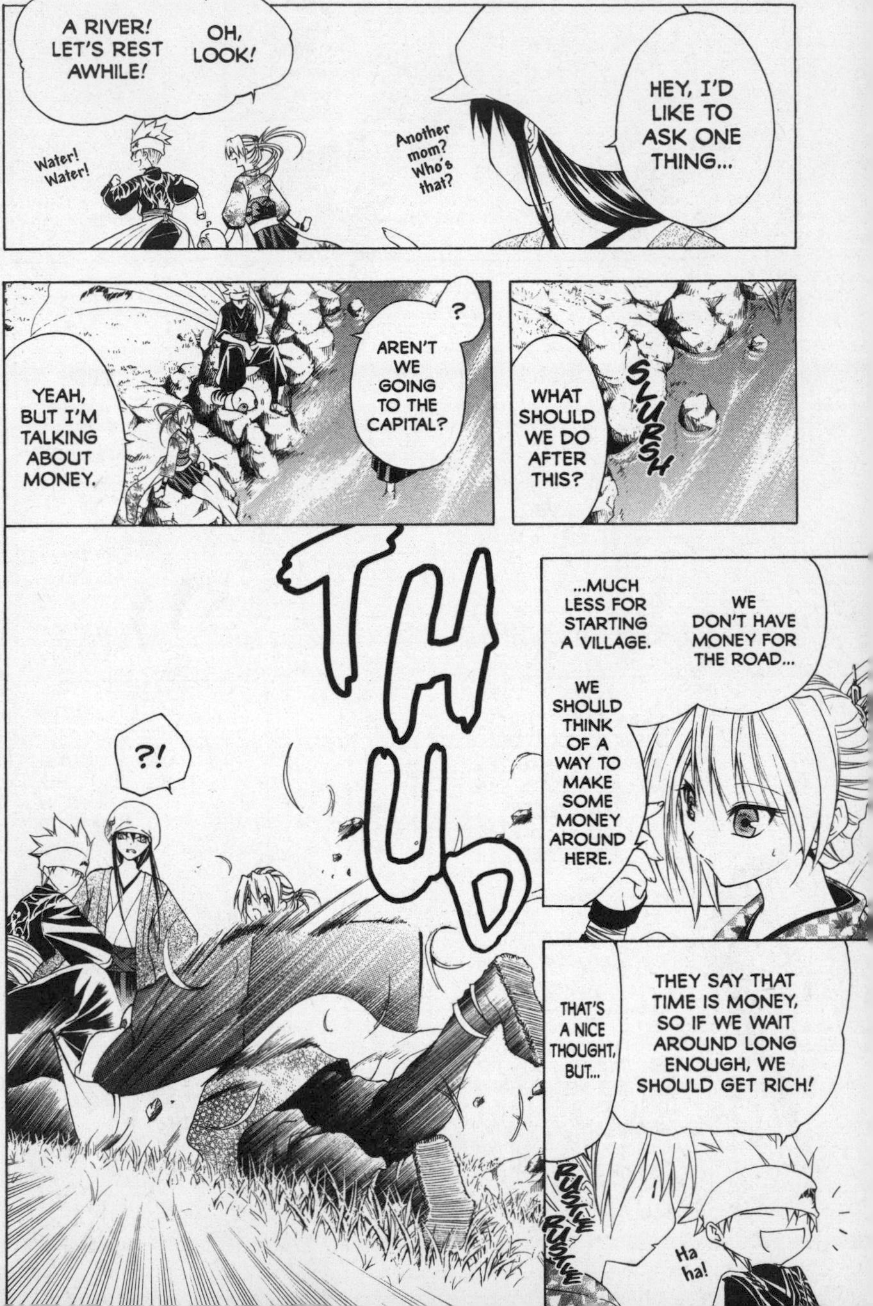
HEY, I'D LIKE TO ASK ONE THING...
Another mom? Who's that?
OH, LOOK!
A RIVER! LET'S REST AWHILE!
Water! Water!
WHAT SHOULD WE DO AFTER THIS?
SLURSH
?
AREN'T WE GOING TO THE CAPITAL?
YEAH, BUT I'M TALKING ABOUT MONEY.
WE DON'T HAVE MONEY FOR THE ROAD...
...MUCH LESS FOR STARTING A VILLAGE.
WE SHOULD THINK OF A WAY TO MAKE SOME MONEY AROUND HERE.
THEY SAY THAT TIME IS MONEY, SO IF WE WAIT AROUND LONG ENOUGH, WE SHOULD GET RICH!
Ha ha!
THAT'S A NICE THOUGHT, BUT...
RUSTLE RUSTLE
THUD
?!

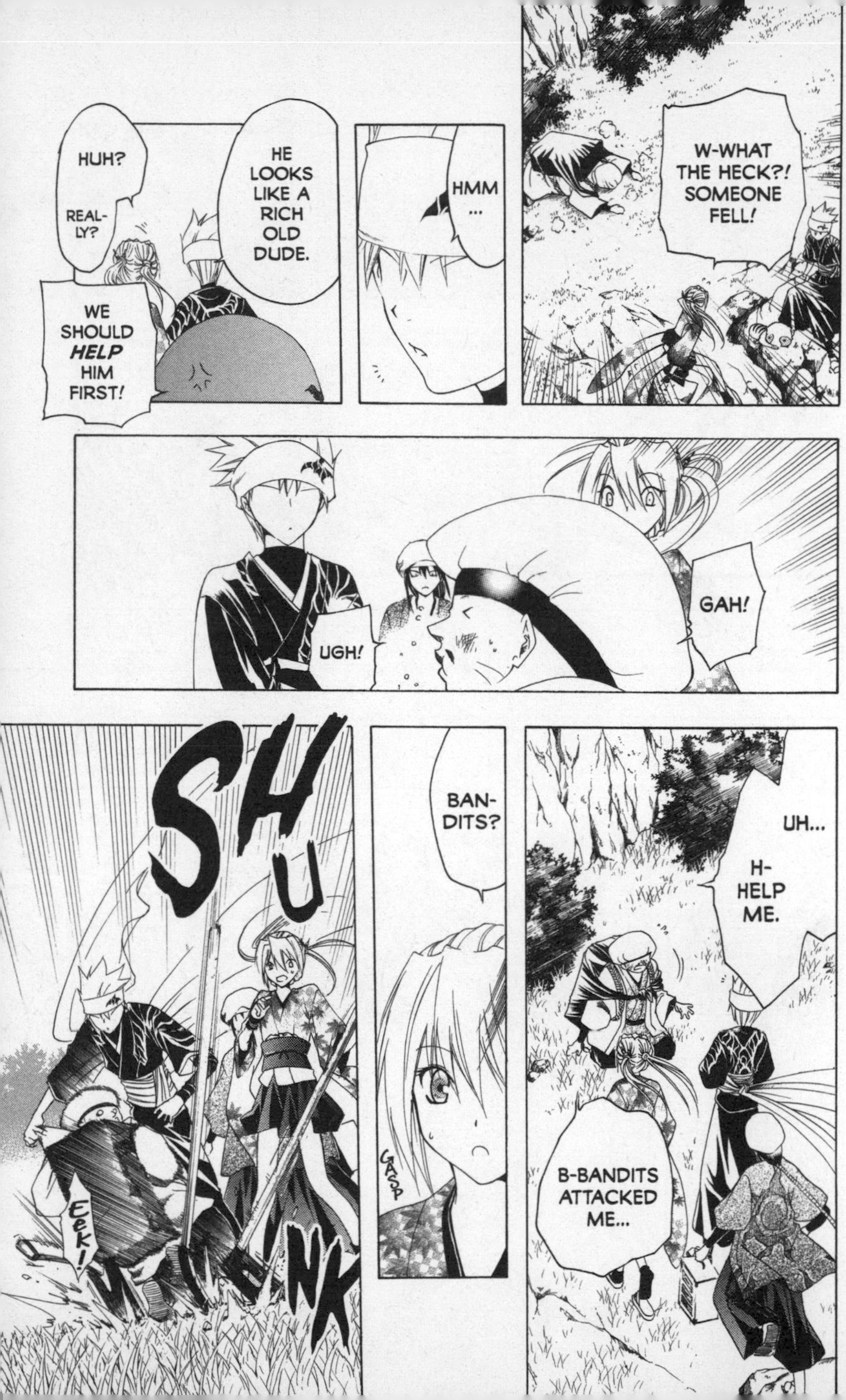
W-WHAT THE HECK?! SOMEONE FELL!
HMM ...
HE LOOKS LIKE A RICH OLD DUDE.
HUH?
REAL-LY?
WE SHOULD **HELP** HIM FIRST!
GAH!
UGH!
UH...
H-HELP ME.
B-BANDITS ATTACKED ME...
BAN-DITS?
GASP
SHUNK
Eek!

FWOOSH

YIKES!

GET DOWN!

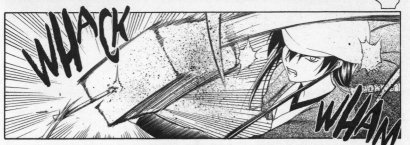

WHACK

WHAM

GRB

YIP!

SHUNK

CHOMP

THOK

OVER THERE!

WHOO

SH

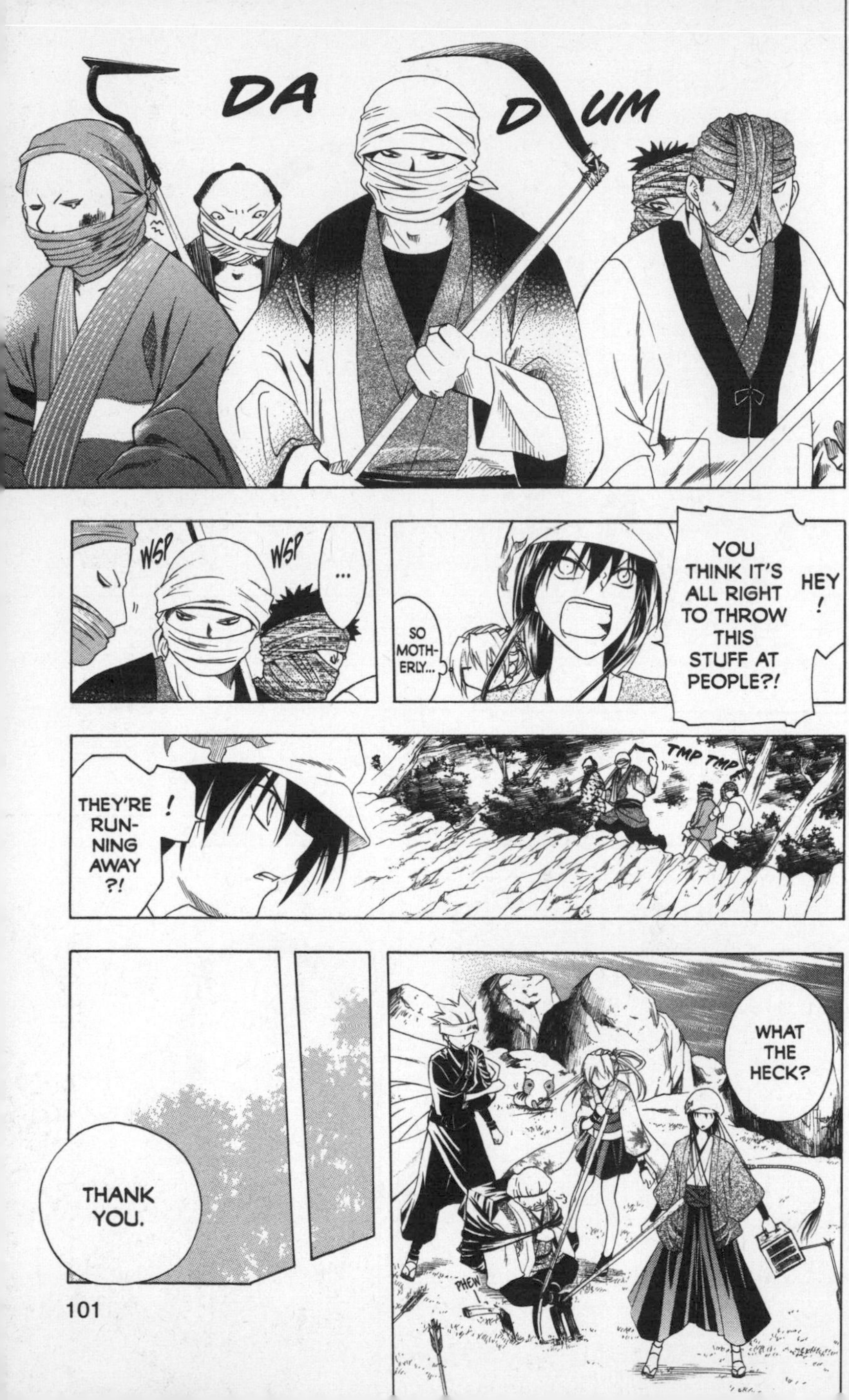
DA DUM
HEY!
YOU THINK IT'S ALL RIGHT TO THROW THIS STUFF AT PEOPLE?!
SO MOTHERLY...
WSP WSP
...
TMP TMP
THEY'RE RUNNING AWAY?!
WHAT THE HECK?
PHEW
THANK YOU.

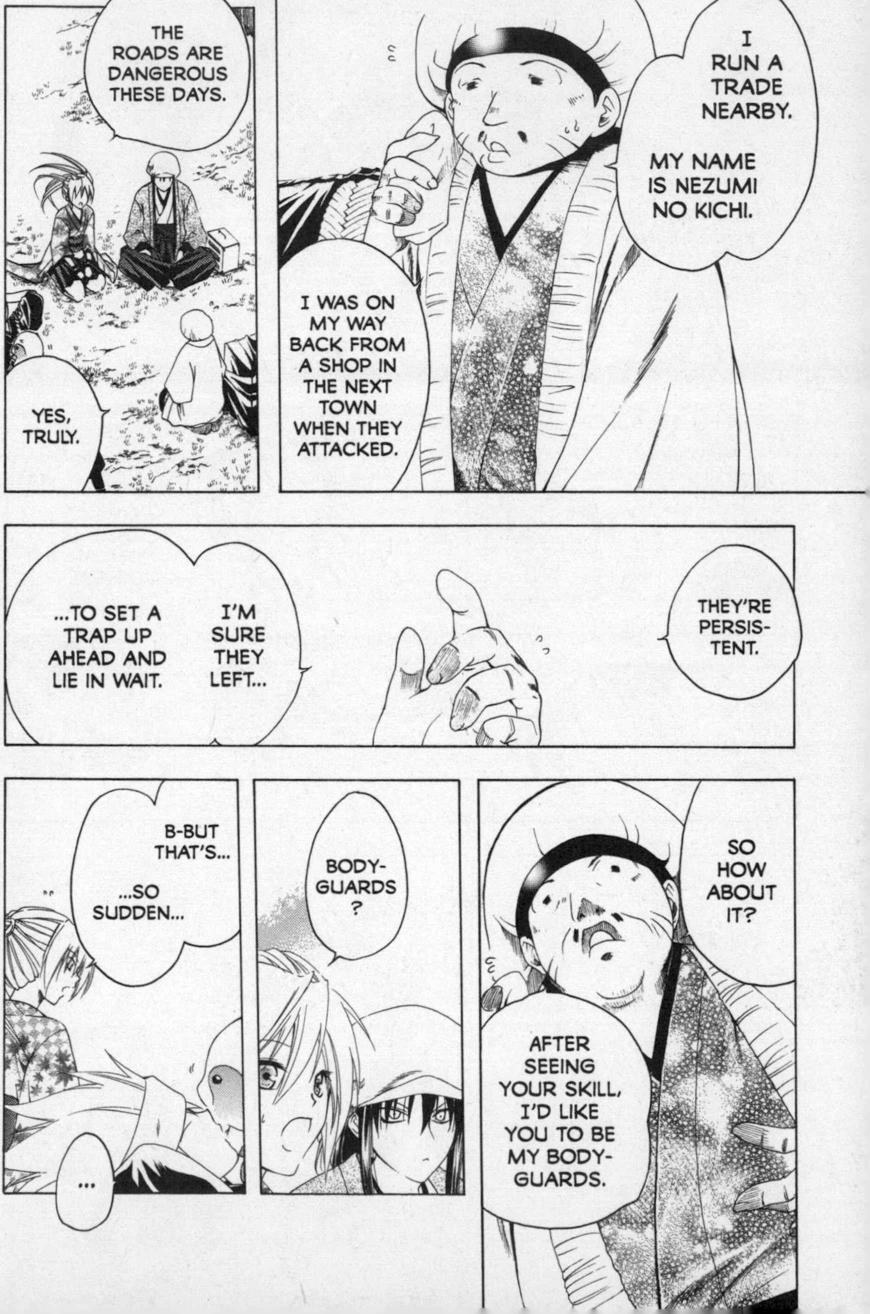
I RUN A TRADE NEARBY.
MY NAME IS NEZUMI NO KICHI.
I WAS ON MY WAY BACK FROM A SHOP IN THE NEXT TOWN WHEN THEY ATTACKED.
THE ROADS ARE DANGEROUS THESE DAYS.
YES, TRULY.
THEY'RE PERSIST-TENT.
I'M SURE THEY LEFT...
...TO SET A TRAP UP AHEAD AND LIE IN WAIT.
SO HOW ABOUT IT?
AFTER SEEING YOUR SKILL, I'D LIKE YOU TO BE MY BODY-GUARDS.
BODY-GUARDS?
B-BUT THAT'S...
...SO SUDDEN...
...

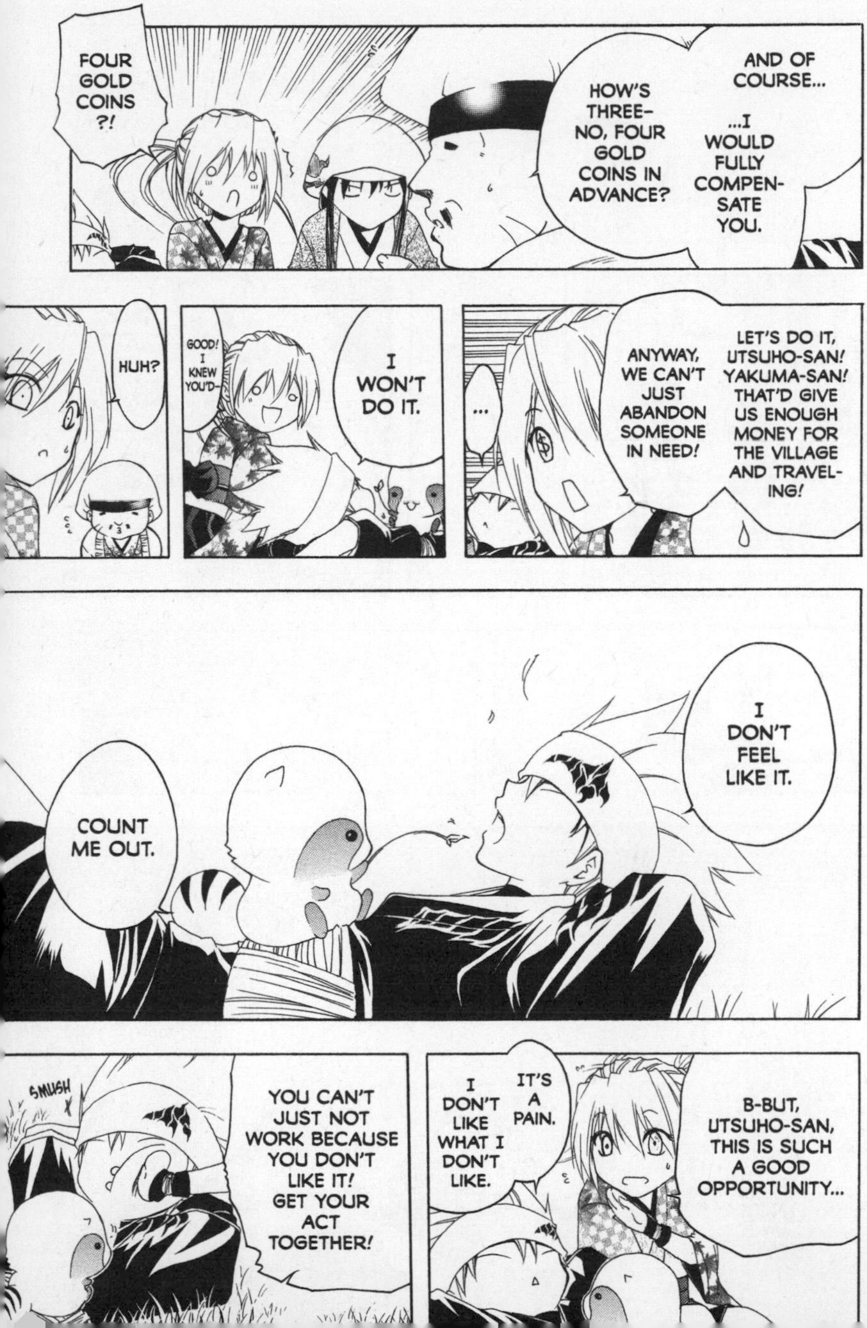
AND OF COURSE... ...I WOULD FULLY COMPENSATE YOU.
HOW'S THREE— NO, FOUR GOLD COINS IN ADVANCE?
FOUR GOLD COINS ?!
LET'S DO IT, UTSUHO-SAN! YAKUMA-SAN! THAT'D GIVE US ENOUGH MONEY FOR THE VILLAGE AND TRAVEL-ING!
ANYWAY, WE CAN'T JUST ABANDON SOMEONE IN NEED!
...
I WON'T DO IT.
GOOD! I KNEW YOU'D—
HUH?
I DON'T FEEL LIKE IT.
COUNT ME OUT.
B-BUT, UTSUHO-SAN, THIS IS SUCH A GOOD OPPORTUNITY...
IT'S A PAIN.
I DON'T LIKE WHAT I DON'T LIKE.
YOU CAN'T JUST NOT WORK BECAUSE YOU DON'T LIKE IT! GET YOUR ACT TOGETHER!
SMUSH

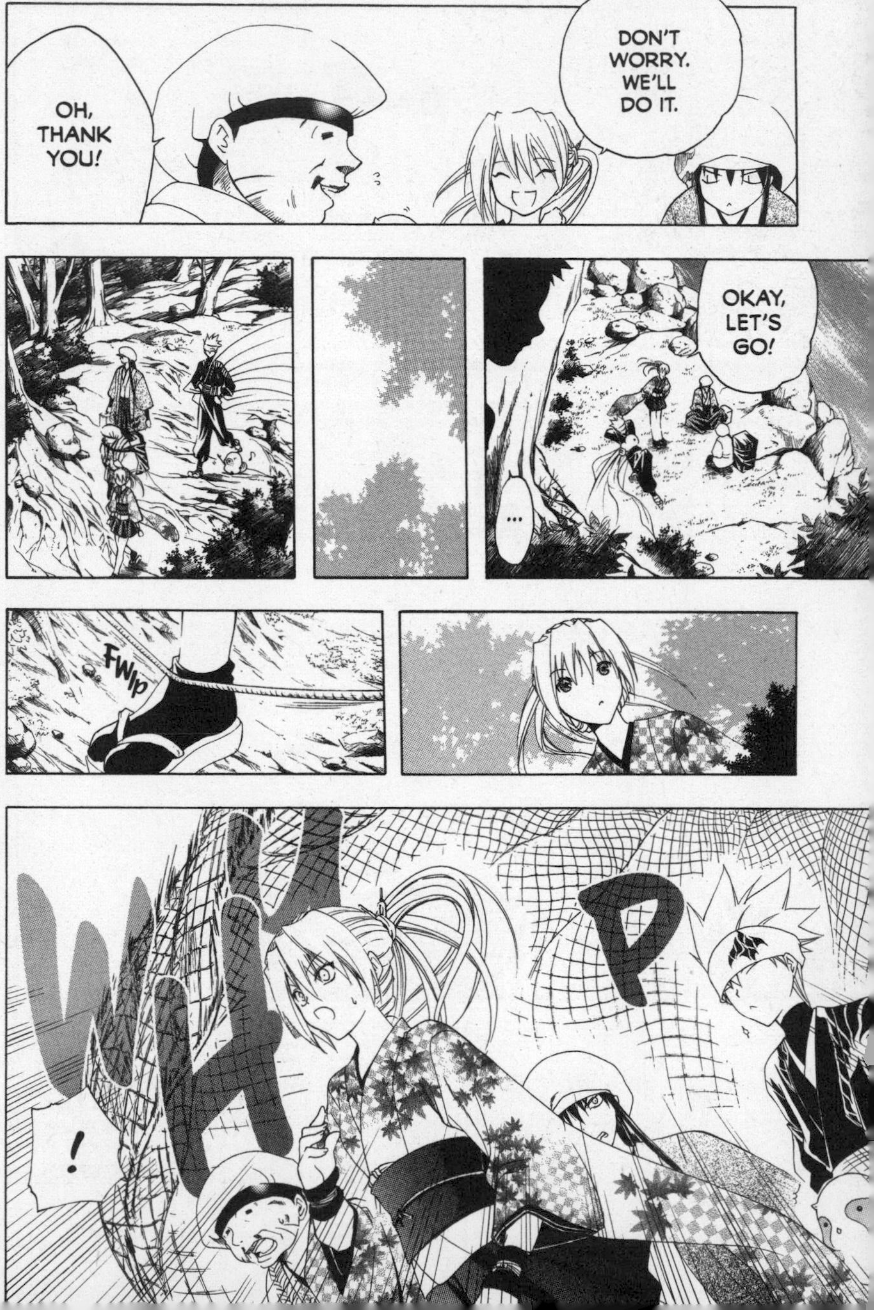
DON'T WORRY. WE'LL DO IT.
OH, THANK YOU!
OKAY, LET'S GO!
...
FWIP
!

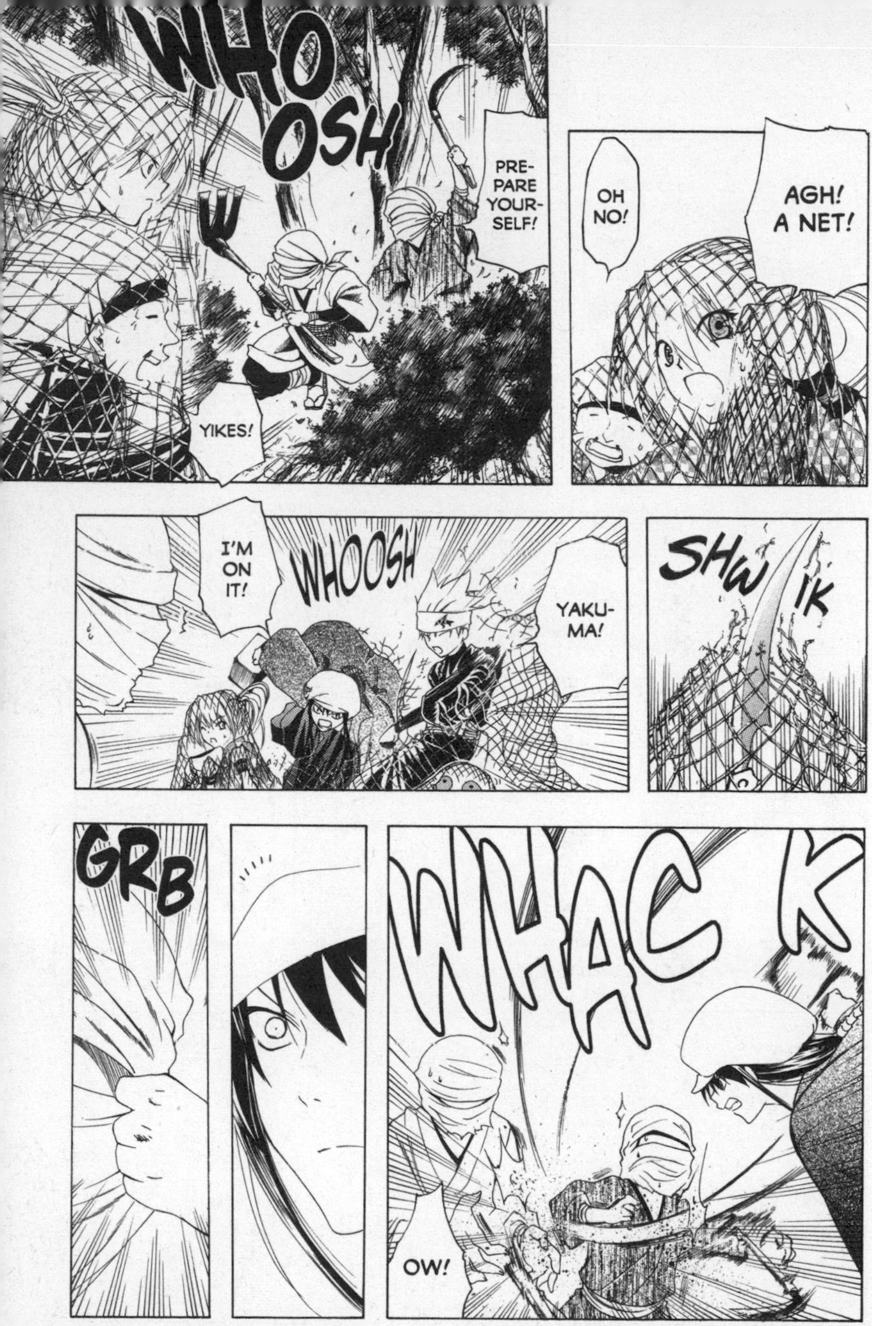
AGH! A NET!
OH NO!
PRE-PARE YOUR-SELF!
WHOOSH
YIKES!
SHWIK
YAKU-MA!
WHOOSH
I'M ON IT!
WHACK
OW!
GRB

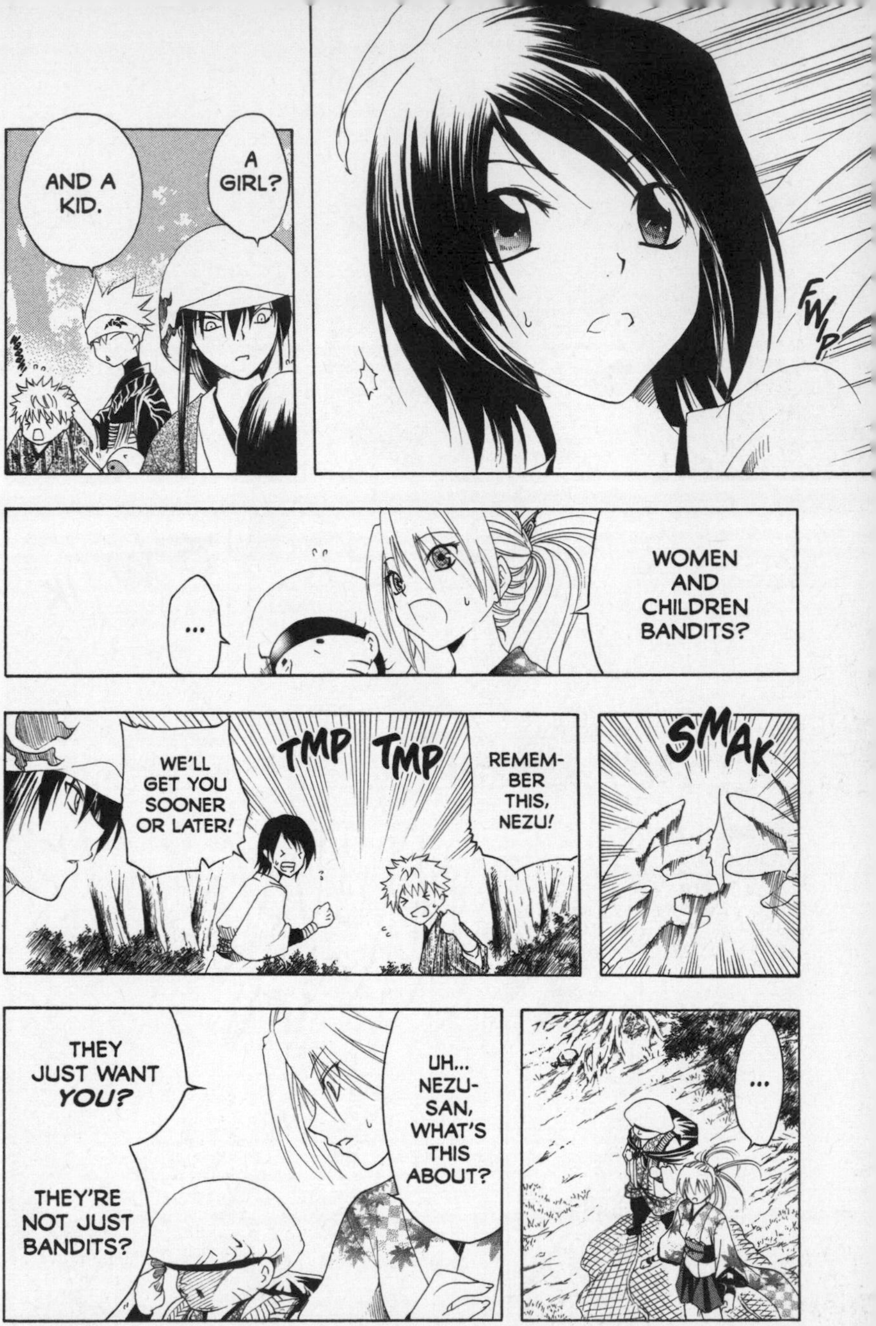
FWIP
A GIRL?
AND A KID.
WOMEN AND CHILDREN BANDITS?
...
SMAK
REMEMBER THIS, NEZU!
TMP TMP
WE'LL GET YOU SOONER OR LATER!
...
UH... NEZU-SAN, WHAT'S THIS ABOUT?
THEY JUST WANT *YOU?*
THEY'RE NOT JUST BANDITS?

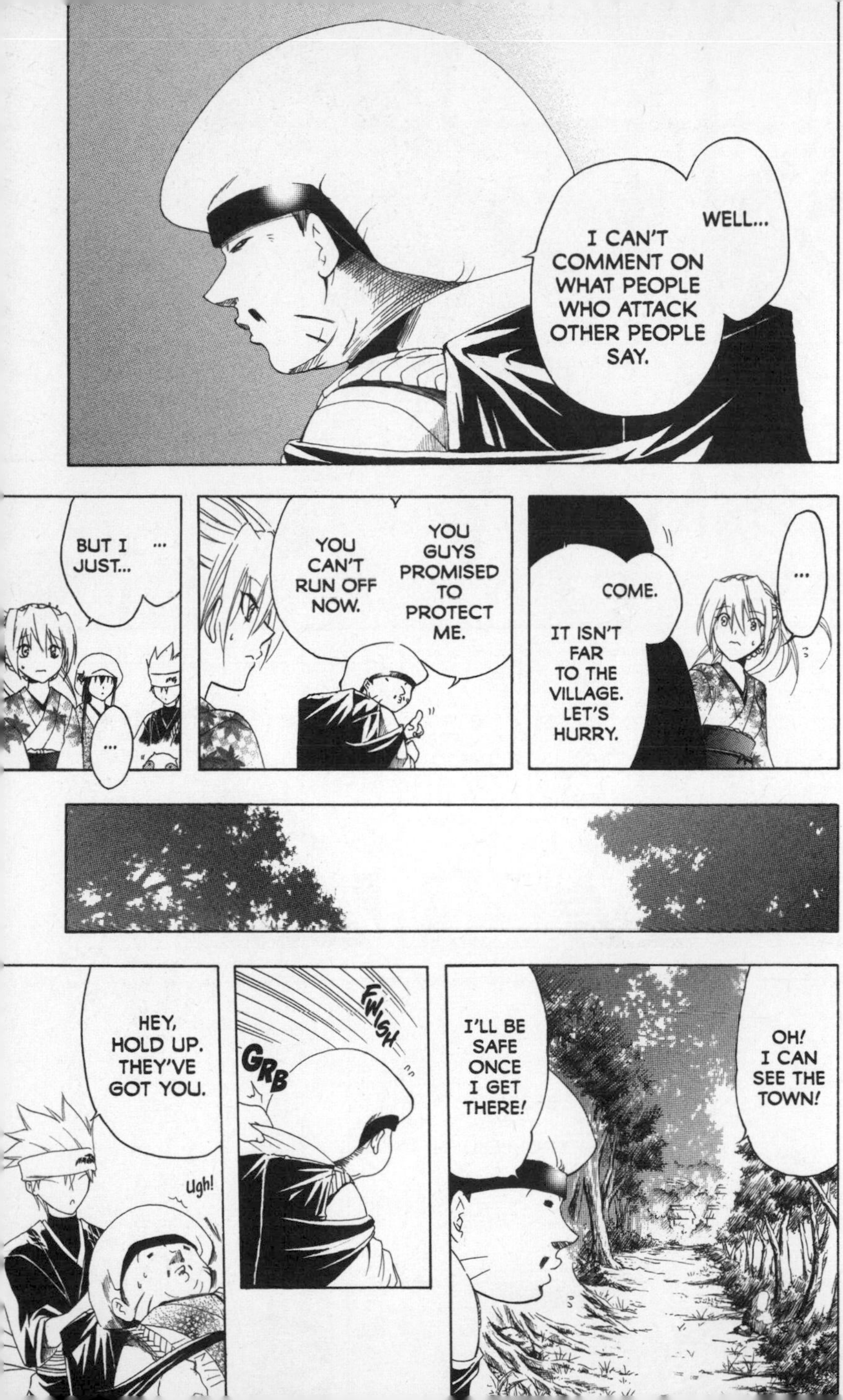
WELL... I CAN'T COMMENT ON WHAT PEOPLE WHO ATTACK OTHER PEOPLE SAY.
...
COME.
IT ISN'T FAR TO THE VILLAGE. LET'S HURRY.
YOU GUYS PROMISED TO PROTECT ME.
YOU CAN'T RUN OFF NOW.
BUT I JUST...
...
...
OH! I CAN SEE THE TOWN!
I'LL BE SAFE ONCE I GET THERE!
FWISH
GRB
HEY, HOLD UP. THEY'VE GOT YOU.
Ugh!

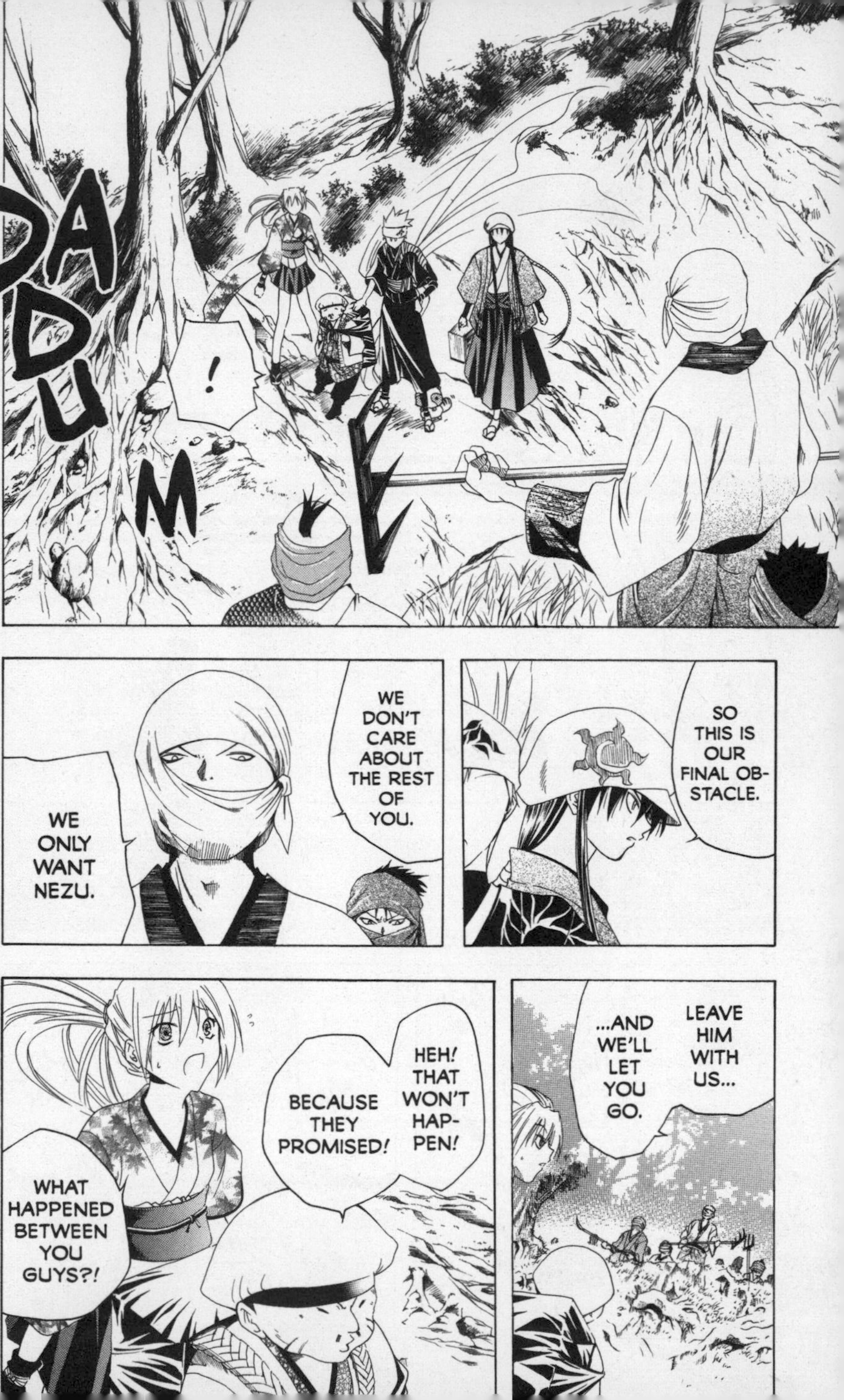
DADUM
!
SO THIS IS OUR FINAL OBSTACLE.
WE DON'T CARE ABOUT THE REST OF YOU.
WE ONLY WANT NEZU.
LEAVE HIM WITH US...
...AND WE'LL LET YOU GO.
HEH! THAT WON'T HAPPEN!
BECAUSE THEY PROMISED!
WHAT HAPPENED BETWEEN YOU GUYS?!

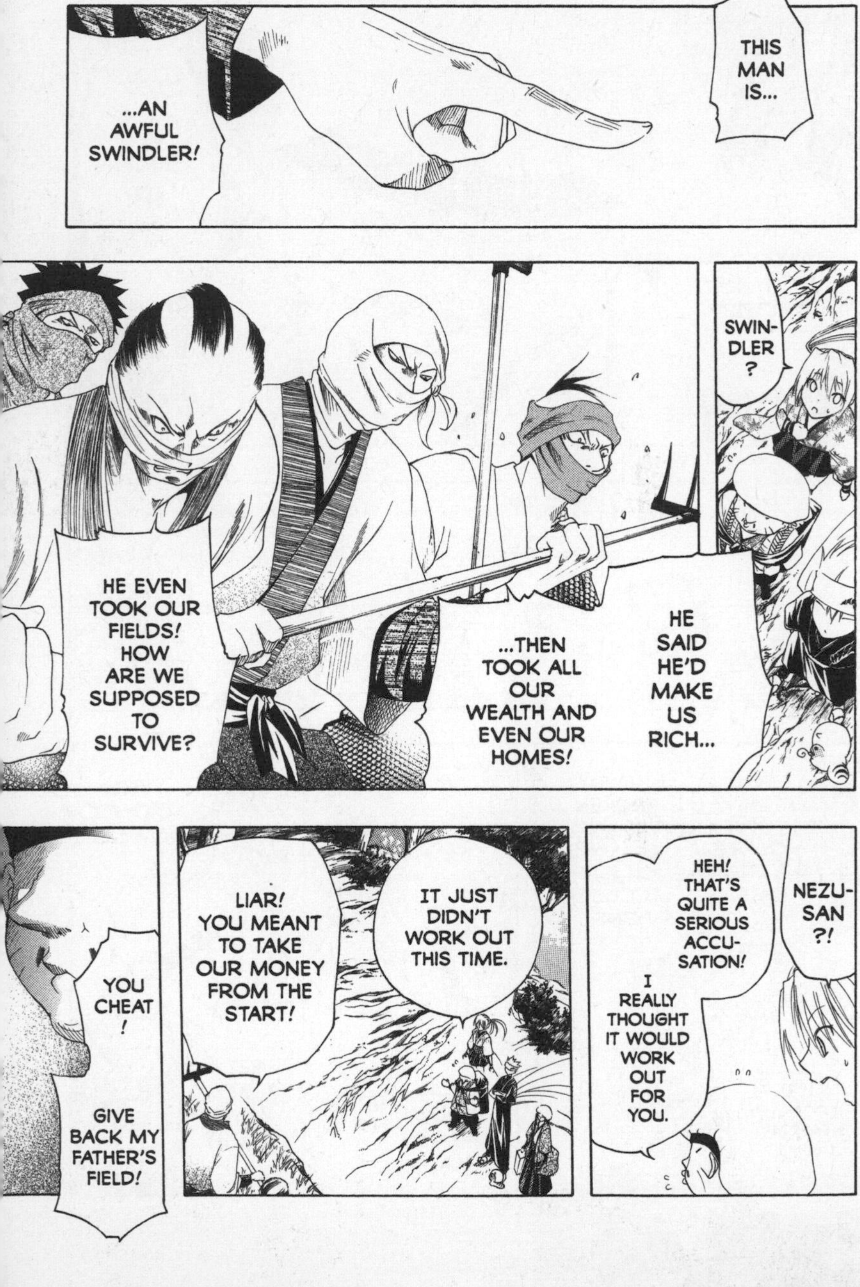
THIS MAN IS...
...AN AWFUL SWINDLER!
SWIN-DLER?
HE SAID HE'D MAKE US RICH...
...THEN TOOK ALL OUR WEALTH AND EVEN OUR HOMES!
HE EVEN TOOK OUR FIELDS! HOW ARE WE SUPPOSED TO SURVIVE?
NEZU-SAN?!
HEH! THAT'S QUITE A SERIOUS ACCU-SATION!
I REALLY THOUGHT IT WOULD WORK OUT FOR YOU.
IT JUST DIDN'T WORK OUT THIS TIME.
LIAR! YOU MEANT TO TAKE OUR MONEY FROM THE START!
YOU CHEAT!
GIVE BACK MY FATHER'S FIELD!

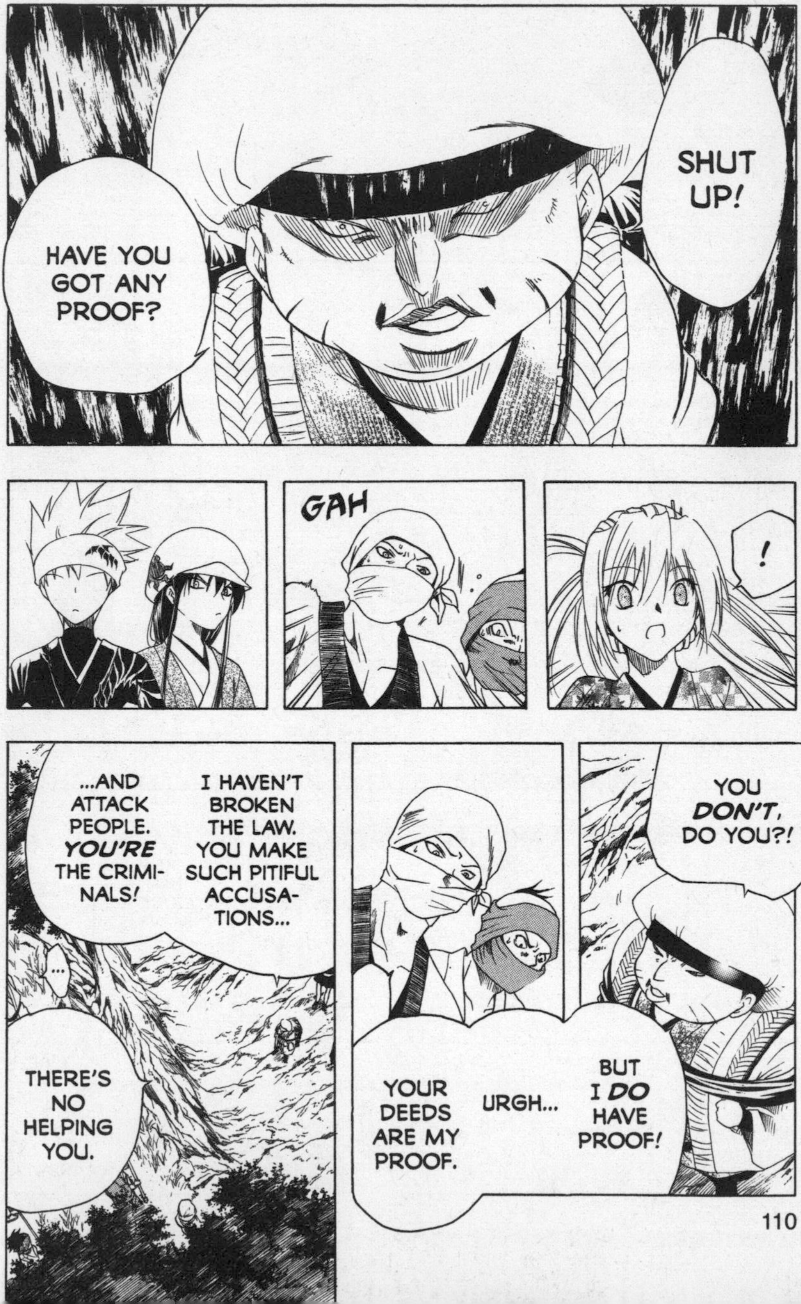
SHUT UP!
HAVE YOU GOT ANY PROOF?
!
GAH
YOU *DON'T*, DO YOU?!
BUT I *DO* HAVE PROOF!
URGH...
YOUR DEEDS ARE MY PROOF.
I HAVEN'T BROKEN THE LAW. YOU MAKE SUCH PITIFUL ACCUSA-TIONS...
...AND ATTACK PEOPLE. *YOU'RE* THE CRIMI-NALS!
...
THERE'S NO HELPING YOU.

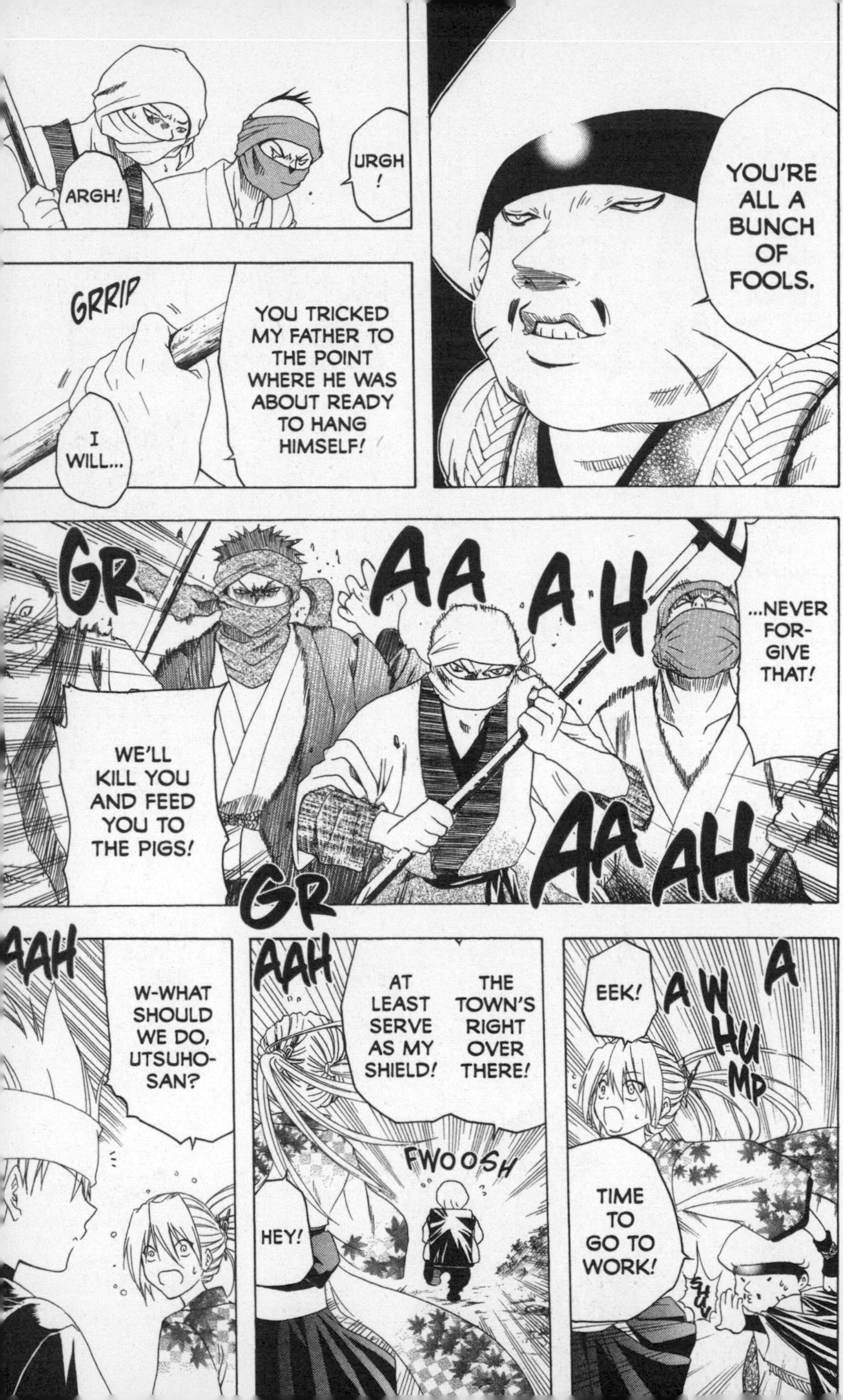
YOU'RE ALL A BUNCH OF FOOLS.
URGH!
ARGH!
GRRIP
YOU TRICKED MY FATHER TO THE POINT WHERE HE WAS ABOUT READY TO HANG HIMSELF!
I WILL...
...NEVER FORGIVE THAT!
AAAH
GR
WE'LL KILL YOU AND FEED YOU TO THE PIGS!
AAAH
GR
AWA
EEK!
WHUMP
TIME TO GO TO WORK!
SHUV
THE TOWN'S RIGHT OVER THERE!
AT LEAST SERVE AS MY SHIELD!
AAH
FWOOSH
HEY!
AAH
W-WHAT SHOULD WE DO, UTSUHO-SAN?

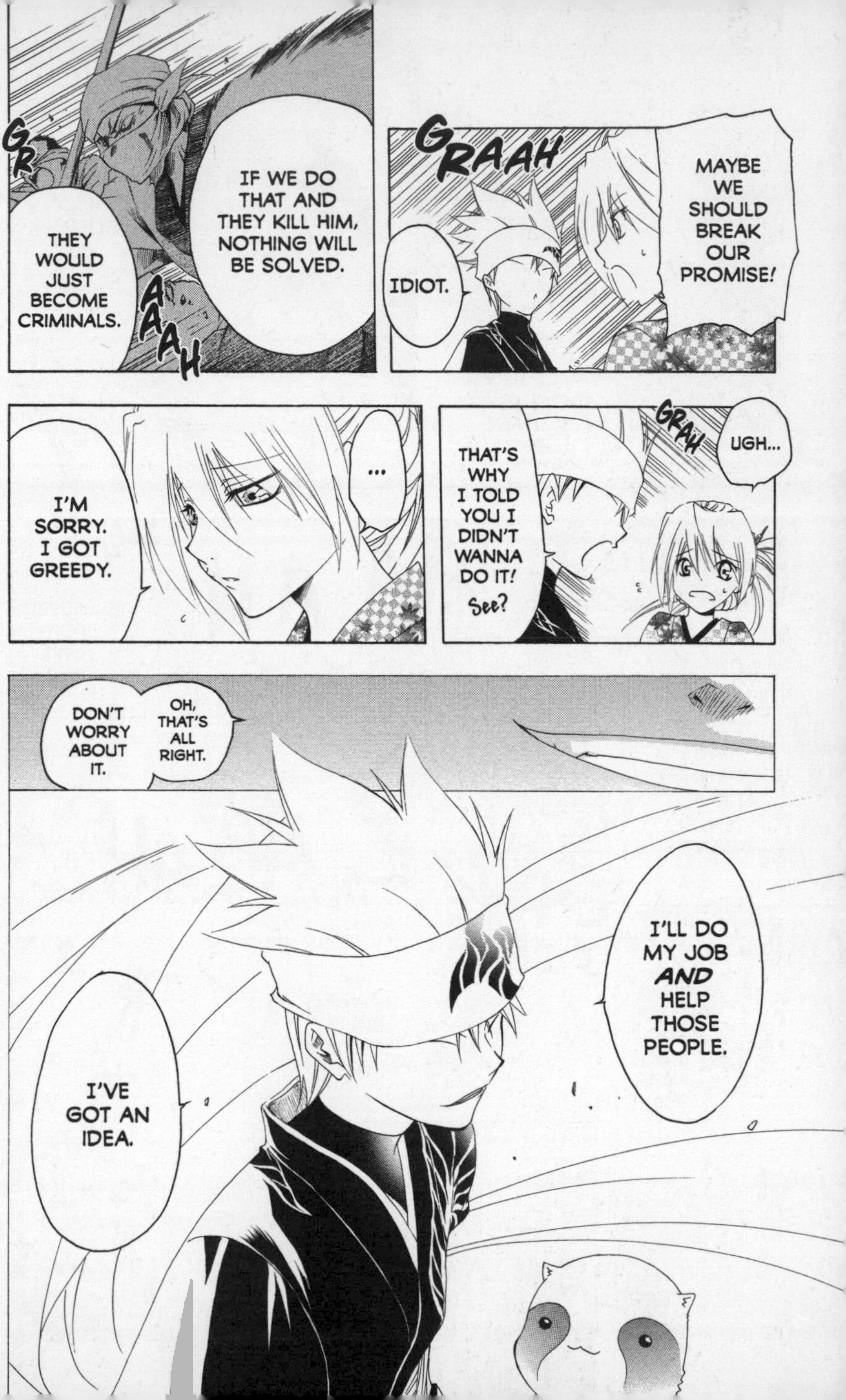
MAYBE WE SHOULD BREAK OUR PROMISE!
GRAAH
IDIOT.
IF WE DO THAT AND THEY KILL HIM, NOTHING WILL BE SOLVED.
GR
THEY WOULD JUST BECOME CRIMINALS.
AAAH
UGH...
GRAH
THAT'S WHY I TOLD YOU I DIDN'T WANNA DO IT!
See?
...
I'M SORRY. I GOT GREEDY.
OH, THAT'S ALL RIGHT.
DON'T WORRY ABOUT IT.
I'LL DO MY JOB AND HELP THOSE PEOPLE.
I'VE GOT AN IDEA.

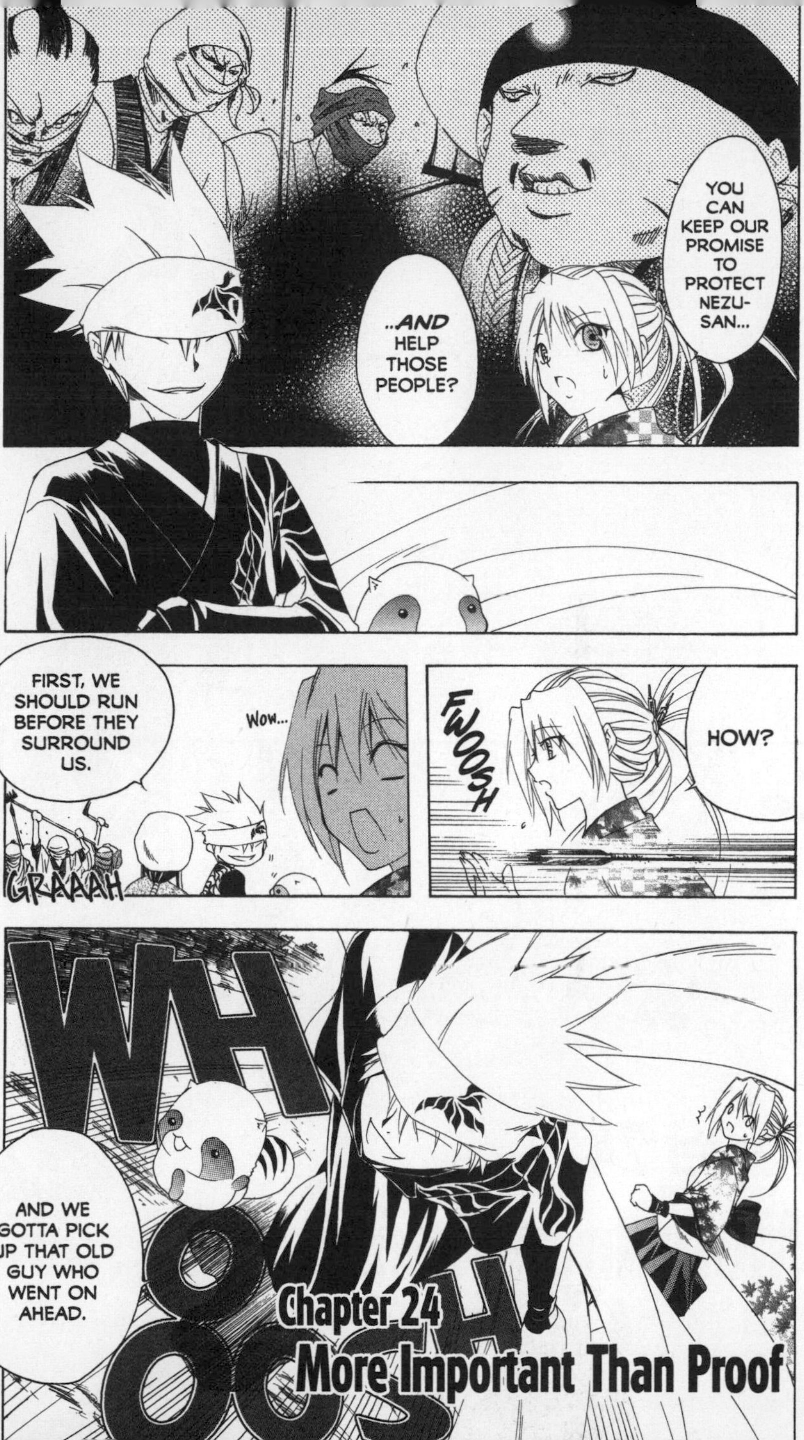
YOU CAN KEEP OUR PROMISE TO PROTECT NEZU-SAN...
...AND HELP THOSE PEOPLE?
HOW?
FWOOSH
FIRST, WE SHOULD RUN BEFORE THEY SURROUND US.
WOW...
GRAAAH
WHOOSH
AND WE GOTTA PICK UP THAT OLD GUY WHO WENT ON AHEAD.
Chapter 24
More Important Than Proof

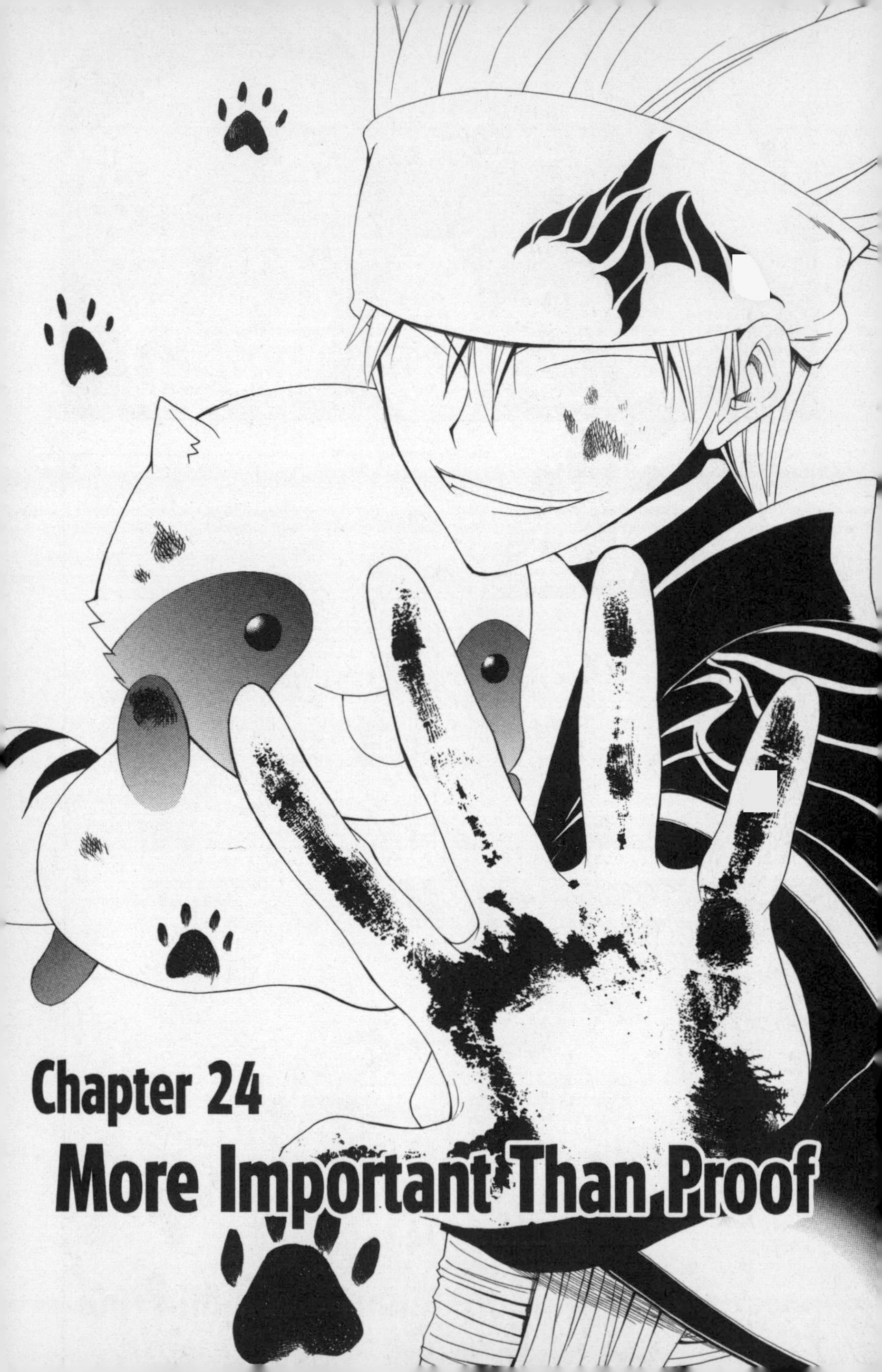
Chapter 24
More Important Than Proof

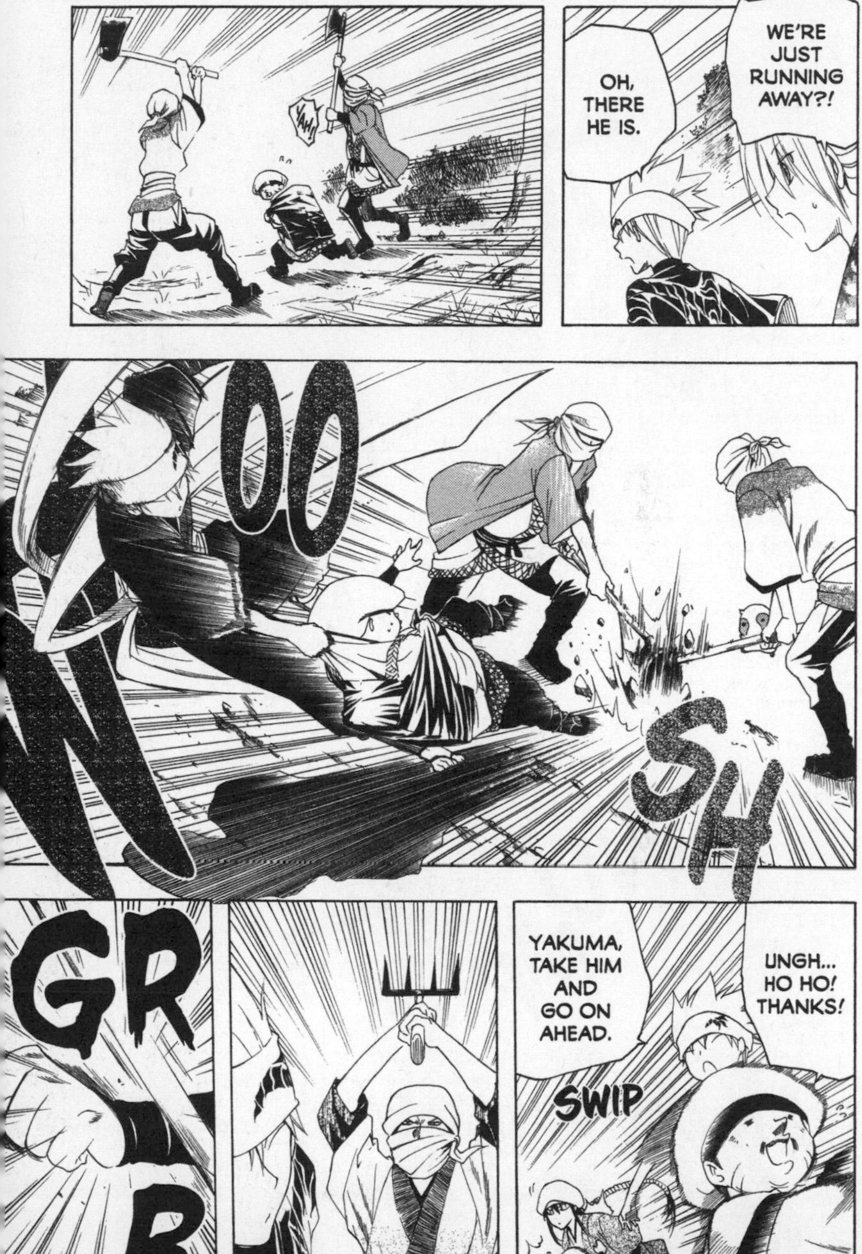
WE'RE JUST RUNNING AWAY?!
OH, THERE HE IS.
YAH!
WOOSH
YAKUMA, TAKE HIM AND GO ON AHEAD.
UNGH... HO HO! THANKS!
SWIP
GRB

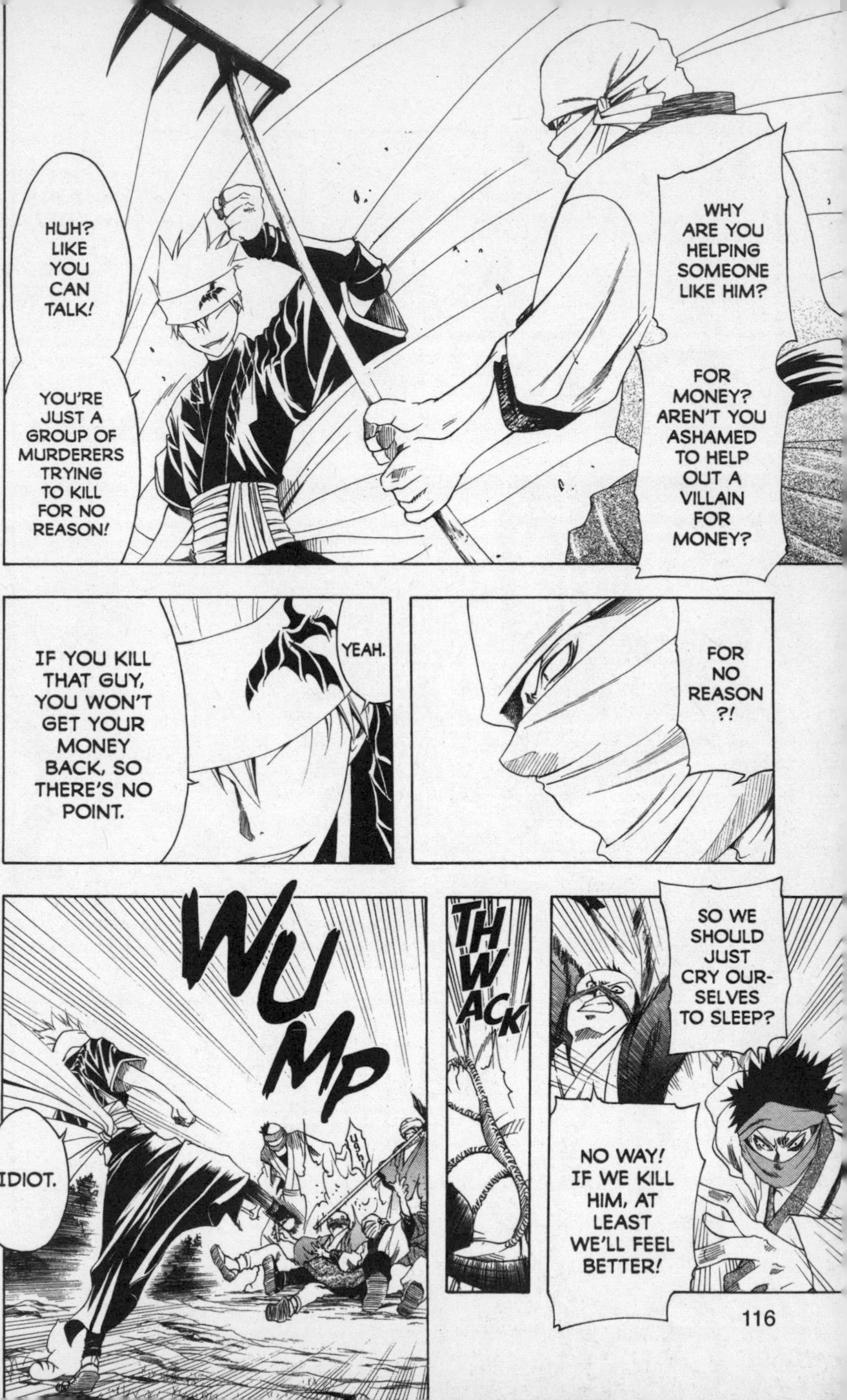
WHY ARE YOU HELPING SOMEONE LIKE HIM?
FOR MONEY? AREN'T YOU ASHAMED TO HELP OUT A VILLAIN FOR MONEY?
HUH? LIKE YOU CAN TALK!
YOU'RE JUST A GROUP OF MURDERERS TRYING TO KILL FOR NO REASON!
FOR NO REASON?!
YEAH.
IF YOU KILL THAT GUY, YOU WON'T GET YOUR MONEY BACK, SO THERE'S NO POINT.
SO WE SHOULD JUST CRY OUR-SELVES TO SLEEP?
NO WAY! IF WE KILL HIM, AT LEAST WE'LL FEEL BETTER!
THWACK
WUMP
IDIOT.

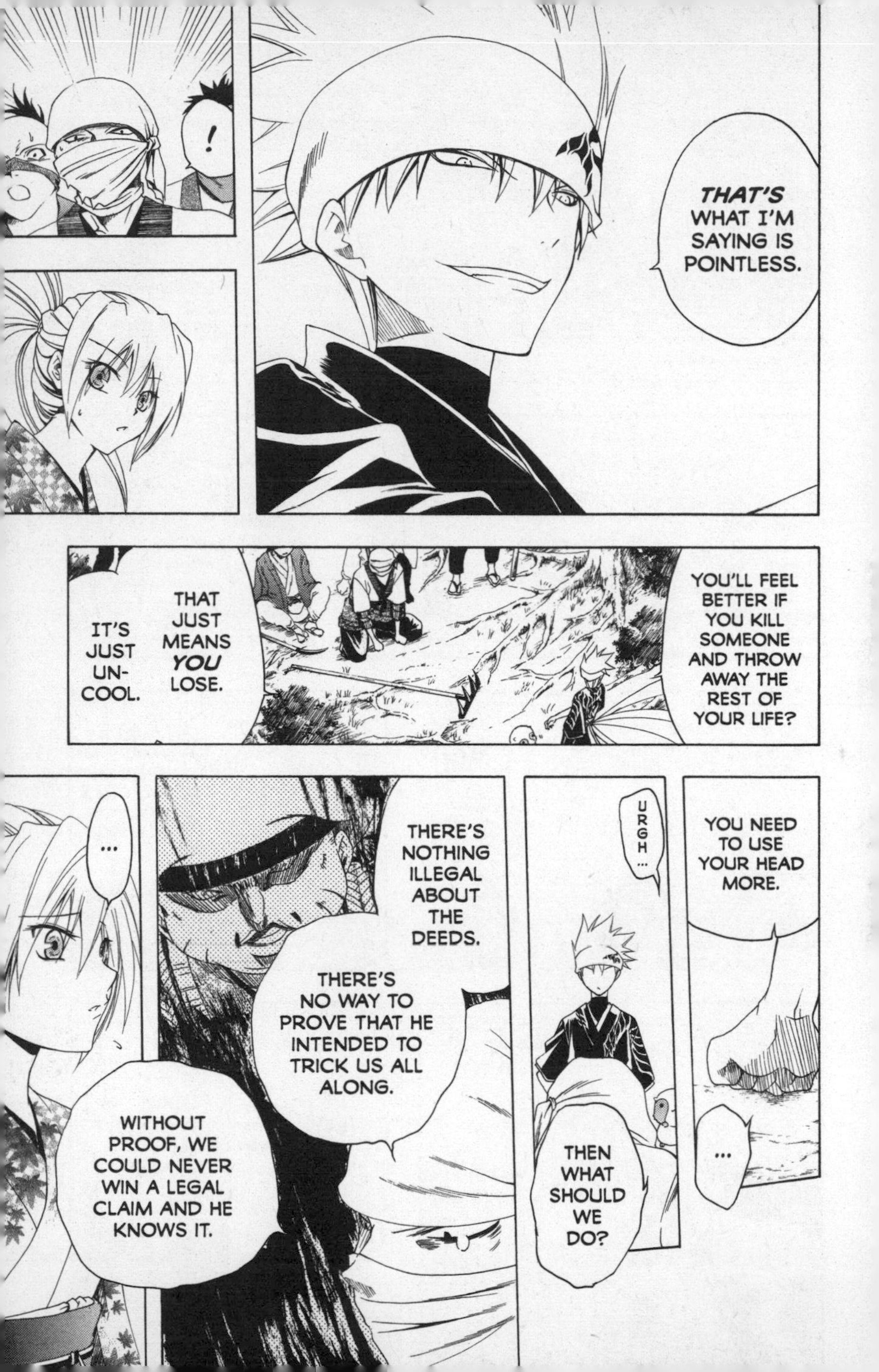
THAT'S WHAT I'M SAYING IS POINTLESS.
YOU'LL FEEL BETTER IF YOU KILL SOMEONE AND THROW AWAY THE REST OF YOUR LIFE?
THAT JUST MEANS YOU LOSE.
IT'S JUST UN-COOL.
YOU NEED TO USE YOUR HEAD MORE.
...
URGH...
THEN WHAT SHOULD WE DO?
THERE'S NOTHING ILLEGAL ABOUT THE DEEDS.
THERE'S NO WAY TO PROVE THAT HE INTENDED TO TRICK US ALL ALONG.
WITHOUT PROOF, WE COULD NEVER WIN A LEGAL CLAIM AND HE KNOWS IT.
...

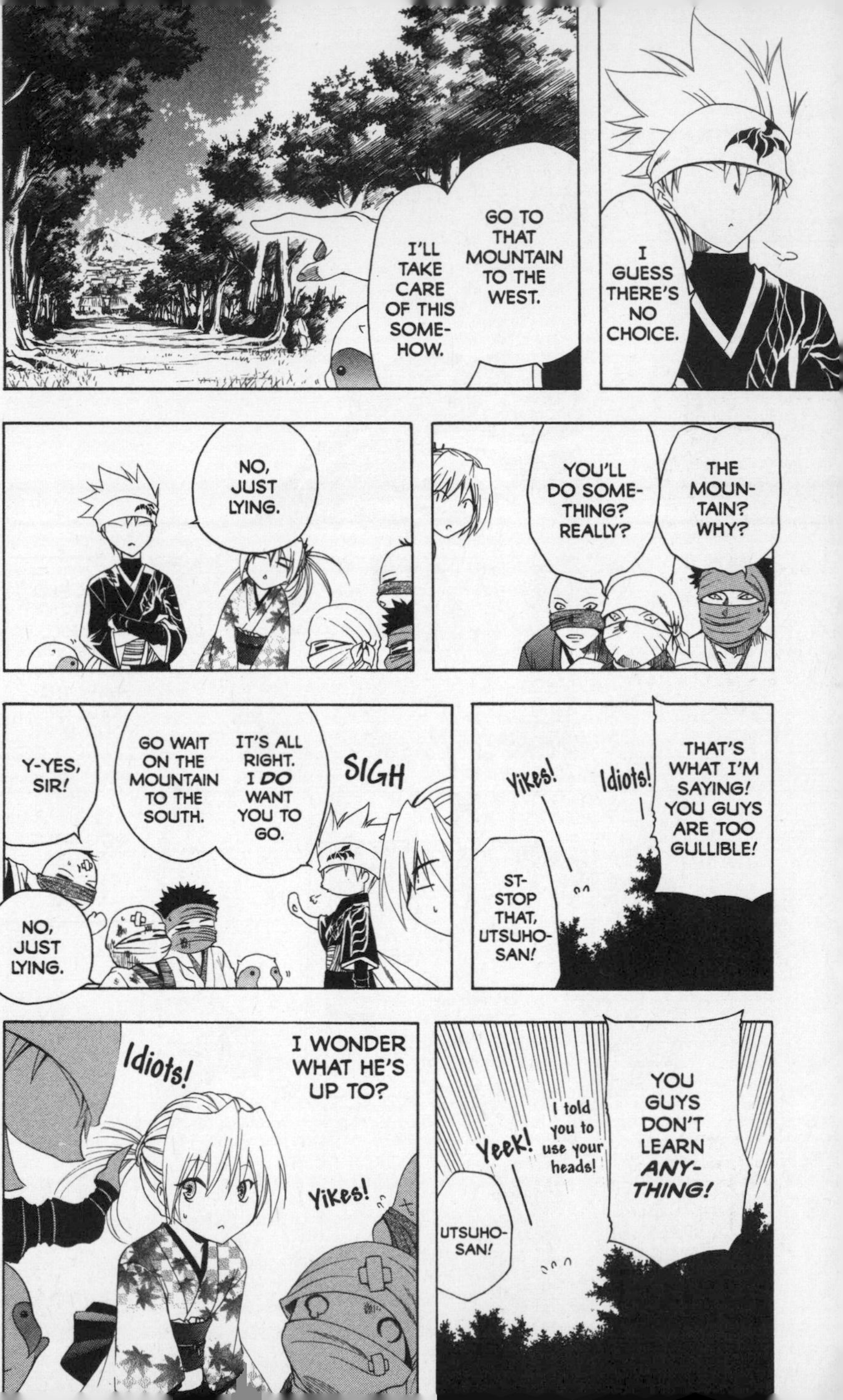
I GUESS THERE'S NO CHOICE.
GO TO THAT MOUNTAIN TO THE WEST.
I'LL TAKE CARE OF THIS SOME-HOW.
THE MOUN-TAIN? WHY?
YOU'LL DO SOME-THING? REALLY?
NO, JUST LYING.
THAT'S WHAT I'M SAYING! YOU GUYS ARE TOO GULLIBLE!
Idiots!
Yikes!
ST-STOP THAT, UTSUHO-SAN!
SIGH
IT'S ALL RIGHT. I *DO* WANT YOU TO GO.
GO WAIT ON THE MOUNTAIN TO THE SOUTH.
Y-YES, SIR!
NO, JUST LYING.
YOU GUYS DON'T LEARN *ANY-THING!*
I told you to use your heads!
Yeek!
UTSUHO-SAN!
I WONDER WHAT HE'S UP TO?
Idiots!
Yikes!

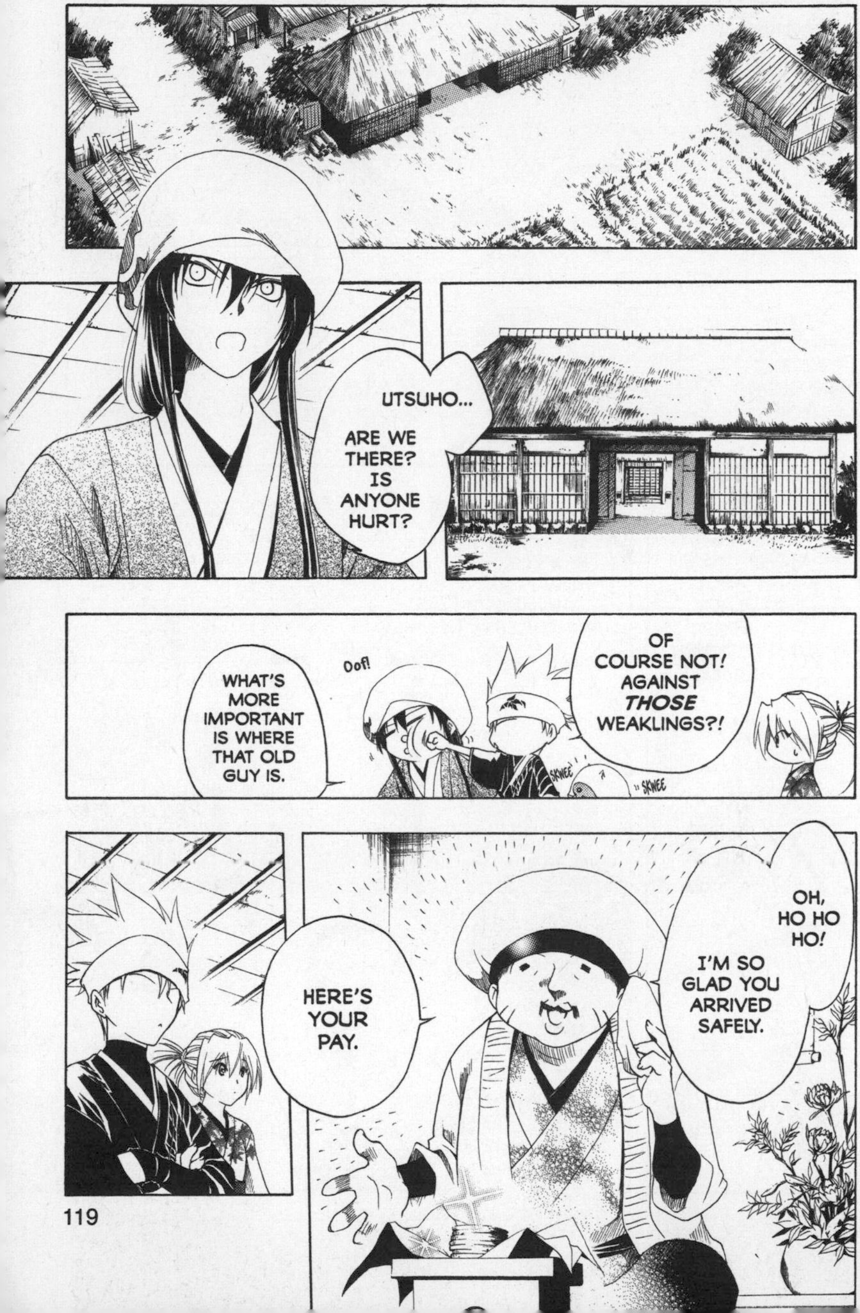
UTSUHO...
ARE WE THERE? IS ANYONE HURT?
OF COURSE NOT! AGAINST *THOSE* WEAKLINGS?!
Oof!
SKWEE
SKWEE
WHAT'S MORE IMPORTANT IS WHERE THAT OLD GUY IS.
OH, HO HO HO!
I'M SO GLAD YOU ARRIVED SAFELY.
HERE'S YOUR PAY.

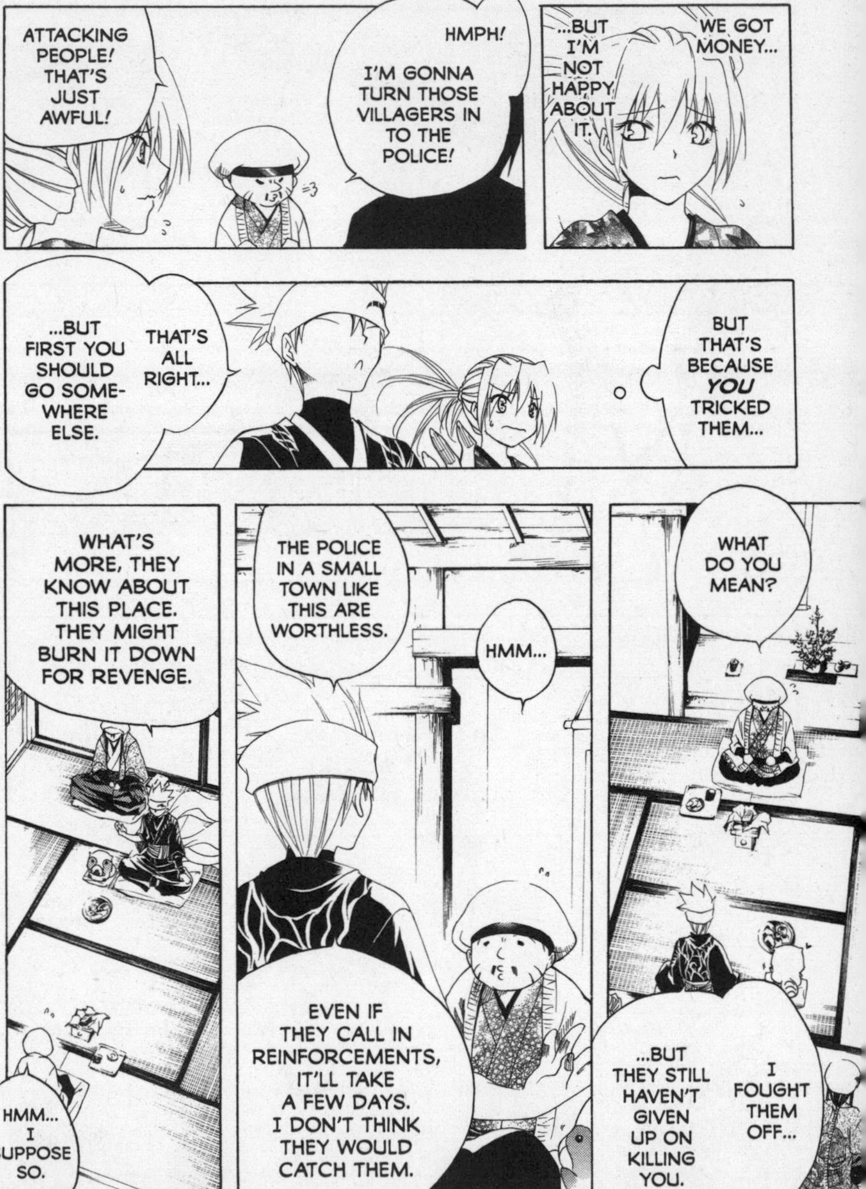
WE GOT MONEY...
...BUT I'M NOT HAPPY ABOUT IT.
HMPH!
I'M GONNA TURN THOSE VILLAGERS IN TO THE POLICE!
ATTACKING PEOPLE! THAT'S JUST AWFUL!
BUT THAT'S BECAUSE *YOU* TRICKED THEM...
THAT'S ALL RIGHT...
...BUT FIRST YOU SHOULD GO SOME-WHERE ELSE.
WHAT DO YOU MEAN?
I FOUGHT THEM OFF...
...BUT THEY STILL HAVEN'T GIVEN UP ON KILLING YOU.
THE POLICE IN A SMALL TOWN LIKE THIS ARE WORTHLESS.
HMM...
EVEN IF THEY CALL IN REINFORCEMENTS, IT'LL TAKE A FEW DAYS. I DON'T THINK THEY WOULD CATCH THEM.
WHAT'S MORE, THEY KNOW ABOUT THIS PLACE. THEY MIGHT BURN IT DOWN FOR REVENGE.
HMM... I SUPPOSE SO.

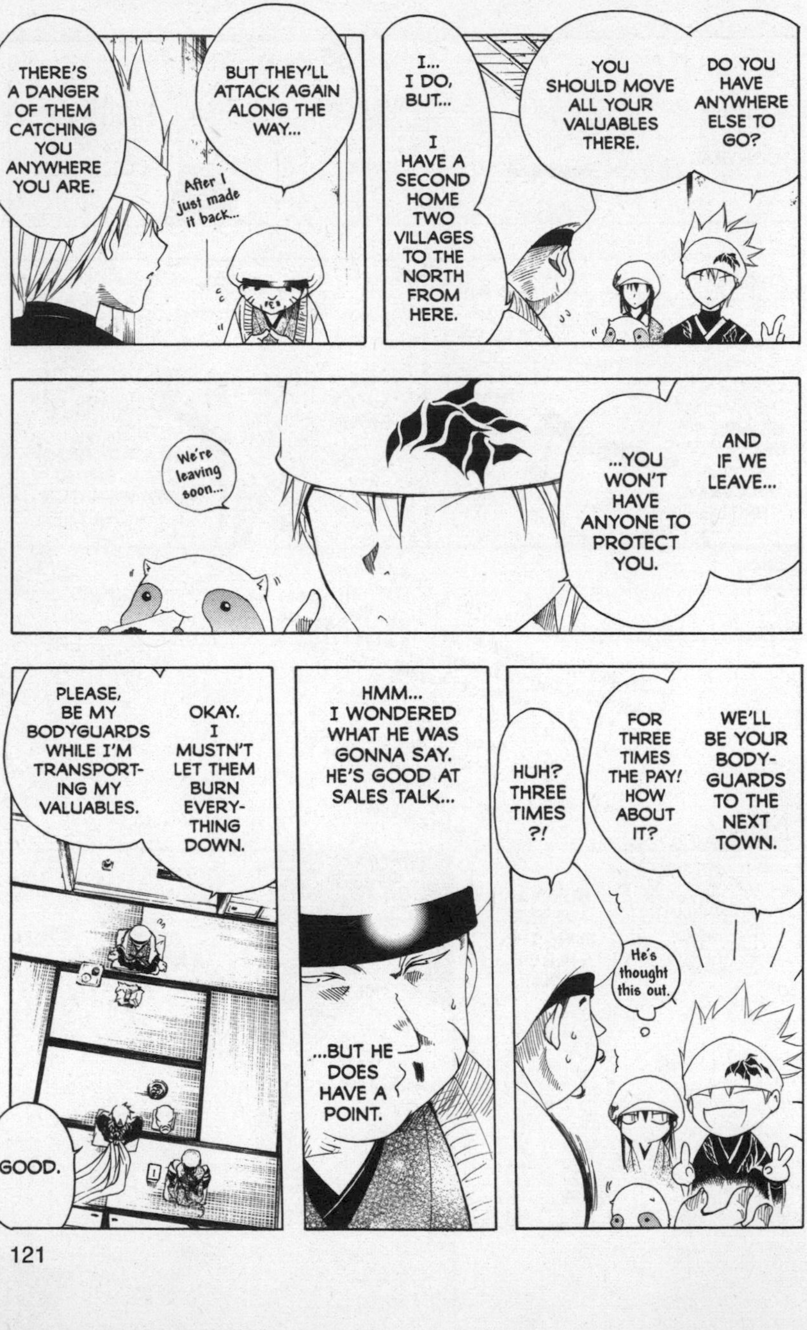
DO YOU HAVE ANYWHERE ELSE TO GO?
I... I DO, BUT... I HAVE A SECOND HOME TWO VILLAGES TO THE NORTH FROM HERE.
YOU SHOULD MOVE ALL YOUR VALUABLES THERE.
BUT THEY'LL ATTACK AGAIN ALONG THE WAY...
After I just made it back...
THERE'S A DANGER OF THEM CATCHING YOU ANYWHERE YOU ARE.
AND IF WE LEAVE...
...YOU WON'T HAVE ANYONE TO PROTECT YOU.
We're leaving soon...
WE'LL BE YOUR BODY-GUARDS TO THE NEXT TOWN.
FOR THREE TIMES THE PAY! HOW ABOUT IT?
HUH? THREE TIMES?!
He's thought this out.
HMM... I WONDERED WHAT HE WAS GONNA SAY. HE'S GOOD AT SALES TALK...
...BUT HE DOES HAVE A POINT.
OKAY. I MUSTN'T LET THEM BURN EVERY-THING DOWN.
PLEASE, BE MY BODYGUARDS WHILE I'M TRANSPORT-ING MY VALUABLES.
GOOD.

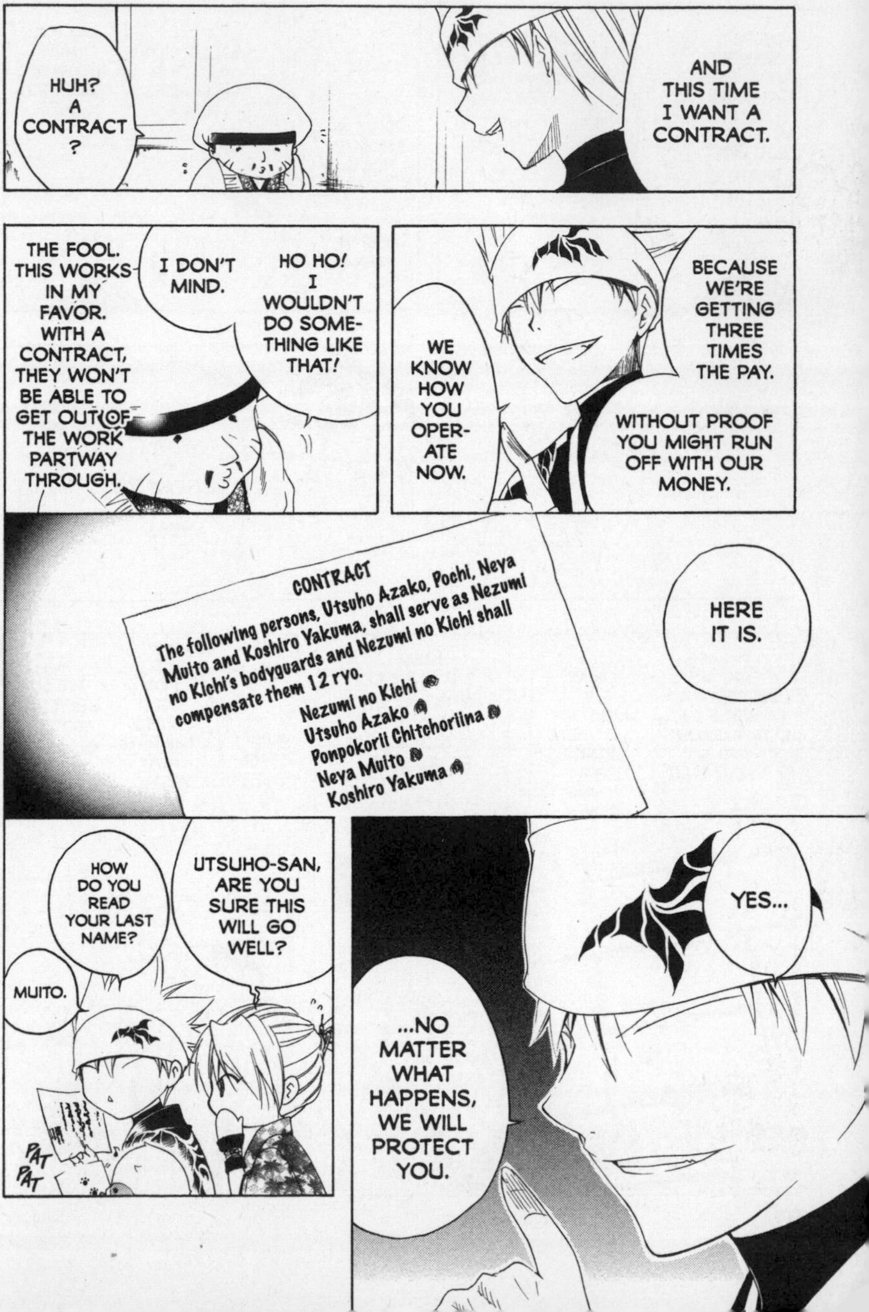
AND THIS TIME I WANT A CONTRACT.
HUH? A CONTRACT?
BECAUSE WE'RE GETTING THREE TIMES THE PAY.
WITHOUT PROOF YOU MIGHT RUN OFF WITH OUR MONEY.
WE KNOW HOW YOU OPERATE NOW.
HO HO! I WOULDN'T DO SOMETHING LIKE THAT!
I DON'T MIND.
THE FOOL. THIS WORKS IN MY FAVOR. WITH A CONTRACT, THEY WON'T BE ABLE TO GET OUT OF THE WORK PARTWAY THROUGH.
HERE IT IS.
CONTRACT
The following persons, Utsuho Azako, Pochi, Neya Muito and Koshiro Yakuma, shall serve as Nezumi no Kichi's bodyguards and Nezumi no Kichi shall compensate them 12 ryo.
Nezumi no Kichi
Utsuho Azako
Ponpokorii Chitchorilina
Neya Muito
Koshiro Yakuma
YES...
...NO MATTER WHAT HAPPENS, WE WILL PROTECT YOU.
UTSUHO-SAN, ARE YOU SURE THIS WILL GO WELL?
HOW DO YOU READ YOUR LAST NAME?
MUITO.
PAT PAT

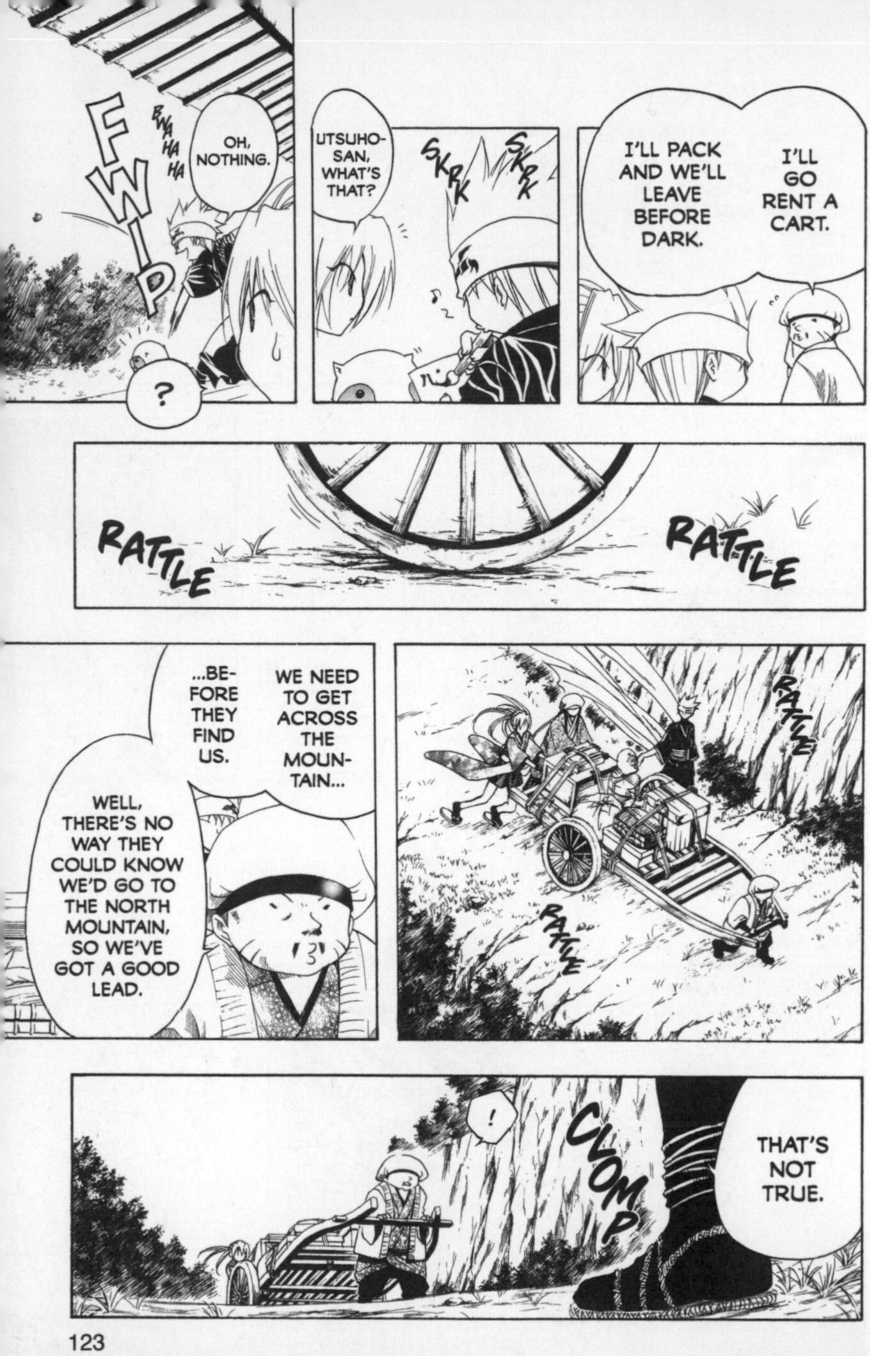
I'LL GO RENT A CART.
I'LL PACK AND WE'LL LEAVE BEFORE DARK.
SKRK
SKRK
UTSUHO-SAN, WHAT'S THAT?
OH, NOTHING.
BWAHAHA
FWIP
?
RATTLE
RATTLE
RATTLE
RATTLE
WE NEED TO GET ACROSS THE MOUNTAIN...
...BEFORE THEY FIND US.
WELL, THERE'S NO WAY THEY COULD KNOW WE'D GO TO THE NORTH MOUNTAIN, SO WE'VE GOT A GOOD LEAD.
THAT'S NOT TRUE.
CLOMP
!

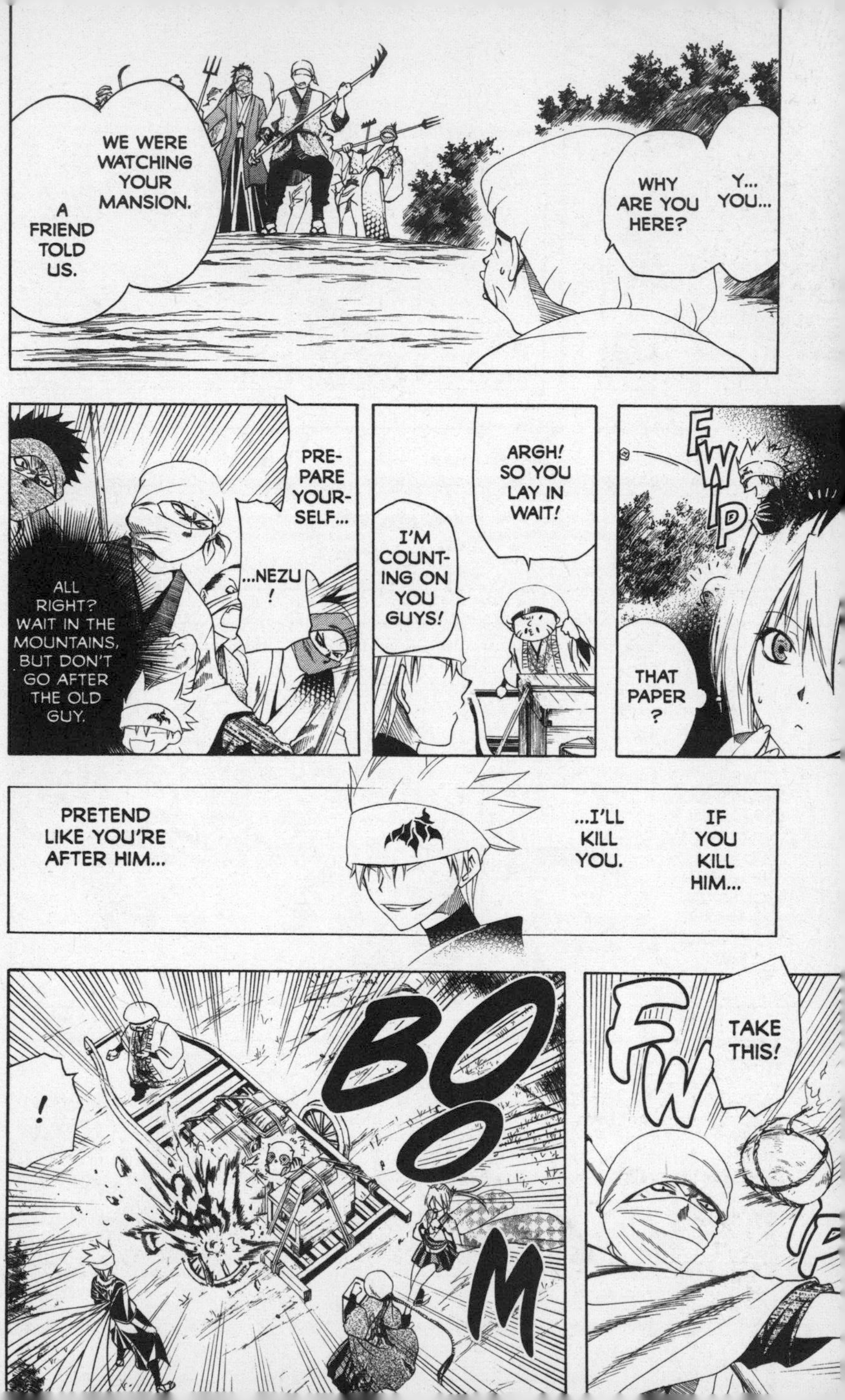
Y... YOU...
WHY ARE YOU HERE?
WE WERE WATCHING YOUR MANSION.
A FRIEND TOLD US.
FWIP
THAT PAPER?
ARGH! SO YOU LAY IN WAIT!
I'M COUNTING ON YOU GUYS!
PRE-PARE YOUR-SELF...
...NEZU!
ALL RIGHT? WAIT IN THE MOUNTAINS, BUT DON'T GO AFTER THE OLD GUY.
IF YOU KILL HIM...
...I'LL KILL YOU.
PRETEND LIKE YOU'RE AFTER HIM...
TAKE THIS!
FWIP
BOOM
!

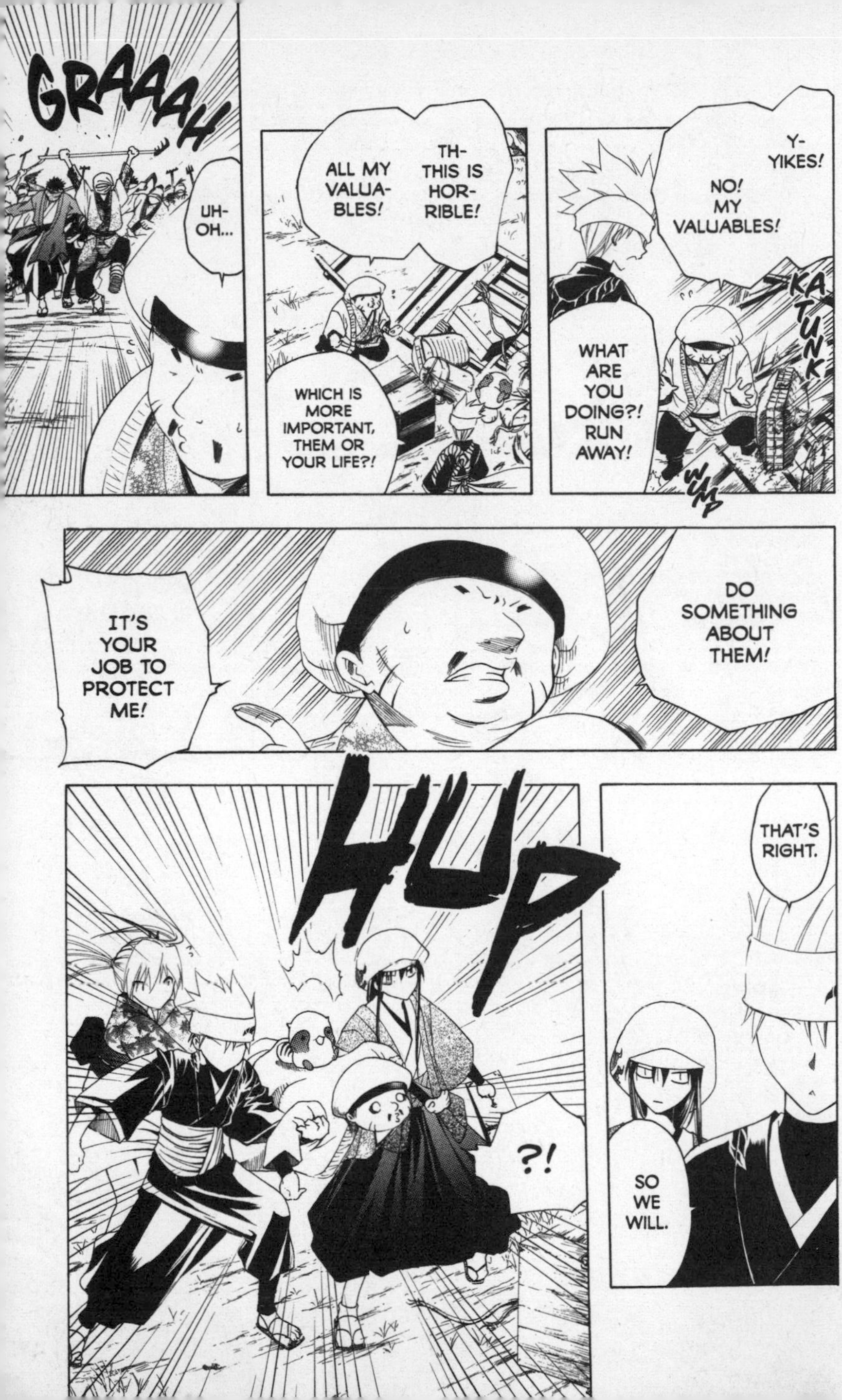
Y-YIKES!
NO! MY VALUABLES!
KATUNK
WHAT ARE YOU DOING?! RUN AWAY!
WUMP
TH-THIS IS HORRIBLE!
ALL MY VALUABLES!
WHICH IS MORE IMPORTANT, THEM OR YOUR LIFE?!
GRAAAH
UH-OH...
DO SOMETHING ABOUT THEM!
IT'S YOUR JOB TO PROTECT ME!
THAT'S RIGHT.
SO WE WILL.
HUP
?!

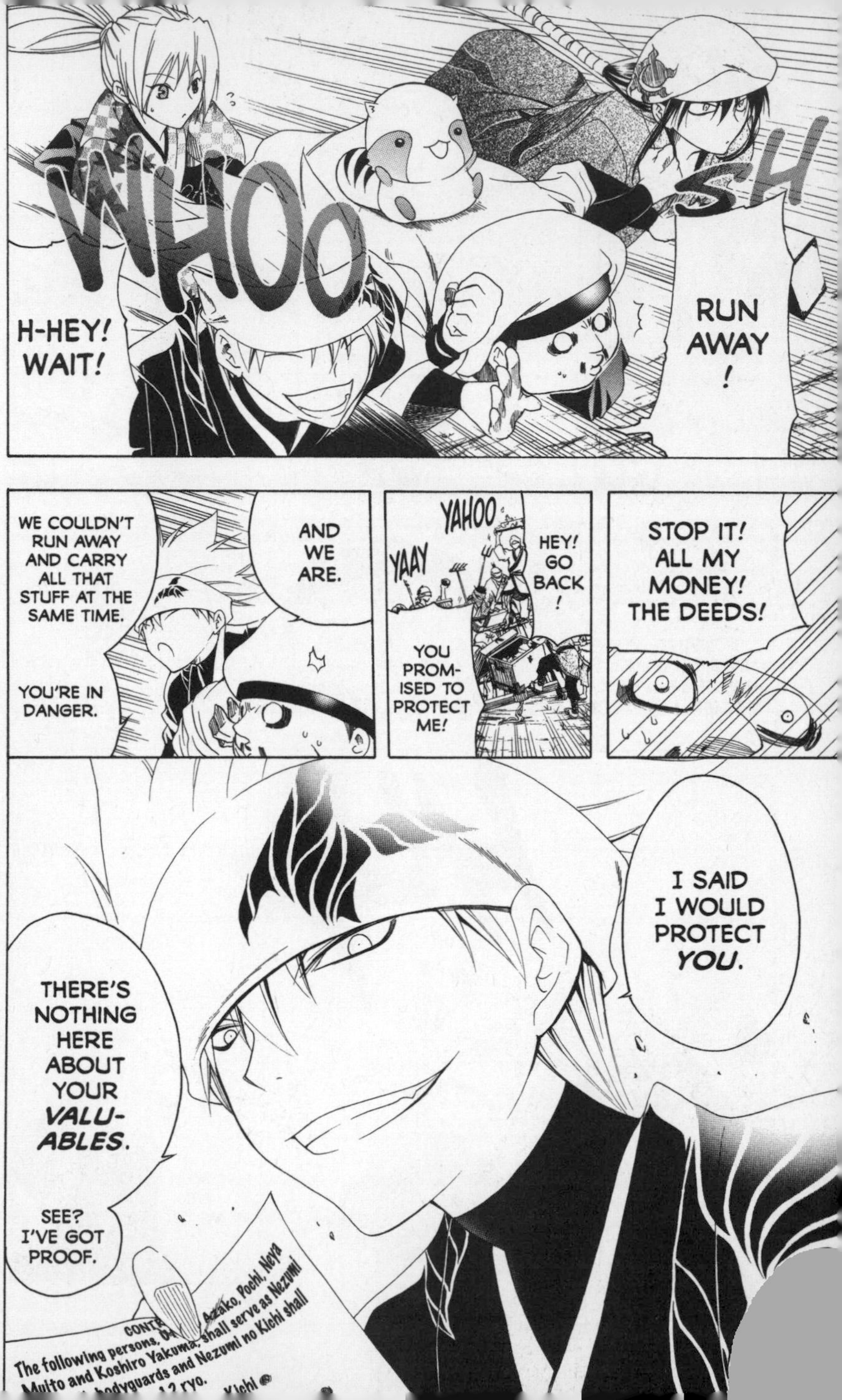
RUN AWAY!
WHOOSH
H-HEY! WAIT!
STOP IT! ALL MY MONEY! THE DEEDS!
HEY! GO BACK!
YAHOO
YAAY
YOU PROMISED TO PROTECT ME!
AND WE ARE.
WE COULDN'T RUN AWAY AND CARRY ALL THAT STUFF AT THE SAME TIME.
YOU'RE IN DANGER.
I SAID I WOULD PROTECT YOU.
THERE'S NOTHING HERE ABOUT YOUR VALUABLES.
SEE? I'VE GOT PROOF.
The following persons,
Azako, Pochi, Neya
Muito and Koshiro Yakuma, shall serve as Nezumi
bodyguards and Nezumi no Kichi shall
12 ryo.
Kichi

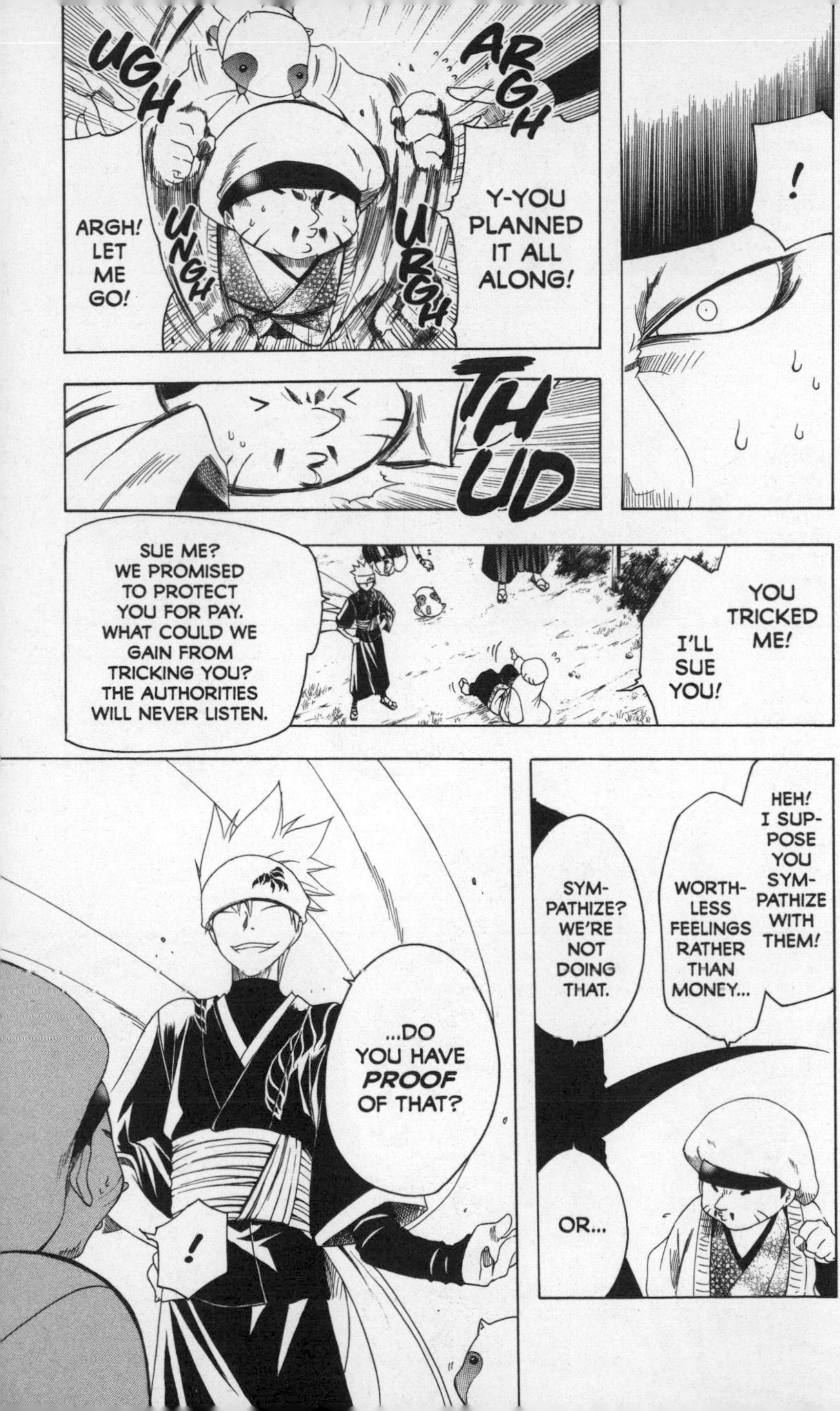
!
ARGH
UGH
Y-YOU PLANNED IT ALL ALONG!
URGH
ARGH! LET ME GO!
UNGH
THUD
YOU TRICKED ME!
I'LL SUE YOU!
SUE ME? WE PROMISED TO PROTECT YOU FOR PAY. WHAT COULD WE GAIN FROM TRICKING YOU? THE AUTHORITIES WILL NEVER LISTEN.
HEH! I SUPPOSE YOU SYMPATHIZE WITH THEM!
WORTHLESS FEELINGS RATHER THAN MONEY...
SYMPATHIZE? WE'RE NOT DOING THAT.
OR...
...DO YOU HAVE *PROOF* OF THAT?
!

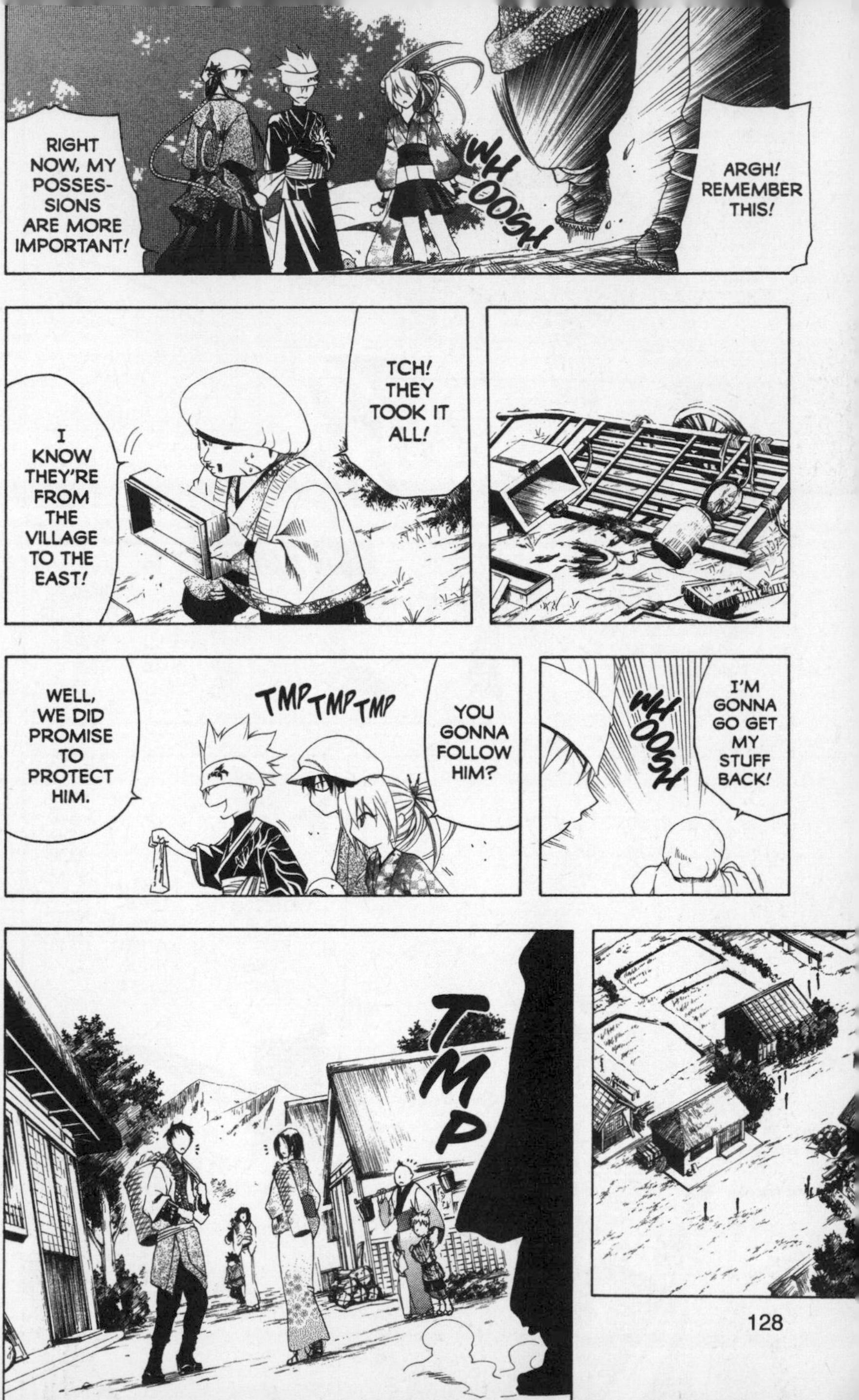
ARGH! REMEMBER THIS!
WHOOSH
RIGHT NOW, MY POSSESSIONS ARE MORE IMPORTANT!
TCH! THEY TOOK IT ALL!
I KNOW THEY'RE FROM THE VILLAGE TO THE EAST!
I'M GONNA GO GET MY STUFF BACK!
WHOOSH
YOU GONNA FOLLOW HIM?
TMP TMP TMP
WELL, WE DID PROMISE TO PROTECT HIM.
TMP
TMP

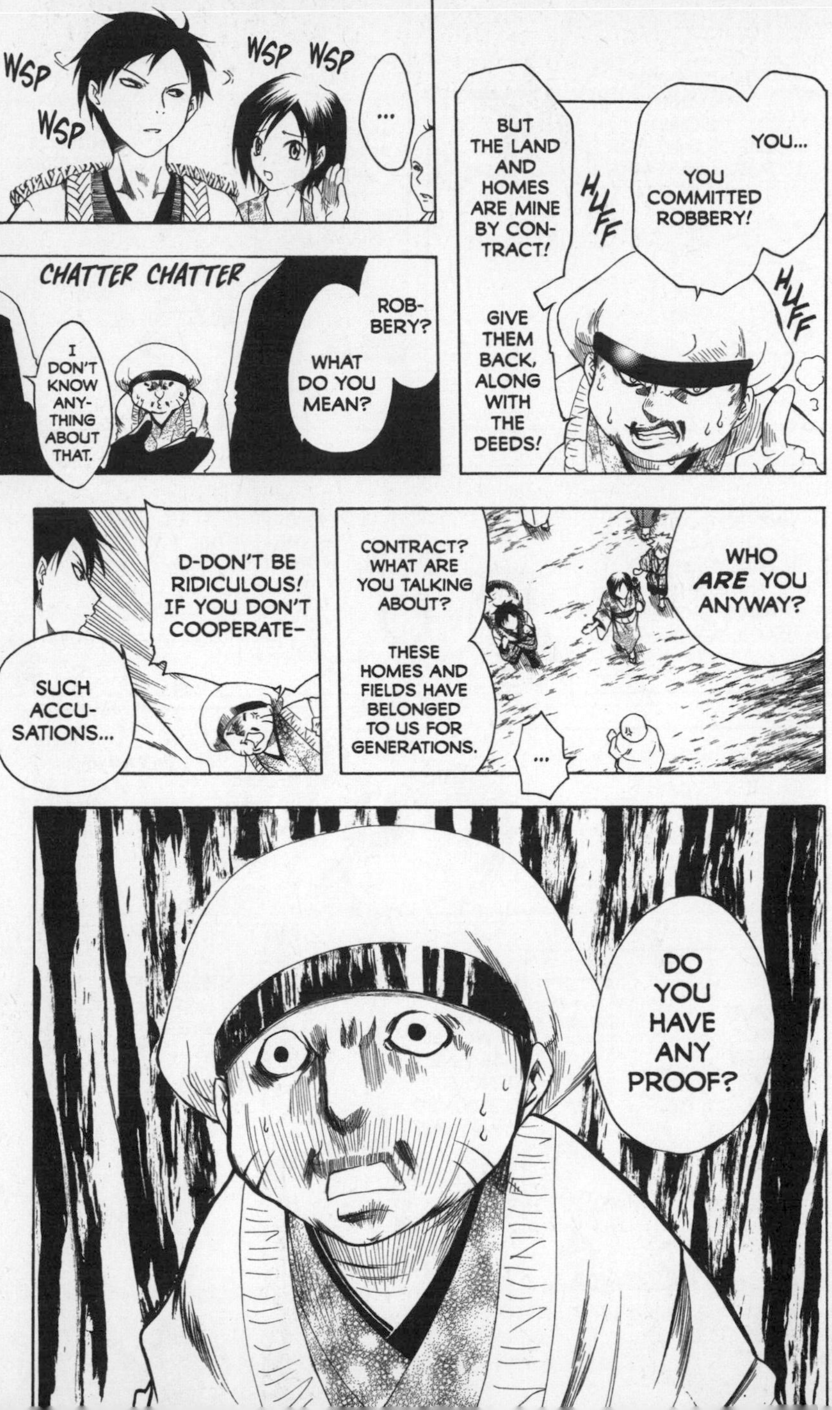
YOU...
YOU COMMITTED ROBBERY!
HUFF
HUFF
BUT THE LAND AND HOMES ARE MINE BY CONTRACT!
GIVE THEM BACK, ALONG WITH THE DEEDS!
WSP WSP
WSP
WSP
...
CHATTER CHATTER
ROBBERY?
WHAT DO YOU MEAN?
I DON'T KNOW ANYTHING ABOUT THAT.
WHO *ARE* YOU ANYWAY?
CONTRACT? WHAT ARE YOU TALKING ABOUT?
THESE HOMES AND FIELDS HAVE BELONGED TO US FOR GENERATIONS.
...
D-DON'T BE RIDICULOUS! IF YOU DON'T COOPERATE–
SUCH ACCUSATIONS...
DO YOU HAVE ANY PROOF?

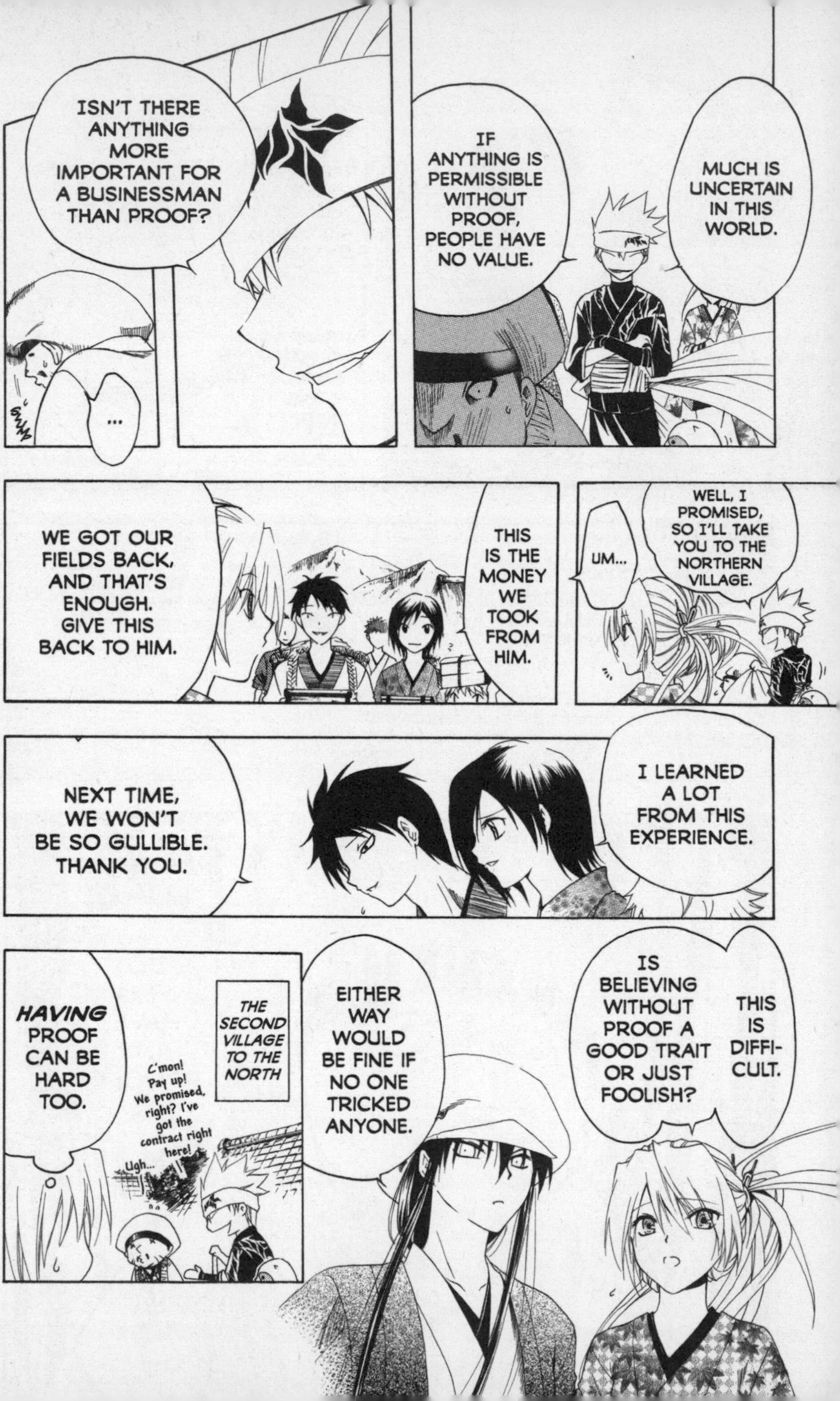
MUCH IS UNCERTAIN IN THIS WORLD.
IF ANYTHING IS PERMISSIBLE WITHOUT PROOF, PEOPLE HAVE NO VALUE.
ISN'T THERE ANYTHING MORE IMPORTANT FOR A BUSINESSMAN THAN PROOF?
...
WELL, I PROMISED, SO I'LL TAKE YOU TO THE NORTHERN VILLAGE.
UM...
THIS IS THE MONEY WE TOOK FROM HIM.
WE GOT OUR FIELDS BACK, AND THAT'S ENOUGH. GIVE THIS BACK TO HIM.
I LEARNED A LOT FROM THIS EXPERIENCE.
NEXT TIME, WE WON'T BE SO GULLIBLE. THANK YOU.
THIS IS DIFFICULT.
IS BELIEVING WITHOUT PROOF A GOOD TRAIT OR JUST FOOLISH?
EITHER WAY WOULD BE FINE IF NO ONE TRICKED ANYONE.
THE SECOND VILLAGE TO THE NORTH
HAVING PROOF CAN BE HARD TOO.
C'mon! Pay up! We promised, right? I've got the contract right here!
Ugh...

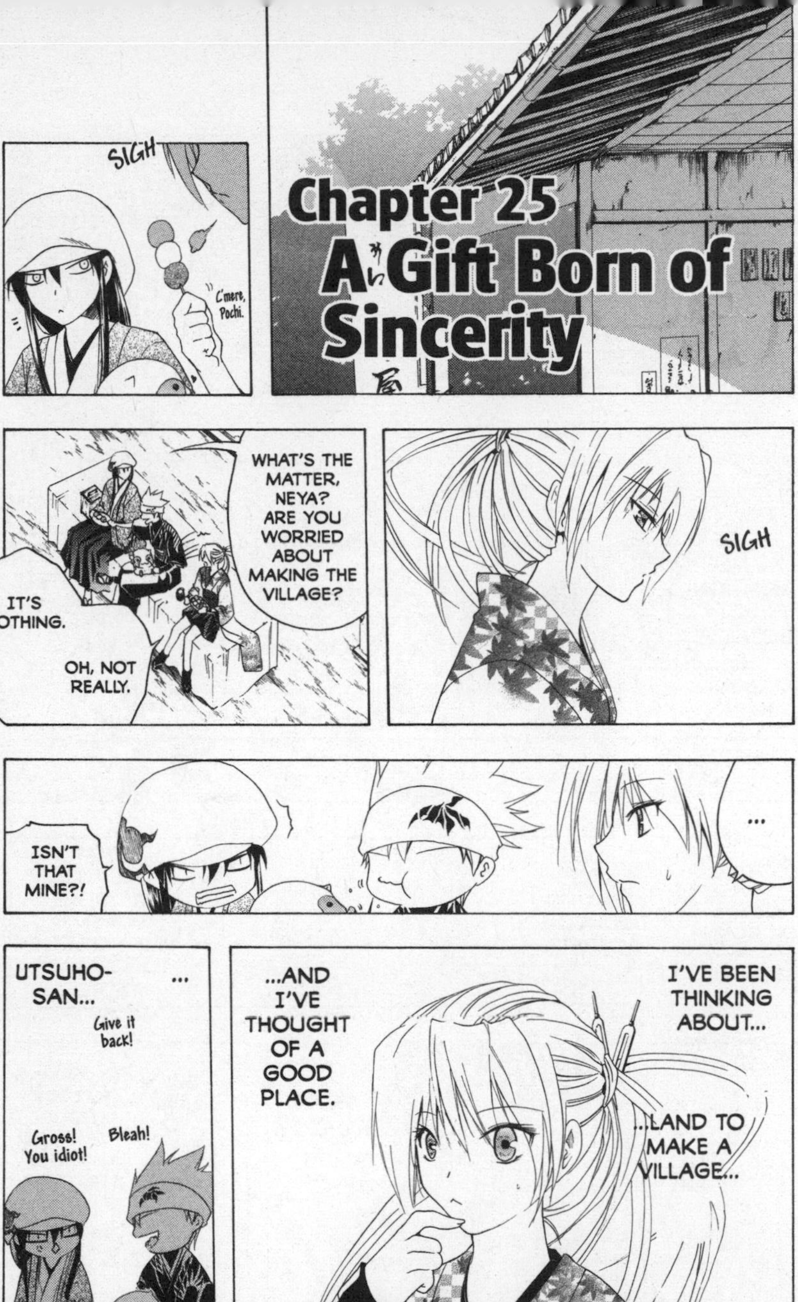
Chapter 25
A Gift Born of Sincerity
SIGH
C'mere, Pochi.
SIGH
WHAT'S THE MATTER, NEYA? ARE YOU WORRIED ABOUT MAKING THE VILLAGE?
IT'S NOTHING.
OH, NOT REALLY.
...
ISN'T THAT MINE?!
I'VE BEEN THINKING ABOUT...
...LAND TO MAKE A VILLAGE...
...AND I'VE THOUGHT OF A GOOD PLACE.
...
UTSUHO-SAN...
Give it back!
Bleah!
Gross! You idiot!

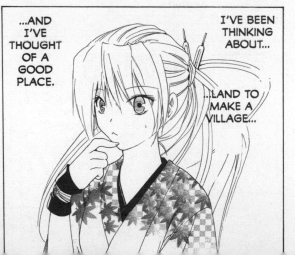

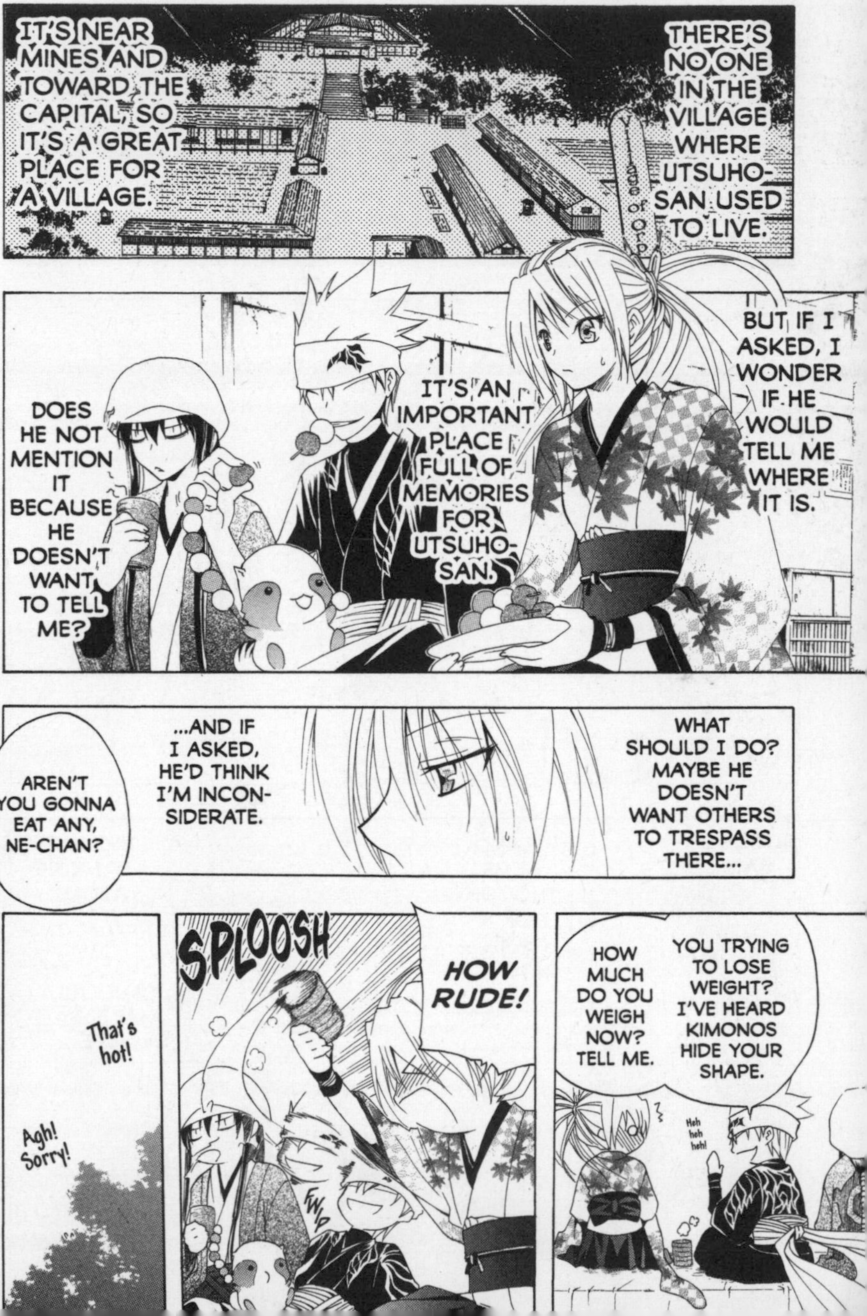
THERE'S NO ONE IN THE VILLAGE WHERE UTSUHO-SAN USED TO LIVE.
IT'S NEAR MINES AND TOWARD THE CAPITAL, SO IT'S A GREAT PLACE FOR A VILLAGE.
BUT IF I ASKED, I WONDER IF HE WOULD TELL ME WHERE IT IS.
IT'S AN IMPORTANT PLACE FULL OF MEMORIES FOR UTSUHO-SAN.
DOES HE NOT MENTION IT BECAUSE HE DOESN'T WANT TO TELL ME?
WHAT SHOULD I DO? MAYBE HE DOESN'T WANT OTHERS TO TRESPASS THERE...
...AND IF I ASKED, HE'D THINK I'M INCONSIDERATE.
AREN'T YOU GONNA EAT ANY, NE-CHAN?
YOU TRYING TO LOSE WEIGHT? I'VE HEARD KIMONOS HIDE YOUR SHAPE.
HOW MUCH DO YOU WEIGH NOW? TELL ME.
Heh heh heh!
HOW RUDE!
SPLOOSH
FWIP
That's hot!
Agh! Sorry!

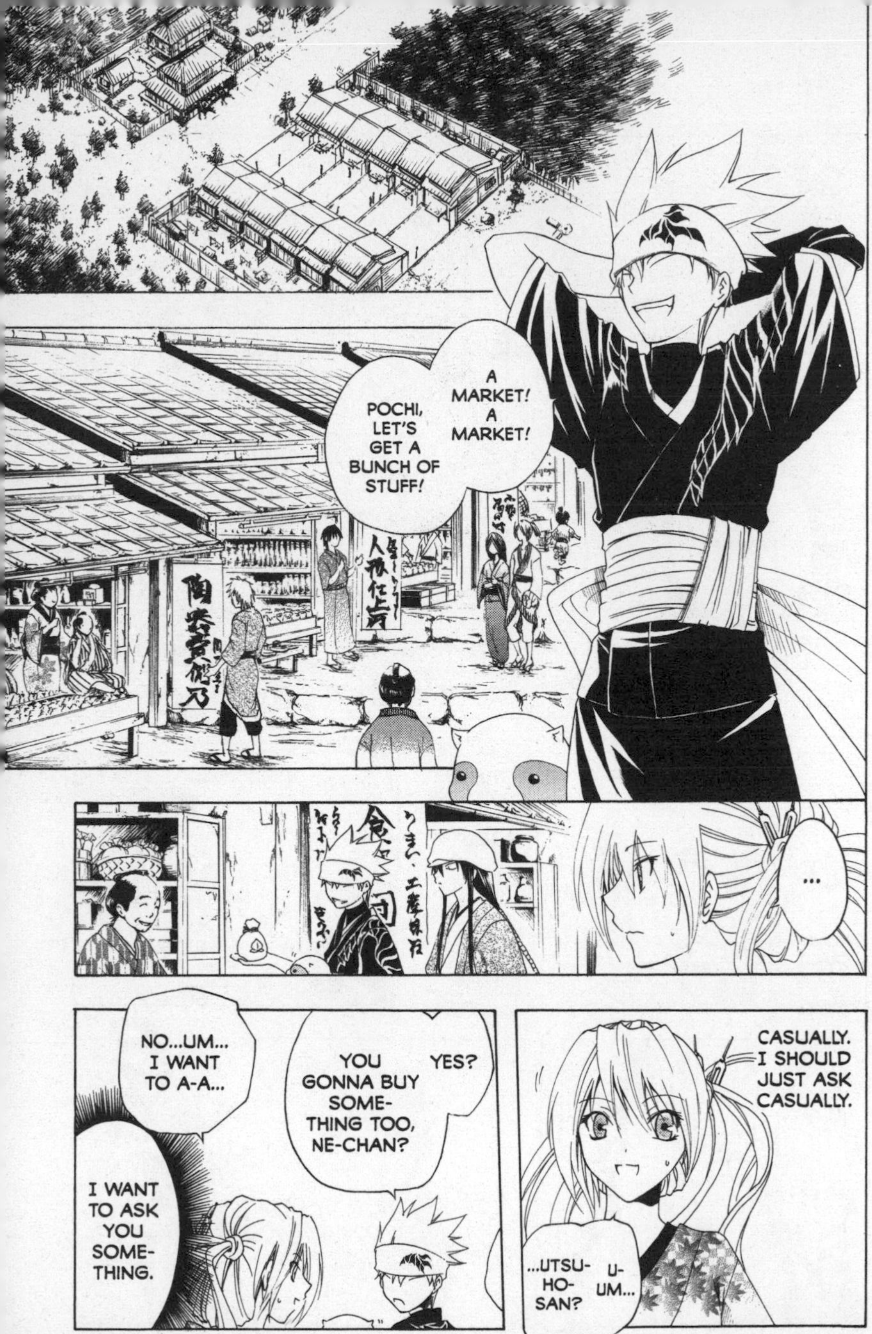
A MARKET! A MARKET!
POCHI, LET'S GET A BUNCH OF STUFF!
...
CASUALLY. I SHOULD JUST ASK CASUALLY.
U-UM...
...UTSU-HO-SAN?
YES?
YOU GONNA BUY SOME-THING TOO, NE-CHAN?
NO...UM... I WANT TO A-A...
I WANT TO ASK YOU SOME-THING.

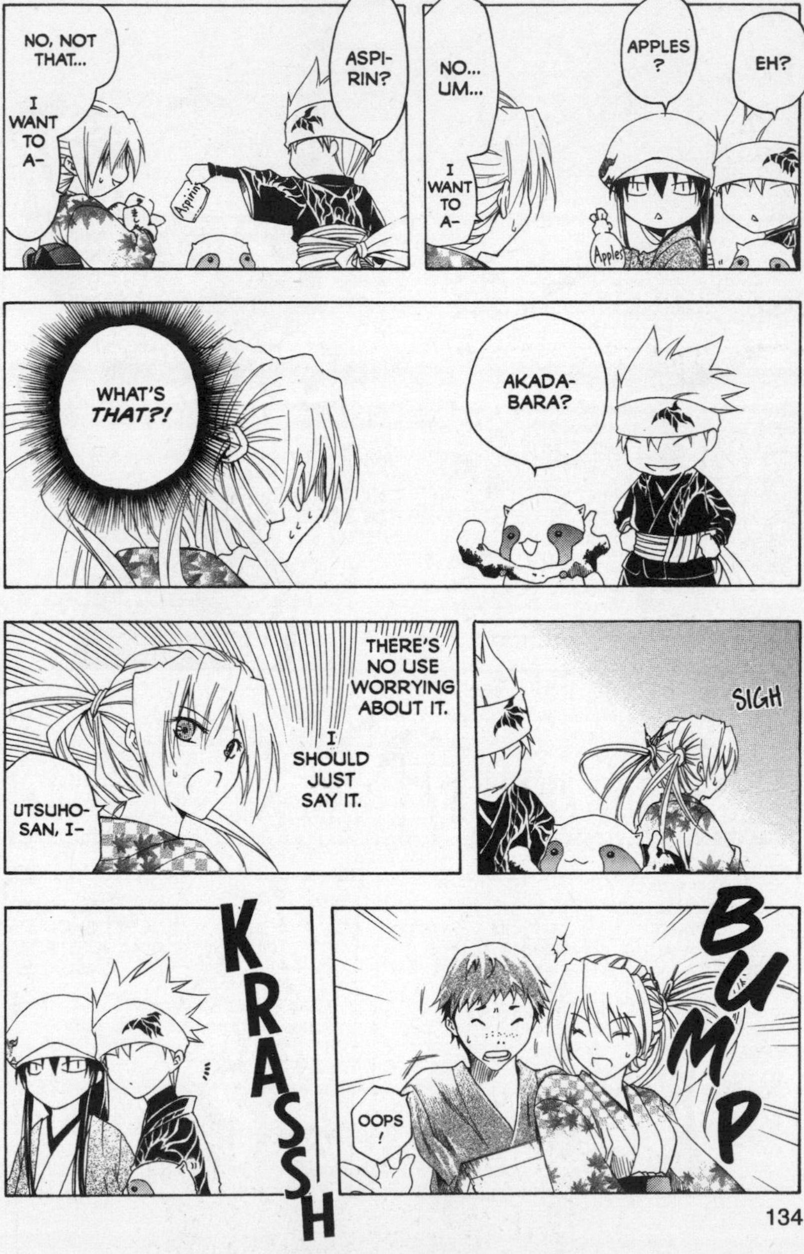
EH?
APPLES ?
Apples
NO... UM...
I WANT TO A-
ASPI-RIN?
Aspirin
NO, NOT THAT...
I WANT TO A-
AKADA-BARA?
WHAT'S *THAT?!*
SIGH
THERE'S NO USE WORRYING ABOUT IT.
I SHOULD JUST SAY IT.
UTSUHO-SAN, I-
BUMP
OOPS !
KRASSH

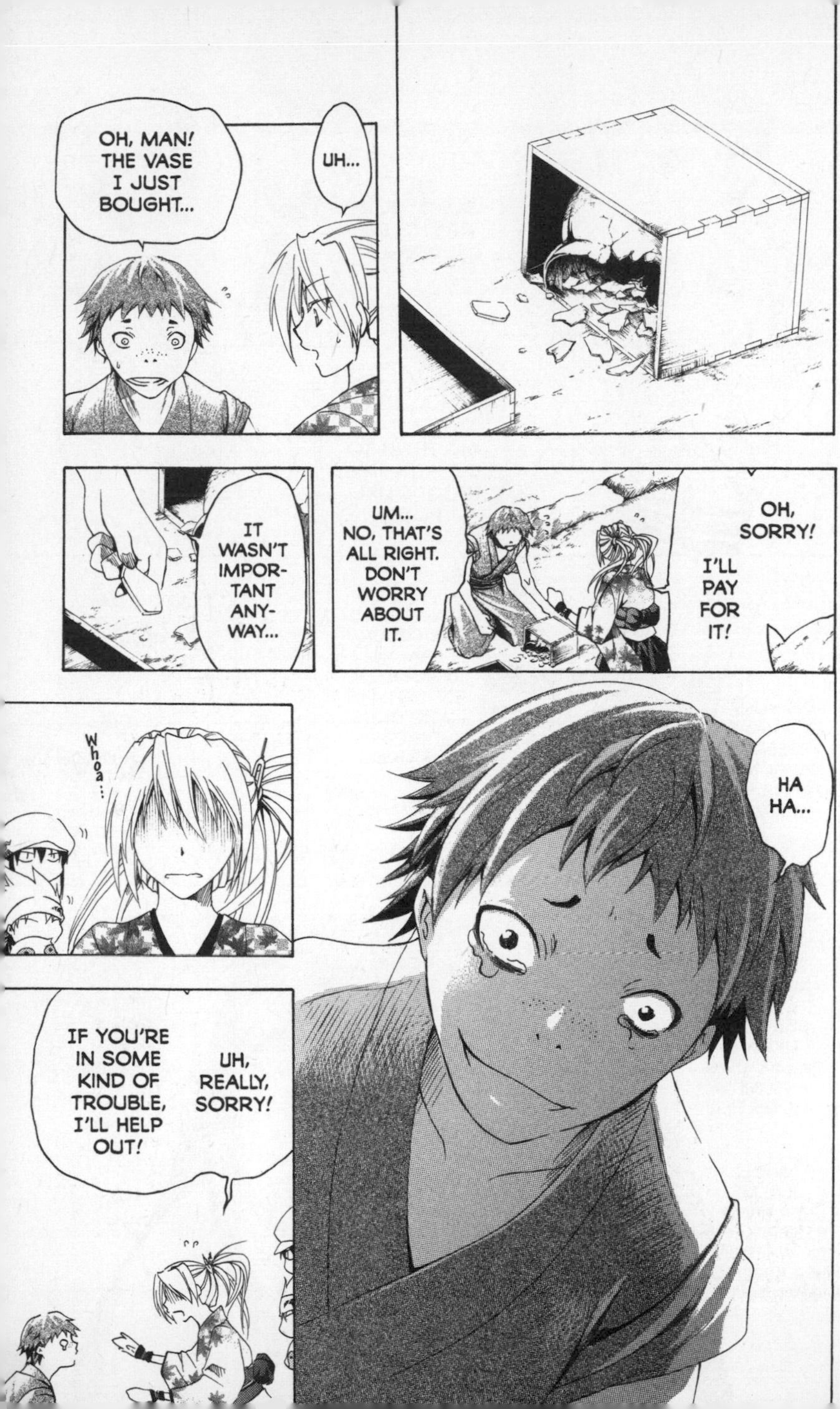
UH...
OH, MAN! THE VASE I JUST BOUGHT...
OH, SORRY! I'LL PAY FOR IT!
UM... NO, THAT'S ALL RIGHT. DON'T WORRY ABOUT IT.
IT WASN'T IMPOR-TANT ANY-WAY...
HA HA...
Whoa...
UH, REALLY, SORRY!
IF YOU'RE IN SOME KIND OF TROUBLE, I'LL HELP OUT!

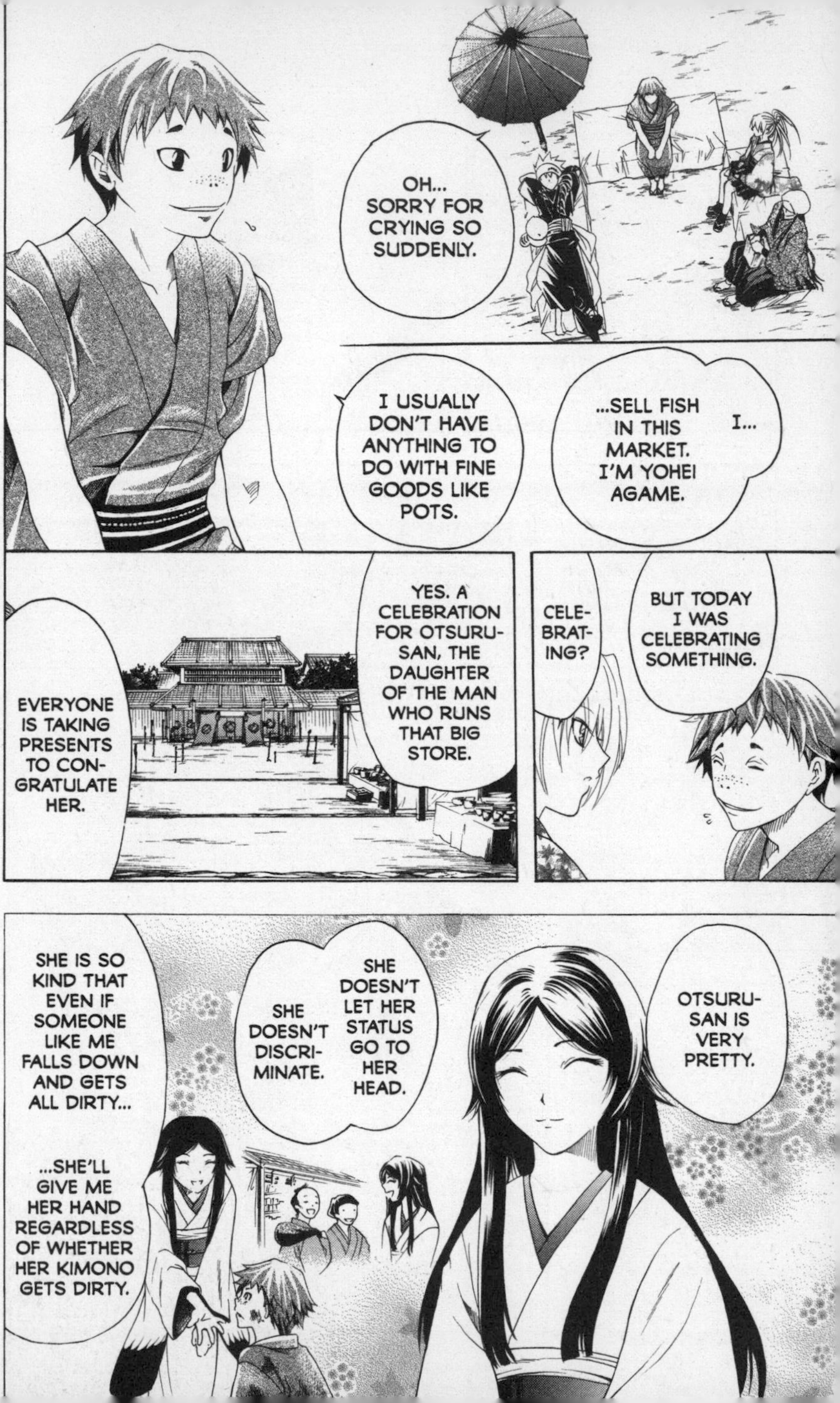
OH... SORRY FOR CRYING SO SUDDENLY.
I...
...SELL FISH IN THIS MARKET. I'M YOHEI AGAME.
I USUALLY DON'T HAVE ANYTHING TO DO WITH FINE GOODS LIKE POTS.
BUT TODAY I WAS CELEBRATING SOMETHING.
CELE-BRAT-ING?
YES. A CELEBRATION FOR OTSURU-SAN, THE DAUGHTER OF THE MAN WHO RUNS THAT BIG STORE.
EVERYONE IS TAKING PRESENTS TO CON-GRATULATE HER.
OTSURU-SAN IS VERY PRETTY.
SHE DOESN'T LET HER STATUS GO TO HER HEAD.
SHE DOESN'T DISCRI-MINATE.
SHE IS SO KIND THAT EVEN IF SOMEONE LIKE ME FALLS DOWN AND GETS ALL DIRTY...
...SHE'LL GIVE ME HER HAND REGARDLESS OF WHETHER HER KIMONO GETS DIRTY.

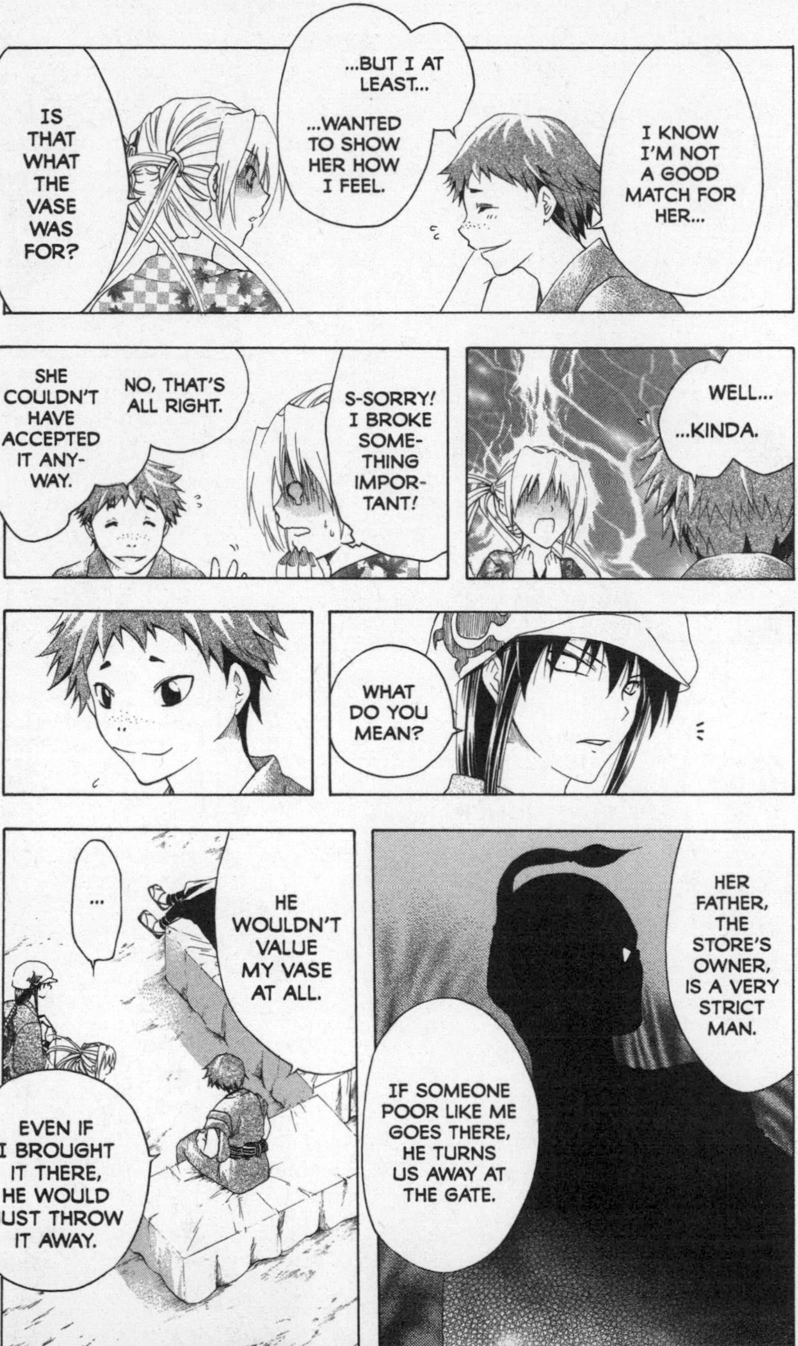
I KNOW I'M NOT A GOOD MATCH FOR HER...
...BUT I AT LEAST...
...WANTED TO SHOW HER HOW I FEEL.
IS THAT WHAT THE VASE WAS FOR?
WELL...
...KINDA.
S-SORRY! I BROKE SOMETHING IMPORTANT!
NO, THAT'S ALL RIGHT.
SHE COULDN'T HAVE ACCEPTED IT ANYWAY.
WHAT DO YOU MEAN?
HER FATHER, THE STORE'S OWNER, IS A VERY STRICT MAN.
IF SOMEONE POOR LIKE ME GOES THERE, HE TURNS US AWAY AT THE GATE.
HE WOULDN'T VALUE MY VASE AT ALL.
...
EVEN IF I BROUGHT IT THERE, HE WOULD JUST THROW IT AWAY.

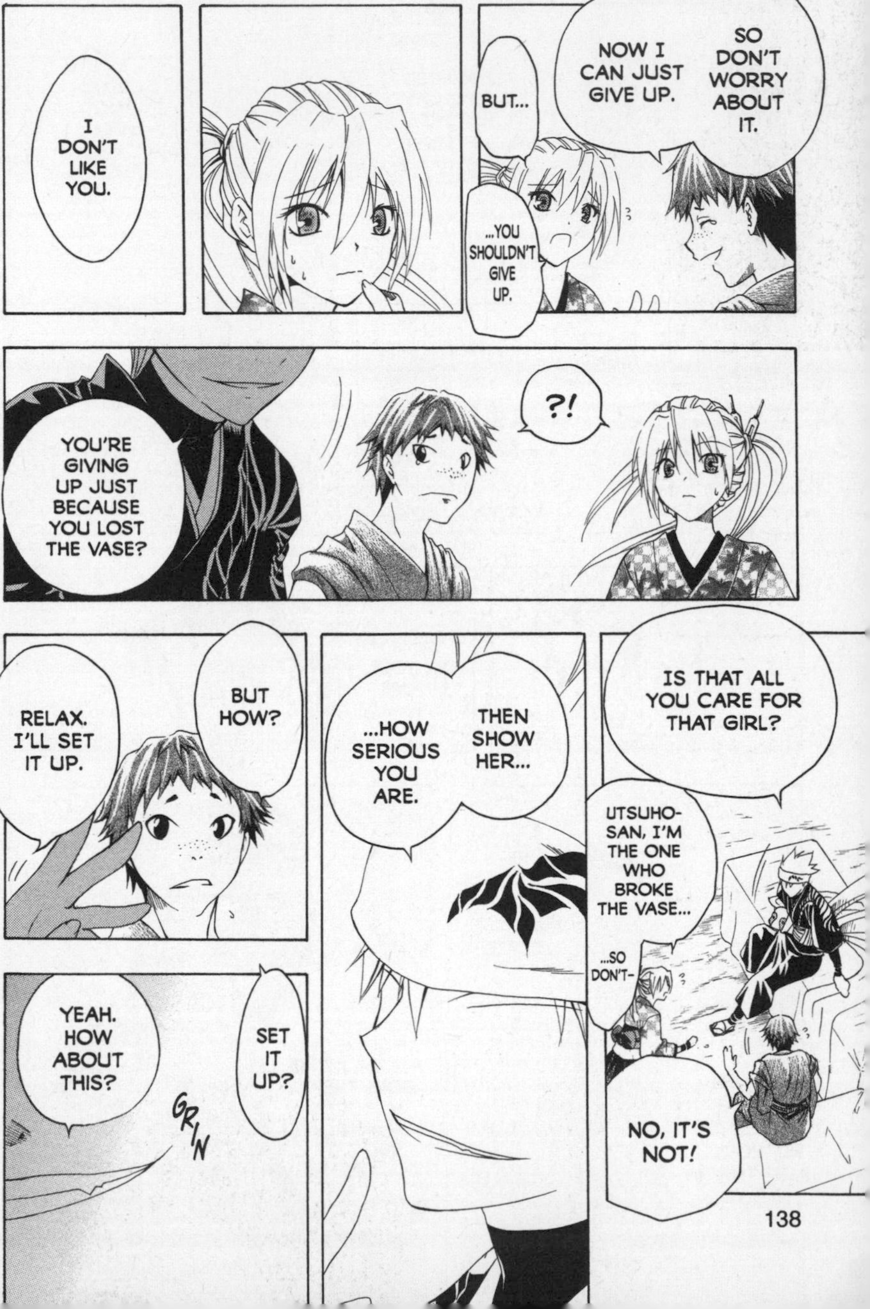
NOW I CAN JUST GIVE UP. SO DON'T WORRY ABOUT IT.
BUT...
...YOU SHOULDN'T GIVE UP.
I DON'T LIKE YOU.
?!
YOU'RE GIVING UP JUST BECAUSE YOU LOST THE VASE?
IS THAT ALL YOU CARE FOR THAT GIRL?
UTSUHO-SAN, I'M THE ONE WHO BROKE THE VASE...
...SO DON'T-
NO, IT'S NOT!
THEN SHOW HER... ...HOW SERIOUS YOU ARE.
BUT HOW?
RELAX. I'LL SET IT UP.
SET IT UP?
YEAH. HOW ABOUT THIS?
GRIN

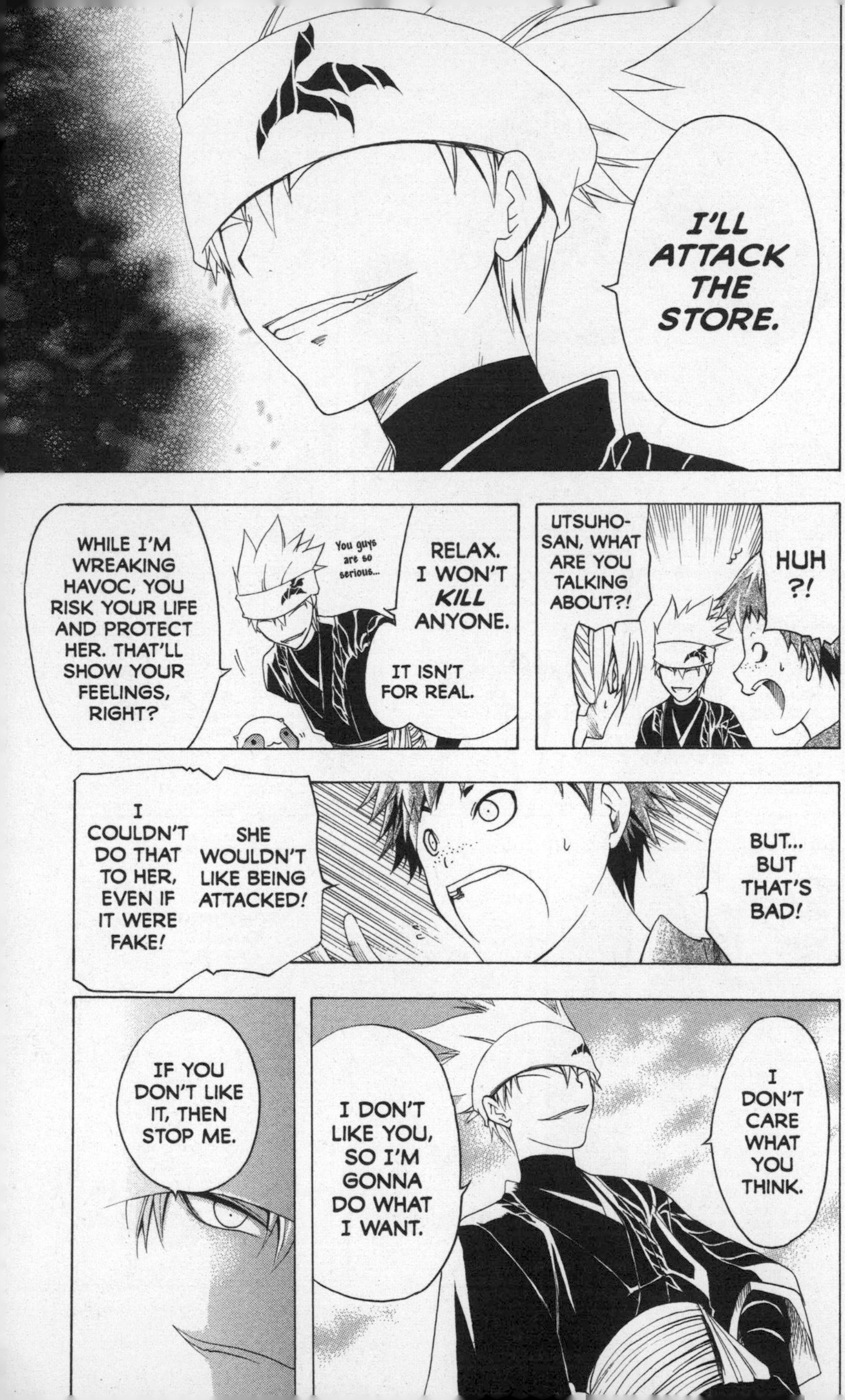
I'LL ATTACK THE STORE.
HUH ?!
UTSUHO-SAN, WHAT ARE YOU TALKING ABOUT?!
RELAX. I WON'T *KILL* ANYONE.
You guys are so serious...
IT ISN'T FOR REAL.
WHILE I'M WREAKING HAVOC, YOU RISK YOUR LIFE AND PROTECT HER. THAT'LL SHOW YOUR FEELINGS, RIGHT?
BUT... BUT THAT'S BAD!
SHE WOULDN'T LIKE BEING ATTACKED!
I COULDN'T DO THAT TO HER, EVEN IF IT WERE FAKE!
I DON'T CARE WHAT YOU THINK.
I DON'T LIKE YOU, SO I'M GONNA DO WHAT I WANT.
IF YOU DON'T LIKE IT, THEN STOP ME.

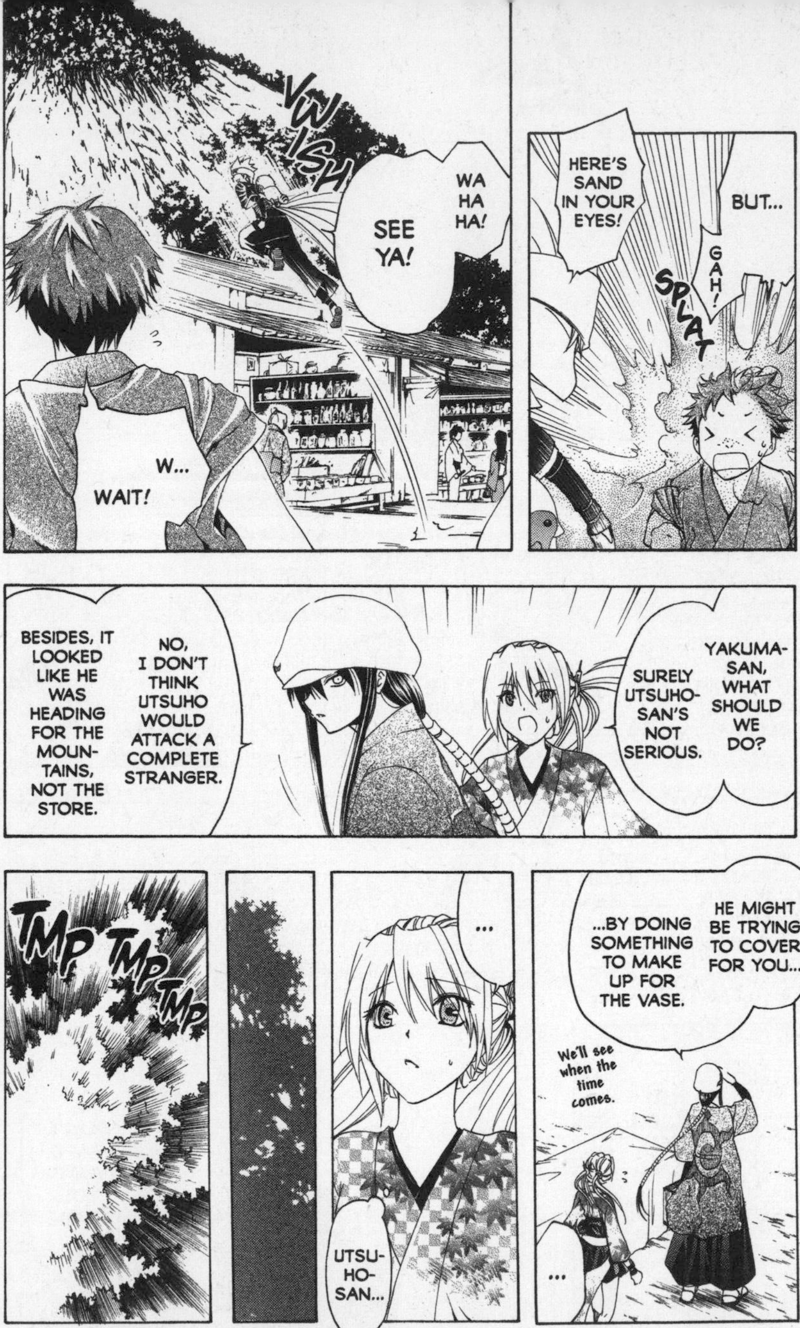
BUT...
HERE'S SAND IN YOUR EYES!
GAH!
SPLAT
VWISH
WA HA HA!
SEE YA!
W...
WAIT!
YAKUMA-SAN, WHAT SHOULD WE DO?
SURELY UTSUHO-SAN'S NOT SERIOUS.
NO, I DON'T THINK UTSUHO WOULD ATTACK A COMPLETE STRANGER.
BESIDES, IT LOOKED LIKE HE WAS HEADING FOR THE MOUNTAINS, NOT THE STORE.
HE MIGHT BE TRYING TO COVER FOR YOU...
...BY DOING SOMETHING TO MAKE UP FOR THE VASE.
We'll see when the time comes.
...
...
UTSUHO-SAN...
TMP TMP TMP

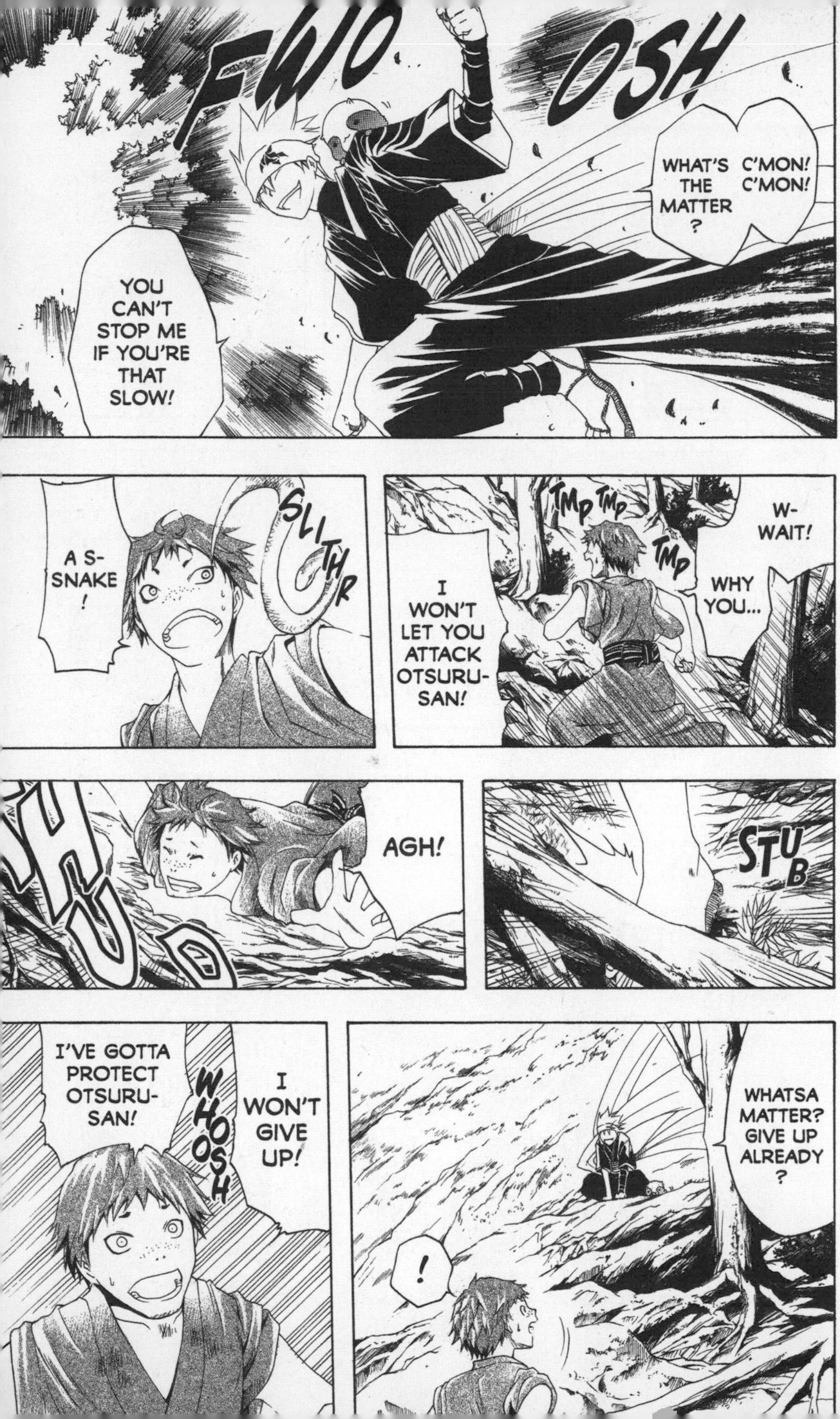
FWOOSH
WHAT'S THE MATTER? C'MON! C'MON!
YOU CAN'T STOP ME IF YOU'RE THAT SLOW!
W-WAIT!
WHY YOU...
TMP TMP TMP
I WON'T LET YOU ATTACK OTSURU-SAN!
SLITHR
A S-SNAKE!
STUB
AGH!
WHATSA MATTER? GIVE UP ALREADY?
!
I WON'T GIVE UP!
WHOOSH
I'VE GOTTA PROTECT OTSURU-SAN!

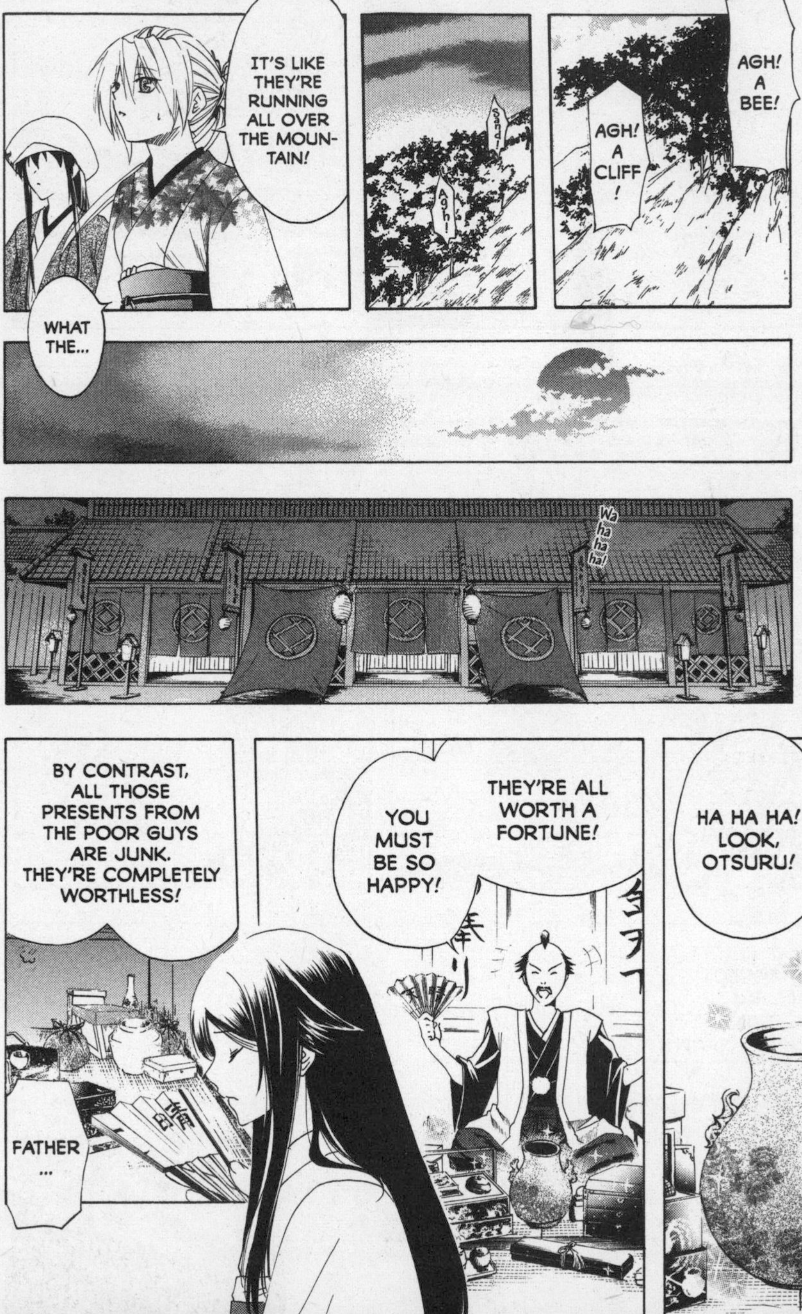
AGH! A BEE!
AGH! A CLIFF!
Sand!
Agh!
IT'S LIKE THEY'RE RUNNING ALL OVER THE MOUN-TAIN!
WHAT THE...
Wa ha ha ha!
HA HA HA! LOOK, OTSURU!
THEY'RE ALL WORTH A FORTUNE!
YOU MUST BE SO HAPPY!
BY CONTRAST, ALL THOSE PRESENTS FROM THE POOR GUYS ARE JUNK. THEY'RE COMPLETELY WORTHLESS!
FATHER ...

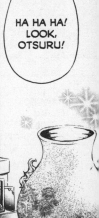

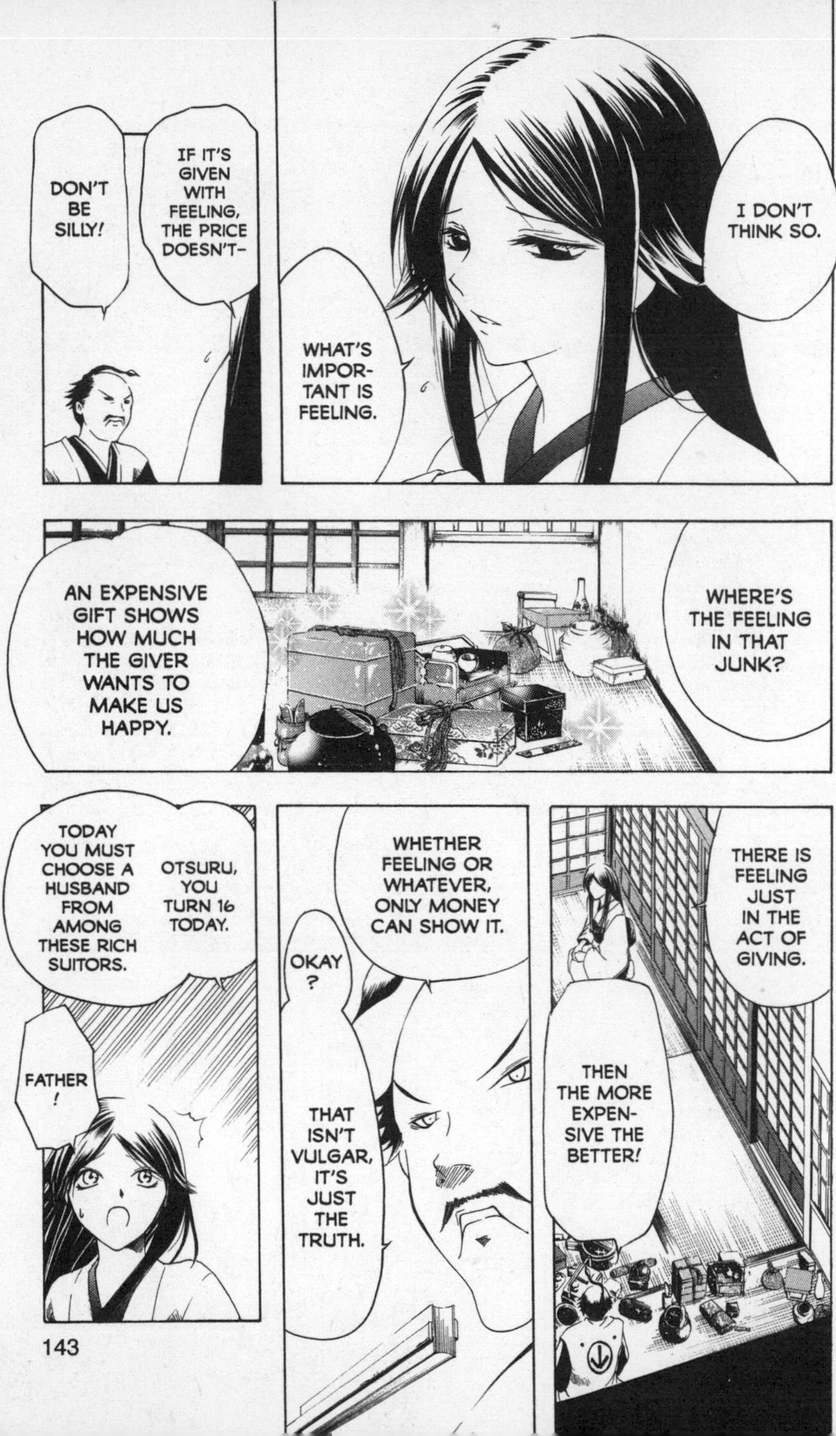
I DON'T THINK SO.
WHAT'S IMPOR-TANT IS FEELING.
IF IT'S GIVEN WITH FEELING, THE PRICE DOESN'T-
DON'T BE SILLY!
WHERE'S THE FEELING IN THAT JUNK?
AN EXPENSIVE GIFT SHOWS HOW MUCH THE GIVER WANTS TO MAKE US HAPPY.
THERE IS FEELING JUST IN THE ACT OF GIVING.
THEN THE MORE EXPEN-SIVE THE BETTER!
WHETHER FEELING OR WHATEVER, ONLY MONEY CAN SHOW IT.
OKAY?
THAT ISN'T VULGAR, IT'S JUST THE TRUTH.
OTSURU, YOU TURN 16 TODAY.
TODAY YOU MUST CHOOSE A HUSBAND FROM AMONG THESE RICH SUITORS.
FATHER!

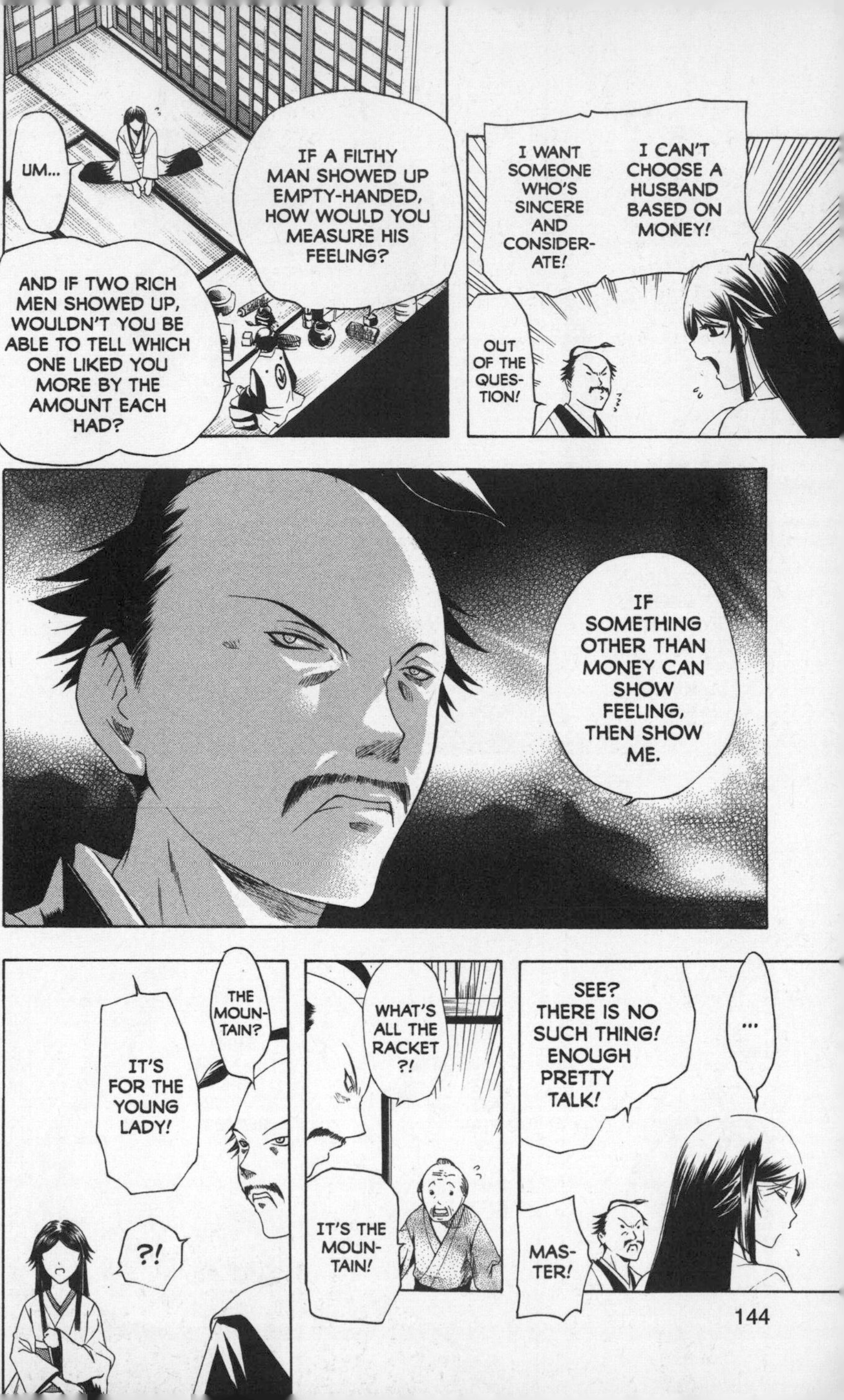
I CAN'T CHOOSE A HUSBAND BASED ON MONEY!
I WANT SOMEONE WHO'S SINCERE AND CONSIDER-ATE!
OUT OF THE QUES-TION!
IF A FILTHY MAN SHOWED UP EMPTY-HANDED, HOW WOULD YOU MEASURE HIS FEELING?
UM...
AND IF TWO RICH MEN SHOWED UP, WOULDN'T YOU BE ABLE TO TELL WHICH ONE LIKED YOU MORE BY THE AMOUNT EACH HAD?
IF SOMETHING OTHER THAN MONEY CAN SHOW FEELING, THEN SHOW ME.
...
SEE? THERE IS NO SUCH THING! ENOUGH PRETTY TALK!
MAS-TER!
WHAT'S ALL THE RACKET ?!
IT'S THE MOUN-TAIN!
THE MOUN-TAIN?
IT'S FOR THE YOUNG LADY!
?!

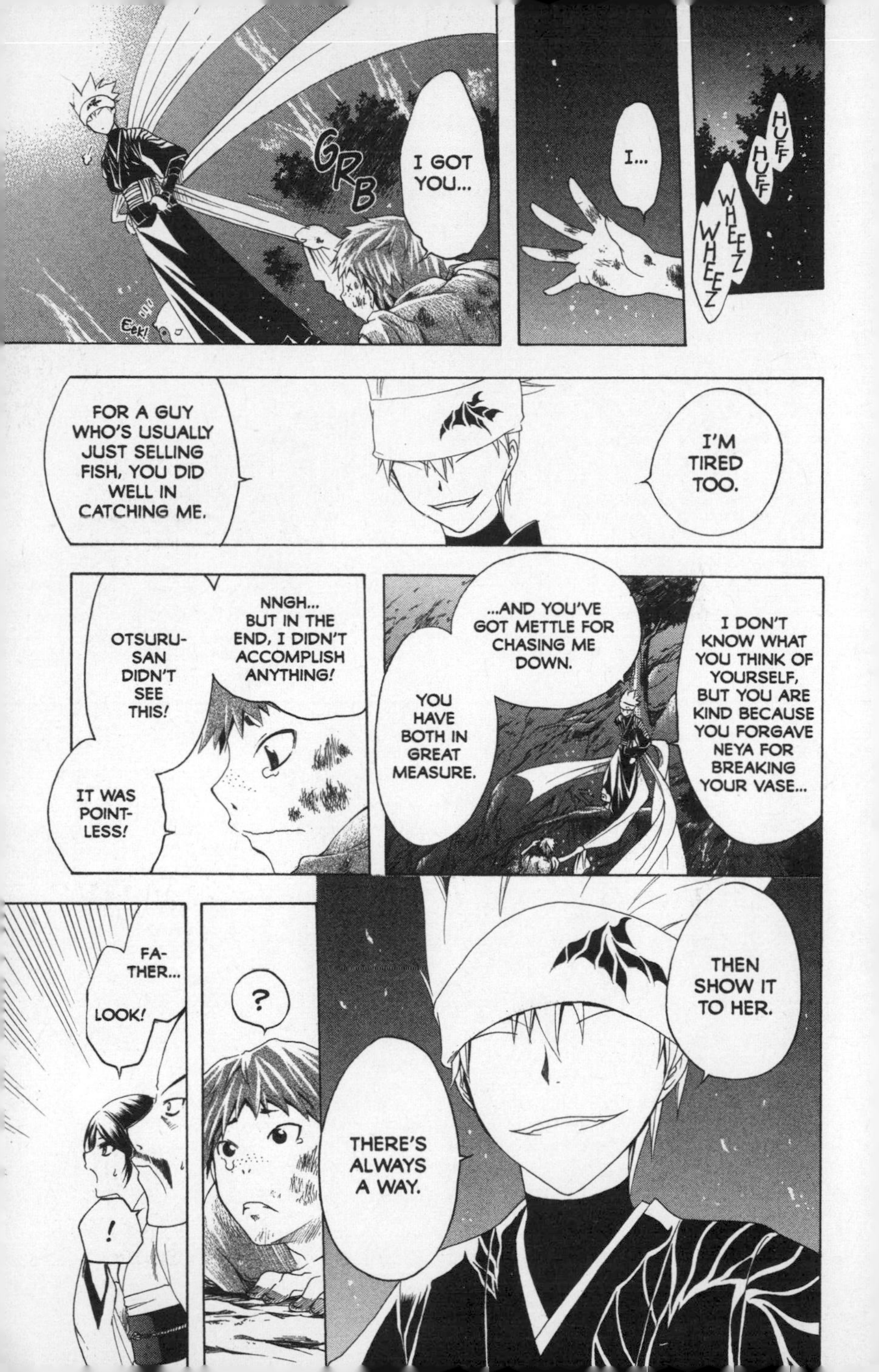
HUFF HUFF
WHEEZ WHEEZ
I...
I GOT YOU...
GRB
Eek!
I'M TIRED TOO.
FOR A GUY WHO'S USUALLY JUST SELLING FISH, YOU DID WELL IN CATCHING ME.
I DON'T KNOW WHAT YOU THINK OF YOURSELF, BUT YOU ARE KIND BECAUSE YOU FORGAVE NEYA FOR BREAKING YOUR VASE...
...AND YOU'VE GOT METTLE FOR CHASING ME DOWN.
YOU HAVE BOTH IN GREAT MEASURE.
NNGH... BUT IN THE END, I DIDN'T ACCOMPLISH ANYTHING!
OTSURU-SAN DIDN'T SEE THIS!
IT WAS POINT-LESS!
THEN SHOW IT TO HER.
THERE'S ALWAYS A WAY.
?
FA-THER...
LOOK!
!

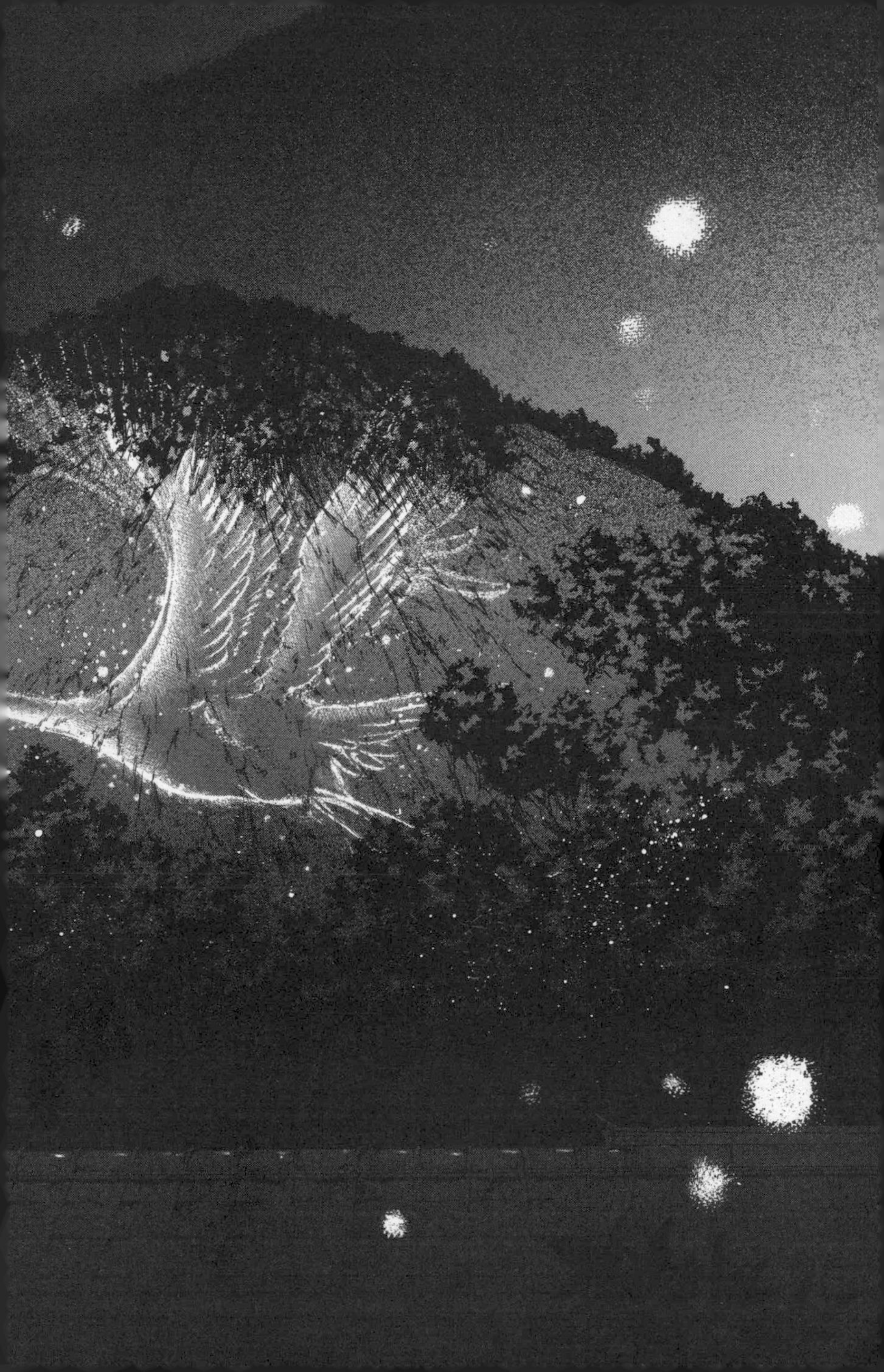

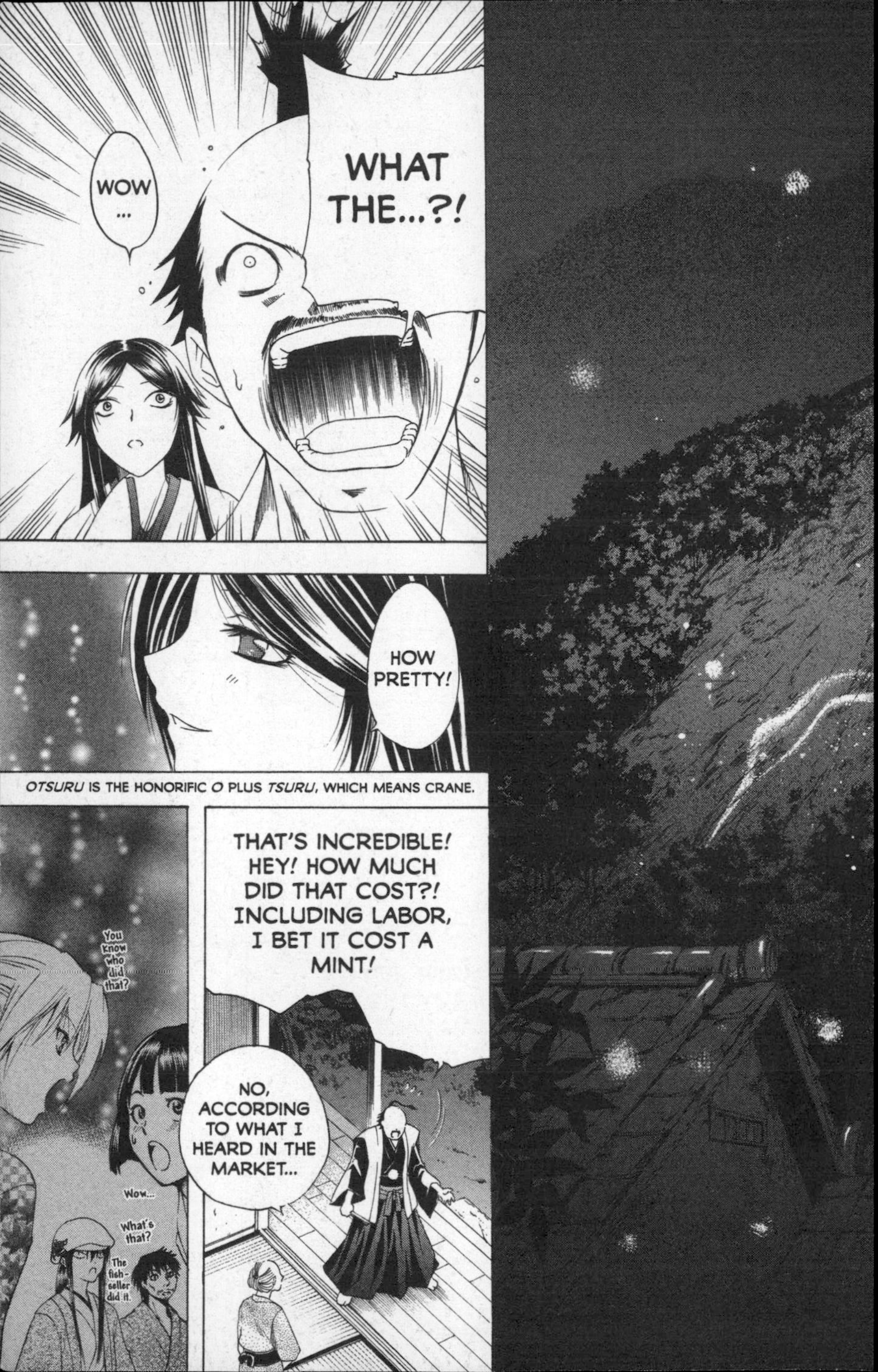
WHAT THE...?!
WOW ...
HOW PRETTY!
OTSURU IS THE HONORIFIC O PLUS TSURU, WHICH MEANS CRANE.
THAT'S INCREDIBLE! HEY! HOW MUCH DID THAT COST?! INCLUDING LABOR, I BET IT COST A MINT!
NO, ACCORDING TO WHAT I HEARD IN THE MARKET...
You know who did that?
Wow...
What's that?
The fish-seller did it.

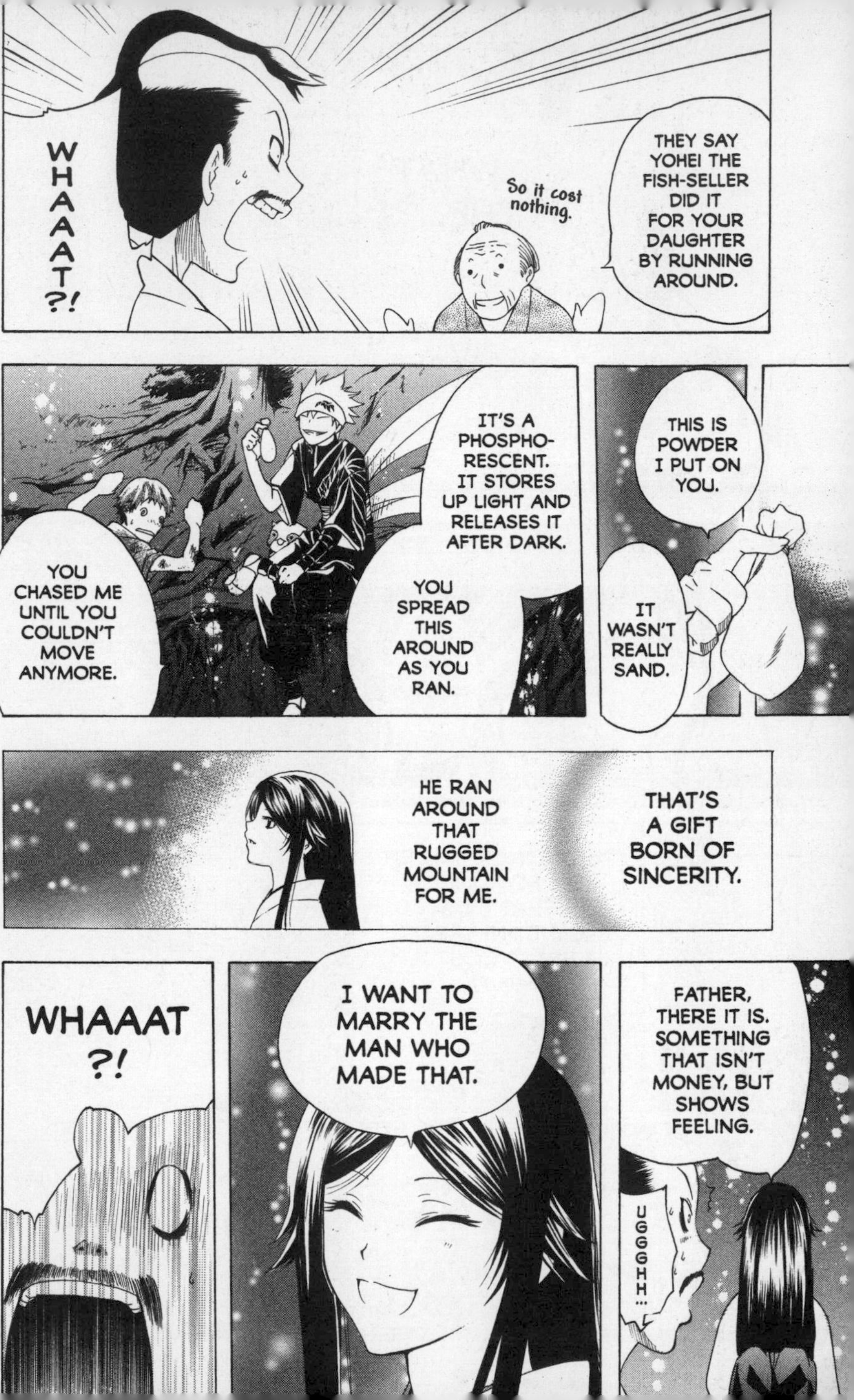
THEY SAY YOHEI THE FISH-SELLER DID IT FOR YOUR DAUGHTER BY RUNNING AROUND.
So it cost nothing.
WHAAAT?!
THIS IS POWDER I PUT ON YOU.
IT WASN'T REALLY SAND.
IT'S A PHOSPHO-RESCENT. IT STORES UP LIGHT AND RELEASES IT AFTER DARK.
YOU SPREAD THIS AROUND AS YOU RAN.
YOU CHASED ME UNTIL YOU COULDN'T MOVE ANYMORE.
THAT'S A GIFT BORN OF SINCERITY.
HE RAN AROUND THAT RUGGED MOUNTAIN FOR ME.
FATHER, THERE IT IS. SOMETHING THAT ISN'T MONEY, BUT SHOWS FEELING.
UGGGH...
I WANT TO MARRY THE MAN WHO MADE THAT.
WHAAAT?!

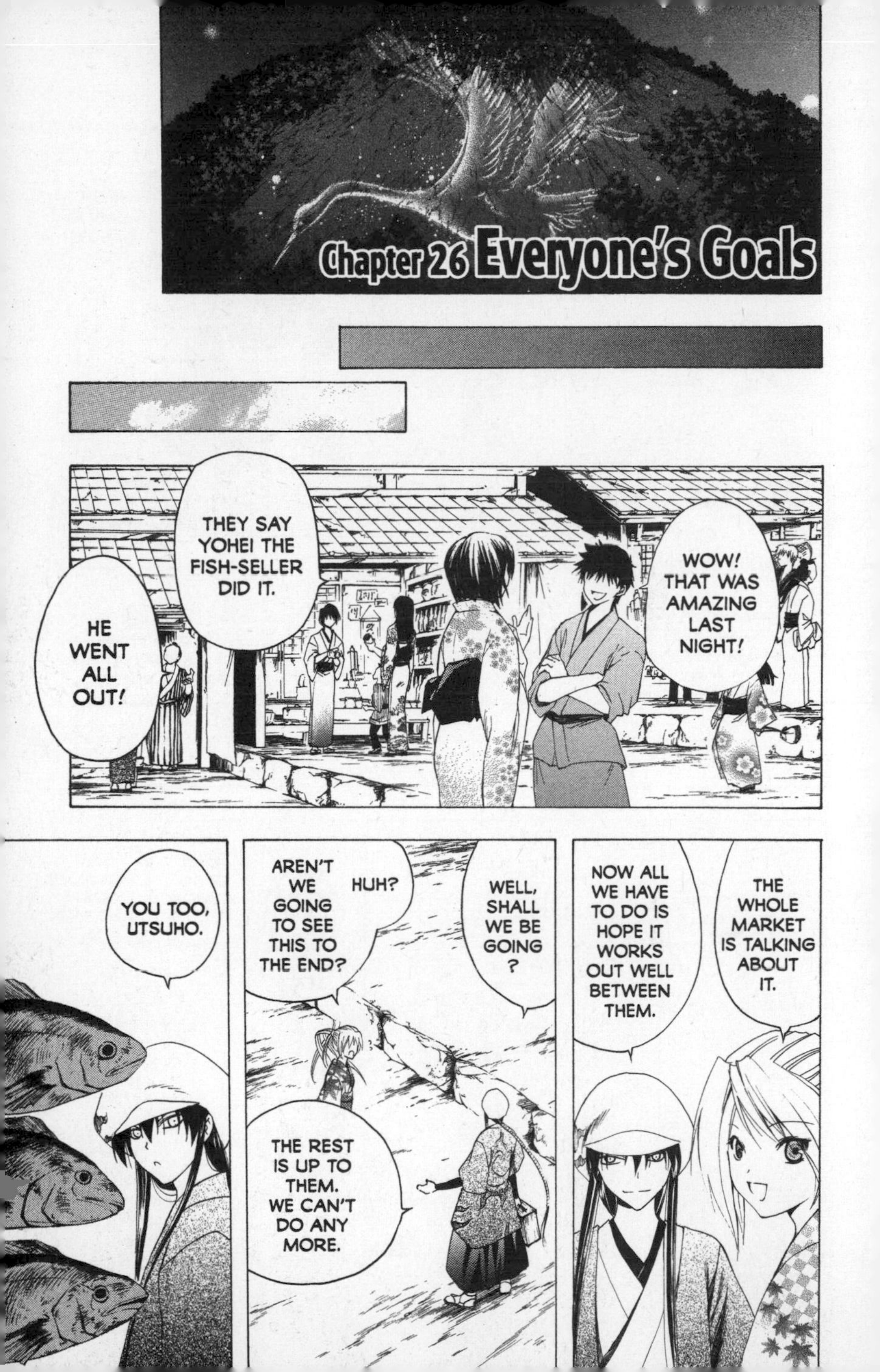
Chapter 26 Everyone's Goals
WOW! THAT WAS AMAZING LAST NIGHT!
THEY SAY YOHEI THE FISH-SELLER DID IT.
HE WENT ALL OUT!
THE WHOLE MARKET IS TALKING ABOUT IT.
NOW ALL WE HAVE TO DO IS HOPE IT WORKS OUT WELL BETWEEN THEM.
WELL, SHALL WE BE GOING?
HUH?
AREN'T WE GOING TO SEE THIS TO THE END?
THE REST IS UP TO THEM. WE CAN'T DO ANY MORE.
YOU TOO, UTSUHO.

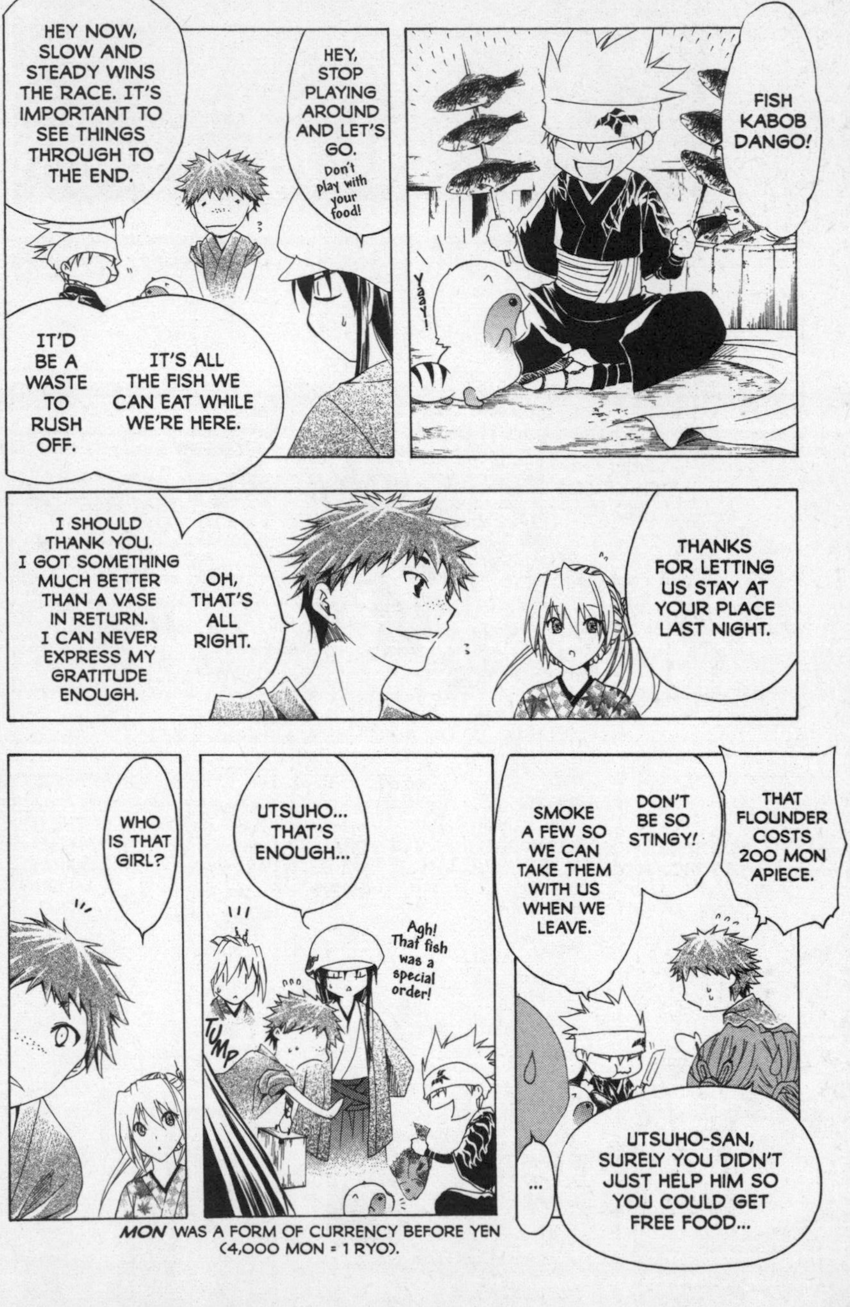
FISH KABOB DANGO!
Yaaay!
HEY, STOP PLAYING AROUND AND LET'S GO.
Don't play with your food!
HEY NOW, SLOW AND STEADY WINS THE RACE. IT'S IMPORTANT TO SEE THINGS THROUGH TO THE END.
IT'S ALL THE FISH WE CAN EAT WHILE WE'RE HERE.
IT'D BE A WASTE TO RUSH OFF.
THANKS FOR LETTING US STAY AT YOUR PLACE LAST NIGHT.
OH, THAT'S ALL RIGHT.
I SHOULD THANK YOU. I GOT SOMETHING MUCH BETTER THAN A VASE IN RETURN. I CAN NEVER EXPRESS MY GRATITUDE ENOUGH.
THAT FLOUNDER COSTS 200 MON APIECE.
DON'T BE SO STINGY!
SMOKE A FEW SO WE CAN TAKE THEM WITH US WHEN WE LEAVE.
UTSUHO-SAN, SURELY YOU DIDN'T JUST HELP HIM SO YOU COULD GET FREE FOOD...
...
UTSUHO... THAT'S ENOUGH...
Agh! That fish was a special order!
TUMP
WHO IS THAT GIRL?

MON WAS A FORM OF CURRENCY BEFORE YEN (4,000 MON = 1 RYO).

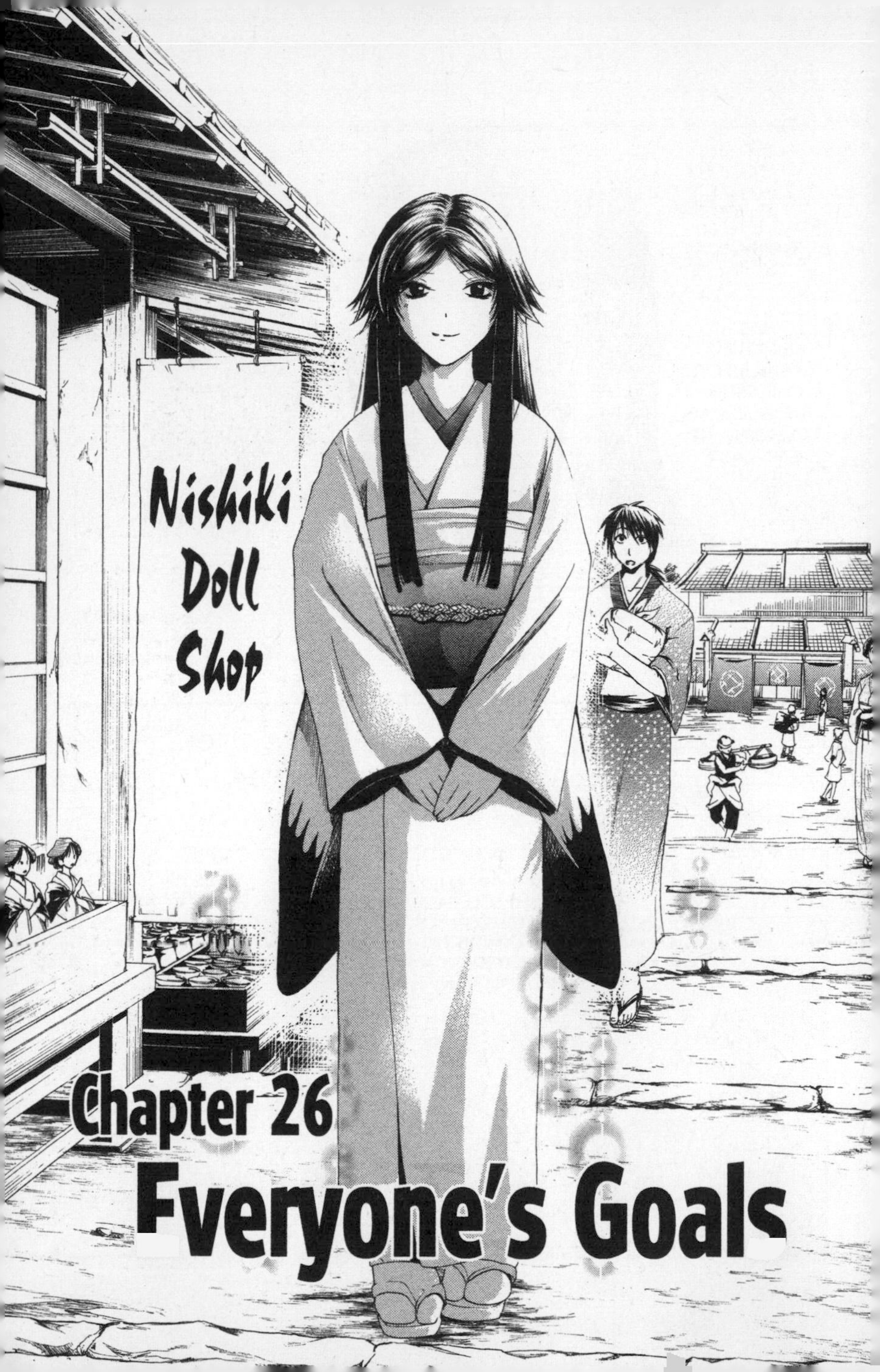
Nishiki Doll Shop
Chapter 26
Everyone's Goals

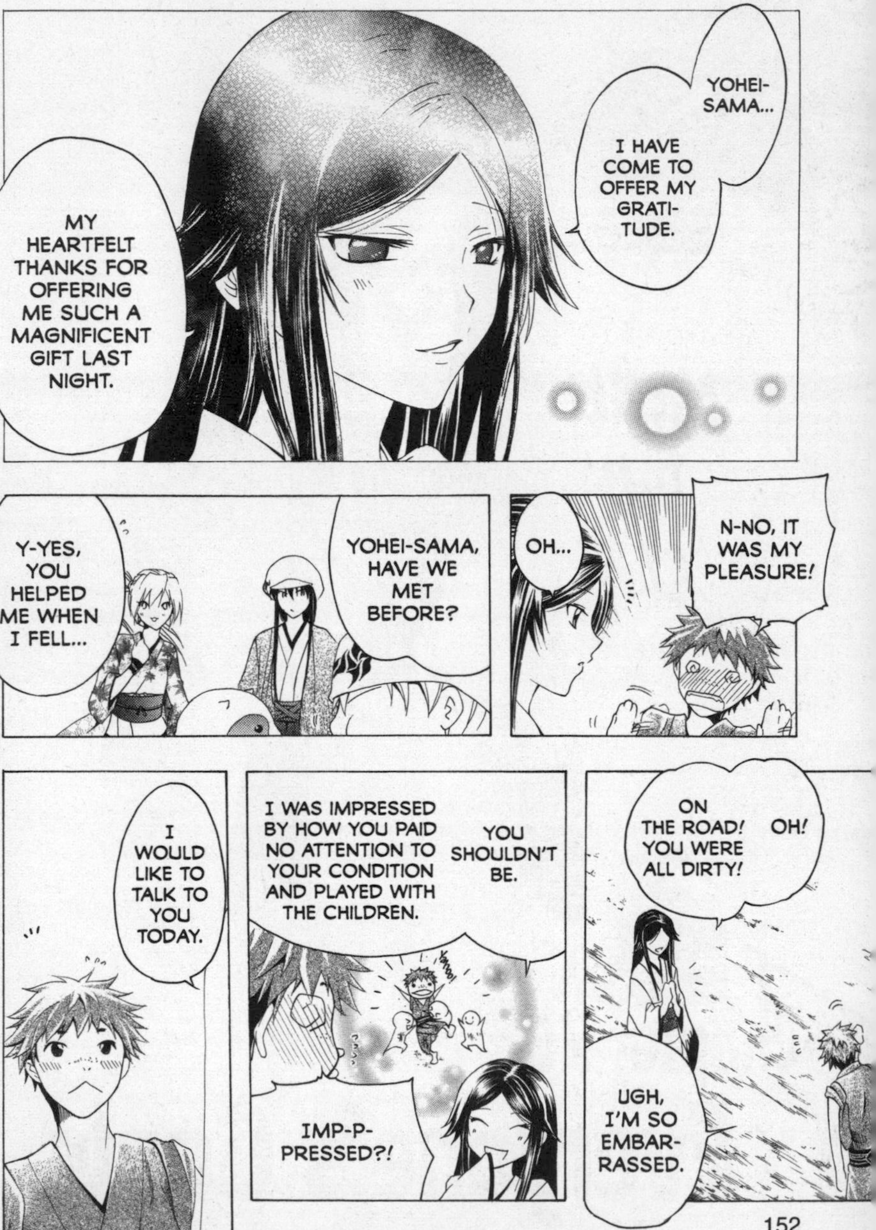
YOHEI-SAMA...
I HAVE COME TO OFFER MY GRATITUDE.
MY HEARTFELT THANKS FOR OFFERING ME SUCH A MAGNIFICENT GIFT LAST NIGHT.
N-NO, IT WAS MY PLEASURE!
OH...
YOHEI-SAMA, HAVE WE MET BEFORE?
Y-YES, YOU HELPED ME WHEN I FELL...
OH!
ON THE ROAD! YOU WERE ALL DIRTY!
UGH, I'M SO EMBARRASSED.
YOU SHOULDN'T BE.
I WAS IMPRESSED BY HOW YOU PAID NO ATTENTION TO YOUR CONDITION AND PLAYED WITH THE CHILDREN.
IMP-P-PRESSED?!
I WOULD LIKE TO TALK TO YOU TODAY.

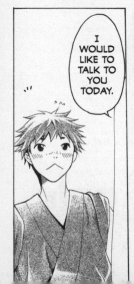

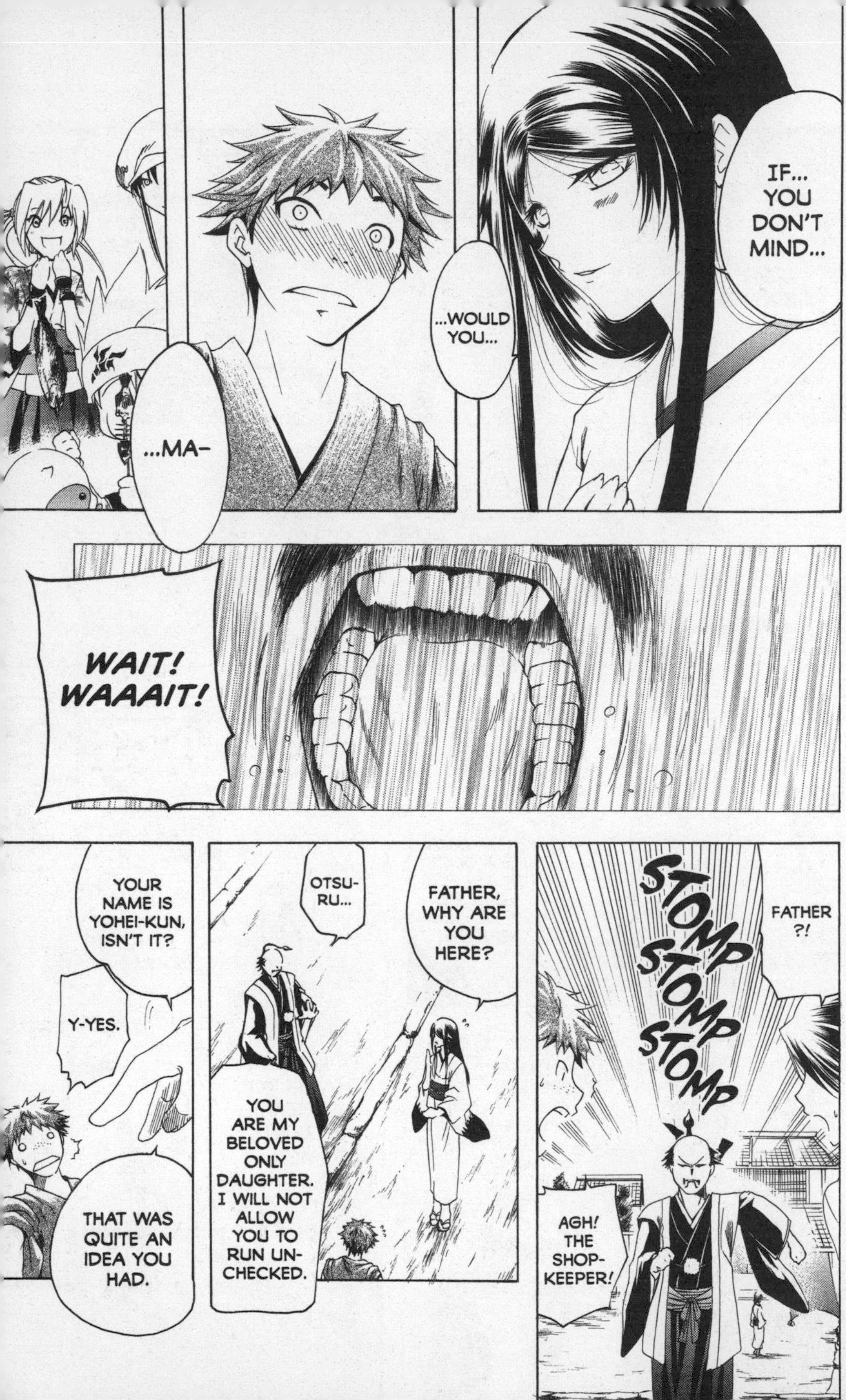
IF... YOU DON'T MIND...
...WOULD YOU...
...MA-
WAIT! WAAAIT!
FATHER?!
STOMP STOMP STOMP STOMP
AGH! THE SHOP-KEEPER!
FATHER, WHY ARE YOU HERE?
OTSU-RU...
YOU ARE MY BELOVED ONLY DAUGHTER. I WILL NOT ALLOW YOU TO RUN UN-CHECKED.
YOUR NAME IS YOHEI-KUN, ISN'T IT?
Y-YES.
THAT WAS QUITE AN IDEA YOU HAD.

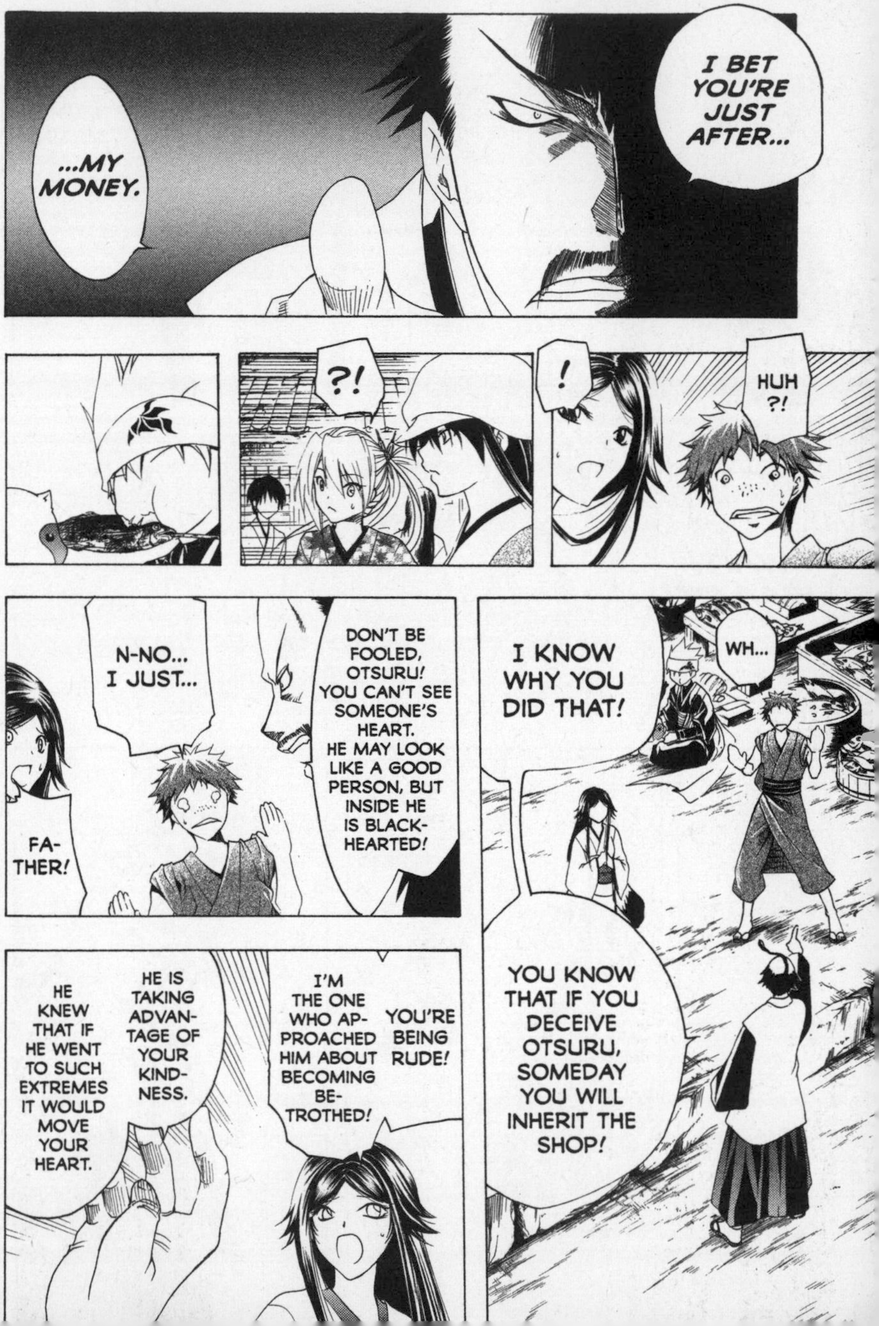
I BET YOU'RE JUST AFTER...
...MY MONEY.
HUH ?!
!
?!
WH...
I KNOW WHY YOU DID THAT!
YOU KNOW THAT IF YOU DECEIVE OTSURU, SOMEDAY YOU WILL INHERIT THE SHOP!
DON'T BE FOOLED, OTSURU! YOU CAN'T SEE SOMEONE'S HEART. HE MAY LOOK LIKE A GOOD PERSON, BUT INSIDE HE IS BLACK-HEARTED!
N-NO... I JUST...
FA-THER!
YOU'RE BEING RUDE!
I'M THE ONE WHO AP-PROACHED HIM ABOUT BECOMING BE-TROTHED!
HE IS TAKING ADVAN-TAGE OF YOUR KIND-NESS.
HE KNEW THAT IF HE WENT TO SUCH EXTREMES IT WOULD MOVE YOUR HEART.

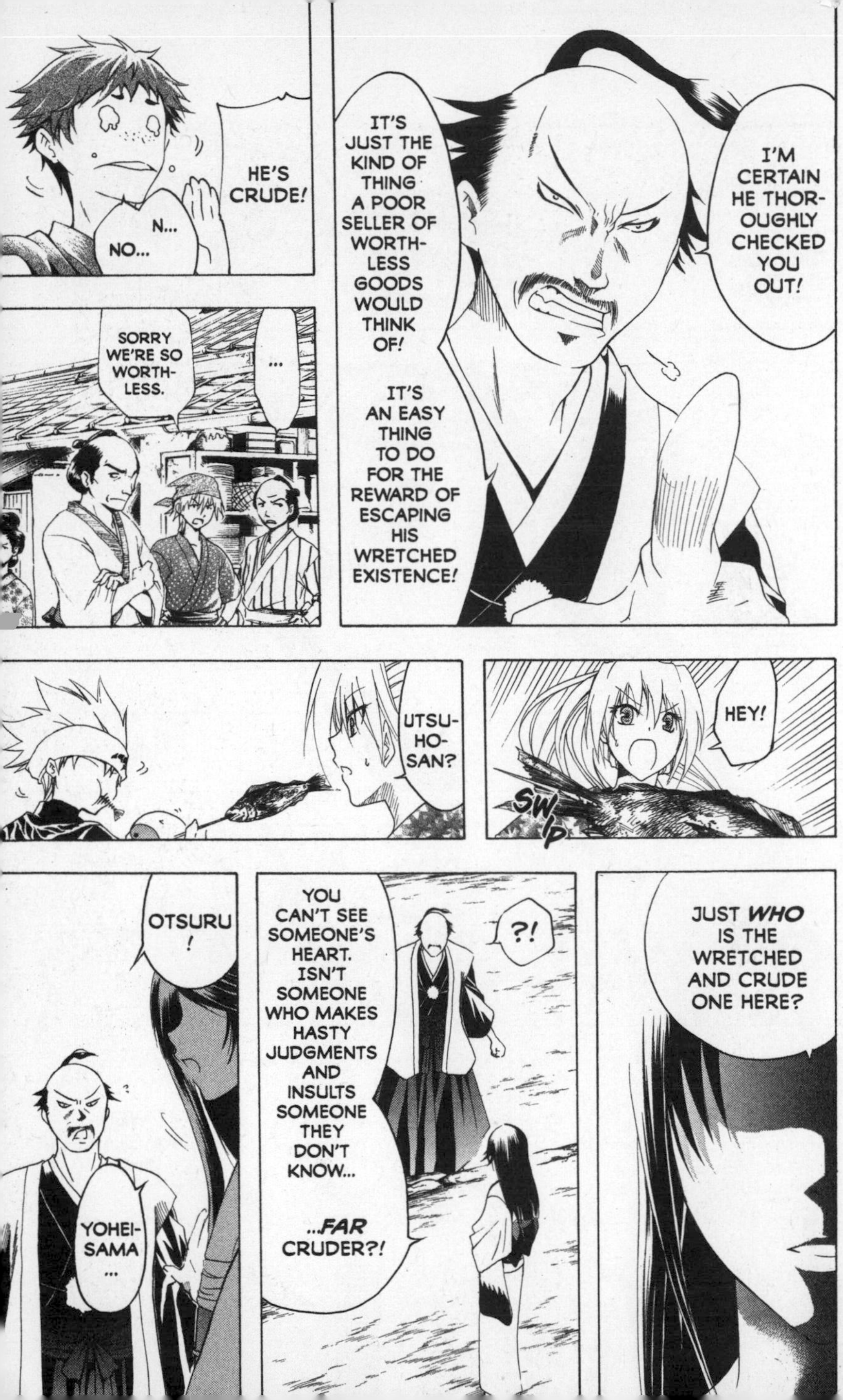
I'M CERTAIN HE THOROUGHLY CHECKED YOU OUT!
IT'S JUST THE KIND OF THING A POOR SELLER OF WORTHLESS GOODS WOULD THINK OF!
IT'S AN EASY THING TO DO FOR THE REWARD OF ESCAPING HIS WRETCHED EXISTENCE!
HE'S CRUDE!
N... NO...
...
SORRY WE'RE SO WORTHLESS.
HEY!
SWIP
UTSU-HO-SAN?
JUST *WHO* IS THE WRETCHED AND CRUDE ONE HERE?
?!
YOU CAN'T SEE SOMEONE'S HEART. ISN'T SOMEONE WHO MAKES HASTY JUDGMENTS AND INSULTS SOMEONE THEY DON'T KNOW...
...*FAR* CRUDER?!
OTSURU!
YOHEI-SAMA...

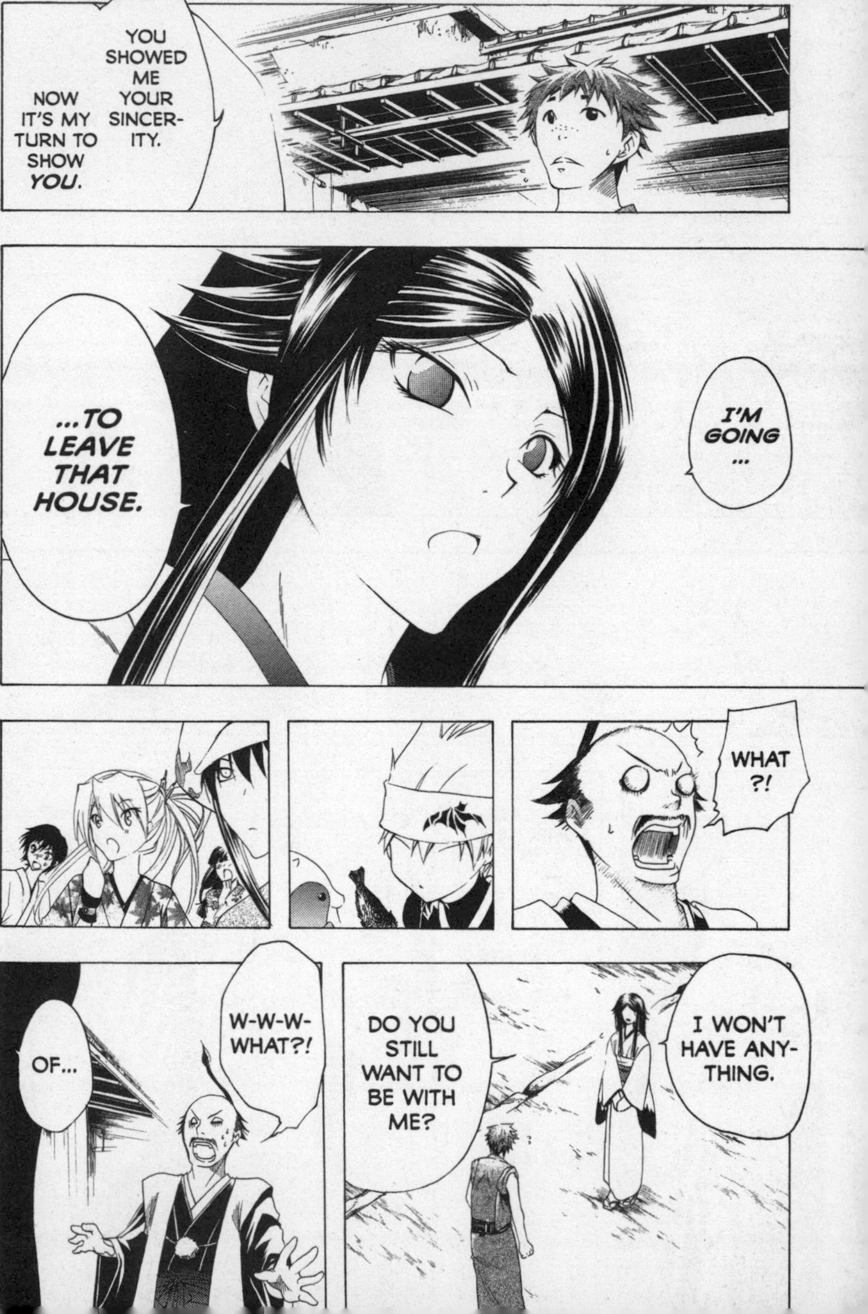
YOU SHOWED ME YOUR SINCER-ITY.
NOW IT'S MY TURN TO SHOW *YOU*.
I'M GOING ...
...TO LEAVE THAT HOUSE.
WHAT?!
I WON'T HAVE ANY-THING.
DO YOU STILL WANT TO BE WITH ME?
W-W-W-WHAT?!
OF...

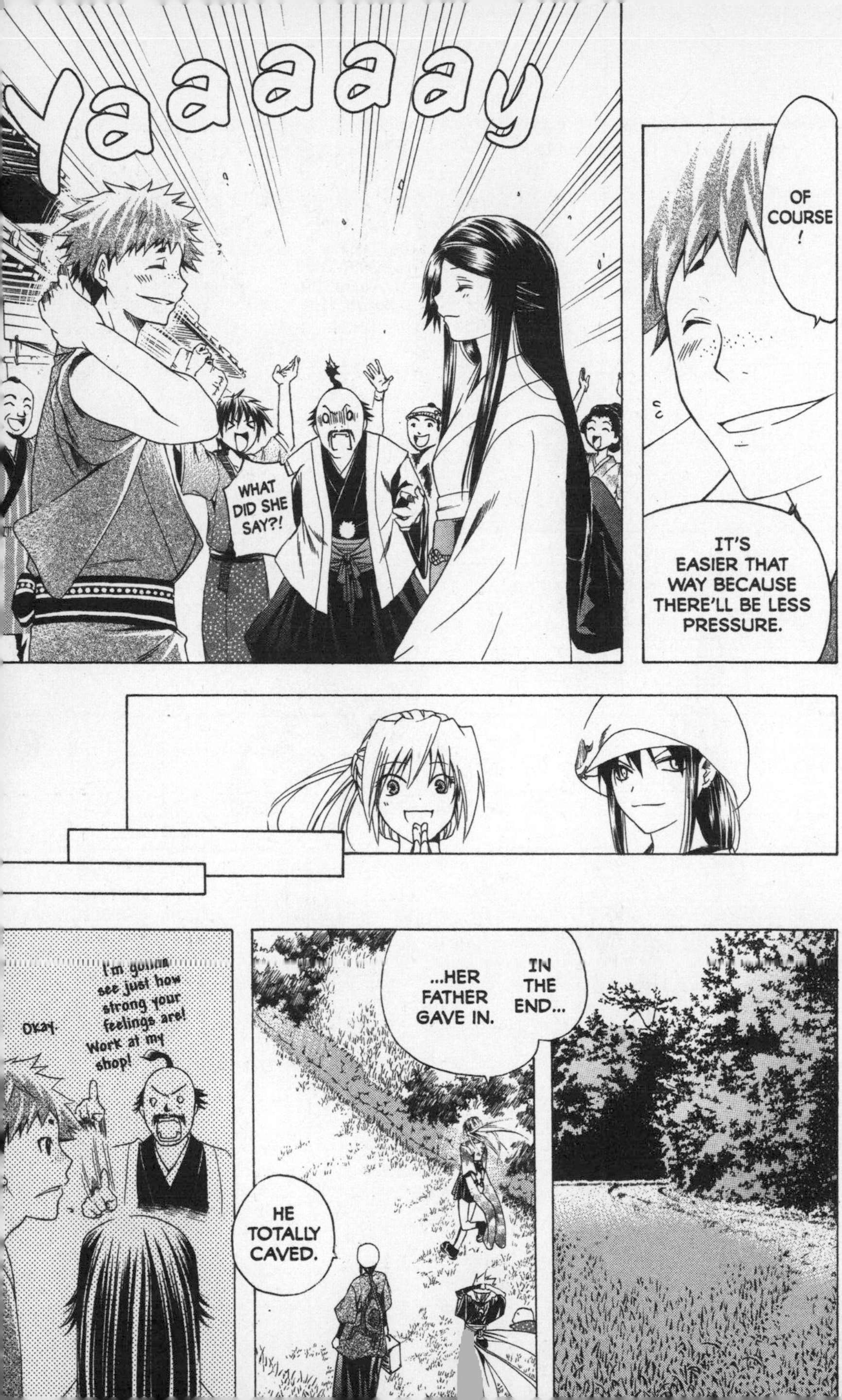
OF COURSE!
IT'S EASIER THAT WAY BECAUSE THERE'LL BE LESS PRESSURE.
Yaaaaaay
WHAT DID SHE SAY?!
IN THE END...
...HER FATHER GAVE IN.
HE TOTALLY CAVED.
I'm gonna see just how strong your feelings are! Work at my shop!
Okay.

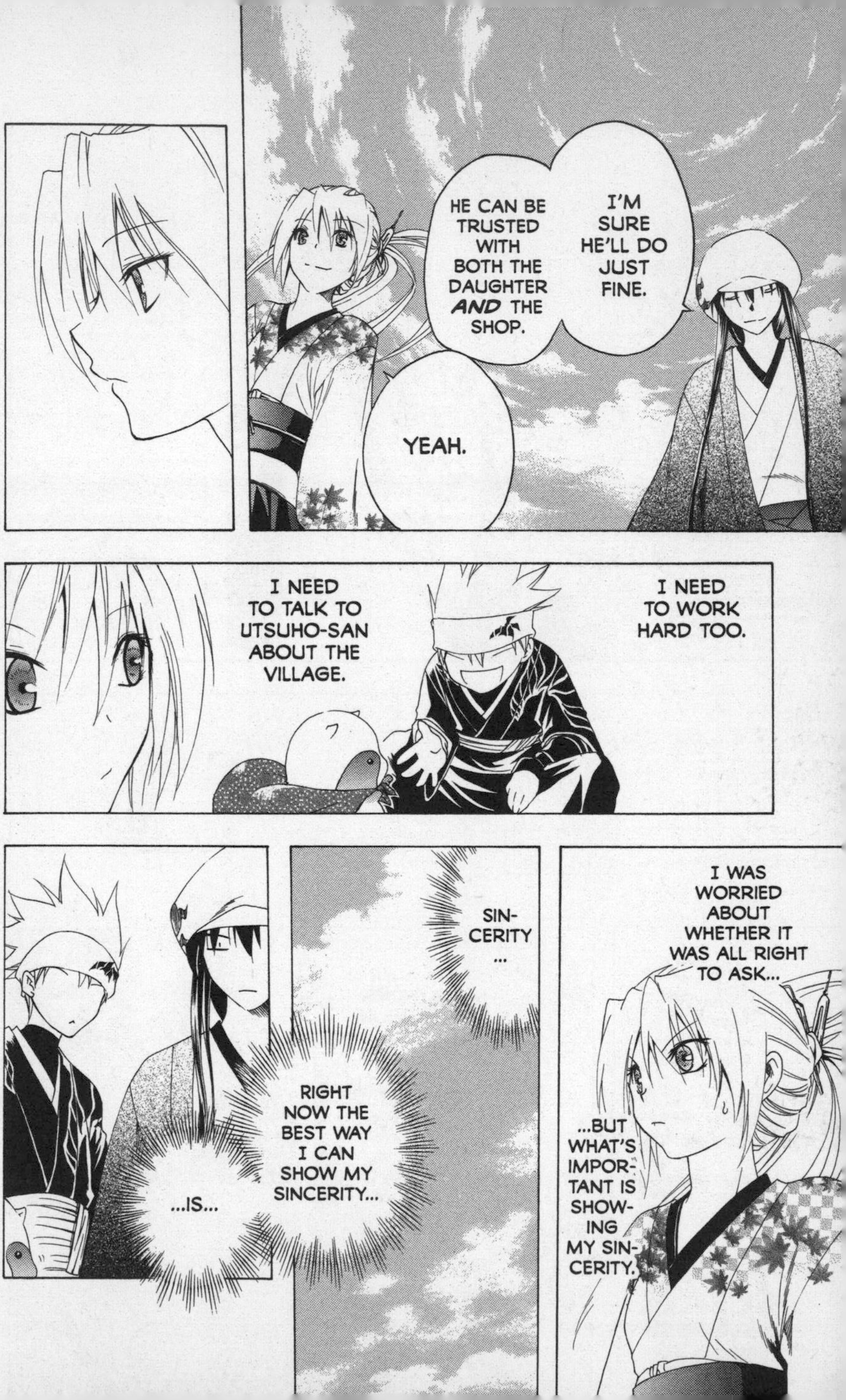
I'M SURE HE'LL DO JUST FINE.
HE CAN BE TRUSTED WITH BOTH THE DAUGHTER *AND* THE SHOP.
YEAH.
I NEED TO WORK HARD TOO.
I NEED TO TALK TO UTSUHO-SAN ABOUT THE VILLAGE.
I WAS WORRIED ABOUT WHETHER IT WAS ALL RIGHT TO ASK...
...BUT WHAT'S IMPOR-TANT IS SHOW-ING MY SIN-CERITY.
SIN-CERITY...
RIGHT NOW THE BEST WAY I CAN SHOW MY SINCERITY...
...IS...

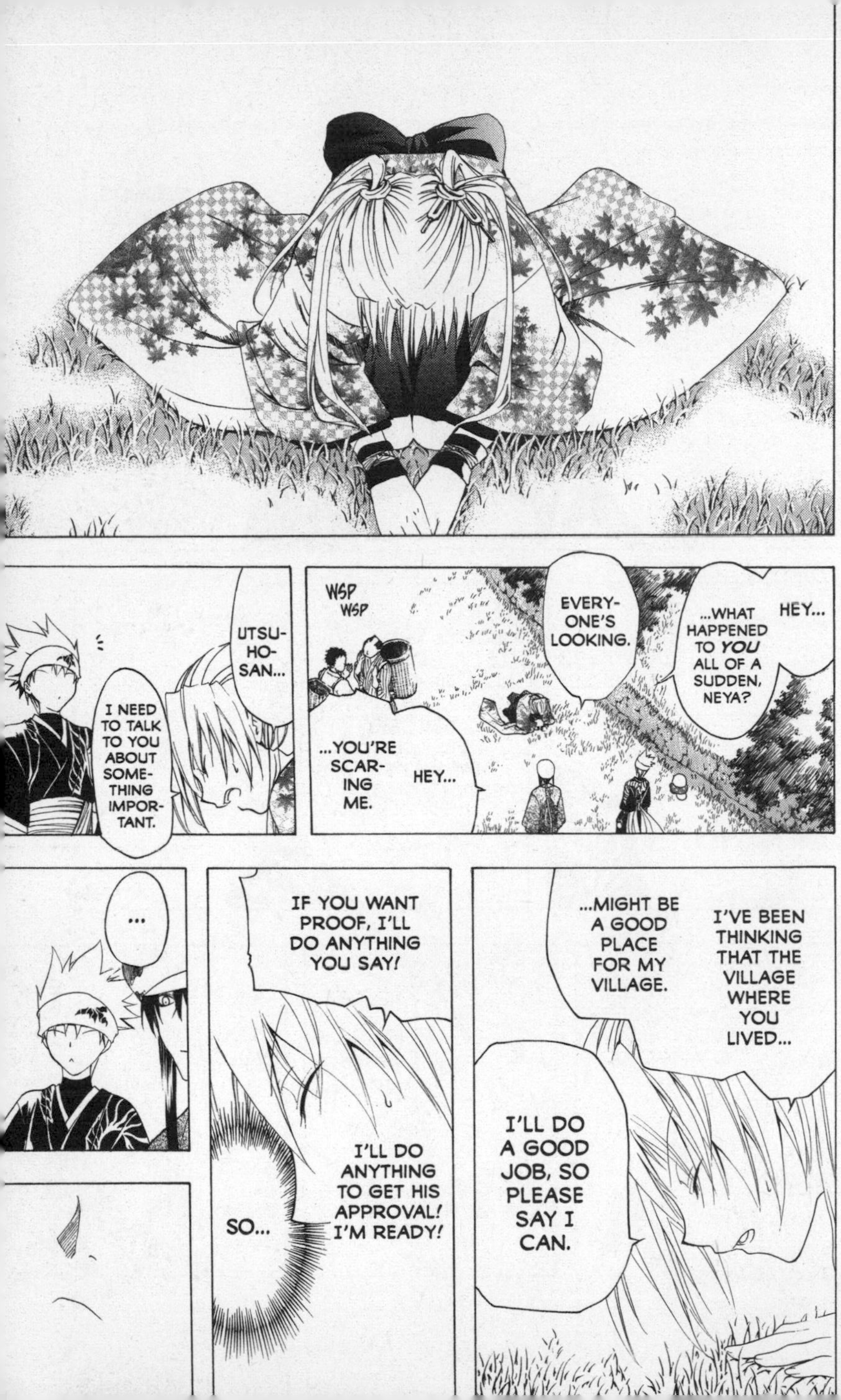
HEY...
...WHAT HAPPENED TO *YOU* ALL OF A SUDDEN, NEYA?
EVERY-ONE'S LOOKING.
WSP WSP
HEY... ...YOU'RE SCAR-ING ME.
UTSU-HO-SAN...
I NEED TO TALK TO YOU ABOUT SOME-THING IMPOR-TANT.
I'VE BEEN THINKING THAT THE VILLAGE WHERE YOU LIVED...
...MIGHT BE A GOOD PLACE FOR MY VILLAGE.
I'LL DO A GOOD JOB, SO PLEASE SAY I CAN.
IF YOU WANT PROOF, I'LL DO ANYTHING YOU SAY!
I'LL DO ANYTHING TO GET HIS APPROVAL! I'M READY!
SO...
...

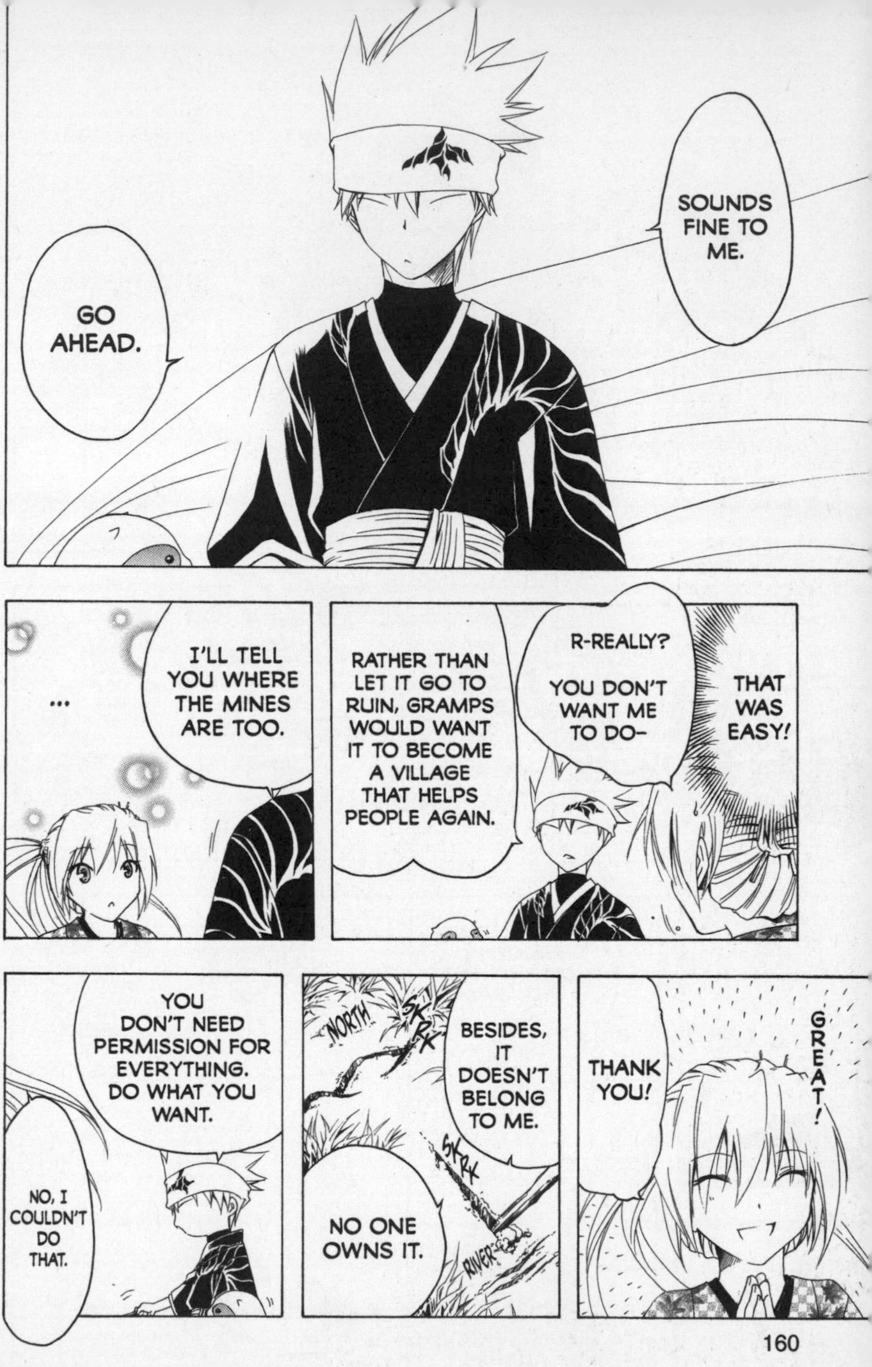
SOUNDS FINE TO ME.
GO AHEAD.
THAT WAS EASY!
R-REALLY?
YOU DON'T WANT ME TO DO-
RATHER THAN LET IT GO TO RUIN, GRAMPS WOULD WANT IT TO BECOME A VILLAGE THAT HELPS PEOPLE AGAIN.
I'LL TELL YOU WHERE THE MINES ARE TOO.
...
GREAT!
THANK YOU!
BESIDES, IT DOESN'T BELONG TO ME.
SKRK
NORTH
SKRK
NO ONE OWNS IT.
RIVER
YOU DON'T NEED PERMISSION FOR EVERYTHING. DO WHAT YOU WANT.
NO, I COULDN'T DO THAT.

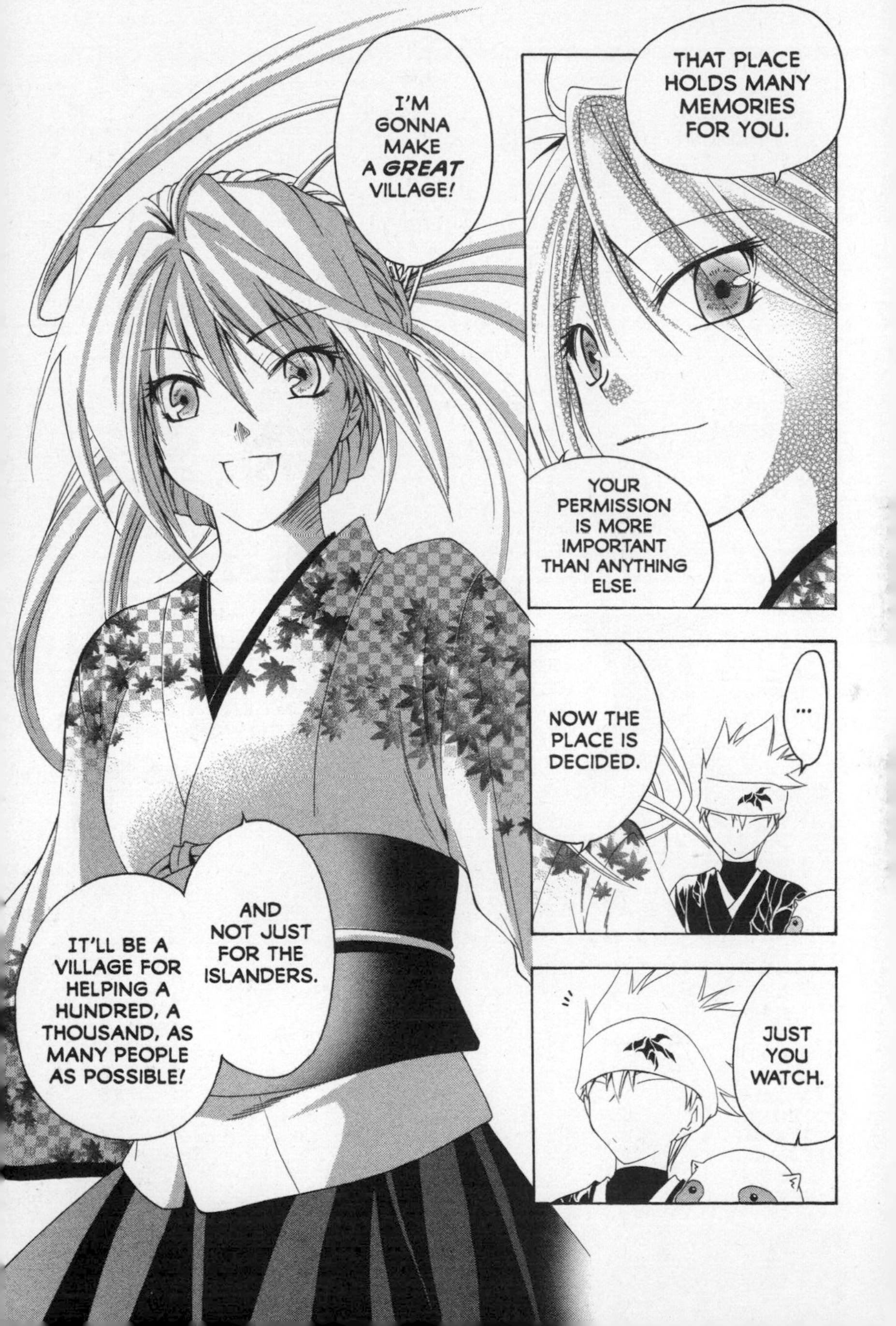
THAT PLACE HOLDS MANY MEMORIES FOR YOU.
YOUR PERMISSION IS MORE IMPORTANT THAN ANYTHING ELSE.
...
NOW THE PLACE IS DECIDED.
JUST YOU WATCH.
I'M GONNA MAKE A *GREAT* VILLAGE!
AND NOT JUST FOR THE ISLANDERS.
IT'LL BE A VILLAGE FOR HELPING A HUNDRED, A THOUSAND, AS MANY PEOPLE AS POSSIBLE!

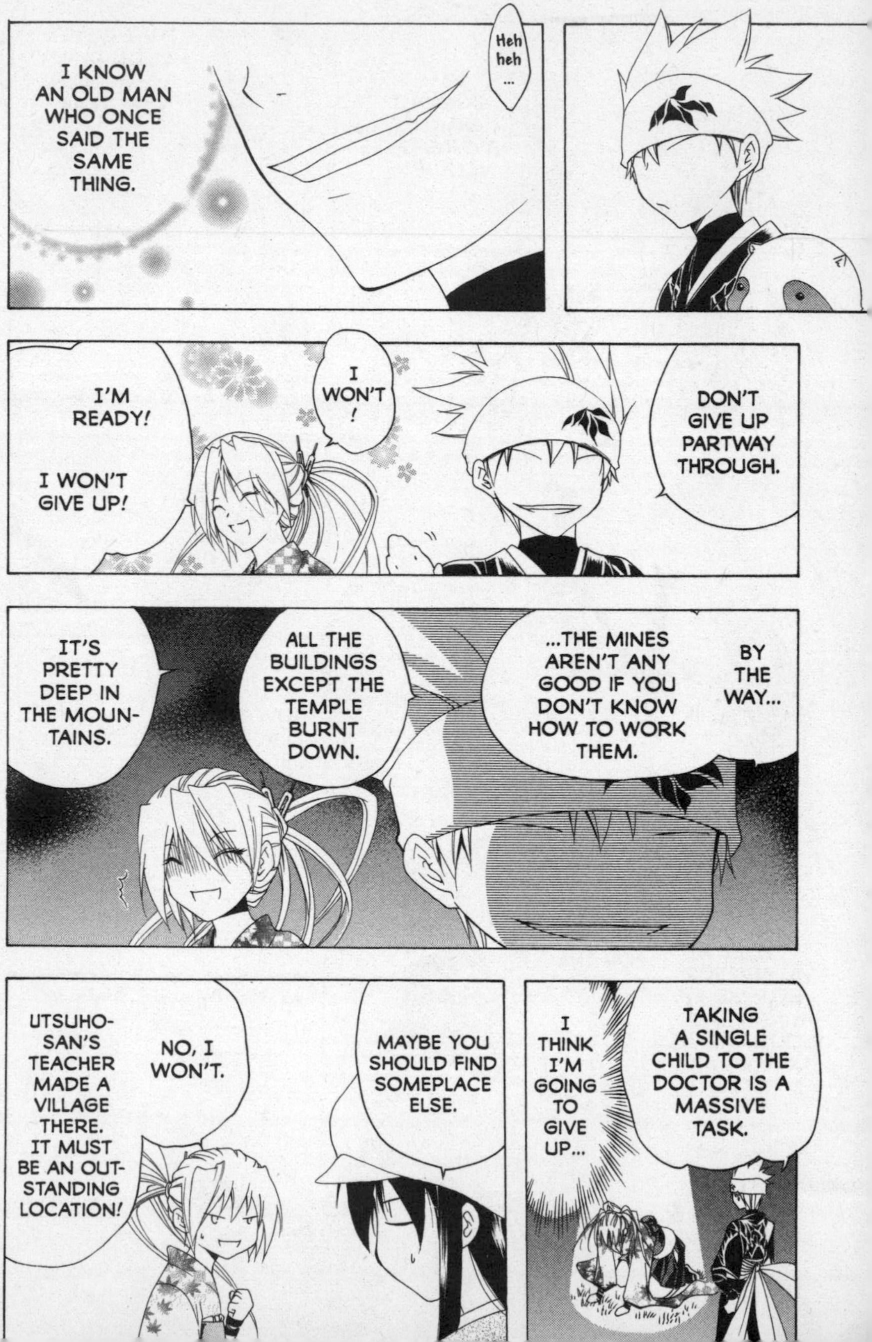
Heh heh ...
I KNOW AN OLD MAN WHO ONCE SAID THE SAME THING.
DON'T GIVE UP PARTWAY THROUGH.
I WON'T!
I'M READY!
I WON'T GIVE UP!
BY THE WAY...
...THE MINES AREN'T ANY GOOD IF YOU DON'T KNOW HOW TO WORK THEM.
ALL THE BUILDINGS EXCEPT THE TEMPLE BURNT DOWN.
IT'S PRETTY DEEP IN THE MOUN-TAINS.
TAKING A SINGLE CHILD TO THE DOCTOR IS A MASSIVE TASK.
I THINK I'M GOING TO GIVE UP...
MAYBE YOU SHOULD FIND SOMEPLACE ELSE.
NO, I WON'T.
UTSUHO-SAN'S TEACHER MADE A VILLAGE THERE. IT MUST BE AN OUT-STANDING LOCATION!

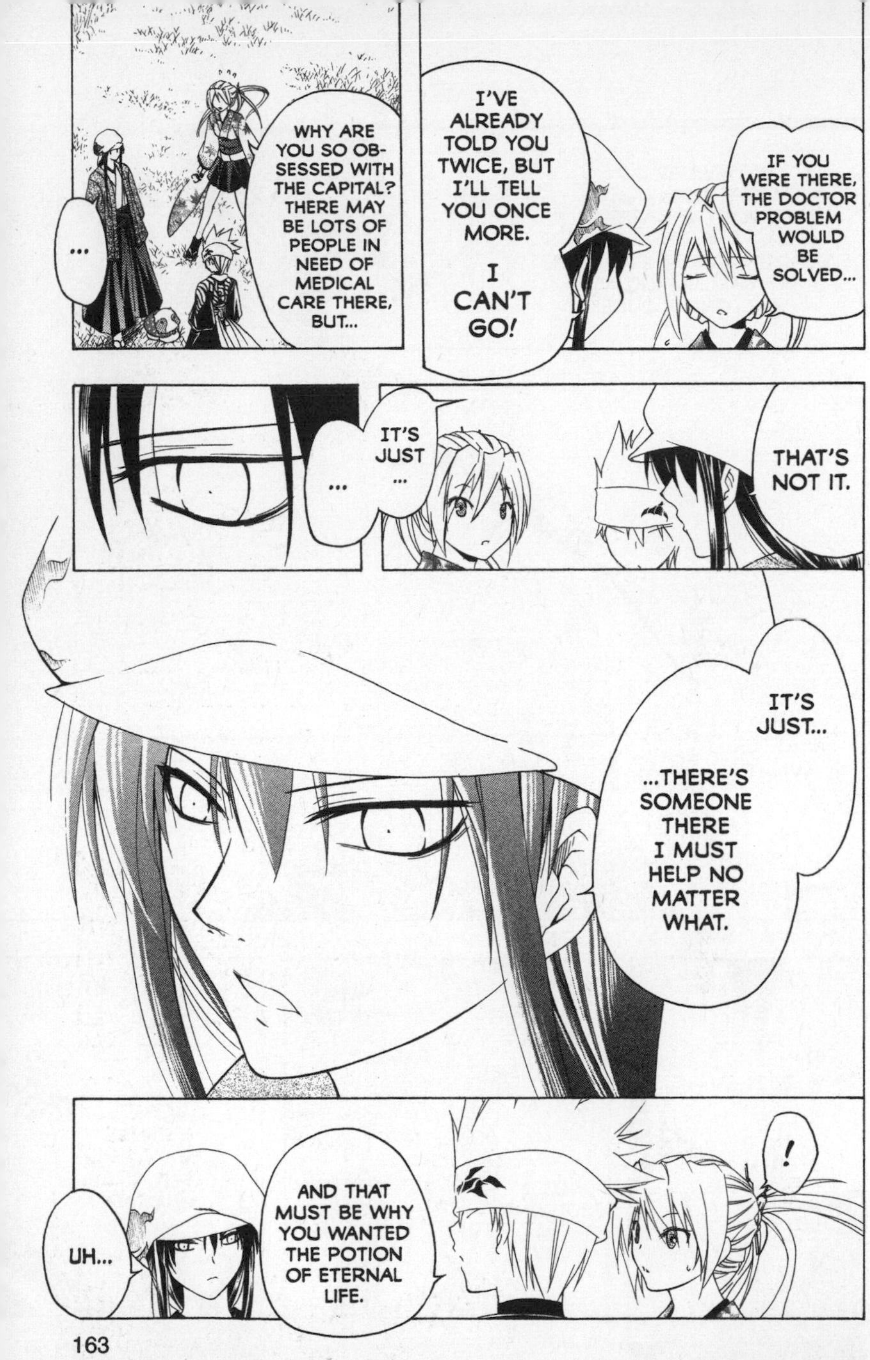
IF YOU WERE THERE, THE DOCTOR PROBLEM WOULD BE SOLVED...
I'VE ALREADY TOLD YOU TWICE, BUT I'LL TELL YOU ONCE MORE.
I CAN'T GO!
WHY ARE YOU SO OB-SESSED WITH THE CAPITAL? THERE MAY BE LOTS OF PEOPLE IN NEED OF MEDICAL CARE THERE, BUT...
...
THAT'S NOT IT.
IT'S JUST ...
...
IT'S JUST...
...THERE'S SOMEONE THERE I MUST HELP NO MATTER WHAT.
!
AND THAT MUST BE WHY YOU WANTED THE POTION OF ETERNAL LIFE.
UH...

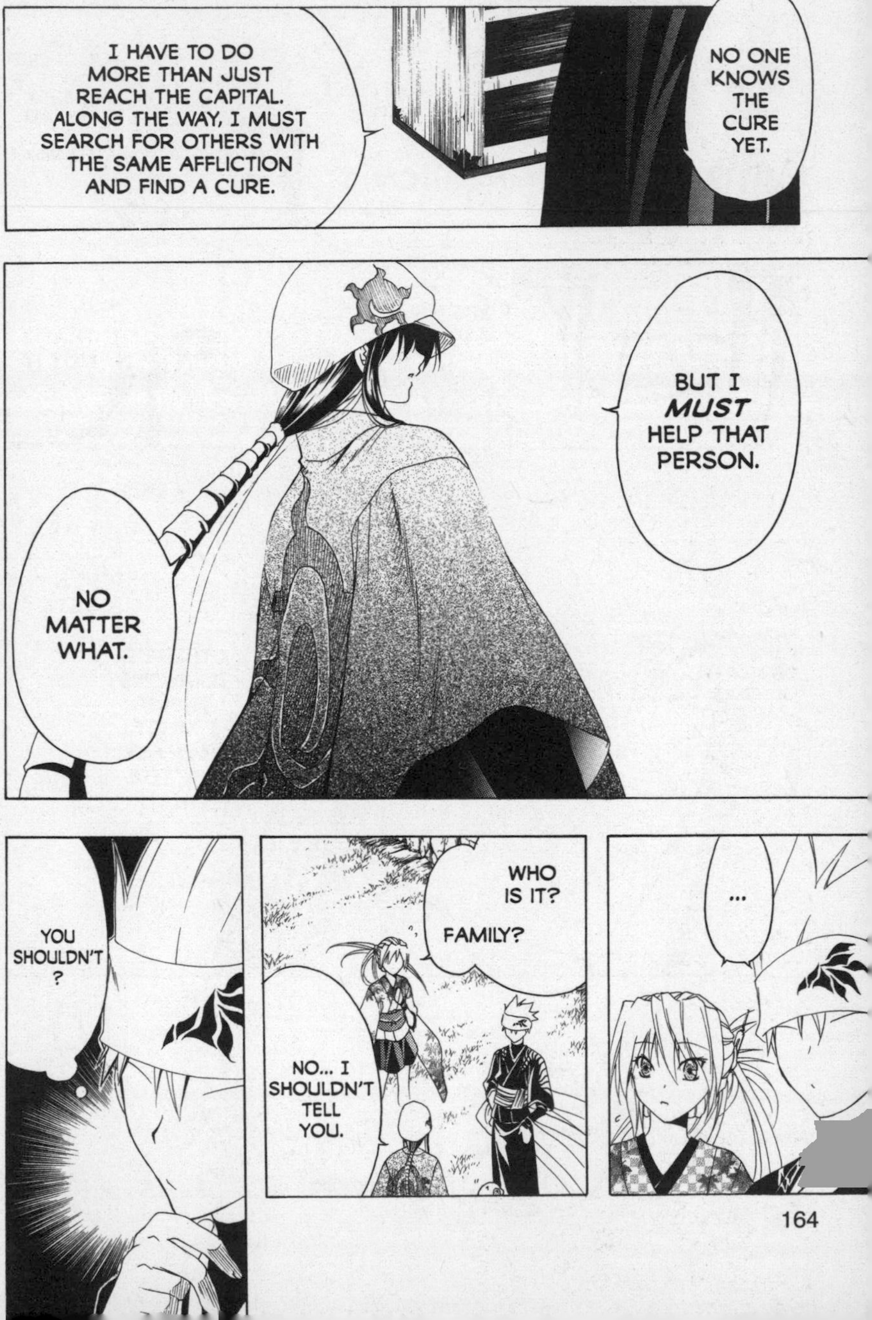
NO ONE KNOWS THE CURE YET.
I HAVE TO DO MORE THAN JUST REACH THE CAPITAL. ALONG THE WAY, I MUST SEARCH FOR OTHERS WITH THE SAME AFFLICTION AND FIND A CURE.
BUT I *MUST* HELP THAT PERSON.
NO MATTER WHAT.
...
WHO IS IT?
FAMILY?
NO... I SHOULDN'T TELL YOU.
YOU SHOULDN'T?

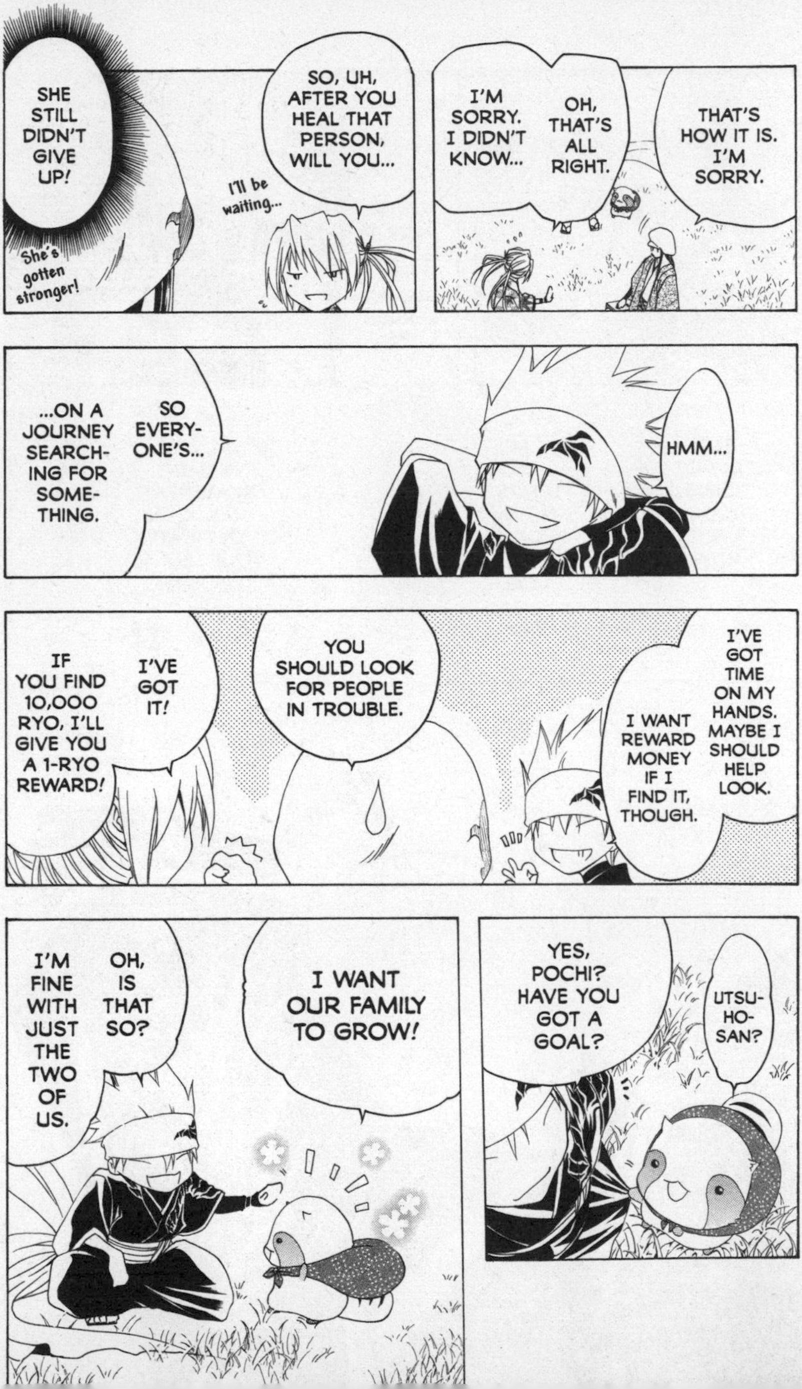
THAT'S HOW IT IS. I'M SORRY.
OH, THAT'S ALL RIGHT.
I'M SORRY. I DIDN'T KNOW...
SO, UH, AFTER YOU HEAL THAT PERSON, WILL YOU...
I'll be waiting...
SHE STILL DIDN'T GIVE UP!
She's gotten stronger!
HMM...
SO EVERYONE'S...
...ON A JOURNEY SEARCHING FOR SOMETHING.
I'VE GOT TIME ON MY HANDS. MAYBE I SHOULD HELP LOOK.
I WANT REWARD MONEY IF I FIND IT, THOUGH.
YOU SHOULD LOOK FOR PEOPLE IN TROUBLE.
I'VE GOT IT!
IF YOU FIND 10,000 RYO, I'LL GIVE YOU A 1-RYO REWARD!
UTSUHO-SAN?
YES, POCHI? HAVE YOU GOT A GOAL?
I WANT OUR FAMILY TO GROW!
OH, IS THAT SO?
I'M FINE WITH JUST THE TWO OF US.

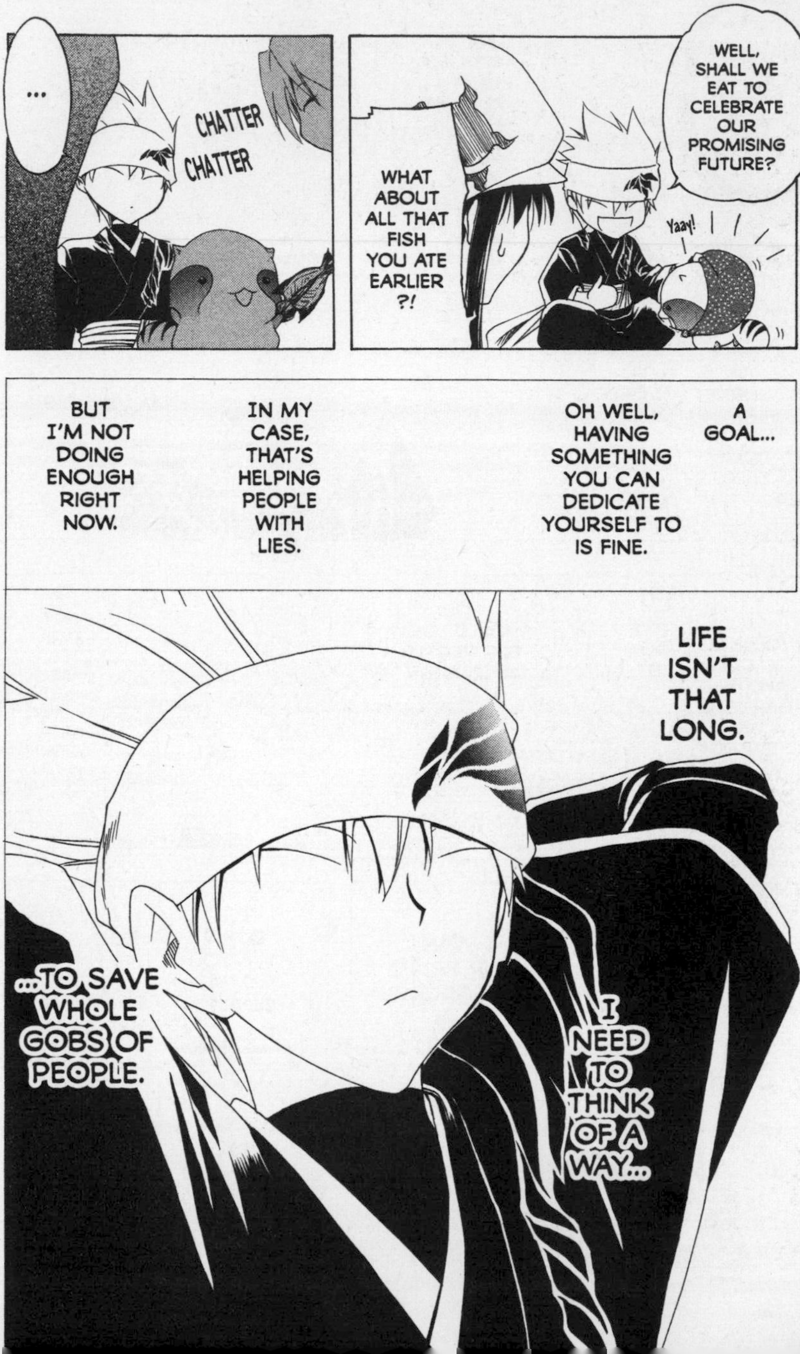
WELL, SHALL WE EAT TO CELEBRATE OUR PROMISING FUTURE?
Yaay!
WHAT ABOUT ALL THAT FISH YOU ATE EARLIER?!
CHATTER
CHATTER
...
A GOAL...
OH WELL, HAVING SOMETHING YOU CAN DEDICATE YOURSELF TO IS FINE.
IN MY CASE, THAT'S HELPING PEOPLE WITH LIES.
BUT I'M NOT DOING ENOUGH RIGHT NOW.
LIFE ISN'T THAT LONG.
I NEED TO THINK OF A WAY...
...TO SAVE WHOLE GOBS OF PEOPLE.

Chapter 27 The Power of a God

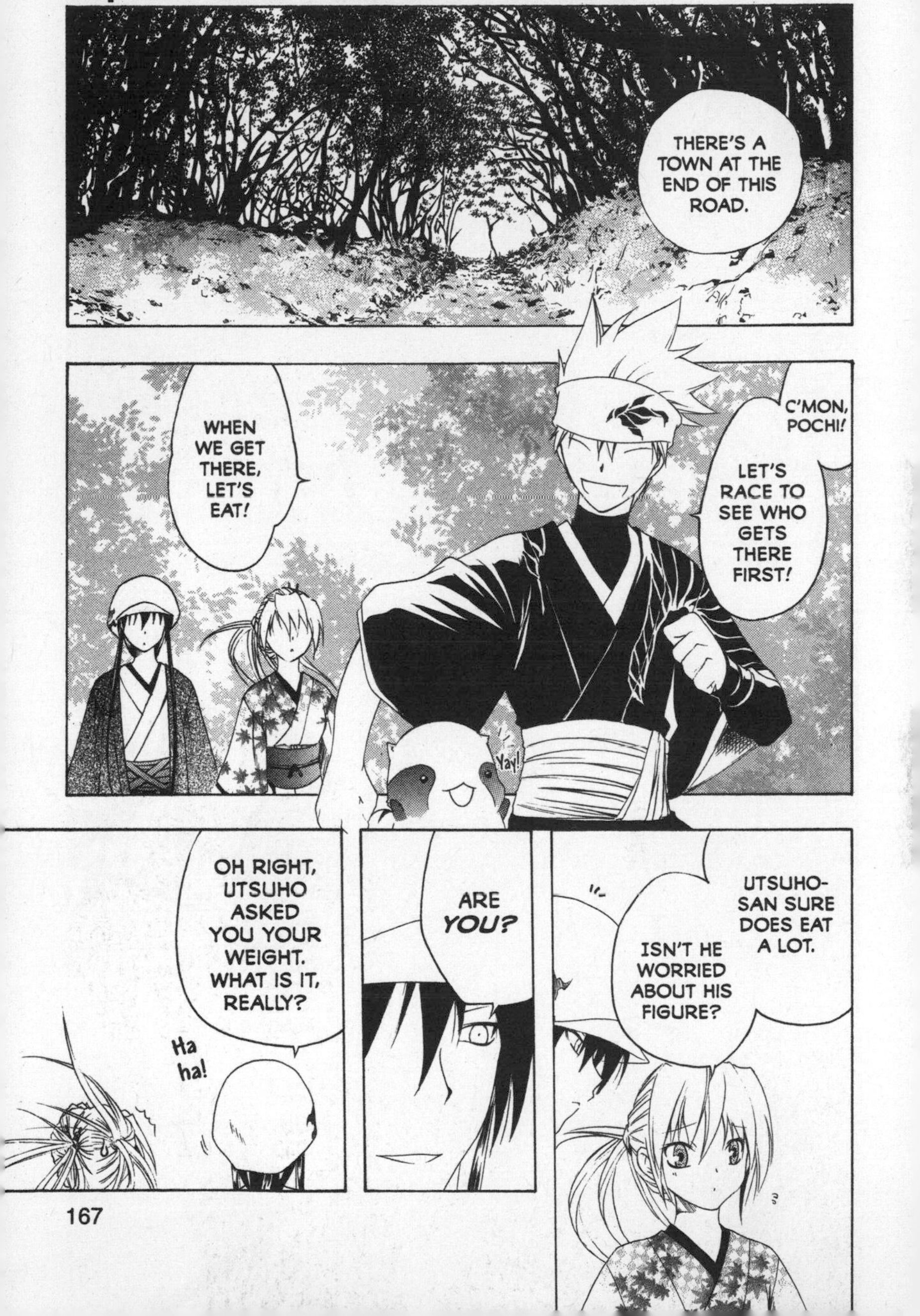
THERE'S A TOWN AT THE END OF THIS ROAD.
C'MON, POCHI!
LET'S RACE TO SEE WHO GETS THERE FIRST!
WHEN WE GET THERE, LET'S EAT!
Yay!
UTSUHO-SAN SURE DOES EAT A LOT.
ISN'T HE WORRIED ABOUT HIS FIGURE?
ARE *YOU*?
OH RIGHT, UTSUHO ASKED YOU YOUR WEIGHT. WHAT IS IT, REALLY?
Ha ha!

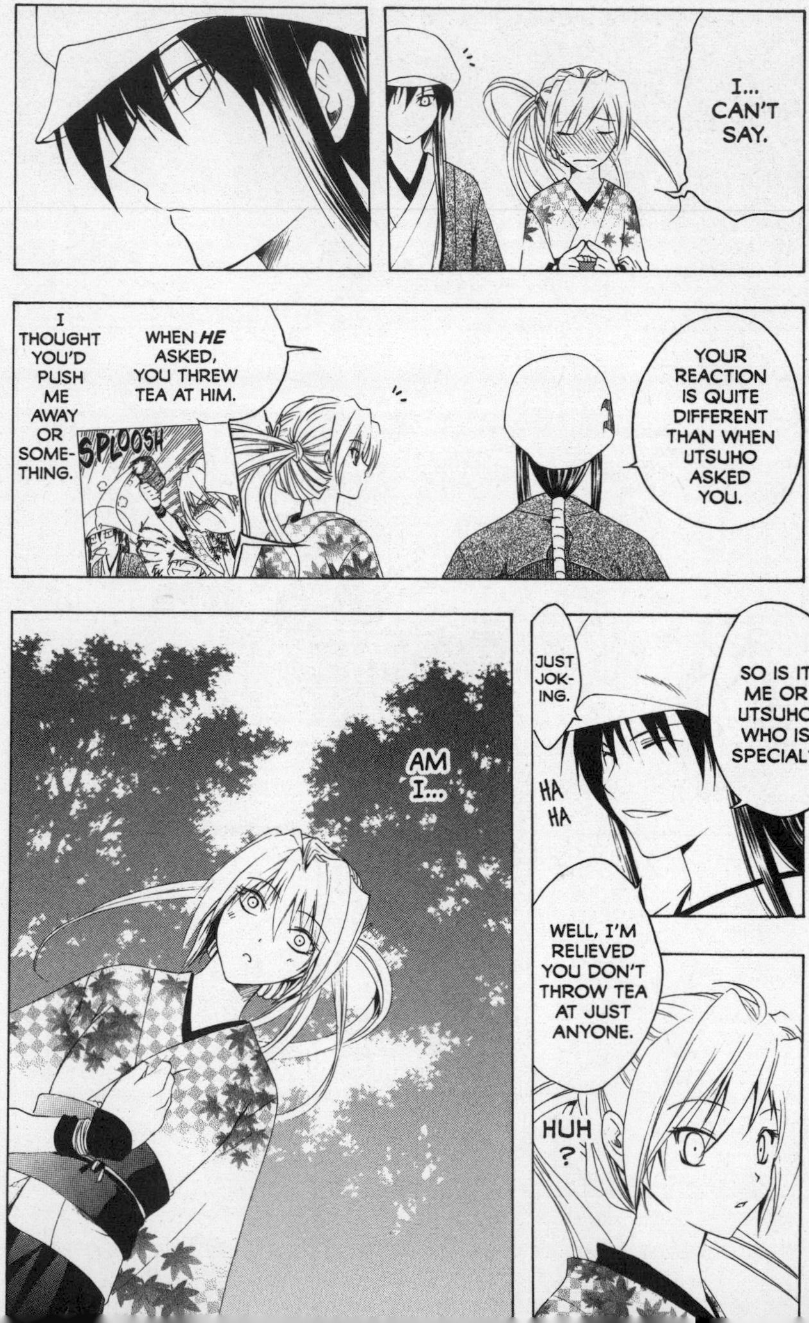
I... CAN'T SAY.
YOUR REACTION IS QUITE DIFFERENT THAN WHEN UTSUHO ASKED YOU.
WHEN *HE* ASKED, YOU THREW TEA AT HIM.
I THOUGHT YOU'D PUSH ME AWAY OR SOME-THING.
SPLOOSH
SO IS IT ME OR UTSUHO WHO IS SPECIAL?
JUST JOK-ING.
HA HA
WELL, I'M RELIEVED YOU DON'T THROW TEA AT JUST ANYONE.
HUH?
AM I...

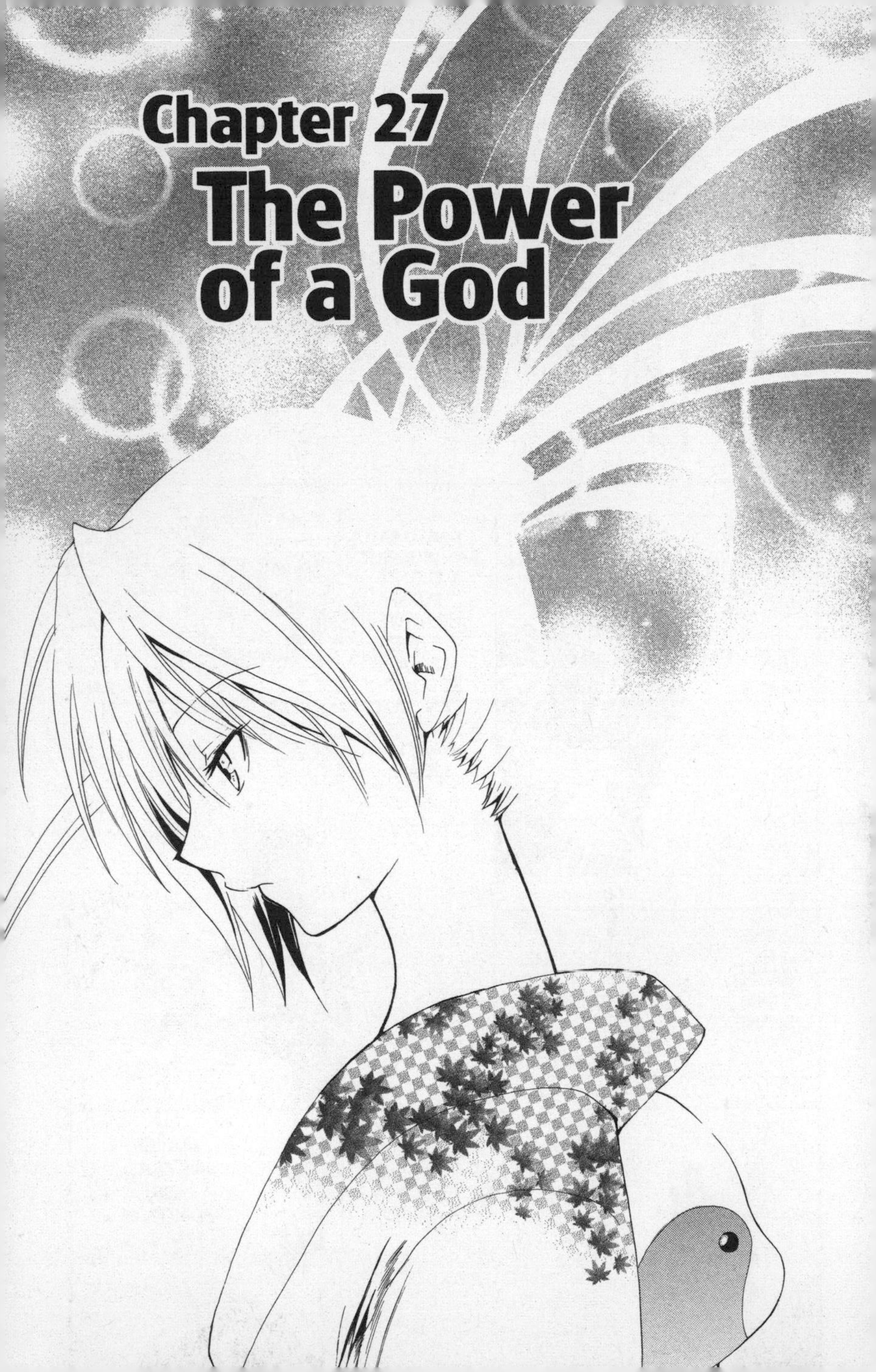
Chapter 27
The Power of a God

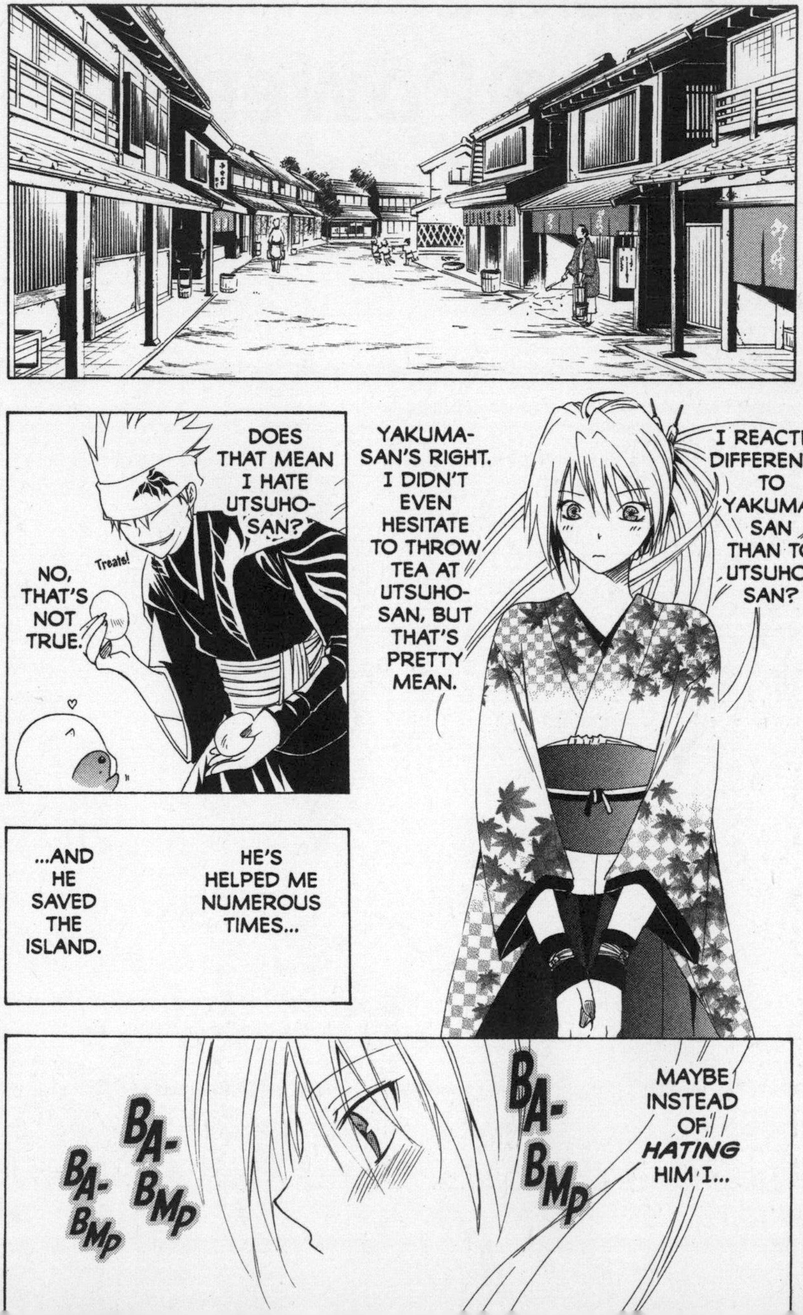
I REACTED DIFFERENTLY TO YAKUMA-SAN THAN TO UTSUHO-SAN?
YAKUMA-SAN'S RIGHT. I DIDN'T EVEN HESITATE TO THROW TEA AT UTSUHO-SAN, BUT THAT'S PRETTY MEAN.
DOES THAT MEAN I HATE UTSUHO-SAN?
Treats!
NO, THAT'S NOT TRUE.
HE'S HELPED ME NUMEROUS TIMES...
...AND HE SAVED THE ISLAND.
MAYBE INSTEAD OF *HATING* HIM I...
BA-BMP
BA-BMP
BA-BMP

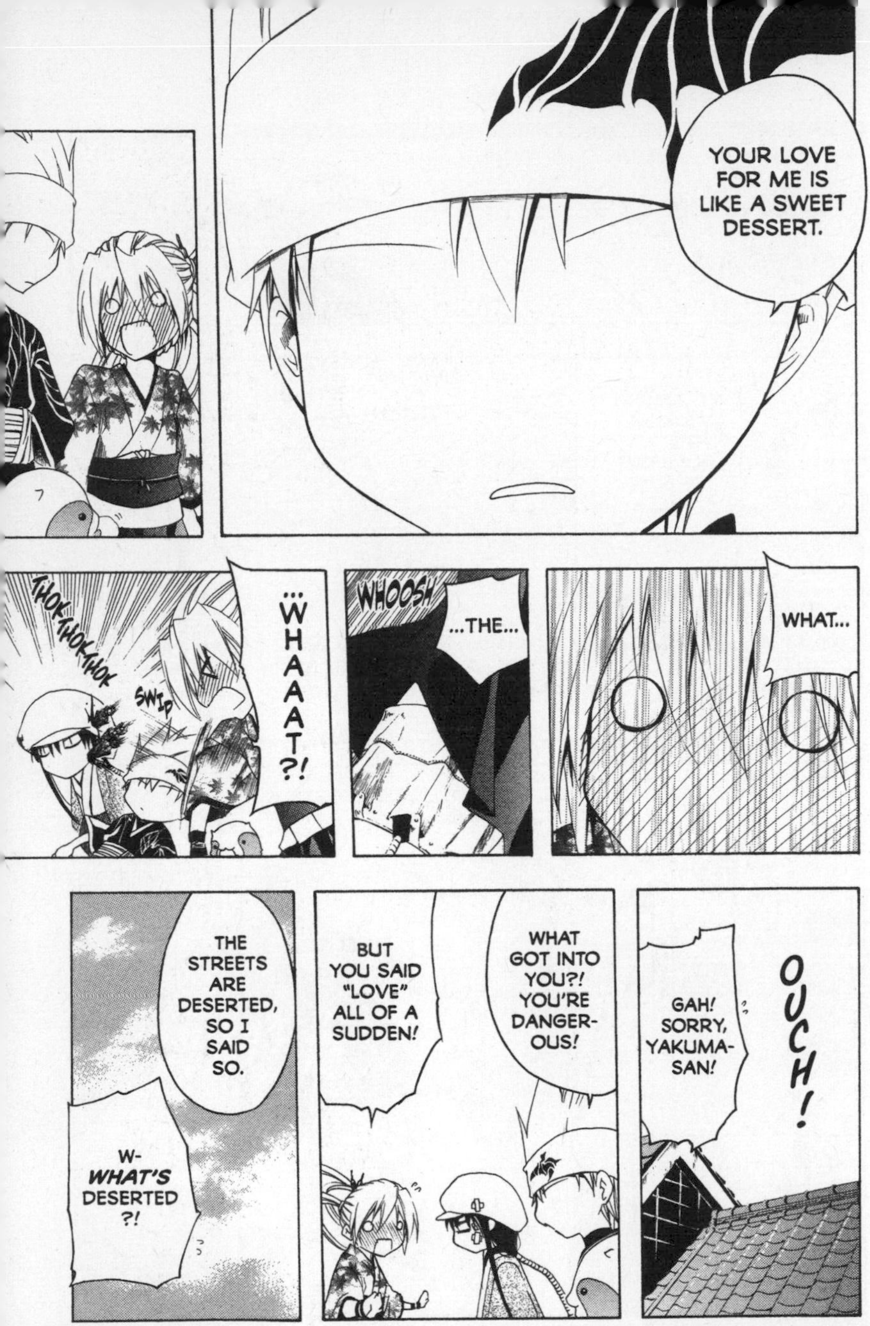
YOUR LOVE FOR ME IS LIKE A SWEET DESSERT.
WHAT...
WHOOSH
...THE...
...WHAAAAT?!
THOK THOK THOK THOK
SWIP
OUCH!
GAH! SORRY, YAKUMA-SAN!
WHAT GOT INTO YOU?! YOU'RE DANGER-OUS!
BUT YOU SAID "LOVE" ALL OF A SUDDEN!
THE STREETS ARE DESERTED, SO I SAID SO.
W-WHAT'S DESERTED?!

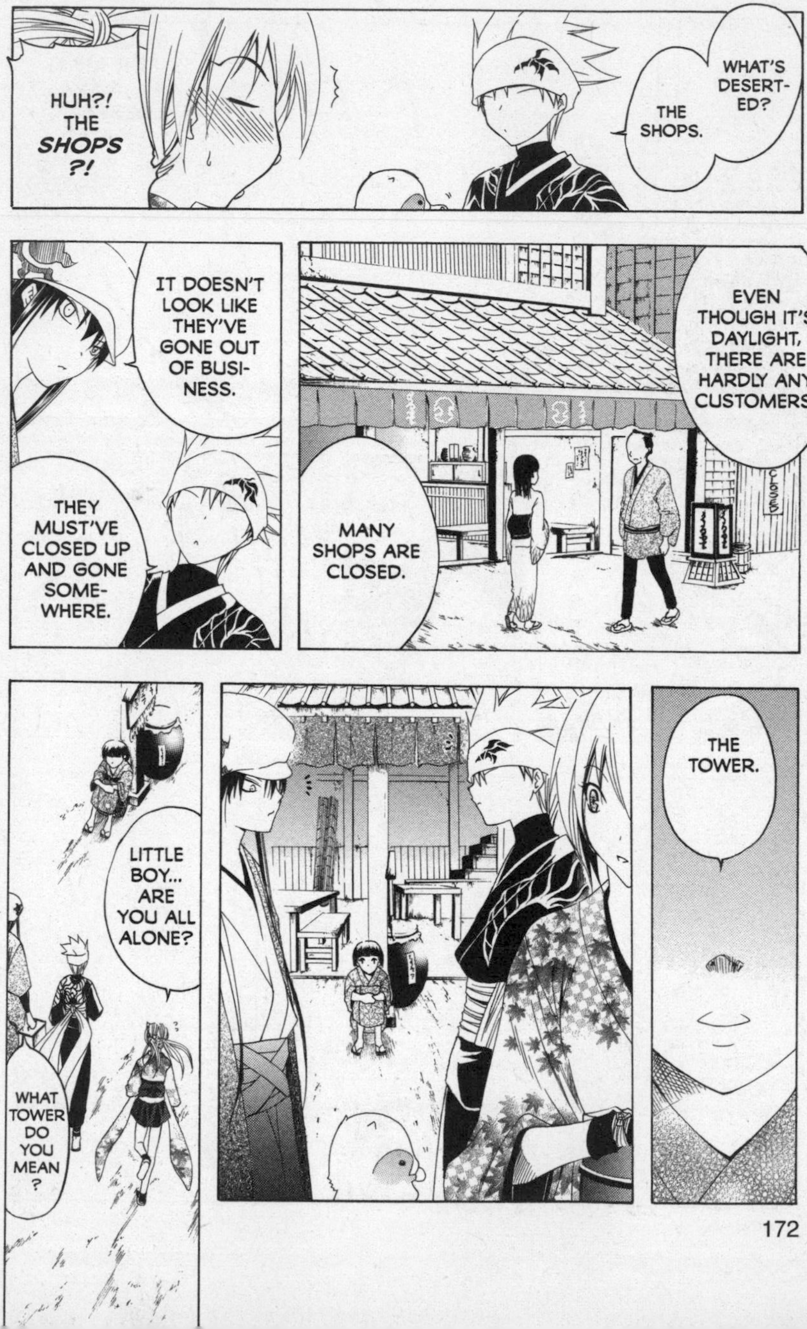
WHAT'S DESERTED?
THE SHOPS.
HUH?! THE *SHOPS* ?!
EVEN THOUGH IT'S DAYLIGHT, THERE ARE HARDLY ANY CUSTOMERS.
CLOSED
MANY SHOPS ARE CLOSED.
IT DOESN'T LOOK LIKE THEY'VE GONE OUT OF BUSINESS.
THEY MUST'VE CLOSED UP AND GONE SOMEWHERE.
THE TOWER.
LITTLE BOY... ARE YOU ALL ALONE?
WHAT TOWER DO YOU MEAN?

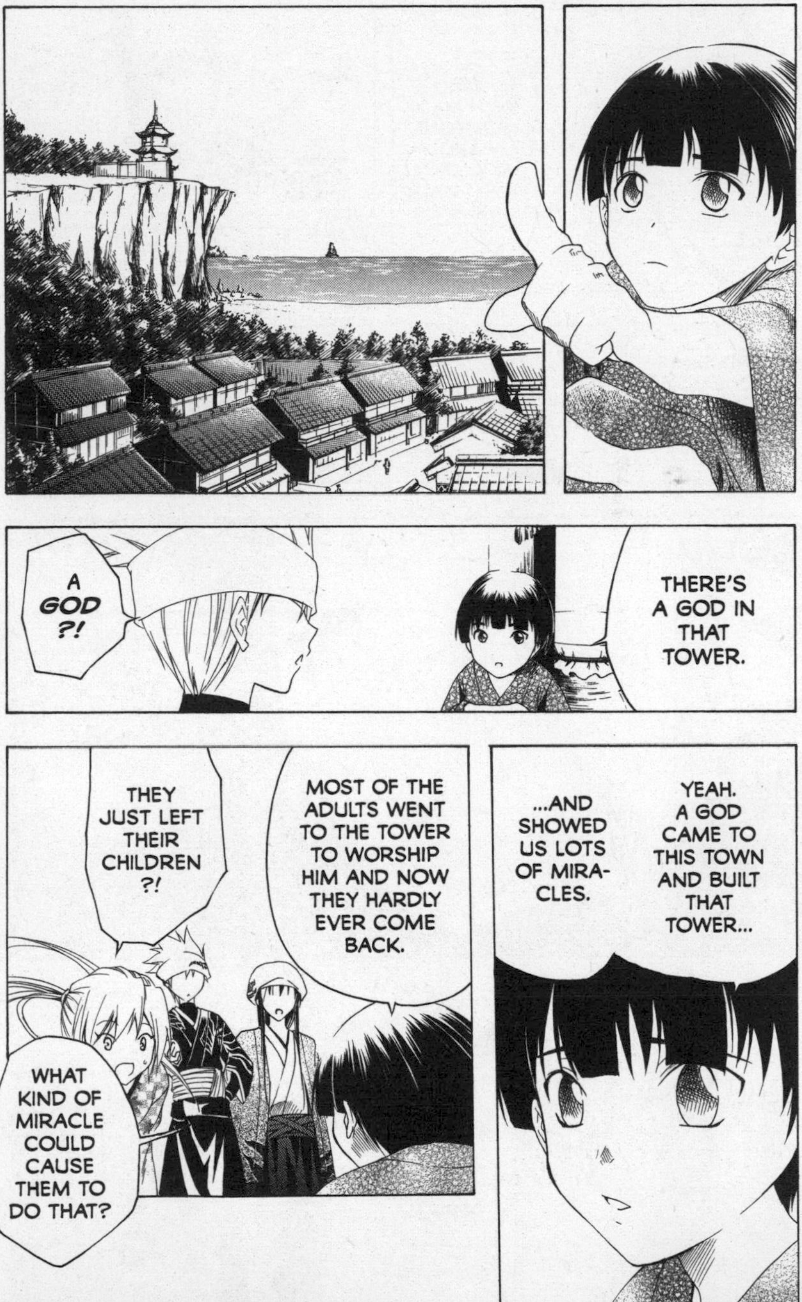
THERE'S A GOD IN THAT TOWER.
A GOD?!
YEAH. A GOD CAME TO THIS TOWN AND BUILT THAT TOWER...
...AND SHOWED US LOTS OF MIRACLES.
MOST OF THE ADULTS WENT TO THE TOWER TO WORSHIP HIM AND NOW THEY HARDLY EVER COME BACK.
THEY JUST LEFT THEIR CHILDREN?!
WHAT KIND OF MIRACLE COULD CAUSE THEM TO DO THAT?

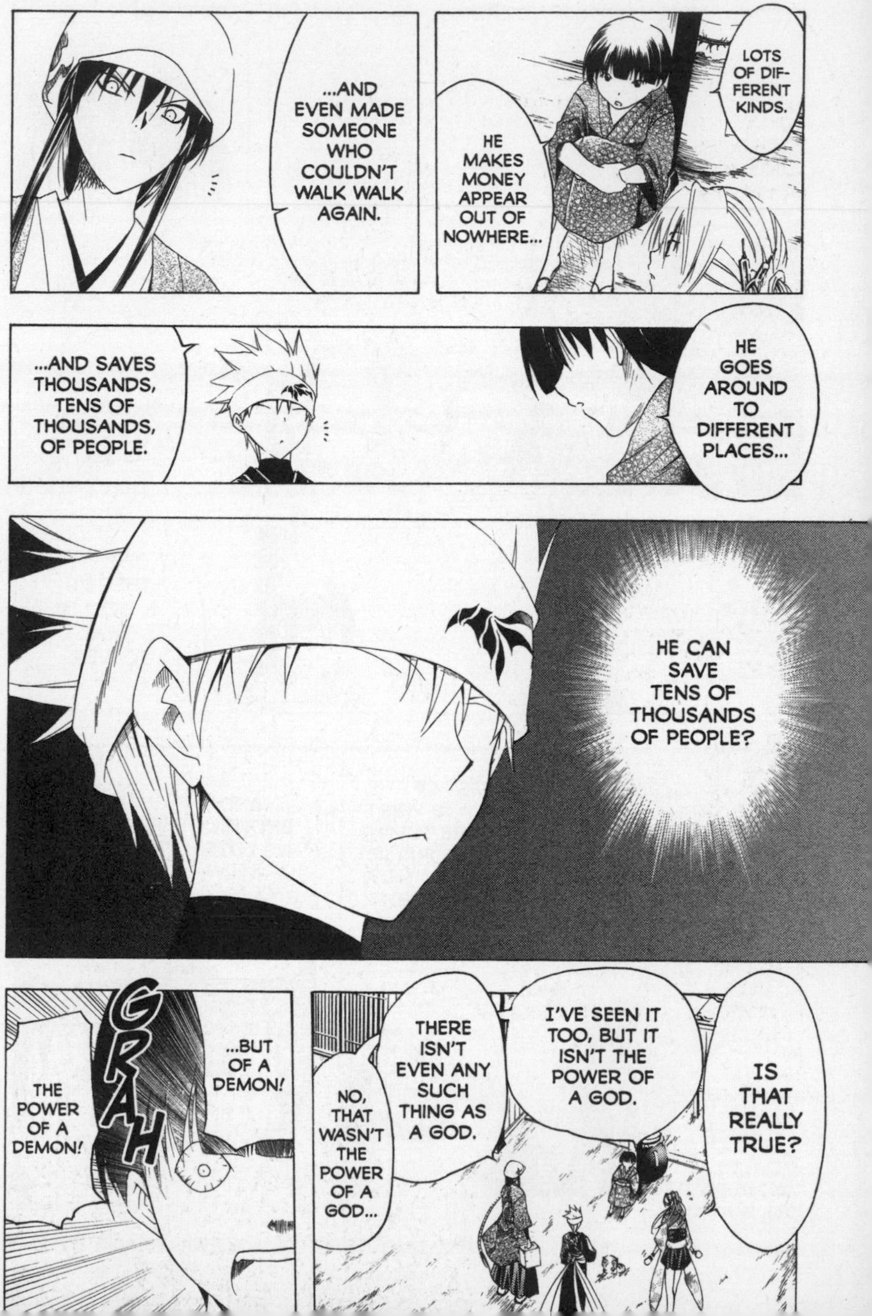
LOTS OF DIFFERENT KINDS.
HE MAKES MONEY APPEAR OUT OF NOWHERE...
...AND EVEN MADE SOMEONE WHO COULDN'T WALK WALK AGAIN.
HE GOES AROUND TO DIFFERENT PLACES...
...AND SAVES THOUSANDS, TENS OF THOUSANDS, OF PEOPLE.
HE CAN SAVE TENS OF THOUSANDS OF PEOPLE?
IS THAT REALLY TRUE?
I'VE SEEN IT TOO, BUT IT ISN'T THE POWER OF A GOD.
THERE ISN'T EVEN ANY SUCH THING AS A GOD.
NO, THAT WASN'T THE POWER OF A GOD...
...BUT OF A DEMON!
GRAH
THE POWER OF A DEMON!

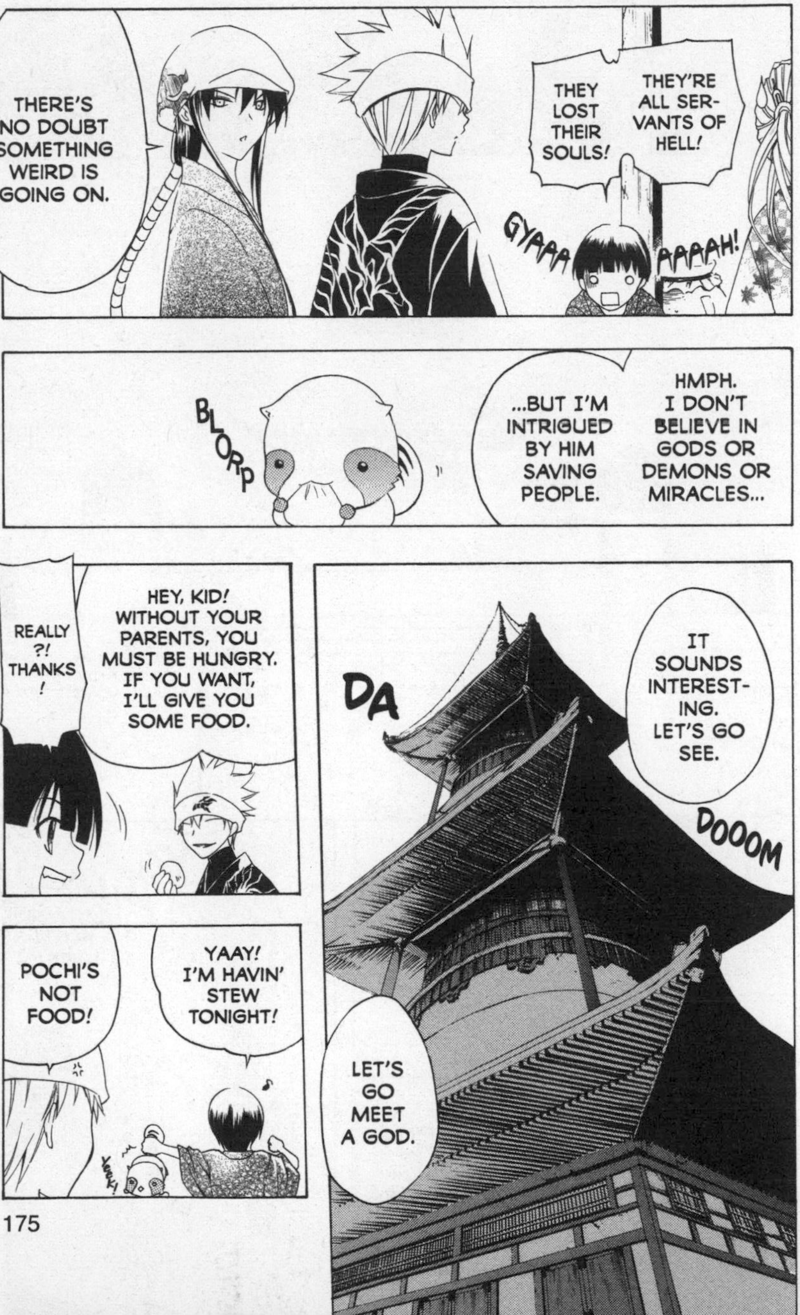
THEY'RE ALL SERVANTS OF HELL!
THEY LOST THEIR SOULS!
GYAAAAAAH!
THERE'S NO DOUBT SOMETHING WEIRD IS GOING ON.
HMPH. I DON'T BELIEVE IN GODS OR DEMONS OR MIRACLES...
...BUT I'M INTRIGUED BY HIM SAVING PEOPLE.
BLORP
IT SOUNDS INTERESTING. LET'S GO SEE.
DA
DOOOM
LET'S GO MEET A GOD.
HEY, KID! WITHOUT YOUR PARENTS, YOU MUST BE HUNGRY. IF YOU WANT, I'LL GIVE YOU SOME FOOD.
REALLY?! THANKS!
YAAY! I'M HAVIN' STEW TONIGHT!
POCHI'S NOT FOOD!

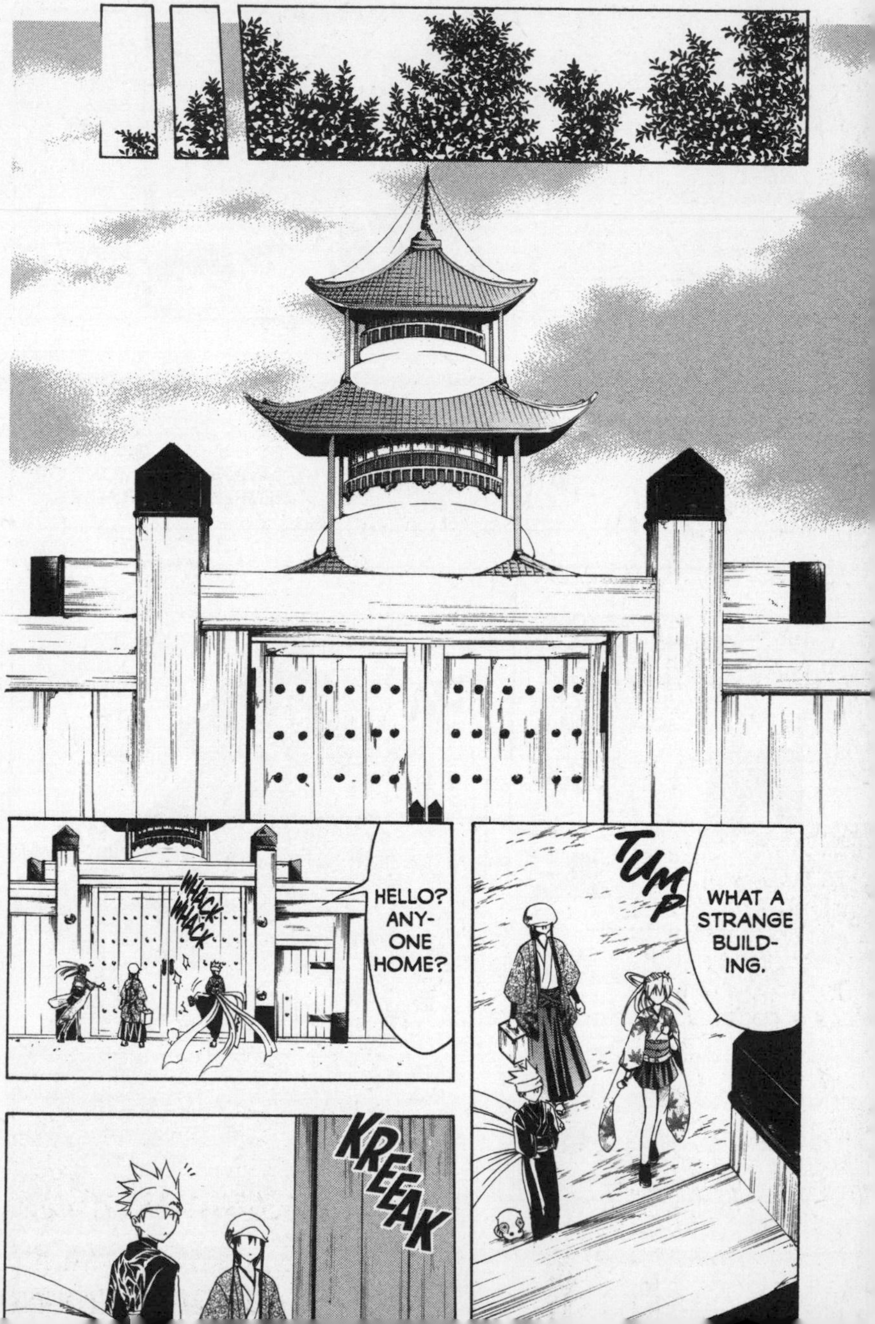
WHAT A STRANGE BUILD-ING.
TUMP
HELLO? ANY-ONE HOME?
WHACK WHACK
KREEAK

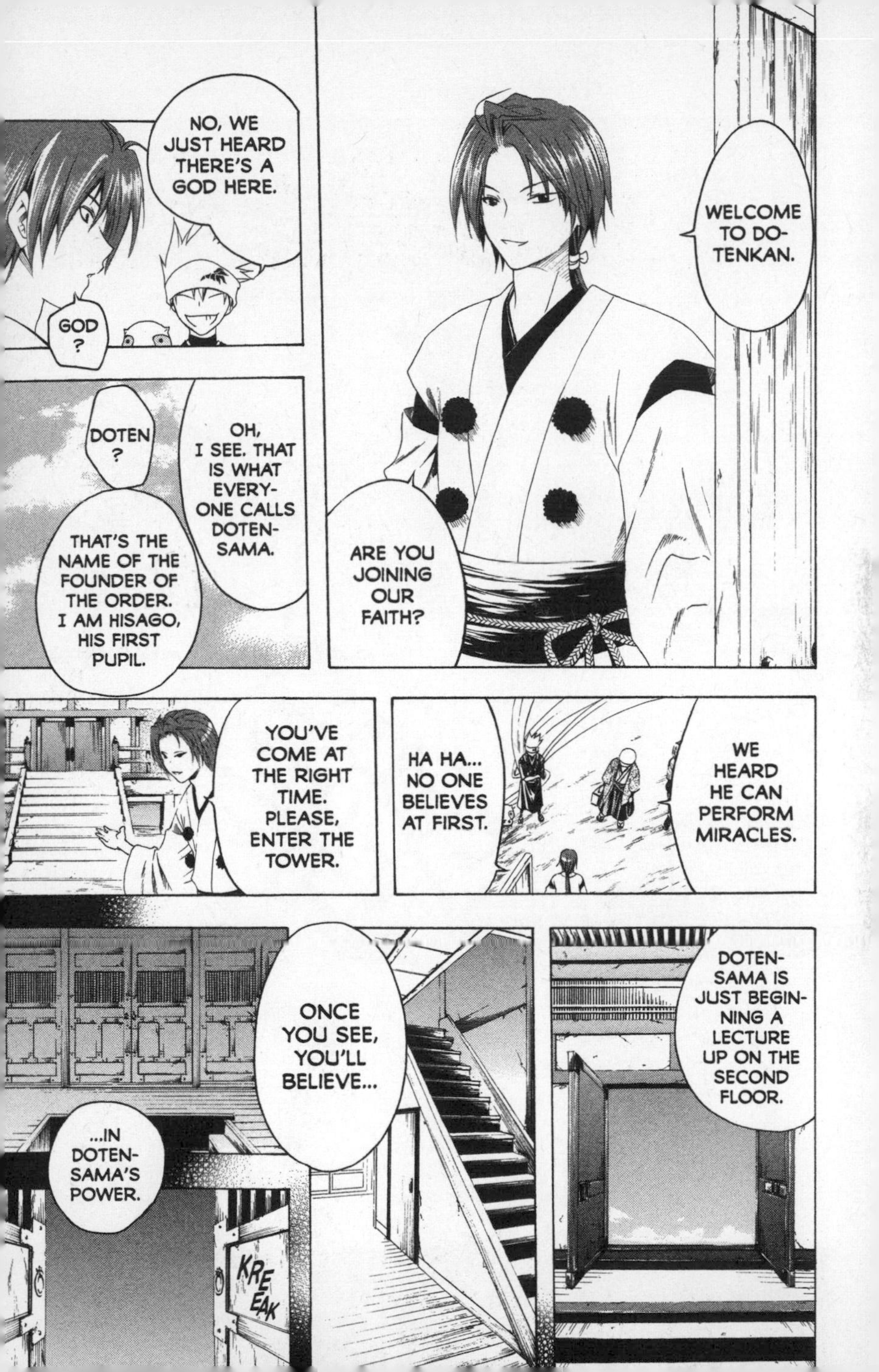
WELCOME TO DOTENKAN.
ARE YOU JOINING OUR FAITH?
NO, WE JUST HEARD THERE'S A GOD HERE.
GOD?
OH, I SEE. THAT IS WHAT EVERYONE CALLS DOTEN-SAMA.
DOTEN?
THAT'S THE NAME OF THE FOUNDER OF THE ORDER. I AM HISAGO, HIS FIRST PUPIL.
WE HEARD HE CAN PERFORM MIRACLES.
HA HA... NO ONE BELIEVES AT FIRST.
YOU'VE COME AT THE RIGHT TIME. PLEASE, ENTER THE TOWER.
DOTEN-SAMA IS JUST BEGINNING A LECTURE UP ON THE SECOND FLOOR.
ONCE YOU SEE, YOU'LL BELIEVE...
...IN DOTEN-SAMA'S POWER.
KREEAK

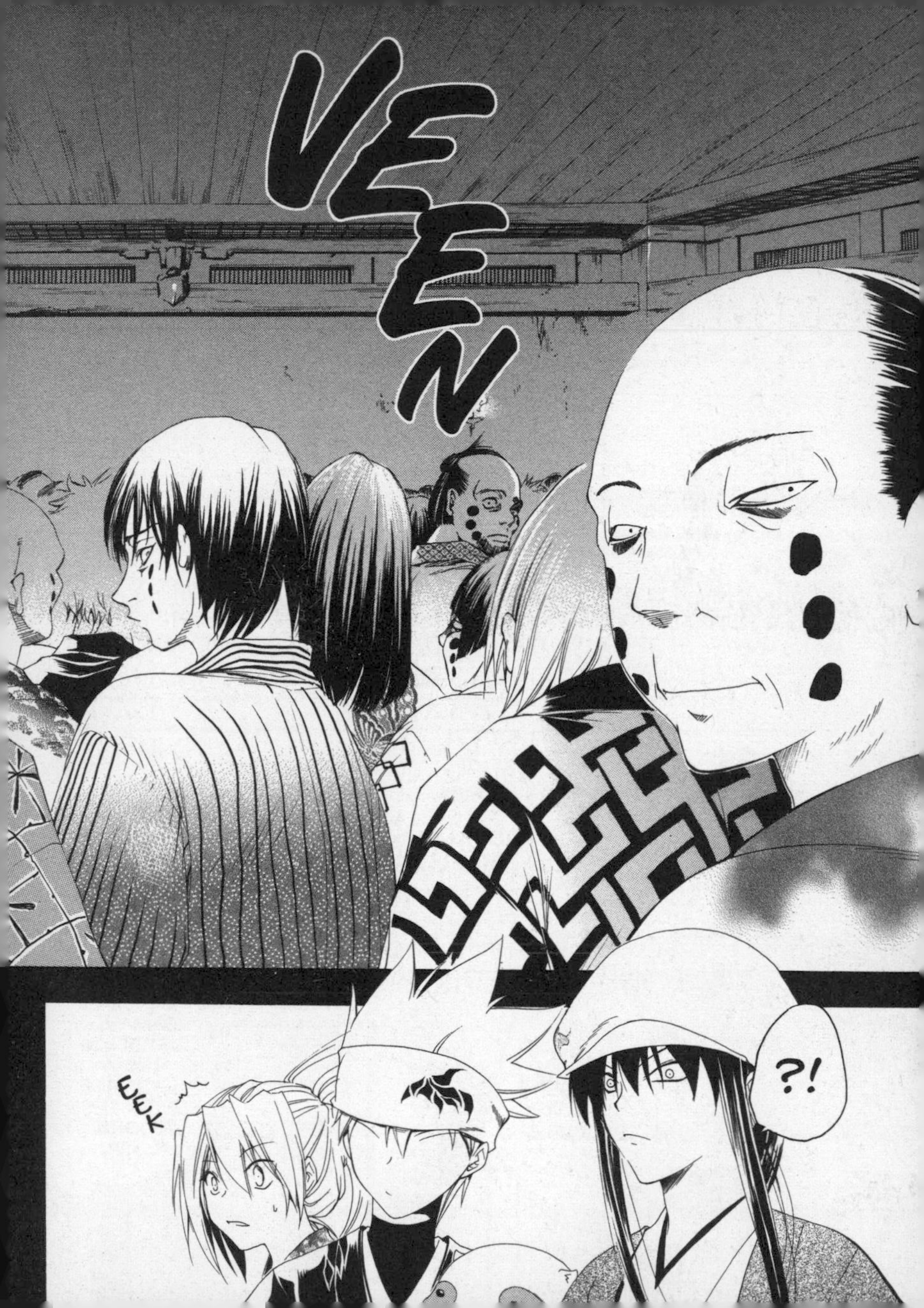
VEEN
?!
EEEK

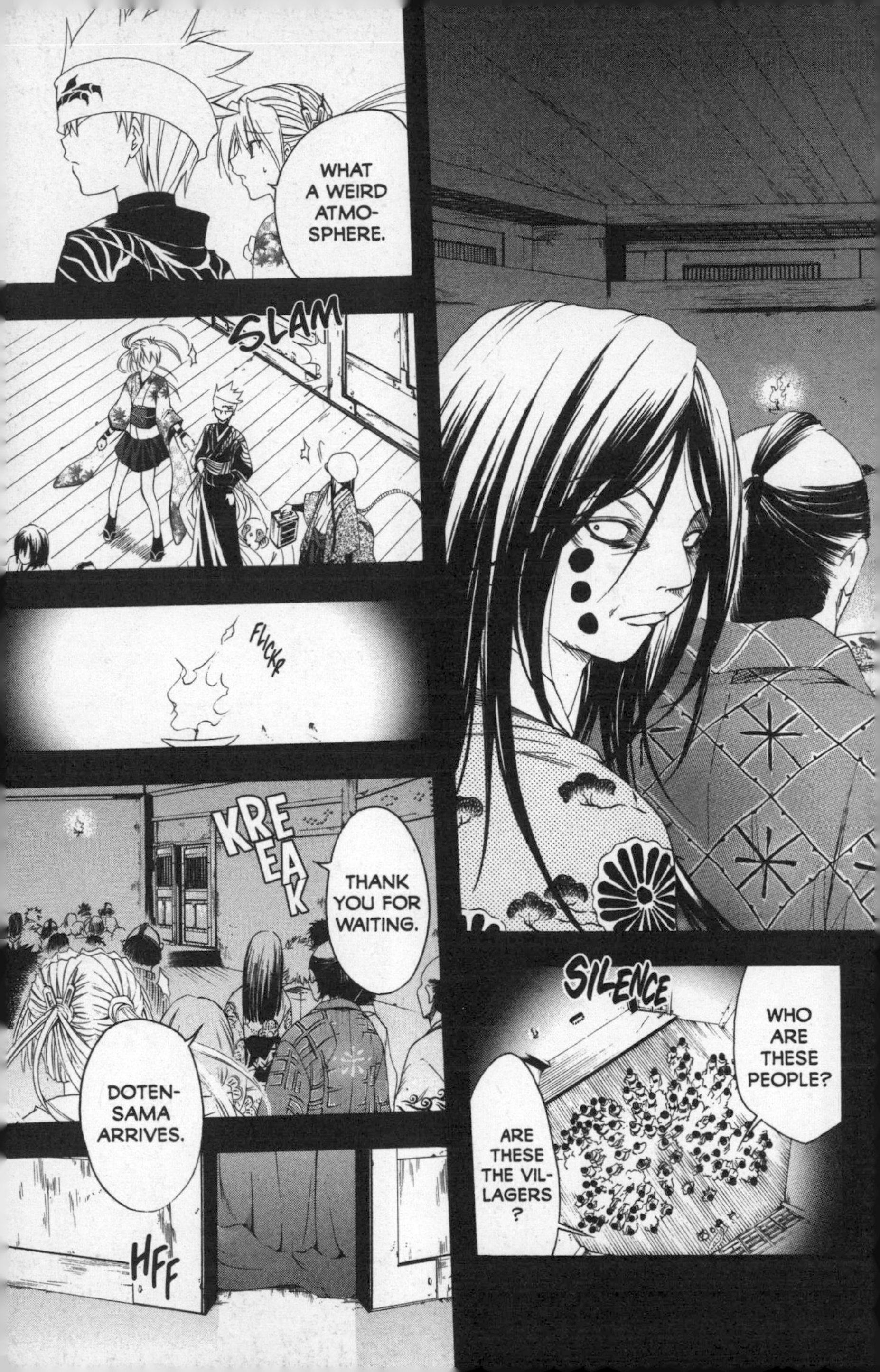
SILENCE
WHO ARE THESE PEOPLE?
ARE THESE THE VILLAGERS?
WHAT A WEIRD ATMOSPHERE.
SLAM
FLICKR
KREEAK
THANK YOU FOR WAITING.
DOTEN-SAMA ARRIVES.
HFF

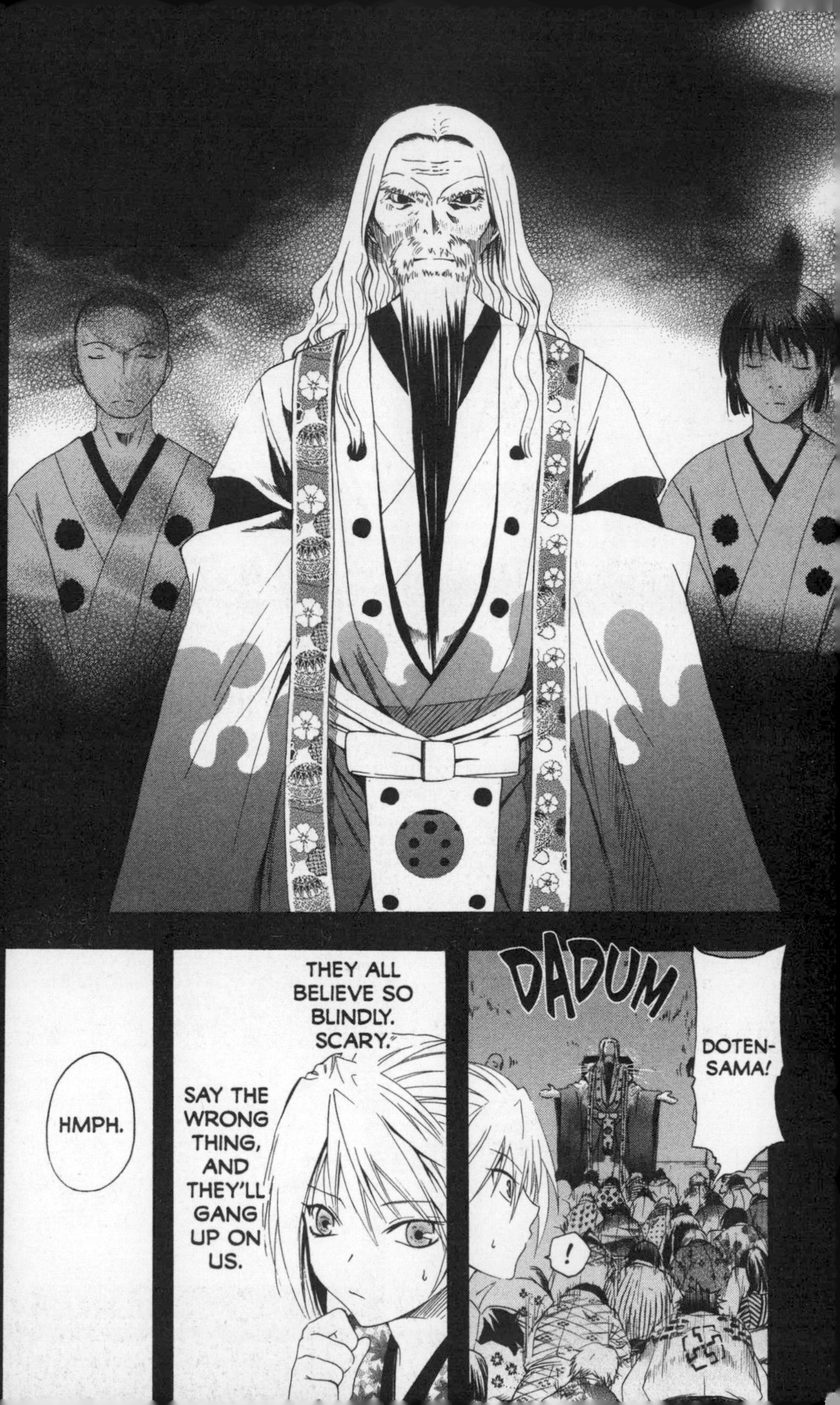
DADUM
DOTEN-SAMA!
!
THEY ALL BELIEVE SO BLINDLY. SCARY.
SAY THE WRONG THING, AND THEY'LL GANG UP ON US.
HMPH.

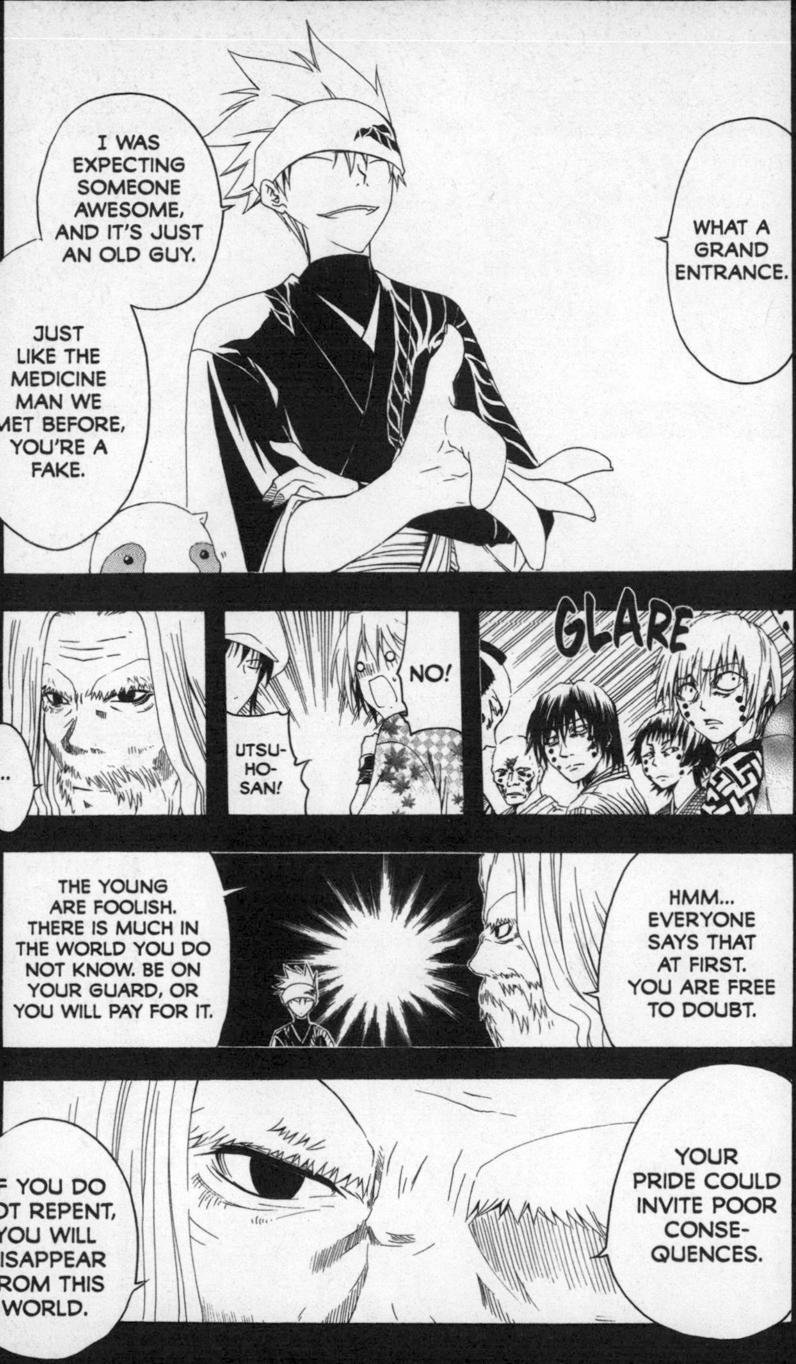
WHAT A GRAND ENTRANCE.
I WAS EXPECTING SOMEONE AWESOME, AND IT'S JUST AN OLD GUY.
JUST LIKE THE MEDICINE MAN WE MET BEFORE, YOU'RE A FAKE.
GLARE
NO!
UTSU-HO-SAN!
...
HMM... EVERYONE SAYS THAT AT FIRST. YOU ARE FREE TO DOUBT.
THE YOUNG ARE FOOLISH. THERE IS MUCH IN THE WORLD YOU DO NOT KNOW. BE ON YOUR GUARD, OR YOU WILL PAY FOR IT.
YOUR PRIDE COULD INVITE POOR CONSE-QUENCES.
IF YOU DO NOT REPENT, YOU WILL DISAPPEAR FROM THIS WORLD.

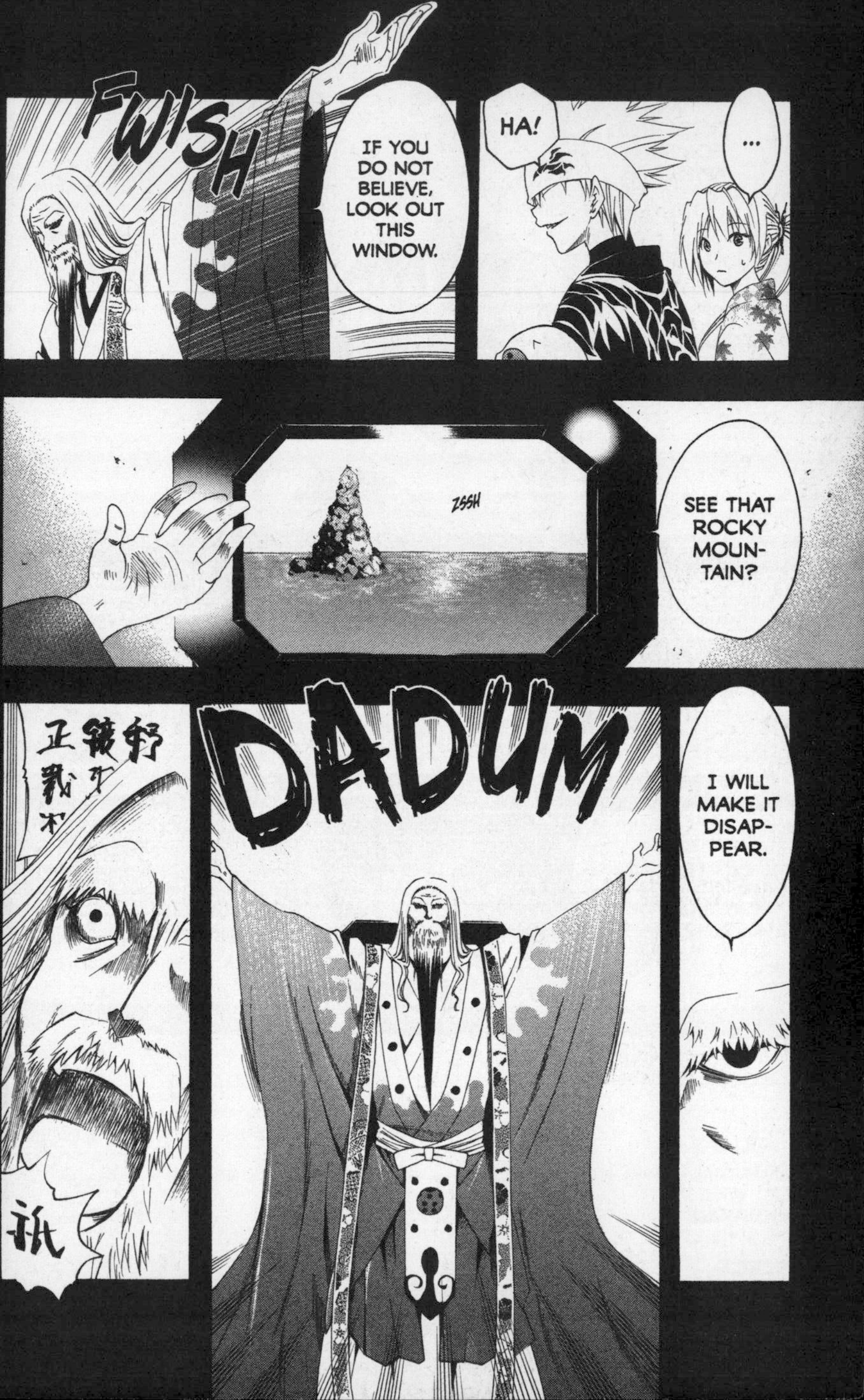
HA!
...
IF YOU DO NOT BELIEVE, LOOK OUT THIS WINDOW.
FWISH
SEE THAT ROCKY MOUNTAIN?
ZSSH
I WILL MAKE IT DISAPPEAR.
DADUM

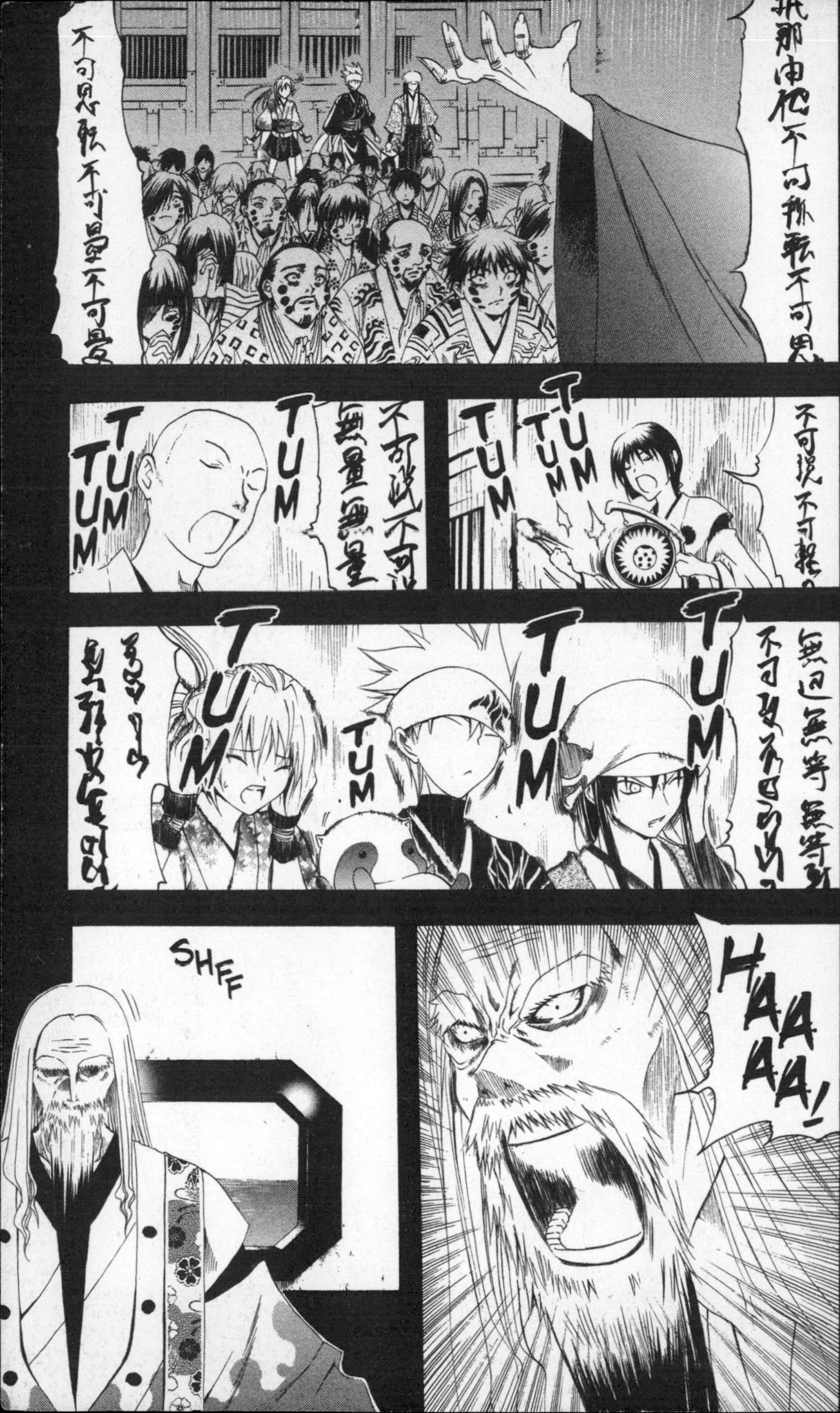
TUM
TUM
TUM
TUM
TUM
TUM
TUM
TUM
TUM
TUM
TUM
TUM
HAAAAA!
SHFF

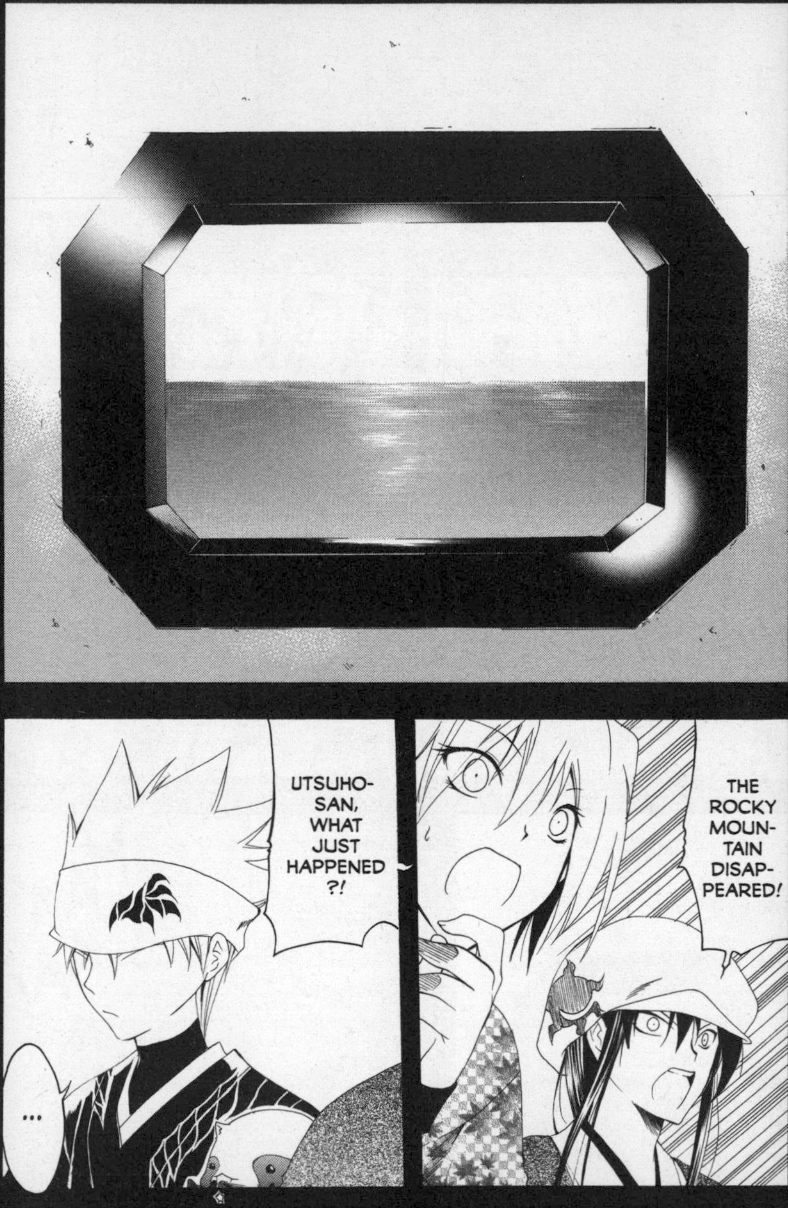
THE ROCKY MOUN-TAIN DISAP-PEARED!
UTSUHO-SAN, WHAT JUST HAPPENED?!
...

◆Bonus Manga◆

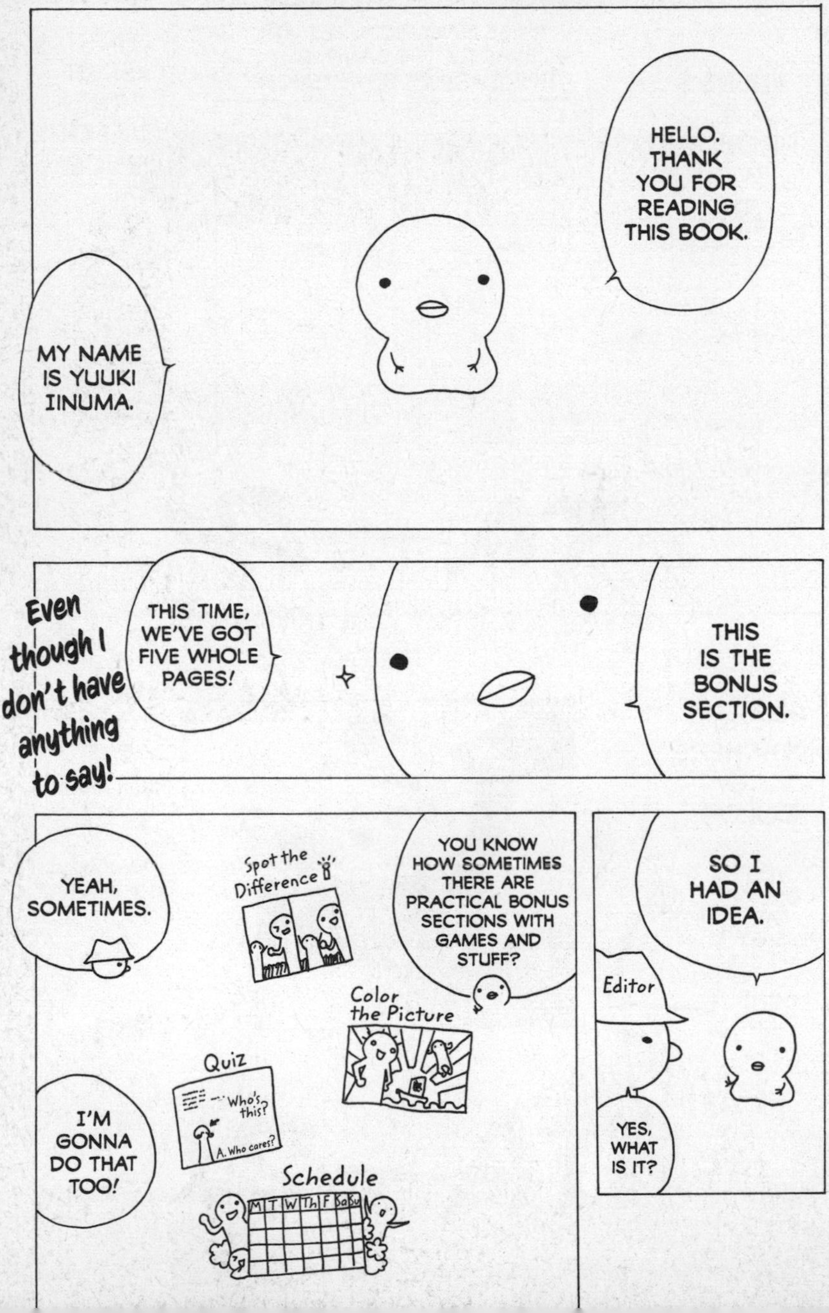
HELLO. THANK YOU FOR READING THIS BOOK.
MY NAME IS YUUKI IINUMA.
THIS IS THE BONUS SECTION.
THIS TIME, WE'VE GOT FIVE WHOLE PAGES!
Even though I don't have anything to say!
SO I HAD AN IDEA.
Editor
YES, WHAT IS IT?
YOU KNOW HOW SOMETIMES THERE ARE PRACTICAL BONUS SECTIONS WITH GAMES AND STUFF?
YEAH, SOMETIMES.
Spot the Difference
Color the Picture
Quiz
Who's this?
A. Who cares?
Schedule
M T W Th F Sa Su
I'M GONNA DO THAT TOO!

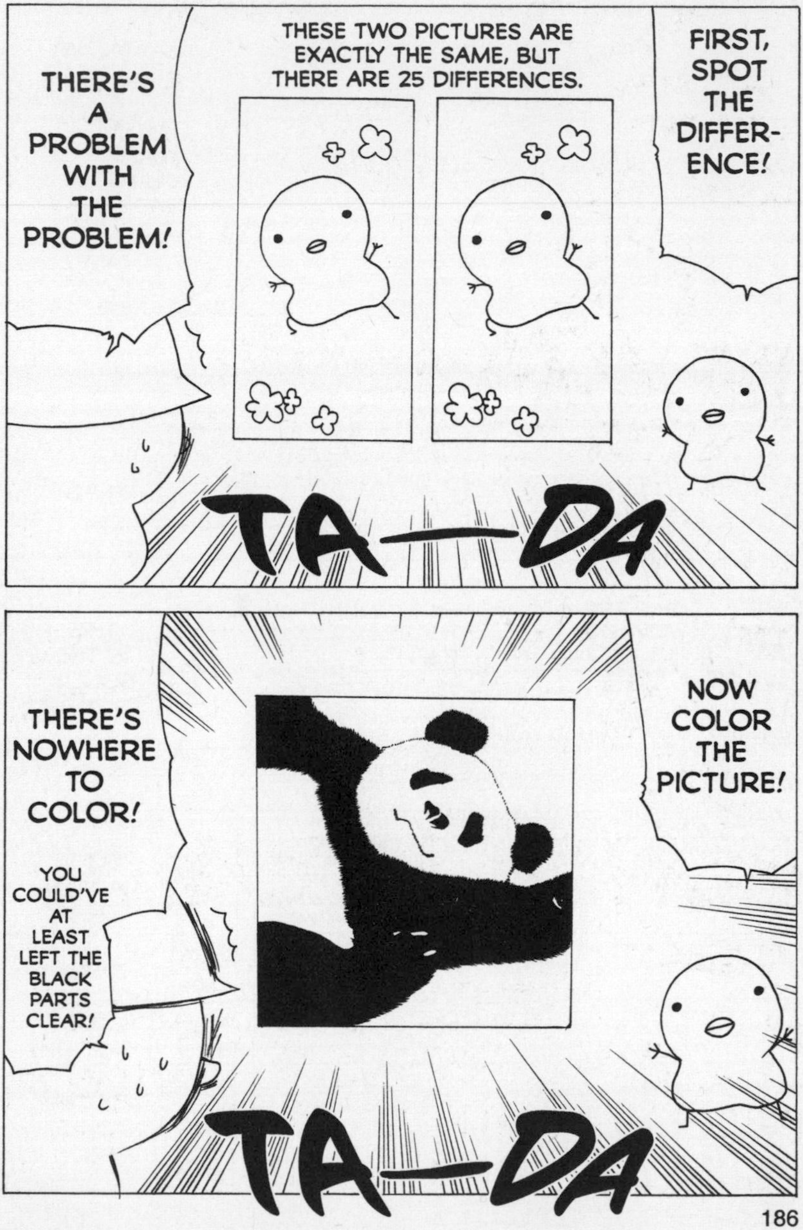
FIRST, SPOT THE DIFFERENCE!
THESE TWO PICTURES ARE EXACTLY THE SAME, BUT THERE ARE 25 DIFFERENCES.
THERE'S A PROBLEM WITH THE PROBLEM!
TA—DA
NOW COLOR THE PICTURE!
THERE'S NOWHERE TO COLOR!
YOU COULD'VE AT LEAST LEFT THE BLACK PARTS CLEAR!
TA—DA

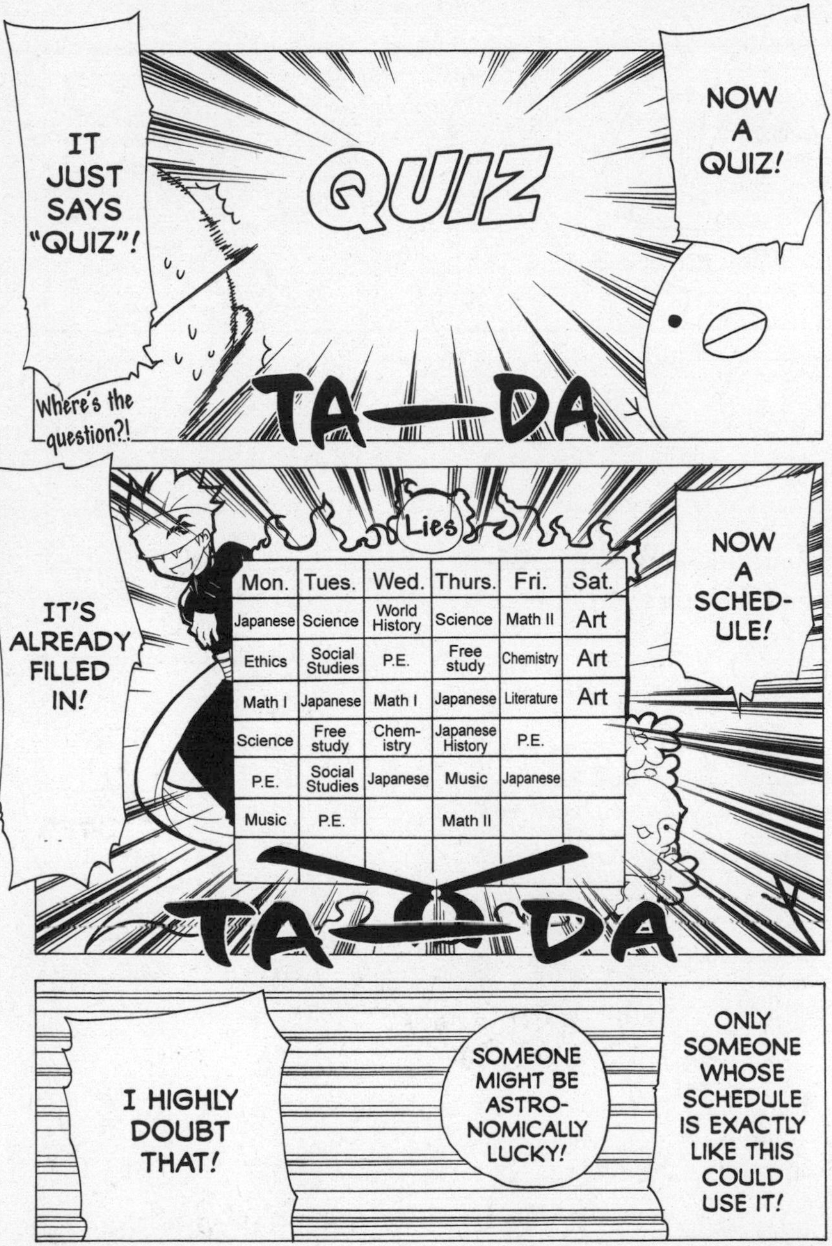
NOW A QUIZ!
QUIZ
IT JUST SAYS "QUIZ"!
TA—DA
Where's the question?!
NOW A SCHEDULE!
Lies
Mon. Tues. Wed. Thurs. Fri. Sat.
Japanese Science World History Science Math II Art
Ethics Social Studies P.E. Free study Chemistry Art
Math I Japanese Math I Japanese Literature Art
Science Free study Chemistry Japanese History P.E.
P.E. Social Studies Japanese Music Japanese
Music P.E. Math II
IT'S ALREADY FILLED IN!
TA—DA
ONLY SOMEONE WHOSE SCHEDULE IS EXACTLY LIKE THIS COULD USE IT!
SOMEONE MIGHT BE ASTRONOMICALLY LUCKY!
I HIGHLY DOUBT THAT!

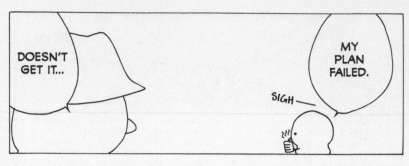

DOESN'T GET IT...

SIGH

MY PLAN FAILED.

There are still pages left...

LET'S SEE...

I'll introduce my rabbit...

PLUMP

SNIF SNIF

MY PRINCESS. THREE YEARS OLD.

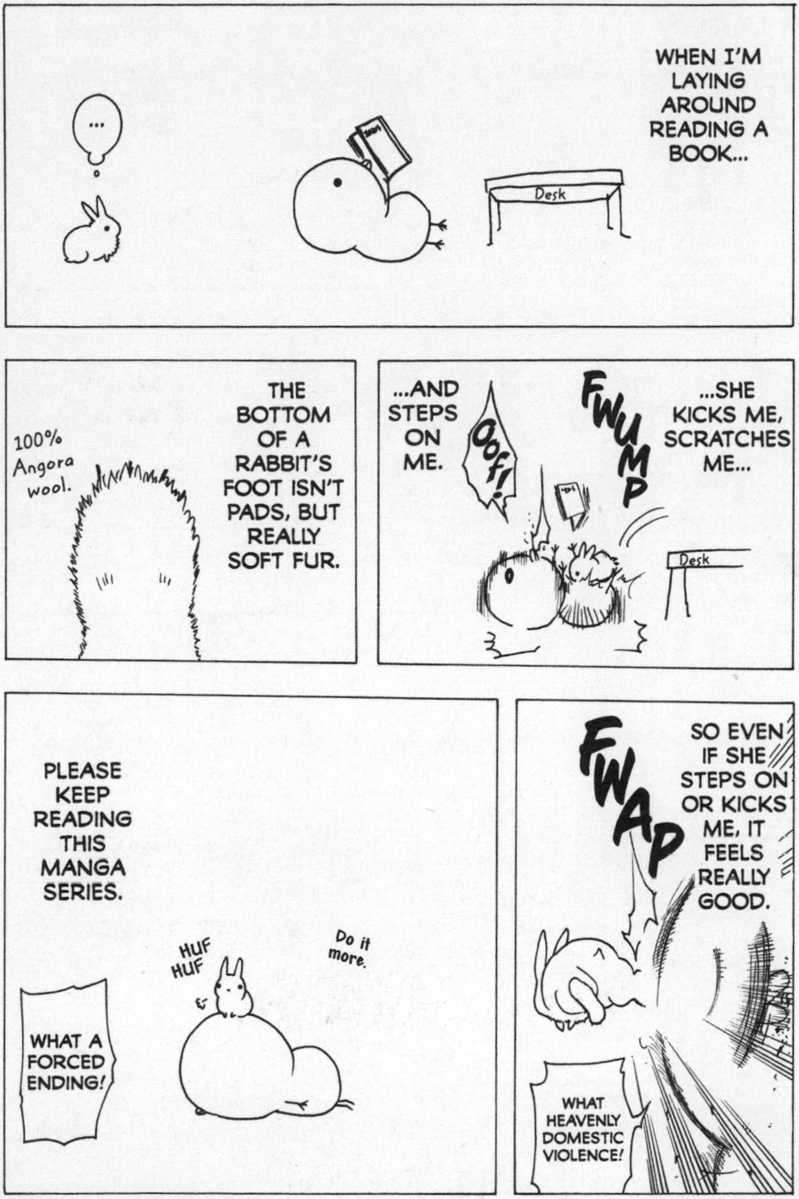
WHEN I'M LAYING AROUND READING A BOOK...
Desk
...
...SHE KICKS ME, SCRATCHES ME...
FWUMP
Desk
Oof!
...AND STEPS ON ME.
THE BOTTOM OF A RABBIT'S FOOT ISN'T PADS, BUT REALLY SOFT FUR.
100% Angora wool.
SO EVEN IF SHE STEPS ON OR KICKS ME, IT FEELS REALLY GOOD.
FWAP
WHAT HEAVENLY DOMESTIC VIOLENCE!
PLEASE KEEP READING THIS MANGA SERIES.
Do it more.
HUF HUF
WHAT A FORCED ENDING!

ITSUWARIBITO
Volume 3
Shonen Sunday Edition

Story and Art by
YUUKI IINUMA

© 2009 Yuuki IINUMA/Shogakukan
All rights reserved.
Original Japanese edition "ITSUWARIBITO UTSUHO"
published by SHOGAKUKAN Inc.

Original Japanese cover design by Shu Anzai & Bay Bridge Studio

Translation/John Werry
Touch-up Art & Lettering/Susan Daigle-Leach
Cover Design/Sean Lee
Interior Design/Matt Hinrichs
Editor/Carrie Shepherd

Printed in the U.S.A.

Published by VIZ Media, LLC
P.O. Box 77010
San Francisco, CA 94107

10 9 8 7 6 5 4 3
First printing, August 2011
Third printing, September 2014

www.viz.com

WWW.SHONENSUNDAY.COM

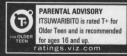